SECTARIAN LAW IN THE DEAD SEA SCROLLS

Number 33

SECTARIAN LAW IN THE DEAD SEA SCROLLS
Courts, Testimony and the Penal Code

by Lawrence H. Schiffman

SECTARIAN LAW IN THE DEAD SEA SCROLLS
Courts, Testimony and the Penal Code

by
Lawrence H. Schiffman

Scholars Press
Chico, California

SECTARIAN LAW IN THE DEAD SEA SCROLLS
Courts, Testimony and the Penal Code

by
Lawrence H. Schiffman

Publication of this book was made possible, in part, by the generosity of the Jewish Federation of Rhode Island. Special thanks go to Mr. Melvin Alperin, President, and Mr. Elliot Cohan, Executive Director.

Library of Congress Cataloging in Publication Data

Schiffman, Lawrence H.
Sectarian law in the Dead Sea Scrolls.

(Brown Judaic studies ; no. 33) (ISSN 0147-927X)
Bibliography: p.
Includes index.
1. Dead Sea scrolls—Criticism, interpretation, etc. 2. Qumran community. 3. Jewish law—Palestine. I. Title. II. Series.
BM487.S313 296.1'55 82-837
ISBN 0-89130-568-8 AACR2
ISBN 0-89130-569-6 (pbk.)

Printed in the United States of America

To my parents

שלשה שותפין הן באדם הקב"ה ואביו ואמו

(B. Qiddushin 30b)

TABLE OF CONTENTS

PREFACE

The present volume represents a continuation of the research undertaken by me in *The Halakhah at Qumran* (Leiden: E. J. Brill, 1975) and in several articles published thereafter. That volume contained two parts. In the first it was shown based on a study of the legal terminology of the Dead Sea corpus that the Qumran sect did not have a concept such as the later tannaitic oral Law and that the sect derived all its laws from what they saw as inspired biblical exegesis. In the second part of the volume the detailed Sabbath Code of the *Zadokite Fragments* was studied in order to demonstrate this thesis and to compare the sect's Sabbath laws to those of other Second Temple sources, tannaitic and amoraic *halakhah*, and the practices of the medieval sect of the Karaites. It was found that the sectarian material represented a unique system of Jewish law which could not be identified with that of any previously known group of Jews.

In the present study, we turn to another area of law altogether. We seek to investigate the sectarian legal system, specifically its courts, court procedure, rules of testimony and the Penal Code. In this way, we can test the conclusions already reached in previous studies and also apply our results to more general questions regarding the nature of the sect. Specifically, this volume attempts to learn not only the legal details of the sectarian code, but also how these details relate to the structure and doctrines of the sects thereby clarifying points of sectarian life previously held in dispute by scholars.

Many are those who have contributed to the completion of this volume. Professor Baruch A. Levine of New York University, teacher and colleague, has been a constant source of encouragement in my work. He shares with me a common interest in Qumran studies, and our many discussions have been most helpful. Professor Francis E. Peters of New York University served as Chairman of the Department of Near Eastern Languages and Literatures for most of the years during which this volume was written. He was likewise of great help in facilitating my research. His wide grasp of Near Eastern history has contributed substantially to my own understanding of the cultural continuum in which the texts studied here were authored. All my colleagues and students at New York University have encouraged and stimulated my research. From the methodological point of view I have benefited immensely from the works of Professor David Halivni of the Jewish Theological Seminary as well as from the many exchanges of ideas we have had over the years. Professor Jacob Neusner of Brown University, through his many works and in numerous conversations, has significantly contributed to the method employed in this volume. Professor Neusner was kind enough to include this volume in this series under his editorship. The inspiration of Professors Alexander Altmann and Nahum M. Sarna of Brandeis University continues to be a guiding force in my work.

The publication of this volume was made possible by a generous grant from the Hagop Kevorkian Fund. I wish to thank Professor R. Bayly Winder, Director of the Hagop Kevorkian Center for Near Eastern Studies at New York University, for his help in this regard.

The Memorial Foundation for Jewish Culture, the American Council of Learned Societies, and the Arts and Science Research Fund of New York University supported this project in its earliest and most crucial stages. The Gottesman Foundation made possible the presentation of part of this research before the World Congress of Jewish Studies in Jerusalem in 1977. Parts of several chapters, here revised and expanded, appeared in *Revue de Qumran* and the *Jewish Law Annual*, the editors of which are thanked for their helpful suggestions. The work was completed while I served as Visiting Associate Professor of Jewish History at Ben-Gurion University of the Negev in Beersheva. Dr. Menahem Schmeltzer, Librarian of the Jewish Theological Seminary of America, Mr. Philip Miller, Librarian of the Hebrew Union College-Jewish Institute of Religion in New York, and Mr. Pinchas Ziv of the library of Ben-Gurion University of the Negev were most gracious in putting the collections under their supervision at my disposal. Dr. Stefan Reif, Director of the Taylor-Schechter Genizah Research Unit at Cambridge University Library, made available to me photographs of the *Zadokite Fragments* from the Cairo *genizah*. My friend and colleague, Dr. Daniel J. Lasker of Ben-Gurion University of the Negev, kindly undertook to read the entire manuscript and to offer helpful suggestions.

My wife, Marlene, typed the manuscript, prepared the material for publication, and compiled the indices. Her many suggestions helped to give the work readability and clarity. Her constant encouragement and support made the completion of this study a much easier task. The volume is dedicated to my parents who first brought me to begin the study of the Torah at the age of six and who have ever since aided my studies in every way possible.

Jerusalem
April 24, 1981

L.H.S.

LIST OF ABBREVIATIONS

For short title references or fuller bibliographic description see the Bibliography.

AJSR	*Association for Jewish Studies Review.*
ANET	J. Pritchard, ed., *Ancient Near Eastern Texts.*
APOT	R. H. Charles, ed., *Apocrypha and Pseudepigrapha of the Old Testament.*
B.	Babylonian Talmud.
BA	*Biblical Archaeologist.*
BASOR	*Bulletin of the American Schools of Oriental Research.*
BDB	F. Brown, S. R. Driver, C. Briggs, *A Hebrew and English Lexicon of the Old Testament.*
Brownlee	W. H. Brownlee, *The Dead Sea Manual of Discipline.*
CBQ	*Catholic Biblical Quarterly.*
CDC	Cairo Damascus Covenant (*Zadokite Fragments* or *Damascus Document*).
DJD I	D. Barthélemy, J. T. Milik, *et al.*, eds., *Qumran Cave I, Discoveries in the Judaean Desert* I.
DJD III	M. Baillet, J. T. Milik, R. de Vaux, *Les 'Petites Grottes' de Qumran, Discoveries in the Judaean Desert* III.
DJD IV	J. A. Sanders, *The Psalms Scroll of Qumran Cave 11, Discoveries in the Judaean Desert* IV.
DJD V	J. M. Allegro, *Qumrân Cave 4, Discoveries in the Judaean Desert* V.
DS	R. N. Rabbinovicz, *Diqduqe Soferim.*
DSD	Dead Sea Discipline (*Manual of Discipline* or *Rule Scroll*).
DSH	Dead Sea Habakkuk Commentary (*Pesher*).
DST	Dead Sea Thanksgiving Scroll (*Hodayot*).

DSW	Dead Sea War Scroll (*Scroll of the War of the Sons of Light against the Sons of Darkness*).
EJ	*Encyclopaedia Judaica*.
Enc. Bib.	*Encyclopaedia Biblica* (*Miqra'it*).
Enc. Tal.	*Encyclopaedia Talmudit*.
Ges.	E. Kautzsch, ed., *Gesenius' Hebrew Grammar*, trans. A. E. Cowley.
H.	*Hilkhot* in M. Maimonides, *Mishneh Torah*.
HAQ	L. H. Schiffman, *The Halakhah at Qumran*.
HTR	*Harvard Theological Review*.
HWT	*Hashlamot We-Tosafot* in Ch. Albeck, ed., *Shishah Sidre Mishnah*.
HUCA	*Hebrew Union College Annual*.
IEJ	*Israel Exploration Journal*.
ILR	*Israel Law Review*.
JAOS	*Journal of the American Oriental Society*.
JBL	*Journal of Biblical Literature*.
JE	*Jewish Encyclopedia*.
JJS	*Journal of Jewish Studies*.
(new) JPS	*The Torah*, new translation by the Jewish Publication Society.
JQR, O.S.; N.S.	*Jewish Quarterly Review*, Original Series; New Series.
JSJ	*Journal for the Study of Judaism in the Persian, Hellenistic and Roman Period*.
JSK	N. Wieder, *The Judean Scrolls and Karaism*.
JSS	*Journal of Semitic Studies*.
KS	*Kiryat Sepher*.
LXX	*Septuaginta*.
M.	Mishnah.
MGWJ	*Monatschrift für Geschichte und Wissenschaft des Judentums*.
MMY	Ḥ. Yalon, *Megillot Midbar Yehudah*.
MT	Masoretic Text.
NEB	*New English Bible*.
NTS	*New Testament Studies*.
P.	Palestinian Talmud.
PAAJR	*Proceedings of the American Academy for Jewish Research*.

Qimron	E. Qimron, *Diqduq Ha-Lashon Ha-ʿIvrit shel Megillot Midbar Yehudah.*
QS	C. Rabin, *Qumran Studies.*
Rabin	C. Rabin, *The Zadokite Documents.*
RB	*Revue biblique.*
REJ	*Revue des études juives.*
RQ	*Revue de Qumran.*
RSV	Revised Standard Version.
Schechter	S. Schechter, *Documents of Jewish Sectaries.*
Segal	M. H. (M. Ṣ.) Segal, "*Sefer Berit Dameseq.*"
Shnaton	*Shnaton La-Miqra' U-Le-Ḥeqer Ha-Mizraḥ Ha-Qadum.*
T.	Tosefta.
ThLZ	*Theologische Literaturzeitung.*
ThZ	*Theologische Zeitschrift.*
TK	S. Lieberman, *Tosefta' Ki-Fshutah.*
TS	Temple Scroll.
Ṭur	Jacob ben Asher, *'Arbaʿah Ṭurim.*
VT	*Vetus Testamentum.*
Wernberg-Møller	P. Wernberg-Møller, *The Manual of Discipline.*
War Scroll	Y. Yadin, *The Scroll of the War of the Sons of Light against the Sons of Darkness.*
1QSa	*Serekh Ha-ʿEdah* (*Rule of the Congregation*).

INTRODUCTION

1. *The Problem*

The study of the Dead Sea Scrolls is still in its infancy. Scarcely three decades have passed since the discovery of a hoard of manuscripts destined to change our perceptions of the history of the Hebrew Bible, Judaism, and Christianity. The publication of many of the texts from Qumran is still awaited. Indeed, manuscripts from Masada, Naḥal Ḥever, and Wadi Murabaat have joined the Qumran corpus in making available to us original sources from a period both enigmatic and central to our understanding of world religions and civilization.

The scrolls have been the object of study from numerous points of view. Scholars have investigated the nature of the Dead Sea sect, its customs, legal traditions, history, theology, and significance for the understanding of Judaism and Christianity. Yet there is still much to learn from this corpus.

Prevalent scholarly opinion has identified the sect with the Essenes of Philo, Josephus, and other Greco-Roman sources. This view is an oversimplification, however. First, Josephus, the primary source on the Essenes, wrote for a Greek and Roman audience and so represented the Essenes as a Greek philosophic school. Second, he himself admits to having included more than one group of sectarians under the heading "Essenes." Judging from the generalizations he made in regard to his "fourth philosophy," it can be seen that several groups may have been described as one by Josephus. When it is realized that a whole constellation of such sects existed in the Second Commonwealth period, we find insufficient the evidence for simply identifying the Essenes of Philo and Josephus with the Dead Sea sect./1/

While it is perfectly legitimate to attempt to prove, as prevalent scholarly opinion has done, that the Essenes are to be identified as the authors of the Qumran scrolls, it is totally illegitimate to use this theory as an axiom upon which to build interpretations of the Qumran texts. Scholarly integrity demands that each corpus—the Hebrew and Aramaic scrolls from the caves of Qumran and the Greek reports on the Essenes of Philo and Josephus—be subjected to separate critical review. Only after the full import of each set of materials has been grasped by us will it be legitimate to draw conclusions regarding the relationship between the Essenes and the Dead Sea sect.

It was in an effort to see the Qumran material from this perspective that this writer began his study of the legal material in the Dead Sea Scrolls with a volume entitled *The Halakhah at Qumran* (1975)./2/ The purpose of that volume was to come to conclusions regarding the conceptual framework behind the legal material in the Qumran corpus, i.e. how the sect derived its law and how its members perceived this process. In order to test these conclusions, the Sabbath code of the *Zadokite Fragments* was studied in detail. That initial study, limited as it was in scope, could not deal with many aspects of the Jewish legal material found at Qumran, and did not relate to the more general issues concerning the nature of the sect, its structure, and self-definition.

For this reason, the present study has begun with aspects of civil law which naturally lend themselves to conclusions of this nature. It was quickly found that the relationship between civil law and aspects of purity, impurity, communality of property, and meals at Qumran was such that it was not possible to study any of these questions without attention to the others. Hence, the volume deals with selected aspects of civil law, and provides them with the necessary "ritual" context as well.

This volume cannot make any claims of completeness. It can only study in depth certain aspects of Qumran life and law which are interrelated and attempt to draw some conclusions about the form of Judaism practiced at Qumran. After treating subjects regarding courts, testimony, and court procedure in the Dead Sea Scrolls, the study turns to the Penal Code of the sect. Since the principles of the Penal Code are intimately linked to the sect's approach to ritual purity and impurity, and since these concepts in turn serve as the basis for the process of entry into the sect, these matters must be taken up as well. Only after the analysis of ritual purity and its place in sectarian life which has been undertaken here, can the place of the communal meals of the sect be understood; hence, the inclusion of this topic as well.

Indeed, the various chapters illustrate well the themes which run through the Qumran legal materials—ritual purity and impurity, sin and atonement, and the attempt of the sect to organize a perfect society in a still-to-be-perfected world. While all these concepts could be illustrated as well from the non-legal materials in the Qumran corpus, we have chosen to investigate these ideals as they are enshrined in sectarian law and in the communal structure of the Qumran sect.

Is it, in fact, possible to study any one aspect of Qumran legal or religious tradition without relating to so many others? The question might be asked as well for biblical or Talmudic law or even for Judaism as a whole. The essential characteristic of Judaism, in each and every one of its pre-modern manifestations, is that it is all-encompassing in its nature. Further, it is organic in that its components are seen as constantly combining and recombining such that no aspect can be studied without recourse to others. One might remark, as a colleague once did, that it is possible to extend any dissertation in Talmudic studies infinitely until it would engulf the entire literature of the Talmud. It is exactly this problem which plagues those who study Qumran literature as well. The system of Jewish life and tradition can indeed be broken down into component parts by the use of systems of classification. But even those systems imposed by the literature of the Jewish tradition, whether at Qumran or in Rabbinic literature, are themselves conscious attempts at oversimplification. This system, composed of interlocking and re-interlocking parts possessed of an organic connection one to another, is never really divisible.

One who would seek to understand Judaism in any one of its manifestations must first turn to what the Rabbis called the *halakhah*, for here is expressed that which is obligatory—the way of life linking God to man. All the other aspects are of secondary importance when compared with the day-to-day expressions of Judaism through law and practice. Therefore, only through the study of the Dead Sea sect's legal texts may we come to any understanding of the real meaning of life to the Dead Sea sectarian. Without this aspect, all our musings on theology, Messianism, communal life, and the rest of the nuts and bolts of the field of Qumran studies, will amount to very little. Ultimately, the sectarian saw himself as a servant of God. Only through an understanding of how he expressed this service, through what format and regulations, will it be possible to evaluate properly this corpus of manuscripts which sheds so much light on the history of Judaism in this period.

But before embarking on this study, it is necessary to examine the sources upon which it rests. What is the primary concern or point of view of each text? What are its component parts or documents, and what developments can be discerned in it? Finally, what kind of a society does it envisage? When we have answered these questions for each source, we will be ready to ask what the interrelation of these texts is and how they may be used to construct a general picture of the teachings of what we have come to call the Dead Sea sect.

2. *The* Manual of Discipline

Although the *Manual of Discipline* as it stands before us is clearly a composite work, we shall first attempt to understand it in its present form, as passed on by its redactor or redactors. Afterwards, we will deal with the theories which have been proposed regarding the evolution of this text.

The *Manual* may best be described as a document envisaging a small, closely-knit society, governed by a specific code, rejecting all outsiders except those seeking admission to the sect. The heart of the text is certainly the legalistic sections of the *Manual*, DSD 5:1–6:13 defining the nature of the structure of the group, DSD 6:13–6:23 dealing with the procedures for the admission of new members of the sect, and DSD 6:24–7:25, 8:16–9:2 the sectarian Penal Code./3/ The remaining sections of the text consist of

(1) the description of the annual covenant renewal ceremony, (2) the theological tract on the two spirits, (1 and 2 serving as the introduction to the legal body) and (3) concluding paeons to the *maskil*, a poem extolling the virtues of life in the sect, and praises of God Himself.

The specific theological and doctrinal presuppositions of the *Manual* need not concern us here. They have been dealt with in many excellent studies. Certainly, though, the structure of this document points up the importance of seeing the theological and doctrinal aspects in light of the legal, and the legal in light of the doctrinal. The redactor has certainly intended us to understand the two as a unity, inseparable in meaning.

The *Manual of Discipline* carries the message that an ideal society can be created and structured so as to express and exemplify the principles which it proposes. This is no mere lip service. We shall see that the doctrines of the sect about purity and impurity, and predestination ("two spirits") are integral parts of the foundation on which the legal sections of the document rest. There is no way to understand one without the other.

Here we are face to face with a document which does not resemble the major texts of the tannaitic legal tradition. Tannaitic texts never set forth the doctrinal bases upon which they rest. The *Manual*, on the other hand, does not leave these principles unsaid. On the contrary, the theological basis for the practice is explicit here, so explicit that the message cannot fail to impress the reader and to leave its mark.

What is the social character of the group envisaged by this text as it now stands? The sect is clearly a group such as that which lived at Qumran and at other proximate locations on the shore of the Dead Sea, a closely-knit society in which each man had his function and rank. According to the *Manual of Discipline*, each member retains title to his own possessions, which are registered in ledgers and made available for communal use. The group lives in a perpetual state of ritual purity, joining together for some meals, as well as maintaining regular sessions for study of Scripture and liturgical praise of God. Each man sees himself as a part of this group which in itself constitutes a sanctuary in exile, a replacement Temple for that which, to the sectarians, was currently in the hands of the evildoers. A dominant role is accorded the priests, although major decisions are made by a sectarian assembly, the *moshav ha-rabbim*. Even if at one time the priests had actually controlled affairs at Qumran, this role seems to be in the process of becoming ceremonial.

J. Murphy-O'Connor has proposed a framework for understanding the history of the development of the *Manual of Discipline*./4/ His proposal is based on what can be determined of the history of the sect. His basic assumption states that the *Manual* is the product of an evolutionary process rather than of the efforts of a redactor who assembled the entire text at one time from its various documents. (Such an evolution is in accord with the way in which Rabbinic literature developed throughout its long and complex history.)

Murphy-O'Connor assigns specific passages to each of four stages in the development of the text. Yet a caveat must be expressed. The specific interpretations which lie behind Murphy-O'Connor's analysis are not always accepted in this study nor by all scholars. While his basic thesis appears valid, there will still be controversy regarding the actual boundaries of the specific passages belonging to one stage or another as the exegesis of the Qumran texts continues to advance.

Murphy-O'Connor identifies DSD 8:1–16a and 9:3–10:8a as comprising the earliest stage. This core served as the basis around which the rest of the material agglomerated. This material is, in his terminology, a manifesto which describes a sect that has not yet come into being. It therefore would antedate the formation of the sect as well as the career of the teacher of righteousness.

The second stage is comprised of DSD 8:16b–19 and 8:20–9:20. These passages make up the earliest penal legislation of the group. Here we see a group close to its origins. The legislation is primitive and meant to react to the problems of the recently formed sect. It was inserted into the manifesto of the first stage.

The third stage contains DSD 5:1–13a and 5:15b–7:25. Here the community is thoroughly institutionalized and has become more democratic. Whereas power was originally limited to the Zadokite priests, it is now shared by all full members of the group. The community is more developed and stable. We hear of new members, a general assembly, and encounter casuistically formulated penal legislation. Further, there is a stronger sense of community. It is to this stage in the development of the *Manual* that the greatest number of correspondences are found with the *Serekh Ha-'Edah*, the *Rule of the Congregation*. This stage in the development of the *Manual* corresponds most probably to the heyday of the sectarian settlement at Qumran, as determined from archaeological evidence. The manuscript of 1QS has been dated palaeographically to 100–75 B.C./5/

The fourth and final stage in the development of the *Manual* is that of the addition of all kinds of originally independent materials. These are intended here to infuse the members with the spirit of the sect. These materials are the ideological framework which surrounds the more procedural or legalistic elements at the center of the document. Murphy-O'Connor sees the addition of these elements as the result of a dimunition of fervor among the community, a development which he also finds in CDC 19:33–20:1b, 20:8b–13, and 20:17b–22b./6/ Most prominent among these additions is the closing poem in the style of the Thanksgiving Hymns (*Hodayot Scroll*).

These stages fit nicely into the archaeological periodization of the occupation of Qumran. The first stage, of course, dates to before the settlement of the group at Qumran. The second stage would correspond to Qumran's period Ia (before 135–104 B.C.). The third and fourth stages would be equivalent to period Ib (ca. 135–31 B.C.). The *Manual* would have been complete already by period II, beginning with the restoration of the settlement after the earthquake of 31 B.C. and ending when the settlement was destroyed by the Romans in 68 A.D./7/

While this theory will be helpful for our comprehension of the development of the sect and its literature, our study seeks to understand the sect after the crystallization of its way of life. By investigating the material as it now stands, we are studying a sect which, by the Hasmonean period, had solidified its position regarding its beliefs, legal system, and practices. This occurred in Murphy-O'Connor's stage three. The non-theological aspects of this text were already in close to present form and constituted a unity. We are therefore entitled to view the material as it stood in this stage and to work from it without hesitation. The materials added in the fourth stage to provide the theological and conceptual framework no doubt existed separately already in the third stage. We may therefore use them to determine the doctrinal and conceptual framework against which to understand the legal material within the *Manual of Discipline*.

3. *The* Rule of the Congregation (Serekh Ha-'Edah)

The *Rule of the Congregation* appears as one of two appendices to the *Manual of Discipline*. (The second, the *Rule of Benedictions* [*Serekh Ha-Berakhot*] is not relevant to this study since it is not a legal text.) *Serekh Ha-'Edah* is a Messianic document picturing the ideal constitution of the sect in the end of days. The text is based upon the same theological and doctrinal presuppositions as is the *Manual of Discipline*. It describes the members of the community by the functions they assume at various stages in their lives. It then pictures an eschatological meeting of the *moshav ha-rabbim* (although this term is not used) emphasizing the ritual purity of the group and the exclusion from it of those afflicted with physical blemishes and imperfections. In keeping with the biblical view such people were excluded, no doubt, since these blemishes were seen as evidence of moral imperfections. Finally, the text describes a banquet at the end of days at which the two Messianic figures expected by the sect preside.

It must be assumed that the events predicted in this text actually constitute a kind of Messianic mirror image of the society described in the *Manual of Discipline*. After all, the sect saw itself as living on the verge of the end of days and must have attempted to realize in the sectarian life of the *Manual* the very same perfection and purity. Indeed, we have seen that the society envisaged in the *Manual* is based on the purity and moral perfection of its members. This text, then, may be used as a key to the understanding of the *Manual*. The community described in the *Manual* is an attempt to create Messianic conditions, even before the beginning of the eschaton. The entire society is structured to realize the sectarians' dreams of the future in the present.

This conclusion will also be central from a methodological point of view. It will allow us to assume that legal materials contained in the *Rule of the Congregation* were actualized in the everyday life of the sect, for their entire society was structured to this end. The difference between the texts is simply that the *Rule of the Congregation* places these legal aspects in a Messianic framework, explaining that the culmination of all that envisaged in the *Manual*, and which to some extent could not be fully realized in the present, pre-Messianic age, could be and would be achieved in the end of days.

4. *The* Zadokite Fragments

If the two documents discussed so far tell us about those living at Qumran and the environs, the *Zadokite Fragments* or *Damascus Document* must be seen in somewhat different light. Since the bulk of the material from this text unearthed at Qumran has yet to be published, our observations here must be based only on the medieval *genizah* manuscripts and the reports by J. T. Milik./8/ The text begins with a long prologue (termed the Admonition by C. Rabin/9/) which seeks to explain the reaction of the sect to those outside its bounds. Over and over we are told that only the sect and its leadership is capable of properly interpreting Jewish law. All other groups and their sins are catalogued so as to explain the necessity for the physical and spiritual separation of the sect from the rest of the people of Israel. We also learn of the role of the *moreh ṣedeq*, the "correct teacher," who, along with the Zadokite priests, led the confused initial members to the path of truth.

While this introduction itself contains much material not paralleled in the *Manual*, its ideology is very close to that of the *Manual*, and could just as easily be attached to it. Yet when we leave the Admonition and turn to the legal materials in this document, we encounter something quite different from what occurs in the *Manual*. Whereas the *Manual* primarily treats the sectarian, organizational aspects of the sect's law, this text treats the full gamut of Jewish legal topics. Within this text are tracts dealing with civil law, oaths, judges, witnesses, lost and stolen property, ritual purity, Sabbath, cult and sacrifices, relations with idolators, *kashrut* of foods, plagues, etc. It seems as if the author wanted to state that only through the sect could one aspire to the correct observance of these laws. He may be polemicizing against the attitude that observance of the law is enough, and that the sectarian framework was not necessary. He states that the ultimate purpose of this society is that of perfection through traditional Jewish observances, and only the sect possesses the correct understanding and rulings allowing for proper observance.

Scattered among these tracts, particularly toward the end of what is preserved in our medieval manuscripts, are materials relating to the organization of the sect. By and large these passages allude to many of the same institutions described in the *Manual*, yet some important differences are to be observed. First, this text seems to envisage two groups within the sect, those living at the center of sectarian life (known by us as Qumran), and those who live scattered throughout the country in "camps." Second, it has been observed that the entrance requirements for the sect in the *Zadokite Fragments* comprise only the first two stages of those described in the *Manual*. In other words, the sectarians of the *Zadokite Fragments* are novices in the view of the *Manual*./10/

The author of the *Manual* clearly wanted to convey that the way of life of the sectarian community was the only path to the attainment of religious perfection. The author of the *Zadokite Fragments* treats this aspect side by side with the traditional subjects of Jewish law, and, in so doing, emphasizes that the communal structure described in the *Manual* serves not only to ensure ritual purity and to create a spiritual Temple, but also to enable the sectarian to observe Jewish law as revealed to the sect through divinely inspired biblical exegesis.

Whereas our manuscripts for most of the *Zadokite Fragments* are medieval and come from the Cairo *genizah*, fragments of eight copies of this text have been found at Qumran. The oldest materials come from cave 4, being dated palaeographically to 75–50 B.C., whereas the cave 6 manuscript is dated to the first century A.D./11/

Murphy O'Connor has also subjected this text to study using a method similar to that which he employed in regard to the *Manual of Discipline*./12/ His study, however, was limited to the Admonition and did not take into account the legal material in the *Zadokite Fragments*. We shall first summarize his findings regarding the literary development of the Admonition, and then attempt to correlate them to what is known about the legal section.

Murphy-O'Connor has suggested that the compiler of the Admonition used four principle sources. The first of these was CDC 2:14–6:1, a "missionary document" which was intended to win over members to the sect. The second was CDC 6:11–8:3, a memorandum written to call members to more faithful observance of the principles of the sect. The third was CDC 8:3–19, a document criticizing the ruling class in Judea for not supporting the sect (which Murphy-O'Connor terms the "Essenes"). Fourth, is CDC 19:33–20:22b, a document intended to stem rising disaffection in the community. In addition, the compiler had before him a fragment of community legislation found in CDC 20:1c–8a and, most probably, a *pesher* on Num. 21:18 which formed the basis of CDC 6:2–11. The compiler added to this the hortatory framework, intending to emphasize the advantages of being part of the community and the consequences of failure to live in accordance with its interpretation of the law.

Murphy-O'Connor has attempted to correlate the various sources before the compiler with the stages in the history of the sect./13/ Since many of his views on the history of the sect are at best unproven, we are left with little choice but to accept his notion of a complex of sources lying behind the composition of the Admonition and to postpone judgment on the specific dating of the individual components. At all events, it can be said with certainty that the full Admonition was in present form by period Ib of the occupation of Qumran, the period by which the sect's way of life, its law and lore, was crystallized.

We have already noted that the compiler of the Admonition intended to create an introduction to the corpus of law which followed. Indeed, the entire thrust of the Admonition is to encourage observance of the Law as interpreted by the sect. If so, we may assume that the various tracts of law were likewise before the compiler who organized them into the text as it now stands.

The still unpublished manuscripts of the *Zadokite Fragments* discovered in cave 4 at Qumran have brought about a new picture of the outline of this text, previously known only from the tenth and twelfth century Cairo *genizah* fragments. J. T. Milik has reconstructed the order as follows: Opening columns (not present in the Cairo manuscripts), CDC 1–8, a missing section only partly preserved in the 4Q fragments, CDC 15–16, CDC 9–14, and the final columns from cave 4 including a penal code and a liturgy for the covenant renewal feast./14/

Each of the legal sections of the *Zadokite Fragments* was apparently redacted as a unit before being placed into the code. It is most likely that this material was the fruit of sectarian study sessions at which the various laws here preserved were deduced from Scripture. After completion of this study, the laws were then assembled into groups of laws on a single topic called *serakhim*. It is these *serakhim* which provided the raw material for the redaction of the legal section as outlined by J. Fitzmyer./15/ There may have been intermediate stages in which *serakhim* were associated into groups, but this process can no longer be traced. What we have before us is the result of the redaction of these *serakhim* into a code which presents a clear idea of the subjects of Jewish law important to the sect, and how these were, in turn, related to the issues of sectarian organization, specifically as they concerned the settlements outside Qumran. The compiler also added the necessary headings, some of which are still preserved in our text.

Detailed textual analysis reveals the Scriptural basis of each prescription and the way in which the biblical passage was interpreted by the sect. It can be seen that laws are derived from various parts of the Bible. Perhaps the study sessions were scheduled or conducted so as to select biblical materials on a particular subject to be compiled into the *serekh*. However, it is more likely that the *serekh* was redacted from the results of many study sessions which took place over a long period of time. It would then be a topical collection, composed and redacted at a later occasion.

CDC 9:2–10:10 constitutes such a code pertaining to the sectarian courts, legal procedure, theft, and testimony. This volume opens with the detailed examination of its prescriptions. Yet it is not enough merely to analyze the individual provisions without regard to the structure or framework in which they appear. Some observations may be made here regarding the literary character of this tract.

The code is preceded by a difficult introductory passage (CDC 9:1) which may have indicated the prohibition on recourse to non-Jewish courts. It serves to emphasize the exclusive validity of the courts and their procedures to be described as the text progresses./16/ The code itself begins with the sectarian process of reproof which requires that prior to being tried for an offense, the offender must be formally reproved before witnesses and the reproof recorded in the records of the sect. After a somewhat parenthetical remark requiring that all oaths be taken only before the judges, the code continues to describe the process of adjuration used to bring about the restitution of property illegally gained and the procedure for returning lost property when the owner cannot be located.

Next comes the detailed law of testimony, specifying the number of witnesses required and the procedure for combining the testimony of a single witness to successive commissions of the same offense. At this point are specified the requirements for the qualifications of witnesses. Finally, the text details the composition of the courts and the attendant qualifications for judges.

The organization of this passage must be noted. After the general requirement that all cases must be tried before Jewish courts, the passage proceeds in an order which begins with the commission of the offense and ends with the trial. For this reason, the first matter treated is reproof which takes place immediately after a crime. If the reproof is duly received and the crime is not repeated, the procedure stops here. If the crime has resulted in the illegal appropriation of property, a method is described which is calculated to bring about its restitution. If the criminal comes forward of his own at this stage, the process is again halted. At this point, the return of lost property appears as a digression, since it is so similar to that of stolen property. If these steps are of no avail, or if the crime is repeated, then the testimony of the witnesses, provided it is legally acceptable, serves as the basis for a formal indictment. Finally, if testimony to the crime must be heard, a court is required which is properly constituted of judges who meet specific qualifications. Now the criminal, after all the preceding conditions and procedures have been fulfilled, finds himself before the bar of justice. The text, then, has taken us from the commission of the offense, to attempts at restitution, to the gathering of testimony, to the final trial.

The order of the passages as they appear in the structure identified here is not conducive, however, to a coherent explication of the foundations of the Qumran legal system. Later laws often contain the exegetical basis or legal details which are necessary for a complete understanding of earlier provisions. Therefore, in this volume the text is not studied in the order of the code but rather in an order which facilitates the explanation of the material.

Whereas the detailed examination of the Sabbath Code of the *Zadokite Fragments* showed its individual provisions to conform to a form and a syntax,/17/ the text under study here does not conform to so rigid a structure. The following table indicates the literary forms of the individual laws before us:

Passage (CDC)	Main Clause	Subsidiary Clause
9:1	כל . . . אשר	
9:2–8	אשר אמר + Scriptural proof-text	אם
9:8–12	על השבועה אשר אמר . . . איש אשר	
9:13–16	כל . . . אשר	וכן . . . אם
9:16–23	כל . . . אשר	אם . . . אם . . . ואם . . . אם
9:23–10:2	ואל + imperfect	
10:2f.	אל + imperfect	
10:4–10	זה סרך ל . . .	ואל

The number of forms here is actually quite limited. The protases of the laws almost always begin with a use of *'asher* if the law is casuistic. This is the case in CDC 9:1, 9:2–8, 9:8–12, 9:13–16, and 9:16–23. These constitute the first five laws in the code. The next two, CDC 9:23–10:2 and 10:2f., as well as the second half of 10:4–10, are apodictic laws of negative character. These are formulated, like the Sabbath Code, with *'al* followed by a verb in the imperfect. Only the last law is formulated as an apodictic *serekh*, a form known from elsewhere in the sectarian corpus. Subsidiary conditions are uniformly introduced with *'im*. *We-khen* is used in CDC 9:13–16 to introduce a prescription similar to the preceding one. These laws are certainly much closer in form to those of the legal sections of the Hebrew Bible than to the laws of the tannaitic corpus.

5. *Relationship of the Texts*

Lest anyone suggest that the *Zadokite Fragments* and the *Manual of Discipline* have no relationship one to another, it must be noted that the common vocabulary itself, specifically the technical terminology, ought to convince us at least of the probability that the sources emanate from related circles. While the finding of fragments of the text of the *Zadokite Fragments* at Qumran, in the very same caves in which fragments of the *Manual of Discipline* were found, would also support this assumption, it cannot be seen as decisive. The Qumran library contained many compositions, including biblical, Apocryphal, pseudepigraphal, and sectarian writings. We cannot view this library as some kind of "canon." Books were collected because either they were regarded as authoritative (whatever that would have meant to the sectarians) or because they were the documents of similar groups. For example, the Enoch and Jubilees materials found at Qumran were by no means composed by the sect. They simply formed a part of its library which, like any library, reflected the interests, beliefs, and predilections of the collector.

Nevertheless, the relationship of these two texts cannot be contested. The hallmark of the sectarian texts is in their approach to the derivation of the law. Both of these texts share the basic principle of Qumran legal formulation that laws are derived from Scripture by a process of inspired biblical exegesis which took place in regularly occurring sessions. Further, and perhaps most important, only when the testimony of the two documents is studied at the many points at which they share common details, can we begin to understand either text. Thus, we are led to the conclusion that despite the somewhat different intentions of the two texts, as well as the different socio-communal background of each, they do, in fact, make up the complementary pieces of one puzzle.

From the point of view of method, though, it will be necessary to distinguish them carefully whenever we move beyond the linguistic stage of inquiry. In this way it will be possible to uncover the specific intent of each document and the relationship of the texts one to another.

It can be determined that the sect outlined in the *Manual* subscribed to the self-image portrayed in the Admonition of the *Zadokite Fragments* and shared in its sacred history. The sectarians shared the principles enunciated in the *Zadokite Fragments* concerning the general topics of Jewish law. The constant calls for proper observance of the law in the *Manual*, probably refer to the very laws contained in the *Zadokite Fragments* and known by us to have been derived entirely from the Scriptural exegesis of the sect.

6. *The Sectarian Community*

We learn from the *Zadokite Fragments* that there were groups of sectarians living as perpetual novitiates in various places throughout the Land of Israel. Although they were physically located within the general Jewish society, they subscribed to the principles of the sect and to as many of its observances as were possible outside a self-contained community of perfect holiness such as that at Qumran, described by the *Manual*.

What was the relationship between the two kinds of communities described in our texts? From a theological and legal point of view, the ideal society of the sect was that described in the *Manual* and constituted at Qumran and perhaps in nearby desert communities. This, at least, was closest to the ideal which could be realized before the end of days in which the Temple would pass into the hands of the sect, and its rituals would be conducted in accordance with sectarian rulings. Those sectarians living outside of this center were by definition deprived of the complete purity and sanctity of the life within this substitute sanctuary in the desert.

Apart from its idealized image, it seems to us that the settlement at Qumran served as a kind of central academy and retreat for the sect. Its most devoted members lived their entire lives in this center, never desiring to return to what they saw as the impurity of the general Jewish society. Others, who were less capable of devoting themselves so extensively to the sect, dwelt elsewhere, but may have come once or several times for periods of study at this center. Only those who came to the headquarters could progress beyond the initial stages of the novitiate and enter full-fledged membership in the sect. Of these, many remained permanently at Qumran. Others, for whatever reasons, returned to their homes.

Such a view of the relationship of the two types of communities helps to deal with another problem—that of celibacy and the absence of women from the sect. Somehow, because of the descriptions of celibate Essenes in Philo and Josephus, the theory still persists that the sect was celibate. This is despite the explicit references in the *Rule of the Congregation* and the *Zadokite Fragments* to marriage as part of the normal course of events in both forms of communal structure.

Among the most important pieces of evidence cited for the celibacy of those at Qumran is the disproportionately small number of women and children buried in the cemetery at Qumran. The theory propounded here provides an explanation for this phenomenon. Most of those at the Qumran center lived there for periods of specific duration during which they progressed through the final stages of the novitiate and participated in extensive study, perhaps even copying parts of the Bible and the sectarian documents. Many of these, no doubt, came before marriage or left their wives and families at home at these periods. Indeed, such was normal procedure for those in ancient times wishing to study various disciplines in the academies. Only those who resided in this center permanently would have brought their wives and children to Qumran. Others would have left them at home in the various places in which they lived. Therefore, only a small number of women and children would have been buried at Qumran, even though the members of the sect were not celibate.

7. *The Enigma of the* Temple Scroll

The discovery of the *Temple Scroll* and its subsequent publication in so handsome a format by Professor Y. Yadin/18/ has done much to spur the study of Qumran legal materials. The scroll describes, in the order of the Torah, beginning with the book of Exodus, the structures and appurtenances of the Temple. Laws related to the rites performed in the sanctuary are discussed in the course of describing its structure, equipment, and furnishings. These cultic laws are interspersed in the description and followed by others of a seemingly non-cultic character originating toward the end of the book of Deuteronomy. The author tells us explicitly that the scroll describes the Temple in which Israel will worship *before* the end of days (TS 29:2–10). This is not a Messianic Temple. Rather, it is an ideal Temple, built upon the principles of Scriptural exegesis and the beliefs of the author(s), and intended for the pre-Messianic age.

We will see that the underlying principle upon which the derivation of law in the Temple Scroll is based is different from that of the rest of Qumran literature. In this respect, as well as in the philological, terminological, and literary aspects,/19/ this text reflects an approach somewhere between that of the sect and that which one may project back upon the Pharisees of this period.

Furthermore, this text concerns matters which are, for the most part, outside the purview of this volume. After all, its intent is to describe a sanctuary, while ours is to understand the relationship between the law and the community. The *Temple Scroll* seeks to define the details of the sacrificial cult and its sanctuary, yet these details were in no way actualized in the life of the sect. Ironically, on the subject of the actualization of Temple practice through the observance of ritual purity in everyday life outside the sanctuary, the *Temple Scroll* itself is curiously silent.

How can we explain the silence of the *Temple Scroll* on precisely those matters which were of greatest concern to the sect? We would suggest, despite its provenance at Qumran and the many points of contact between it and the sectarian literature, that it is not a composition authored by the members of the sect. Had the sectarians composed a scroll on Temple practice, we would have expected the strong polemic against the cult as currently conducted, familiar to us from the *Zadokite Fragments*. Such a book would also have attempted to relate the cult to the lives of the sect. We cannot dismiss these omissions by saying that this was not the concern of the author. An ancient author always betrays the community in which and for which he writes. The author of the *Temple Scroll*, however, does not write like a sectarian. He writes like a member of the "priestly circles" which transmitted and studied the cultic writings of the Pentateuch. He sees no need to relate the cult to society. The cult in and of itself is his main preoccupation. Through it, and only through it, may one attain holiness and perfection. The only society that he envisages is one in which the king of Israel manages secular affairs and the priests and Levites, from their central and unique sanctuary, provide almost vicariously for the religious needs of the people. There is no room here for purity in the home, let alone in the sect. And this picture, he emphasizes, is not Messianic, it is his ideal for the present. Who wrote this scroll and why is an enigma we cannot solve, but, even bearing in mind the divergences between the various texts of the sect, it certainly does not fit the framework in which we have been able to locate the *Manual of Discipline*, *Rule of the Congregation*, *Zadokite Fragments*, and the many other compositions of the Qumran sectarians.

8. *The Derivation of Law*

The legal materials of the Dead Sea sect are the result of sectarian biblical exegesis. This exegesis, described in the *Manual of Discipline*, took place in regular study sessions which were part of the life of the sect at its main center. The results of the decisions reached at such sessions were assembled into lists (*serakhim*), and it is in these lists of sectarian legal statements that many of the component parts of the *Manual of Discipline* and the *Zadokite Fragments* had their origins.

What was the method used by the sect in deriving laws from legal *midrashim*? The usual technique was to take words and expressions of the biblical verses which served as the basis of the legal derivation and to weave these into legal statements. Only through textual study, therefore, is it possible to unravel these statements and to uncover their Scriptural basis. Almost never do we find an explicit quotation of the proof-text for a law. Our study of the Sabbath law/20/ has demonstrated this technique unquestionably, and we shall see here that it can be applied to the other areas of law as well.

The sect believed that its interpretations were arrived at under some form of divine inspiration by which God's will would be discovered. According to the Qumran sect, the Law fell into two categories, the *nigleh* ("revealed") and the *nistar* ("hidden"). The *niglot* are those laws rooted in Scripture whose interpretations are obvious to anyone. The *nistarot*, on the other hand, are those commandments the correct interpretation of which is known only to the sect. The sectarian interpretation of the *nistarot* is the result of a process of inspired biblical exegesis, a sort of divinely guided *midrash*. Study sessions were regarded as a medium through which God made known to the sect the correct interpretations of His commandments.

To the sect, all necessary guidance in matters of the Law was available through this process. Two of the most important terms for this exegesis found at Qumran are *perush* and *midrash*. Both of these terms refer specifically to the exegetical process which took place when the written text of the Scriptures was interpreted by the *'ish ha-doresh*, a member of the sect appointed to serve in turn as expounder of the law at a particular session./21/ According to the scrolls, at all times some member of the sect expounded the law. The sect also held meetings of their assembly, the *moshav ha-rabbim*, at which they studied the Bible, explained it, and fixed the law. In their view God inspired the expounder of the law so that he would properly explain each passage. These correct interpretations, the *nistar* ("hidden"), God had kept secret from the Sons of Darkness. Only the members of the sect, the Sons of Light, understood the Scriptures and their legal traditions correctly. The Sons of Darkness knew only the *nigleh* ("revealed"), which they interpreted for themselves in an incorrect manner. Although the sect would not divulge its interpretations to those outside of its ranks, the rest of Israel was regarded by them as culpable for violations of the *nistarot*.

It is true that the sect believed that the Torah was properly understood in the days of the *rishonim*, apparently before the onset of the Hellenistic period. But they laid no claim to a tradition from that period. On the contrary, they claimed that the tradition had been lost. Only they, with divine help, had succeeded in rediscovering the real meaning of Scripture and only they lived in accord with it./22/

The interpretations of the Qumran sect have been likened by many to the Rabbinic concept of oral Law. The Rabbinic point of view assumes that at Sinai, along with the revelation of the written Law, an oral Law was also revealed which was then transmitted orally from Moses, and from generation to generation, until it reached the tannaim. The concept has two main components: the dual revelation and the aspect of tradition./23/ Neither of these beliefs is claimed by the sect for its interpretations. On the contrary, the sect sees the revelation of those laws which are not part of the written Torah as taking place in its own study sessions, not as having been given to Moses on Sinai. Moses received a written Torah only. Further, the Qumranites never attribute any authority to tradition. On the contrary, they assert that, although the correct interpretation of the Torah was once known to the *rishonim*, "the early ones," it has been lost, and the sect must recover the correct interpretation through inspired biblical exegesis.

While both the sect and the later Rabbinic tradition agreed that God granted man the wisdom to interpret Scripture, a point of contention exists here as well. To the Rabbis, God gave this interpretation to Moses on Sinai, and henceforth the tradition flowed. There was only one revelation in the Rabbinic view, at Sinai. Thereafter, it was the responsibility of the Rabbis only to explain and transmit that which they had received at Sinai, in writing and orally. To the sect, God's revelation was eternal and continual, so that in each generation the expounders of the law could derive from Scripture the regulations to be followed in their time.

But of course the Rabbinic dual Torah concept as we have described it cannot be shown to have existed in the early Hasmonean period when the sectarian teachings were taking shape. It is first in evidence in the tannaitic tradition. While the exact dating of the origin of this concept is in fact unavailable, the earliest contexts in which it appears in present form are post-70 A.D. Even if one wanted to take at face value the tannaitic attribution of the concept to the period of Hillel and Shammai,/24/ there would still be a chronological and historical gap between the tannaim and the Pharisees of the Hasmonean period.

Here Josephus, if properly understood, can fill the gap. Josephus in his descriptions of the Pharisees speaks about the Pharisaic traditions of the fathers./25/ He is asserting that the Pharisees had traditions, external to those in the Bible, which they claimed to have received from their fathers. Here there is no claim of Mosaic revelation for these traditions, or even of hoary tradition. Nor is it ever stated that these traditions were oral. It is simply the existence of extra-biblical legal traditions that is asserted. Properly understood, this evidence informs us that the Pharisees had not yet developed the oral Torah concept as it appears later on in the tannaitic tradition, but that the concept of a tradition of law was already present among the Pharisees when the sect's teaching was being developed. Whereas the sect saw the source of its extrabiblical traditions as divinely inspired exegesis, the Pharisees had not yet begun at this time to claim divine authority or even that of hoary antiquity for their extrabiblical practices.

A different approach may be identified in the *Temple Scroll*. Whereas the other texts from Qumran see the extrabiblical material as derived from inspired biblical exegesis, the author of the *Temple Scroll* sees it as inherent in the biblical text. He weaves his extrabiblical material into the text in several ways. Often, in constructing his material from the various biblical verses, he hints at *midrashim* which demonstrate his point of view. On the other hand, he often adds directly to the text statements which have no basis in Scripture. The author is making the claim, then, that the "extrabiblical" traditions are not extrabiblical. He claims that they are an integral part of the text and have the same status as the text.

The approach of the *Temple Scroll* is like that of the Pharisees of Josephus in that the author of the Scroll believes the "extrabiblical" material to be authoritative. Like the later Rabbinic concept of oral Law, he sees the material as having been given at Sinai. Hence he includes it directly in his "Torah." His approach may be contrasted with that of the other Qumran materials, which see the extrabiblical material as originating in an inspired exegetical process, not in the Sinaitic revelation. In this respect, the author of the *Temple Scroll* appears closer to what would eventually become the tannaitic viewpoint that to that of what we have come to call the Dead Sea sect.

9. *The Method*

The study presented in this volume is the result of the application of a specific method to the interpretation of the material before us. The method may be described as both philological and historical, both synchronic and diachronic. Each text is understood first as an individual passage, then within the context of its document and of the Qumran corpus in general. It is then compared to other Jewish legal texts and traditions in an effort to provide a wider background for its explanation and in order to fix its place in the history of Jewish law.

Let us explain each of these steps in greater detail, so that the chapters that follow will be better understood. The first step in investigating any passage is the fixing of its correct reading. To this end the philological notes indicate alternate readings as well as emendations where advisable. These notes are based both on the investigation of the photographs and published plates of the original manuscripts as well as on the various editions and commentaries on the scrolls.

Once the text is established, notes attempt to present relevant philological data, including explanation of the linguistic usages, legal terminology, and parallel passages in the Hebrew Bible. This last step is most important since research in the legal texts of the Dead Sea Scrolls must be founded upon an understanding of the role of Scriptural exegesis in the material before us. By the careful dissection of the texts, it can be determined which biblical texts served as the bases for the Qumran material, and how these texts were interpreted by the sect.

The importance of the philological notes cannot be over emphasized. It has become evident that only in the process of preparing such notes could a passage really be understood. While it might be argued that there is no need to present all these notes, it is, in fact, obligatory for a scholar to make completely clear the road he traveled in arriving at his conclusions. Since the basic ingredient of these conclusions will always be our understanding of the simple meaning of the text, such data is extremely important. Further, it is hoped that by laying out the full basis of our study, others may be better stimulated to add to the debate.

Once the passage is so understood, it must be looked at in the context of the document in which it appears. While the importance of eventually reaching conclusions about the manner in which the various documents were compiled or authored cannot be denied, the most important task for us will be the understanding of the material in its final form, as it represents the thought of the sect when it reached its maturity. Therefore, the passage is first understood in context. Then it may be illuminated by additional material from the other documents of the sect.

Once we understand the text in its own context and in the context of the parallels from the Qumran corpus, it is appropriate to compare it with other corpora of Jewish law. Of course, biblical law must always serve as the basis where its evidence is available. We will want to compare carefully traditions of the Second Temple sources such as Philo, the Apocrypha and pseudepigrapha, as well as Josephus's reports regarding the Second Commonwealth period. We shall also search the vast corpus of the *halakhah* as found in Rabbinic literature, as well as the schismatic traditions of the Karaites and other groups to aid us in our study. These comparative texts represent widely different time periods. Most relevant will be the Second Commonwealth and Talmudic sources, especially those which can be dated to the tannaitic period. Other sources must be used with greater caution.

Comparative sources serve several purposes. First, comparison of the sectarian materials to other corpora establishes the relationship of the groups one to another. Second, these sources often suggest ways of better understanding the Qumran material, since so often they react to the same issues in very similar ways. Comparison will also help us to fill in missing details where this seems reasonable, but always with extreme caution. Finally, comparative sources allow us to place the Qumran material in historical context. Even though it is not possible, by any means, to assume a linear development from biblical tradition to the Qumran corpus to Rabbinic sources, we will nonetheless attempt to arrange the material in chronological order, as it facilitates understanding, and can often help in clarifying the general picture.

In trying to establish a chronological "history of *halakhah*" we are limited by a serious gap in our knowledge. We would like to know the Pharisaic *halakhah* in the Hasmonean period in order to compare it with the material in our text. Unfortunately, our material regarding the Pharisees stems from post-70 A.D. sources. Whether this material appears in Josephus or in the tannaitic materials, we must reckon with its tendentiousness. Also to be taken into account is the great chronological leap between the period in which these later sources were compiled and the period they describe. Further, even if these sources had attempted to represent to us that which their authors had received in complete faithfulness, the impact of the destruction of the country and its central sanctuary in 66–74 A.D. must have wrought vast changes in the form and even content of these materials. These considerations must be kept in mind in reaching conclusions about the history of the *halakhah*.

The legal materials from the Dead Sea caves also serve as an excellent source for an understanding of several aspects of the communal structure and way of life of the sect, as the daily life of the sectarian and of the sect as a whole was regulated closely by the legal texts of the group. The legal texts of any society open a window into its daily life unavailable elsewhere. From law we can learn social history, and this is the case with the Qumran material. Many debates about issues such as celibacy, attitude to outsiders, position of the priests, etc. can best be clarified by detailed investigation of the legal material in the scrolls.

A study of this nature also reveals the self-definition of the sect and the manner in which its law and ritual expressed this attitude. There can be no question that the only proper way to come to an understanding of that all-encompassing phenomenon we call Judaism in any of its manifestations is to understand the legal and ritual tradition, that which is called *halakhah* in Rabbinic Judaism. Thus, the sectarian legal materials, alongside those of theological or doctrinal import, will begin to elucidate how the sect defined itself and what its place was among the constellation of sects and trends which made up the Judaism of the Second Jewish Commonwealth.

NOTES

/1/ See my "Jewish Sectarianism in Second Temple Times," *Great Schisms in Jewish History*, ed. R. Jospe, S. Wagner (1981), 1–46.

/2/ Henceforth abbreviated *HAQ*. The introduction to that volume discusses bibliographical and methodological considerations which are presumed by the present study.

/ 3/ On the organization and literary structure of the *Manual of Discipline*, see P. Guilbert, "Le plan de la 'Règle de la Communauté,'" *RQ* 1 (1958–59), 323–344. While his view of the *Manual* as a unitary composition cannot be accepted, it is difficult to quarrel with his analysis of the literary structure.

/ 4/ "La genèse littéraire de la Règle de la Communauté," *RB* 76 (1969), 528–549.

/ 5/ F. M. Cross, "The Development of the Jewish Scripts," *The Bible and the Ancient Near East*, ed. G. Wright (1965), 198 n. 116.

/ 6/ J. Murphy-O'Connor, "A Literary Analysis of Damascus Document XIX, 33–XX, 34," *RB* 79 (1972), 544–564.

/ 7/ R. de Vaux, *Archaeology and the Dead Sea Scrolls* (1973), 3–41. Cf. J. H. Charlesworth, "The Origin and Subsequent History of the Authors of the Dead Sea Scrolls: Four Transitional Phases among the Qumran Essenes," *RQ* 10 (1980), 213–233.

/ 8/ *Ten Years of Discovery in the Wilderness of Judaea*, trans. J. Strugnell (1959), 151f.

/ 9/ *The Zadokite Documents* (1954), x.

/10/ G. Forkman, *The Limits of the Religious Community* (1972), 64.

/11/ M. Baillet in *Les 'Petites Crottes' de Qumrân, DJD* III (1962), 129, Milik, *Ten Years*, 58, F. M. Cross, *The Ancient Library at Qumran* (1961), 82 n. 46.

/12/ He summarizes his results in "A Literary Analysis of Damascus Document XIX, 33–XX, 34," *RB* 79 (1972), 562–564. Cf. his "A Literary Analysis of Damascus Document VI, 2–VIII, 3," *RB* 78 (1971), 210–232; "An Essene Missionary Document? CD II, 14–VI, 1," *RB* 77 (1970), 201–229; and "The Critique of the Princes of Judah," *RB* 79 (1972), 200–216.

/13/ See his "The Essenes and their History," *RB* 81 (1974), 215–244, largely reprinted as "The Essenes in Palestine," *BA* 40 (1977), 100–124.

/14/ *Ten Years*, 151f.

/15/ "Prolegomenon" to S. Schechter, *Documents of Jewish Sectaries* (1970), 18f.

/16/ CDC 9:1 has been the source of much discussion. We cannot be certain, however, if it is fully preserved. According to Milik (see above, 9), the still unpublished cave 4 MSS of the *Zadokite Fragments* indicate that CDC 9 actually came after CDC 16. Since the end of CDC 16 is so fragmentary, we cannot be certain that it did not constitute the beginning of a passage the continuation of which was preserved in CDC 9:1. Whatever its exact meaning, it is certainly based on the legal exegesis of Lev. 20:23, 27:28f., and Gen. 9:6. This latter passage has escaped the attention of scholars dealing with our passage. Cf. the discussions of P. Winter, "Ṣadokite Fragments IX, 1," *RQ* 6 (1967–69), 131–136, Z. Falk, "*Beḥuqey hagoyim* in Damascus Document IX, 1," *RQ* 6 (1967–69), 569, I. Rabinowitz, "The Meaning and Date of 'Damascus' Document IX, 1," *RQ* 6 (1967–69), 433–435, and M. Delcor, "The Courts of the Church of Corinth and the Courts of Qumran," *Paul and Qumran*, ed. J. Murphy-O'Connor (1968), 72f. The same article appeared in French as "*Les tribunaux de l'église de Corinthe et les tribunaux de Qumrân*," *Studiorum paulinorum congressus internationalis catholicus* (1961), 535–548. Y. Yadin,

Megillat Ha-Miqdash (1977) I, 292 sees this passage as dealing with Molekh worship. It is hoped that the further publication of Qumran fragments of our text may illuminate this passage.

/17/ *HAQ*, 80–83.

/18/ *Megillat Ha-Miqdash*, 3 vols. (1977).

/19/ See my article, "The *Temple Scroll* in Literary and Philological Perspective," *Approaches to Ancient Judaism* II, ed. W. S. Green (1980), 143–155 and B. Levine, "The Temple Scroll: Aspects of its Historical Provenance and Literary Character," *BASOR* 232 (1978), 5–23.

/20/ *HAQ*, 84–133.

/21/ *HAQ*, 22–76.

/22/ See M. D. Herr, "*Ha-Reṣef She-Be-Shalshelet Mesiratah shel Ha-Torah*," *Sefer Zikkaron Le-Yitzhak Baer*, ed. H. Beinart, S. Ettinger, M. Stern (1980), 51–55.

/23/ See J. Neusner, "Rabbinic Traditions about the Pharisees before A.D. 70: The Problem of Oral Tradition," *JJS* 22 (1971), 1–18, *The Rabbinic Traditions about the Pharisees before 70* (1971) III, 143–179, and "Oral Tradition and Oral Torah, Defining the Problematic," *Studies in Jewish Folklore*, ed. F. Talmage (1980), 251–271.

/24/ A *baraita'* in B. Shabbat 31a.

/25/ *Ant*. 13, 10, 6 (297–98).

CHAPTER ONE
JUDGES AND THEIR QUALIFICATIONS

1. *The Law of Judges*

The Qumran legal system was both detailed and complex. If our texts do not fully reveal this complexity, it is probably because in the period which they represent, the application of the law was primarily entrusted to judicial discretion. For this reason the courts occupied a central place in the sect, dedicated as it was to exacting conformity to its perception of Jewish law.

In order to ensure the correct application of the law, the sect insisted that its courts conform to specific regulations regarding the number of judges constituting a court, the composition of the courts, the selection of judges, their terms of service, and their minimum and maximum ages. These laws are brought together in CDC 10:4–10:

> **וזה סרך לשפטי העדה עד עשרה אנשים ברורים מן העדה לפי העת ארבעה למטה לוי ואהרן ומישראל ששה מבוננים בספר ההגו וביסודי הברית מבני חמשה ועשרים שנה עד בני ששים שנה ואל יתיצב עוד מבן ששים שנה ומעלה לשפוט את העדה כי במעל האדם מעטו ימו ובחרון אף אל ביושבי הארץ אמר לסור את דעתם עד לא ישלימו את ימיהם**

> And this is the rule of the judges of the congregation, up to ten men, chosen/1/ from the congregation/2/ according to the time, four of the tribe of Levi and Aaron,/3/ and from Israel six, learned/4/ in the *Sefer He-Hagu*/5/ and in the teachings/6/ of the covenant, from twenty-five years old to sixty years old. But let no one over sixty years old take his stand/7/ to judge the congregation. For because of man's transgression,/8/ his days/9/ diminished, and because of God's wrath/10/ with the inhabitants of the earth, He decided to remove/11/ their understanding before/12/ they complete their days.

The text before us outlines the basic structure of the sectarian court. It is to consist of ten chosen men, four of the tribe of Levi and Aaron, and the remainder Israelites. All judges must be conversant with the *Sefer He-Hagu* and with the teachings of the sect. Judges must be between twenty-five and sixty years old when appointed and must retire at sixty. Further, the passage provides an explanation of the upper age limit set. We are told that as a result of man's transgression, his life span was reduced, and senility was to set in before the end of his life.

2. *The Number of Judges on a Court*

This passage requires the appointment of ten judges of the community. Since the text indicates the specific composition of the group, it is certain that these judges constituted a court.

While it is well known that later tannaitic tradition legislated a series of courts of three and twenty-three and a high court of seventy-one,/13/ the court of ten is not unprecedented in Jewish law./14/ Ecclesiastes 7:19 speaks of the ten magistrates (*shaliṭim*) of the city. In Ruth 4:2 Boaz, intending to perform the "redemption" (*ge'ulah*) of Ruth's ancestral holdings and thereby to make possible his (levirate?) marriage to her, assembles ten "elders" (*zeqenim*). In verse 9 it is stated that these "elders" are to serve as witnesses (*'edim*) to the legal procedure Boaz is performing. Now it might be assumed that this is simply a case of the requirement of a large number of witnesses, as found in the Elephantine papyri and often in Mesopotamian and Demotic legal practice./15/ Yet one cannot escape the impression that this is a court, albeit convened on an *ad hoc* basis, which *qua* court, is to certify the procedure. It is not unusual in Jewish law for the court to bear witness to the correct discharge of a legal procedure or obligation./16/

Josephus testifies to courts of seven./17/ Even though he attempts to attribute such a procedure to Mosaic revelation, there can be little question that he is reflecting the usage of his own day./18/

Ginzberg/19/ suggests that the passage under discussion may be compared with the Hellenistic δέκα πρῶτοι, the ten men who ruled the city. He sees this as an example of Hellenistic influence on the sect's legal system. These ten men ruled in the Hellenistic cities of Phoenicia and may be presumed to have had a role in the affairs of the Hellenistic cities of Palestine. Josephus's reference to a delegation of ten such men, the high priest, and treasurer/20/ may indicate that such a system was in use in the governance of Jerusalem and the Temple in the period of the procurator Festus (60–62 A.D.)./21/ But it must not be forgotten that these are not judges, but representatives.

Since as a rule the sect and its writings represent the least Hellenized group in all of Palestinian Judaism in the Second Commonwealth period,/22/ it is difficult to accept Ginzberg's assertion of Hellenistic influence, especially in light of the parallel from Ruth. While the Essenes are known to have had courts consisting of at least one hundred,/23/ it is possible that Josephus refers to an Essene court of ten./24/

In cases of *'arakhin* ("valuations"), the donation of the value of a specific field to the Temple, the Mishnah requires that the appraisal of real property must be carried out by ten men, one of whom must be a priest./25/ Ginzberg rightly notes that this body serves only to appraise the property and, therefore, cannot really be called a court./26/ Nonetheless, amoraic sources/27/ contain some indications that courts of ten may have had a place in Palestinian and Babylonian Jewish practice. Joshua ben Levi (Palestinian) refers to "ten who sit in judgment." Rav Huna's (Babylonian) statement, however, that when a case came before him, he would assemble ten rabbis from the academy to share the responsibility with him seems irrelevant. Such a practice would result in a total of eleven judges./28/

Two late midrashic sources, Exodus Rabbah 15:20 and Pirqe Rabbi 'Eli'ezer 8/29/ prescribe the presence of ten judges for the intercalation of the year. Earlier sources, however, contain a debate as to whether three or seven judges are sufficient for the conclusion of the procedure./30/

Ruth 4:2 served for Anan ben David, the eighth century Karaite, to indicate that the minimum number of judges on a court was ten./31/ It is difficult to be certain if Benjamin of Nahawend accepted or rejected this view./32/ Certainly, it is known that no such requirement was normative in medieval Karaite practice./33/ Ginzberg,/34/ perhaps caught up in the effort to disprove the claims of Karaite authorship of the *Zadokite Fragments*,/35/ disputes even the attribution of such a requirement to Anan, but his argument is based primarily on later sources. Since later Karaites often rejected Anan's views and even saw him as fanatical,/36/ such sources cannot be used to establish his views, except when they are directly quoting him.

DSD 8:1f. mentions a group of fifteen sectarians, twelve "people" (*'ish*) and three priests. This group is termed there *'aṣat ha-yaḥad*, the "council of the community." While some scholars have seen the text as referring to a court of twelve of which three are priests, a fragment from cave 4, as reported by J. T. Milik, indicates that a total of fifteen are intended./37/

Some commentators have seen this group of fifteen as a body within the sect, perhaps made up of its core leadership./38/ On the other hand, the continuation of the passage (DSD 8:2–10) reads like a general description of the sect. The text does not mention any executive, judicial, or legislative function for this group./39/ It is probable, then, that the text indicates here the minimum number of members and required composition for the sect. Indeed, E. F. Sutcliffe has suggested that this text reflects the earliest stage when the sectarian settlement at Qumran was about to be founded. The fifteen, in his view, were to be the initial pioneers in the new community. They would found the sectarian settlement under the direction of the teacher of righteousness./40/ His view is in agreement with the theory offered by J. Murphy-O'Connor for the development of the *Manual of Discipline*./41/

Whether Sutcliffe's theory is accepted or not, there can be no question that this text deals only with a minimum number of members for the sect or for a particular settlement of its members. This group can in no way be seen as a court or representative body.

There are, however, indications of other judicial bodies in the sectarian literature. The *moshav ha-rabbim*, the sectarian legislative and judicial assembly, most probably functioned as the highest court,/42/ much as the Great Sanhedrin is said to have functioned according to tannaitic sources./43/ But another small court may be described in 4Q Ordinances, Fragment 2–4 (lines 4–6):/44/

עשר]ה אנשים
וכוהנים שנים ונשפטו לפני שנים העשר האלה] וכל[
דבר בישראל על נפש על פיהם ישאלו ואשר ימרה[ ]
יומת אשר עשה ביד רמה

[te]n men/45/
and two priests, and there shall be judged before these twelve [and every]/46/
case/47/ concerning anyone/48/ in Israel, according to them shall they ask/49/
and anyone who rebels/50/ [ ]
He will be put to death/51/ one who transgresses intentionally./52/

While the missing sections (the ends of the lines) probably account for some fifty per cent of the fragment, some tentative conclusions can be drawn. This passage refers to a court of twelve of which two are to be priests and ten Israelites. This court is to have jurisdiction in capital matters and those who rebel, presumably against its decisions, will be punished. Since no other information is available, there is no way of knowing if this court of twelve is part of the same judicial system as the court of ten. Perhaps 4Q Ordinances represents another view or a different historical period within the legal corpus of Qumran literature.

The number ten manifests itself once more in DSD 6:3f. which is of some interest here:

ובכול מקום אשר יהיה שם עשרה אנשים מעצת היחד אל ימש מאתם
איש כוהן ואיש כתכונו ישבו לפניו וכן ישאלו לעצתם לכול דבר

In every place in which there are ten men from the council of the community,/53/ there should not be absent from them a priest, and each man according to his proper place shall sit before him, and thus shall they be asked for their counsel on any matter.

This text does not actually deal with a court. Apparently, the sect had some small groups of members scattered throughout Palestine. This text requires that every group of ten must include at least one priest to undertake the leadership of the local group. This is in accord with what is otherwise known of the role of the priests in the sect. No doubt, the priests in these small groups did exercise some quasi-judicial functions, but they did not serve as judges *per se*.

3. *The Composition of the Court*

In view of what is known about the structure and makeup of this sect, there is no reason to be surprised at the requirement that both members of "the tribe of Levi and Aaron" and Israelites are to be represented on the bench. Indeed, it appears from many passages that the sect was mustered and conducted its affairs in four groups: priests, Levites, Israelites, and proselytes./54/ Since many passages make clear that the conduct of the affairs of the sect was primarily in the hands of the Zadokite priests,/55/ it would be logical to assume that these judges were Zadokites. Nonetheless, there is no proof of this. Indeed, the phrase *le-maṭeh lewi we-'aharon*, "from the tribe of Levi and Aaron," is so unusual as to offer no clue as to the identity of these judges./56/

Even more enigmatic is the requirement that the positions be apportioned in the ratio of six Israelites to four members of "the tribe of Levi and Aaron." A solution to this problem has been suggested by J. T. Milik who points out that the organization of the tribe of Levi in the *War Scroll* may be of help in understanding the composition of the court./57/ In the *War Scroll* the Levites were divided into the priests (referred to there as sons of Aaron) and the Levitical families of Kohath, Gershon, and Merari. Indeed, Yadin had noted that this division was based on the organization of the tribe in the desert period as described in Numbers./58/ Milik suggests that the four members of the "tribe of Levi and Aaron" in our passage would be, therefore, one each corresponding to the three Levitical families and the Aaronide priests. It is not necessary in order to accept Milik's view to assume that all Levites knew the families from which they were descended. The correspondence need not have been literal but may have been only figurative.

There can be no question that priests occupied a central role in the judicial process in biblical times since the Temple serves as the location of the highest court. This practice was apparently still in effect when Alexander the Great came to Palestine (332–331 B.C.) as is evident from a fragment of the *Aegyptiaca* of Hecataeus of Abdera./59/ He describes the priests as "judges in all major disputes."

Tannaitic sources also indicate that priests were often part of the judicial system. Indeed, the *Sifre* requires that priests and Levites be part of the high court of seventy-one (Great Sanhedrin). Nonetheless, the *Sifre* concludes that if they are unavailable, their absence does not render the court invalid./60/ The *bet din shel kohanim* mentioned in tannaitic sources/61/ apparently had jurisdiction only over matters of the Temple and priesthood. Nonetheless, it probably had its origins at a time when the priests served as the primary members of the judiciary. When this was no longer the case, the priestly courts continued to function in cultic matters.

Josephus, when discussing the seven judges who served in his day, indicated that each judge was assigned two Levitical *shoṭerim*./62/ Josephus's statement, however, does not provide us with a parallel to a court composed of both Levites and Israelites since the function of the *shoṭerim* was only to summon the litigants and enforce the decisions of the court. These Levites were by no means judges.

Those serving on the sectarian court, regardless of whether Levites or Israelites, were required to be schooled in both the *Sefer He-Hagu* and the *yissure ha-berit* ("teachings of the covenant"). (It will not be necessary to discuss these terms in detail since they have been analyzed fully elsewhere.)/63/ The *Sefer He-Hagu* here is probably the biblical text, and the *yissure ha-berit* are the regulations which emerged from the sectarian exegesis of the Bible. These two corpora are analogous to the *nigleh* and *nistar*, which likewise refer to Scripture and its sectarian exegesis./64/ Indeed, these were the two foundations of the sect's legal system. It is therefore to be expected that all judges of the sect would be required to be learned in this material.

4. *Selection and Terms of Judges*

The meaning of *berurim . . . le-fi ha-'et*, "chosen . . . according to the time," in our passage is difficult to establish. Clearly, Ginzberg is correct that *berurim* must be understood as referring to the legal selection of judges./65/ Indeed, tannaitic usage employs the *qal* of *brr* to refer to the act of selecting judges./66/

Tannaitic *halakhah* seems to have envisioned two kinds of courts of three. One would be appointed, presumably by the *nasi'*, with the approval of the court of seventy-one, just as the courts of twenty-three were appointed./67/ The other would be an *ad hoc* court set up to adjudicate financial matters whenever any dispute might arise. Judges for these *ad hoc* lower courts were selected (*brr*) by a process wherein each litigant would choose a judge, and the two judges, in turn, would choose a third. These *ad hoc* courts of three had jurisdiction only in *dine mamonot*, "money matters." While it seems that the court of ten in this Qumran passage is a centrally appointed court and that it must have been set up by the *moshav ha-rabbim*, the sectarian assembly,/68/ it is not impossible that such courts were convened on an *ad hoc* basis, like the tannaitic court of three.

Philo may also provide a parallel to the term *berurim*. In discussing the general qualifications of a judge, Philo refers to them as "chosen by lot or by election."/69/ This passage has engendered some discussion. I. Heinemann remarks on this passage that elsewhere Philo tells us that the Jews did not choose judges by lot, as did the Greeks./70/ But actually, the passage referred to/71/ relates to the rulers (ἀρχῆς) who functioned in "executive" rather than "judicial" capacities. This latter Philonic passage is based on the law of the king in Deut. 17:15 and certainly could not have been understood by Philo to refer to judges. Nonetheless, the strong attack by Philo on the use of lots to select the magistrates/72/ would mitigate against his having looked positively on the selection of judges in this manner. Indeed, he praises Moses for not having used such a technique for the appointment of authorities./73/ If so, the original passage may simply have been reflecting the reality of the Alexandrian Jewish community of his day,/74/ even if he himself did not approve of that reality.

The matter is further complicated by the phrase *le-fi ha-'et*, "according to the time." Ginzberg,/75/ after citing Ben Sira 6:8 which he translates "as long as is convenient," and which literally means "temporarily,"/76/ translated our passage as "as long as they are fit." In both our passage and Ben Sira, *le-fi ha-'et* has the neutral meaning of "temporarily," and no motivation or reason is inherent in the expression. Only context can supply the correct interpretation. It should be noted that Ginzberg's interpretation regarding fitness would apparently mean that the judges would serve until they were unfit by virtue of age, according to the requirements described below in this text. A more likely possibility is that *le-fi ha-'et* be taken with *berurim* to indicate that judges served for some specific term or occasion. In other words, they were selected to serve temporarily. If so, the possibility again is raised that what is being described here may be an *ad hoc* court of ten convened whenever its services were needed.

CDC 14:12–16 describes the social welfare function of the examiner and the judges./77/ Hence, according to this second passage, the status of judge did not begin and end with a particular case. Rather, the judges were regular appointees who were available whenever cases demanded their attention and who handled other matters as well. It is possible that *berurim le-fi ha-'et* refers to their having been selected to serve a specified term which would end at a predetermined time, but no parallel to such a practice may be cited from any other Jewish legal source.

The *Manual of Discipline*, unfortunately not available to Ginzberg when he proposed his interpretation, shows that the term *'et* had a specific connotation in the literature of the Dead Sea Sect. DSD 9:13–14 exemplifies this usage:

לעשות אש רצון אל ככול הנגלה לעת בעת ולמוד אש כול השכל הנמצא לפי העתים ואת חוק העת

> To do the will of God according to everything that is revealed from time to time/78/ and to learn/79/ all the knowledge which is derived/80/ according to the times, and the law of the time.

To the sectarian the continual process of revelation took place through the medium of inspired biblical exegesis. As the law was revealed in this way to the sectarians in their sessions of the *moshav ha-rabbim*, it was codified in their texts. It was believed by them that the law of the times reflected the present state of that which had been revealed to them through exegesis, but that future study would inevitably cause changes in the law.

This same concept is found in DSD 9:18–20 which refers to *kol ha-nimṣa' la-'asot ba-'et ha-zot*, "all which is derived (for them) to do at this time." This motif is encountered over and over again in the sectarian literature./81/ Also to be noted is CDC 12:19–22 in which it appears in conjunction with the *mishpaṭ*, the sectarian regulations which would have played so important a role in the deliberations of the judges (*shofeṭim*) of the community.

Analysis of the term *'et* in its sectarian usage suggests perhaps that *le-fi ha-'et* in the rule for choosing judges of the congregation might refer to the existing law about the procedure as it was derived by sectarian exegesis. If so, judges would be chosen in accord with the current requirements of the sectarian legal system.

5. *Minimum Age of Judges*

It is now time to turn to the age limits set by this passage. In order to understand fully these age requirements, it is necessary to compare other Qumran legislation dealing with age limits. A detailed account of the ages of the men in various military units is given in the *War Scroll* (DSW 6:13–7:3). The required minimum age for military service is twenty-five, and the maximum is sixty.

1QSa 1:6–19 contains a similar listing of the ages and classifications of the members of the sect in the "end of days." While earlier stages in life are indeed mentioned, twenty-five appears as the required minimum for service (lines 12–13):/82/

> **ובן חמש ועש[ר]ים שנה יבוא להת[יצ]ב ביסודות עדת הקודש לעבוד את עבודת העד[ה]**
>
> And at twen[ty]-five years of age he will come to take his sta[n]d among the units/83/ of the holy congregation to perform the service of the congrega[tion].

This text does not specify a maximum age of service. Nevertheless, Licht has concluded from the parallels under discussion here and from context that service would have ended at sixty.

It is furthermore questionable as to what kind of service is implied. Because of the parallel in the *War Scroll*, Licht rightly assumes that military service is being discussed. Despite the frequent use of military terms for cultic service, it is unlikely that the passage refers to the age of participation in cultic service, since the text seems to fix twenty as the age of majority for such purposes (1QSa 1:9f.).

Two other age limitations must be noted here. CDC 14:6–9 specifies the ages for the *kohen 'asher yifqod 'et ha-rabbim* (elsewhere called the *paqid*) as between thirty and sixty. The *mevaqqer* (examiner) over all the camps must be between thirty and fifty years old.

In evaluating these parallels, it must be remembered that the sect saw itself as living on the verge of the end of days. They therefore organized themselves in "this world" (to borrow the Rabbinic phrase) on the model of how they were to be organized in the future age. Furthermore, they saw themselves as an army about to do battle with the forces of evil (Sons of Darkness) for which they were ever preparing. Hence, it is in no way surprising that the minimum age for judging was the same as that for military service. Nor is it strange to find agreement between the *War Scroll* and *Rule of the Congregation* (*Serekh Ha-'Edah*) since they describe aspects of the same end of days.

Yet these parallels are not sufficient explanation for the ages given for both military and judicial function. It must be asked how the sect arrived at these numbers.

Yadin has discussed the ages of conscription in detail in his introduction to the *War Scroll*./84/ He notes that the "general age of conscription" in the Pentateuch is twenty./85/ He explains that the sect, in fixing the minimum age at twenty-five, understood the Bible to mean "that no one is mustered below the age of twenty, but that men are not necessarily conscripted at this age."/86/ In other words, there was no positive commandment, in their view, that a qualified young man serve in the army from the age of twenty. Yadin advances two explanations for the minimum age set by the sect. First, he suggests that since it was composed of priests, Levites, and Israelites, and the sect desired to "equalize the tasks and rights of its members," it had to set the minimum age for all members at twenty-five since this was the age set by the Torah for Levitical service./87/ A second reason Yadin gives is the desire to keep young people out of the camps, to prevent, according to him, impurity and homosexuality.

Yadin's second reason is unlikely. 1QSa 1:9f. specifies the age of sexual maturity and marriage as twenty. There is no reason to apply the fears which Yadin has mentioned, therefore, to those between the ages of twenty and twenty-five. As to the first reason, the idea of equal rights, it seems from all other texts of the sect that these three groups did *not* enjoy equal rights. The members were mustered in the order of priests, Levites, Israelites, and this mustering indicated their order of status in regard to following orders and speaking in the sectarian assembly, the *moshav ha-rabbim*./88/ The Zadokite priests were accorded special preference above all. The entire sect was structured on a system of gradual promotion in status, regarding both entrance to the sect, and status within it. Little credence, then, ought to be given to the motive of equalization of rights and duties.

A better explanation would take its cue from the sect's self-conception and would offer an explanation as well for the fixing of the same minimum age for both judicial and military service. The sect no doubt accepted the legitimacy of only the Zadokite priesthood. Nevertheless, in its way of life, it attempted to extend the requirements of the priesthood to all men. At times, one is not sure if the title "Sons of Zadok" in Qumran writings refers to the priests of such lineage or the sect as a whole. Certainly, the long exegesis of Ezek. 44:5 found in CDC 3:21–4:4 understands the Sons of Zadok as equivalent to the sect. This would be natural considering the pre-eminent part the Zadokites had in the conduct and life of the Qumran group. In this context we also can understand the requirement of pure food in the Qumran sect as well as in the Pharisaic *ḥavurah*./89/

It may therefore be proposed that the sect took the minimum age for Levitical service as prescribed in Num. 8:24 as the rule for both military and judicial service. (The sect does not accept the maximum age given in this same verse, as will be discussed below.) The fixing of the ages of military service at twenty-five, then, was not undertaken out of a desire to grant equal rights and duties to all, but because the sect sought to elevate all its members to the highest status of Levitical sanctity and, in so doing, to ensure the holiness of their courts and military camps.

Num. 4:3, 23, 30, 35, 39, 47 would seem, as noted by Yadin, to prescribe an age of thirty for Levitical service. The tannaim resolved this contradiction by explaining that from twenty-five the Levite was in training, and that he would enter full service only at thirty./90/ Such an explanation would fit the sect's military organization as well. Even though one began to serve from the age of twenty-five, this service was, in the words of Yadin, as "service troops" who "despoil the slain, collect the booty, cleanse the land, guard the arms, prepare the provisions." Only above the age of thirty did one enter actual combat./91/

Indeed, Licht has correctly interpreted 1QSa 1:14f. as indicating that a minimum age of thirty was required for serving in battle as an officer. We will see that this passage clearly refers to active offensive units which were to be made up only of those above thirty./92/ M. 'Avot 5:21 should be understood similarly. *Ben 'esrim li-redof, ben sheloshim la-koaḥ* means that military service begins at twenty (according to the Rabbinic view) but initial service involves only pursuit (*li-redof*) and despoiling of the enemy after the initial offensive confrontation. Only from thirty does one participate in the offensive (*koaḥ*).

In the case of judges, no such distinction was made by the sect. Once twenty-five one might serve as a judge. It can only be surmised here that the sect felt that those called upon to serve, albeit in secondary military functions, had the right to be considered responsible members of the sect, and, hence to serve as judges. It must be remembered that the large courts of the sect comprised of a minimum of ten members representative of the three major classes of the sect—priests, Levites, and Israelites—functioned like juries, and so the danger of allowing those with limited experience resulting from youth to serve on the court was much less than might otherwise be the case.

6. *Maximum Age of Judges*

If the minimum age of judicial and military service was based on the Pentateuchal requirements for Levitical service, how can the maximum age of sixty be explained? After all, Num. 4:3, 23, 30, 35, 39, 47 fix the end of Levitical service at age fifty. Yadin correctly notes that according to Num. 8:25f., while active service for Levites ceased at fifty, certain subsidiary duties were continued after fifty. Such is the case in the *War Scroll* as well. Those reaching the age of fifty no longer went forth to active battle. They might continue to serve militarily in the subsidiary position of *sorekhe ha-maḥanot*, camp prefects. Such service had to end at sixty. Others, it should be noted, from age fifty, served as part of the *mishmarot* (or *ma'amadot*) (DSW 2:4f.). The text of the *War Scroll* specifies no mandatory retirement from this function, although we might assume sixty in light of the parallels./93/

Whereas the Qumran texts give no explicit rationale for the minimum age of twenty-five, either for judicial or military service, the maximum age is in marked contrast. CDC 10:7–10 specifically states that judges must be retired at sixty because senility develops beginning at this age. Senility, along with the shortened life span of man, is seen as a punishment for man's transgressions.

One might be tempted to explain our text as referring to Adam's fall as a result of his sin in the Garden of Eden. Indeed, numerous Rabbinic sources attest to the notion that Adam's powers and size were considerably reduced after the fall./94/ Yet the parallel in Jub. 23:11 links the conditions of old age and senility with Abraham. Rabbinic parallels can be adduced for the idea that with Abraham, man's life span was reduced and senility began to occur./95/ At any rate, it is not necessary to look for a particular sin committed by Abraham which would be the cause of these developments. After all, our text makes clear that God's anger was directed against mankind in general (*ha-'adam yosheve ha-'areṣ*). This last point supports the notion that our text does not refer to the fall of Adam, as *yosheve ha-'areṣ*, "the inhabitants of the earth," would hardly be an appropriate expression with which to describe Adam and Eve.

1QSa 2:7f. lists the feeble old man (*'ish za*[*qen*] *koshel*) among those afflicted with impurities or physical defects who may not take their place among the congregation. It is clear from ll. 9f. that congregation (*'edah*) here refers to the assembly of the community. The text specifically states that the reason for exclusion of such people is that the holy angels are among the community. Those with disabilities would not be permitted to be in the presence of the angels.

Indeed, the very same explanation appears in DSW 7:6 for the exclusion from going to war of women, young men, and those with various types of physical blemishes or impurities./96/ Nevertheless, this passage does not mention the feeble old man. Of course, it is known from other passages in the *War Scroll* that no one over sixty was allowed to have any role in the military service of the sect. Perhaps to some extent this desire to ensure maximum purity and perfection was operating in the exclusion of old men from the military, although the practical military considerations would be paramount./97/

In an effort to explain the basis on which military service ceased at sixty, Yadin cites Lev. 27:3, which he translates, "Then thy valuation shall be for the male from twenty years old even unto sixty years old." Such a derivation would certainly violate the context of the Scriptural passage in question, but context was never a deterrent to the sect nor to the Rabbinic interpreters of the Bible. Indeed, as Rabin/98/ notes, this passage prescribes sixty as the "limit of full value."

Lev. 27:3 would have served to indicate for the sect the upper limits of military service. They would have used it in a legal *midrash* to interpret Num. 8:25 where it is indicated that subsidiary Levitical service might continue beyond fifty, but where no age limit was set. This verse would have allowed the sect to assume a limit of sixty years of age for this subsidiary service. Accordingly, the sect would allow no one, neither judge, soldier, nor official, to serve beyond sixty. The ultimate reasons for forbidding such over-aged service would be, as explained in the Dead Sea texts, the need to ensure the ritual purity of the military camp and to avoid the effects of senility which so often came with old age and which would have severely diminished the abilities of a judge or sectarian official.

7. *Ages of Other Sectarian Officials*

It is appropriate here to compare the ages of two officials of the sect as specified in the *Zadokite Fragments*. CDC 14:6f. reads:

והכהן אשר יפקד אש הרבים מבן שלושים שנה עד בן ששים

And the priest who shall muster/99/ the assembly/100/ (shall be) from thirty to sixty years old.

CDC 14:8f. requires that:

והמבקר אשר לכל המחנות מבן שלשים שנה עד בן חמשים שנה

And the examiner/101/ of all the camps/102/ (shall be) from thirty years old to fifty years old./103/

These officials may be appointed to their responsibilities only after reaching age thirty. This is consistent with the conclusion reached above that only from the age of thirty was it permitted for young men to enter the offensive troops of the sect. Before that age they were limited to training status and to pursuit and despoiling the enemy.

As mentioned above, a difficult passage in 1QSa 1:14f. also indicates the same minimum age of thirty for service as an official or officer of the sect:

ובן שלושים שנה יגש לריב ריב [ומשפ]ט ולהתיצב בראשי אלפי ישראל לשרי מאות שרי ח[מ]שים [ושרי] עשרות

And at the age of thirty years old he shall draw near to struggle for the cause of [justi]ce/104/ and to take his stand/105/ at the head of/106/ the thousands/107/ of Israel, as officers of hundreds, officers of fi[f]ties, [and officers] of tens . . ./108/

While some might choose to see the beginning of this passage as referring to participation in the legal process, this is certainly not its meaning./109/ First, the context shows that this passage concerns the combined organizational and military duties of a sectarian. Second, the continuation of the passage indicates without doubt its military rather than judicial connotation./110/ Third (and this must remain a secondary argument to avoid falling into the trap of harmonization), it is known from elsewhere that the sect already allowed full participation in the judicial process to those who reached twenty-five. The right to testify in capital matters was granted to those at least twenty, and the right to serve as a judge to those over twenty-five. Certainly, then, this requirement of age thirty cannot refer to judicial matters, but, once again, reflects sectarian military organization. Finally, the parallel phraseology of lines 20f. also shows without doubt that the subject is that of the eschatological military organization of the sect.

What emerges from the analysis of this passage is once again a parallel between the minimum age for officials of the sect, officers in its army, and full service in the offensive troops of the eschatological war. The sect had structured its own organization to fulfill its prophecies of the soon-to-dawn end of days, and its system of age limits fit into this scheme of things.

What can be the justification behind the maximum ages prescribed for the officials by the *Zadokite Fragments*? The age of sixty, the maximum age for "the priest who shall muster the assembly," is easily understood. This restriction is in line with the fear of senility mentioned above. No doubt, the work of this official required careful attention to detailed records and the ability to recall those details. Regarding the age of fifty which is specified as the maximum retirement age of the examiner, the probable basis is the maximum age of Levitical service specified in the Torah./111/ The sect believed that its communal structure constituted a kind of holy temple. Its highest official, then—the examiner with central executive authority over all the camps—had to conform to the requirements of Levitical service, even when other officials were allowed to serve until sixty.

A question might arise as to how these ages were calculated. Were they based on a New Year, either Tishre or Nisan, like the regnal years of the First Temple period, or did they depend on the actual intervals after birth of the particular individual? There is no certain answer, but a suggestion can be advanced based on the probable use of Lev. 27:3 as a basis for the maximum age of sixty. A *baraita'* in B. 'Arakhin 18b, as interpreted in an amoraic passage there, indicates that the calculation was made by the number of one-year intervals beginning with the actual birth date of the individual./112/ While one might say that this amoraic interpretation is not necessarily correct, the Tosafot/113/ make a convincing argument based on logic that this is the only possible explanation of the *baraita'*. If we remember that the area of cultic practice was extremely conservative, it may be assumed that this tannaitic method of calculation would probably reflect the custom in Second Temple times. Hence, the ages would be based on one-year intervals counting from the actual date of birth.

8. *Rabbinic Parallels*

P. Sanhedrin 4:7 (9, 22b)/114/ reports in the name of the third century Palestinian amora Rabbi Johanan that for capital cases a judge had to be at least twenty years of age and had to have the physical signs of the onset of puberty. Nevertheless, in money matters, one below twenty or lacking these signs might serve as a judge. It is to be assumed that a minimum age of *bar miṣwah*, thirteen years and one day, would be required for judging money matters. No doubt this passage reflected the practice in Palestine in the third century A.D.

In regard to the twenty year age requirement for judging capital cases in the Palestinian Talmud, it should be noted that CDC 10:1 imposes the same minimum age on witnesses in capital matters./115/ L. Ginzberg/116/ and Ch. Albeck/117/ have argued that these passages and many others indicate that originally the age of legal majority was twenty, not thirteen. Anan ben David, the early Karaite, seems to have accepted twenty as the age of religious majority./118/

Some medieval authorities have understood an *'aggadah* attributed to R. Jonathan, an early third century Palestinian amora, to indicate that it was forbidden to judge before reaching the age of eighteen./119/ This *'aggadah* in B. Shabbat 56b states that Josiah made restitution for all payments made as a result of his judgments *mi-ben shemoneh 'ad shemoneh 'esreh*. This phrase is interpreted to refer to the period between his eighth birthday, when he ascended the throne,/120/ and his eighteenth year when the book of Deuteronomy was found./121/ Josiah made the payments for fear that he had erred in judgment because the book of Deuteronomy had not been available to him. Therefore, the passage has nothing to do with any requirement that a judge be eighteen years old. The medieval views which found an age requirement of eighteen represent a reinterpretation of the passage.

Do Rabbinic sources offer any information about the maximum age of a judge? Rabin refers to M. Horayot 1:4 and a *baraita'* in B. Sanhedrin 36b which, he says, indicate that a *zaqen*, "elder," must not serve in the highest court./122/ He understands the passage to mean, "one who is an elder or who is a eunuch or childless." In reality, the reading of these sources is highly questionable. The *baraita'* as found in T. Sanhedrin 7:5/123/ omits mention of the elder, and MS Florence of the Babylonian Talmud reads *qaṭan*, although medieval citations of the *rishonim*/124/ support the reading *zaqen*.

Further, even if the reading *zaqen* is accepted, we can translate the *baraita'* in B. Sanhedrin 36b as follows: "We do not seat (appoint) in the Sanhedrin an elder who is a eunuch or childless. R. Judah adds even (an elder) who is cruel." Thus, there would be no tannaitic parallel here to the sect's refusal to appoint an elder as judge. Most elders were allowed to serve with the exception of those enumerated. At all events, the passage refers only to capital cases./125/

M. Horayot 1:4 deals with ways in which the high court (Sanhedrin) can be disqualified so that there would be no need to offer the *par he'elem davar shel ṣibbur*, the bull sacrificed to atone for an erroneous ruling by the high court followed by the majority of the people (Lev. 4:13–21). One of the cases involves the presence of a *zaqen she-lo' ra'ah banim*, an elder who had had no children./126/ Rashi notes that such a person would not have the necessary compassion for service in the Sanhedrin.

This *mishnah*, then, disqualifies elders from sitting on the court only when they have had no children. There is no blanket prohibition based on age here./127/ From our point of view, there is no tannaitic tradition which indicates explicitly and unquestionably that elders could not serve as judges. On the contrary, the members of the Sanhedrin are called *zeqenim*./128/

We should add that Talmudic sources give no maximum age for military service. It can be assumed that service would have ceased, according to the Rabbis, at fifty as is indicated in the Pentateuch.

9. *Some Functions of Judges*

An account of the specific duties of the judges of the Qumran community would have been extremely valuable. Unfortunately, such a passage is lacking. There are, however, two passages which cast light on the functions of the judge. These reports must be taken as incidental and in no way should be seen as characteristic or representative.

CDC 14:12–16 describes the social welfare system of the sect.

> ו[וה] סרך הרבים להכין כל חפציהם שכר [ש]ני ימים לכל חדש למ[מ]עט ונתנו על יד המבקר והשופטים ממנו יתנו בעד [יתו]מים וממנו יחזיקו ביד עני ואביון ולזקן אשר [יגו]ע ולאיש אשר ינוע ולאשר ישבה לגוי נכר ולבתולה אשר [א]ין לה ג[ואל ו]לעל[מה א]שר אין לה דורש
>
> And [this] is the rule for the community to provide for all their requirements:/129/ [t]wo days salary per month mi[ni]mum./130/ And they shall give (it) to the examiner (*mevaqqer*) and the judges. From it they shall give for [orp]hans and from it they shall sustain/131/ the poor and needy, the old man who is about to die,/132/ the man who wanders,/133/ the one who is taken captive by a foreign people,/134/ the young woman/135/ who has no close relative/136/ and the unmarried girl/137/ for whom no one cares . . ./138/

Here the judges (and the examiner) are empowered to collect at least eight percent of the income of each member of the sect (not a tithe) to be used for social welfare or charitable purposes./139/ Philo points out that the Essenes fulfilled these needs out of common property,/140/ however, our sect must collect a special fund/141/ since communal use, but not ownership, was the pattern at Qumran./142/ But like the Essenes, the sect dispensed charity communally. In fact, similar practices were the norm in the tannaitic period, and such customs persisted even up to the modern period in Jewish communities./143/

What is especially interesting for this study is that the funds were administered by the examiner (*mevaqqer*) and the judges. It was a function of the combined executive and judicial bodies of the sect to take care of the needy. The needs are seemingly "their" needs, those of the members of the sect. The needy, we may suppose, were members of the sect.

Why should it be that the judges particularly should be so involved in the dispensing of charity to the less fortunate? Perhaps light can be shed on this subject with the aid of a passage in Philo. The last element in Philo's description of the ideal judge is his emphasis on the requirement that the needy or unfortunate *not* be given special treatment before the bar of justice./144/ This is, of course, a Jewish motif entirely, and it is derived from Ex. 23:3. At this point Philo launches into a long discourse on the importance of charity, again emphasizing particularly Jewish values. The only possible explanation for this juxtaposition is that Philo sought to make the point that although charity has no place in the courtroom, it is certainly a primary obligation. This passage suggests that the Qumran materials before us may reflect the same dilemma. How can it be that those charged with enforcing and representing the highest standards of justice in the community should be commanded to ignore the particular needs of the poor? In order to obviate this problem and to be certain that the judges would set the proper example here, the sect legislated participation of the judges in the administration of its social welfare system.

CDC 9:8–10 emphasizes that all oaths must be taken before the judges:

על השבועה אשר אמר לא תושיעך ידך לך איש אשר ישביע על פני השדה
אשר לא לפנים השפטים או מאמרם הושיע ידו לו

Concerning the oath:/145/ As to that which he said,/146/ "You shall not find redress for yourself with your own hand,"/147/ a man who adjures (another)/148/ in the open field,/149/ not before/150/ the judges or (according to) their command,/151/ has found redress for himself with his own hand./152/

Apparently, the seriousness with which the sect looked upon oaths caused them to forbid the taking of an oath outside of court. In this way, vain or false oaths could be avoided.

Licht notes the amoraic argument as to whether a man may do justice for himself./153/ From context it is clear that the Rabbis are questioning whether a man may go on to the property of another to remove (without his permission or the permission of the court) property which he claims rightfully belongs to him. The argument, according to the attributions, must be dated to late third century Babylonia. In the discussion a tannaitic view (attributed to Ben Bag Bag) is cited/154/ saying that a person should not do this lest he appear like a thief. The relevance of all this, however, is doubtful. First, it does not apply at all to oaths./155/ Second, limitations on the powers of the Jewish courts in Babylonia may have led to a situation where such action became necessary and so engendered this amoraic discussion.

What is most interesting about our passage from the *Zadokite Fragments*, however, is the quotation at the beginning. Ginzberg, dealing with the *Zadokite Fragments* before the discovery of the Dead Sea Scrolls, concluded that this passage must be a quotation from the *Sefer He-Hagu*, which he took to be a book of sectarian laws. While later research has shown that the *Sefer He-Hagu* is most probably Scripture, Ginzberg's original conclusion, namely that this was not a quotation of 1 Sam. 25:26, somehow corrupted textually, still stands. This quotation is ultimately derived from some unknown sectarian source. DSD 6:25–27 is likewise based on this quotation:

ואשר ישיב אש רעהו בקשי עורף ודבר בקוצר אפים לפרוע את יסוד עמיתו באמרות את פי רעהו הכתוב לפניהו [הו]שיעה ידו לוא ונענש שנה אח[ת

> Whoever/156/ answers/157/ his neighbor/158/ stubbornly/159/ and speaks impatiently/160/ to reject/161/ the teaching/162/ of his colleague/163/ by disobeying/164/ the command/165/ of the neighbor/166/ listed/167/ before him,/168/ his own hand [has found] redress for him,/169/ and he shall be fined/170/ for on[e]/171/ year./172/

It has been established that the sect followed a complex ranking system in which each member had his own position. This system was used for the purpose of voting in the sectarian assembly (*moshav ha-rabbim*) so as to guarantee each member the right to speak in turn. DSD 5:23 and CDC 14:3–6 give considerable data on this list. It seems that in general the order was priests, Levites, "children of Israel," and proselytes. Within each group, members were placed in order according to their knowledge and deeds./173/

This ranking system was also used for the day to day conduct of affairs. Each member of the sect was obligated to follow instructions from anyone of higher rank. While such a system might seem cumbersome, it was able to function smoothly since the group was so dedicated to their ideals and to the authority structure.

The present law concerns one who, because of stubbornness or impatience, refuses to accept the instructions of a superior and disobeys him. Such a person is described as having taken the law into his own hands and is punished since all actions were to be subject to the divine Law. Only those interpretations of the Law derived and accepted by the sect were correct. Each link in the sectarian chain of authority represented the dissemination of God's word as revealed through the "inspired" biblical exegesis. Further, the sect's leadership was regarded as elected by God. So any member who rejected the instructions or commands of his superior was rejecting a sectarian decision, tantamount to rejecting God's command.

Now what is important for the purpose of this study is that this passage from the *Manual of Discipline* likewise makes reference to this "apocryphal" quotation and indicates that one who violated this law is also violating this quotation. The usage of this quotation is similar to the Rabbinic statements including the clause *'alaw ha-katuv 'omer*, or *ma'aleh 'alaw ha-katuv*, "Scripture says of him," or "Scripture attributes it to him." Licht is certainly correct that the occurrence of this quotation in the *Zadokite Fragments* and its use in the *Manual of Discipline* show that in this case both texts drew from a common source. Not only is this a confirmation of the general thesis that the two works can be used to explain each other, but it is of great significance for the history of the sect as it shows that the documents before us do not represent the earliest phase of sectarian thought and law. Rather, the materials as they are now preserved are the result of an evolutionary process which took place before and during their composition and redaction.

10. *Summary*

The ten judges of Qumran procedure have parallels in the biblical, Hellenistic, and Talmudic periods. These judges served for a specified term. One priest and three Levites (representing the major Levitical families) and six Israelites, all of whom understood both Scripture and its sectarian interpretation, served on the bench.

Study of the age limits set by the *Zadokite Fragments* for judges has shown them to be similar to those for military service. Indeed, the sect attempted to elevate all its members to the status of Levites serving in the Temple. These limits were in consonance with the sect's own interpretations of the relevant biblical material in Num. 8:24f. and Lev. 27:3. Rabbinic parallels were investigated and were shown to provide no real correspondence to the limits set by our text. Nor was it possible to locate any other real parallels. These limits, then, constitute an independent derivation by the sect and were unique to it as far as is known.

It has been seen that the judges played a part in dispensing help to the needy. Also, all oaths had to be taken before them. The taking of oaths outside the court constituted a violation of the precepts of a source quoted in two places but otherwise unknown to us.

NOTES

/1/ See BDB, *s.v. brr*. P. Qiddushin 4:5 (66a) (cited by Schecter) seems to be a parallel usage, although the commentaries translate "pure" in the sense of having proper lineage. (Cf. *Sifre* Num. 92, p. 93 and *Midrash Tanna'im* to Deut. 17:15 (ed. Hoffman, p. 104.) L. Ginzberg, *An Unknown Jewish Sect* (1976), 47f., sees as a closer usage the occurrence of this root in M. Sanhedrin 3:1. Indeed, this usage refers to the process whereby, according to tannaitic law, the judges were selected by the litigants to serve on the bench on *ad hoc* courts of three. The same usage as appears in our text is also found in TS 57:8 (on which see the comments of Yadin) and probably in the broken 3Q 5 frag. 2 (*DJD* III, 97). On this term, see below, 28.

/ 2/ See A. Hurwitz, "*Le-Shimusho shel Ha-Munaḥ 'Edah Be-Sifrut Ha-Miqra'it*," *Tarbiz* 40 (1970/1), 261–267.

/ 3/ For *maṭeh lewi*, see Num. 1:49; 3:6; 17:18; 18:2 (cf. Num. 1:47) in which *maṭeh* is used by the Torah in the sense of "tribe." *Maṭeh 'aharon* occurs in Ex. 7:12; Num. 17:21, 23, 25, all of which use *maṭeh* in the sense of "staff." These usages have been conflated to produce an anomalous phrase, on which see below, 27.

/ 4/ *Mevonanim* is a *polal*, pl. participle, passive in meaning, of the root *byn*. See Ges. sec. 72m and paradigm M. Cf. Deut. 32:10. Note the same usage in the singular in CDC 14:6–8. (Cf. *HAQ*, 44 and notes.)

/ 5/ Scripture (cf. *HAQ*, 44 n. 144).

/ 6/ Reading *yswry* (*yissure*) for MS *yswdy* (*yesode*), against Rabin and Schechter, with Brownlee. Cf. CDC 7:8 (MS A) and 19:4 (MS B) for the confusion of these words (*HAQ*, 46 n. 160). The confusion would have occurred in the *Vorlage* of our copyist as his *dalet* is clear. Cf. CDC 14:6–8 in which parallel *mishpeṭe ha-torah* replaces *yissure ha-berit*.

/ 7/ For the forensic use of the *hitpa'el of yṣb*, see Num. 11:16 (Rabin). Note also Job 33:5 where it is used for answering a charge (BDB).

/ 8/ Rabin (to CDC 19:23) comments that this is an "abstract noun used for inf. constr. (a procedure not uncommon in medieval Hebrew of all periods)." He translates our passage, "when man sinned . . . when God waxed wroth . . ." He is taking the preposition *be-* in a temporal sense while our translation reflects a causal relation, the *bet pretii* (Ges. sec. 119p).

/ 9/ Phonetic spelling of the plural possessive (without *yod*) is common at Qumran. Its presence in our text is not surprising in light of the probable origin of CDC at Qumran. Rabin notes the same form in CDC 2:12 (*meshiḥaw*). It is probable, however, that Y. Yadin's suggestion ("Three Notes on the Dead Sea Scrolls," *IEJ* 6 [1956], 158f.) that we read *meshiḥe* (emending *waw* to *yod*) is correct. Cf. J. Licht, *Megillat Ha-Serakhim* (1965), 47f.; Ḥ. Yalon, *Megillot Midbar Yehudah* (1967), 61f. (first published as "*Megillat Yisha'yahu 'A*," *KS* 27 (1950/1), 163–172), E. Y. Kutscher, *Ha-Lashon We-Ha-Reqa' Ha-Leshoni shel Megillat Yisha'yahu Ha-Shelemah Mi-Megillot Yam Ha-Melaḥ* (1959), 38.

/10/ Schechter's emendation to *be-ḥarot* (cf. Ps. 124:3) is ill-advised in light of the parallelism with *ma'al*, a noun, not an infinitive. In the Bible, the phrase *ḥaron 'af* occurs either with the Tetragrammaton or with a pronoun, only once with *'elohim* (Ezra 10:14) and never with *'el*. No doubt, our text is following the Qumran custom of avoiding the Tetragrammaton. See below, 134. On *ḥaron 'af*, cf. M. Gruber, *Aspects of Nonverbal Communication in the Ancient Near East* (1980) II, 491–502.

/11/ Segal's suggestion that we read *la-sir*, *hif'il* with elided *he'*, is supported by what we now know about this phenomenon at Qumran (Licht, *Serakhim*, 46, cf. Ges. sec. 53q) as well as by the similarity of the letters *waw* and *yod* in the Dead Sea Scrolls (see *HAQ*, 30f. n. 61). This is certainly the simplest interpretation. Nevertheless, if Rabin is correct in seeing this clause as a quotation from Jub. 23:11, his analysis as a *qal* and translation "He commanded that their understanding should depart . . ." would be better. Rabin notes that the Latin: *et erunt transeuntes ab ipsis spiritus intellectus eorum* (see R. H. Charles, *The Ethiopic Version of the Hebrew Book of Jubilees* [1895], *ad loc.*) supports his view. He suggests that the peculiar Hebrew form of accusative with infinitive may lie behind this Latin text. Rabin rejects reading *la-sir* since then *'amar* "could only mean 'He intended.'" I fail to see why this understanding of *'amar* would be objectionable.

/12/ See Prov. 8:26 (Segal). Rabin compares Targumic *'ad la'* and Christian Palestinian Aramaic *'adla' de-* as opposed to Syriac, Galilean, Babylonian *'ad dela'*. His suggestion that the Hebrew has here conditioned the Aramaic usage is unlikely in light of the already established influence of Aramaic on Qumran Hebrew (Licht, *Serakhim*, 44f.).

/13/ M. Sanhedrin 1.

/14/ Cf. Ginzberg, *Sect*, 47, 85, 118, 392.

/15/ R. Yaron, *Introduction to the Law of the Aramaic Papyri* (1961), 17–24.

/16/ Cf. the conversion procedure and my analysis in "At the Crossroads: Tannaitic Perspectives on the Jewish-Christian Schism," *Jewish and Christian Self-Definition* II, ed. E. P. Sanders (1981), 115–156, 338–352.

/17/ *Ant.* 4, 8, 14 (214); *War* 2, 20, 5 (570–571). Note that according to *Ant.* 4, 8, 14 (214) each judge was to have two Levitical officers alloted to him. Presumably these are the equivalent of the *shoṭerim* of Deut. 16:18. Indeed, *Sifre* Deut. 144 (ed. Finkelstein, p. 197) prescribes that the *shoṭerim* be Levites. Cf. 2 Chron. 19:11, *we-shoṭerim ha-lewiyyim*, and M. Weinfeld, "Judge and Officer in Ancient Israel and in the Ancient Near East," *Israel Oriental Studies* 7 (1977), 83–86.

/18/ Cf. the Talmudic expression *shiv'ah ṭove ha-'ir* in amoriac sources (B. Megillah 26a–b). The assertion in E. Schürer, *The History of the Jewish People in the Age of Jesus Christ* II, ed. G. Vermes, F. Millar (1979), 186f., that courts of seven are intended in M. Sanhedrin 3:1 is impossible and contradicts the text completely. Note that seven judges complete the intercalation of the year in M. Sanhedrin 1.

/19/ *Sect*, 85.

/20/ *Ant.* 20, 8, 11 (194).

/21/ Schürer II (1979), 213f. See also M. Stern, "The Herodian Dynasty and the Province of Judea at the End of the Period of the Second Temple," *The Herodian Period*, ed. M. Avi-Yonah (1975), 156 and 358 n. 60. E. E. Urbach, "*Bate-Din shel 'Esrim U-Sheloshah We-Dine Mitot Bet Din*," *Proceedings of the Fifth World Congress of Jewish Studies* (1972), p. 43 nn. 25, 26 and 48 n. 48 assembles sources on courts of ten in Ptolemaic Egypt and Rome.

/22/ See my "Jewish Sectarianism," 1–46.

/23/ *War* 2, 8, 9 (145).

/24/ *War* 2, 8, 9 (146); cf. Ginzberg, *Sect*, 118 n. 42.

/25/ M. Sanhedrin 1:3.

/26/ *Sect*, 47 n. 131. I do not follow the reference to M. Megillah 4:4 as a parallel.

/27/ B. Sanhedrin 7b; B. Horayot 3b.

/28/ Cf. Maimonides, H. Sanhedrin 2:13.

/29/ Cf. David Luria's commentary in ed. Warsaw (1851/2), n. 42, *ad loc.*

/30/ M. Sanhedrin 1:2; T. Sanhedrin 2:1; B. Sanhedrin 10b; P. Sanhedrin 1:2 (18c). Cf. the mention of five in *Wa-Yiqra' Rabbah* 29:4 (to 23:24) and Margaliot, *ad loc.* Apparently, the reference there is to the second stage of the process, according to the view of Simeon ben Gamliel in M. Sanhedrin 1:2. Geonic and medieval halakhic sources speak of the imposition of oaths and adjurations in the presence of ten men. See B. Cohen, *Jewish and Roman Law* (1966) II, 728f., 731. Here the ten function as a ritual quorum in order to render the ceremony public.

/31/ S. Poznanski, "*Anan et ses écrits*," *REJ* 45 (1902), 67. Anan ben David, *Sefer Ha-Miṣwot* in A. Harkavy, *Mi-Sifre Ha-Miṣwot Ha-Rishonim Li-Vene Miqra'* (Zikkaron La-Rishonim VIII, 1903), 171f. The Rabbis took the story of Ruth to indicate that a quorum of ten was necessary (at least before the fact, *le-khatḥilah*) at the ceremony of *ḥaliṣah* (the removal of the shoe to indicate the declining of the brother of the deceased to fulfill the commandment of levirate marriage). See *Pirqe Rabbi 'Eli'ezer* 19 (and the comments of David Luria, *ad loc.*) and *Midrash Tehillim* 92 (ed. Buber, pp. 203b–204a). This quorum functioned only to ensure the public character of the ceremony, not as judges or witnesses.

/32/ See Ginzberg, *Sect*, 150 n. 175 and Benjamin of Nahawend, *Mas'at Binyamin*, 1b.

/33/ Cf. Y. Hadassi, *'Eshkol Ha-Kofer*, 146d, and Aaron ben Elijah of Nicomedia, *Gan 'Eden*, 193b, 194b.

/34/ *Sect*, 150f.

/35/ The new English edition contains an entire chapter devoted to this purpose (338–408). Most of the arguments are directed against A. Büchler, "Schechter's 'Jewish Sectaries,'" *JQR* N.S. 3 (1912/13), 429–485.

/36/ L. Nemoy, "Anan ben David," *EJ* 2, 920.

/37/ For a survey of views see Wernberg-Møller, *ad loc.* and E. F. Sutcliffe, "The First Fifteen Members of the Qumran Community," *JSS* 4 (1959), 134f. On the fragments see J. T. Milik, "*Megillat milḥemet bene 'or bivne ḥošek* by Y. Yadin," (review) *RB* 64 (1957), 589. The text is described in Milik's *Dix ans de découvertes dans le désert de Juda* (1957), 111.

/38/ Sutcliffe, 135f. and M. Weinfeld, "*Defusim 'Irguniyyim We-Taqqanot 'Oneshim Bi-Megillat Serekh Ha-Yaḥad*," *Shnaton* 2 (1977), 63.

/39/ Licht, *ad loc.* and P. Guilbert, in J. Carmignac, P. Guilbert, *Les textes de Qumran* (1961) I, 55.

/40/ Sutcliffe, 137f.

/41/ Above, 4–6.

/42/ *HAQ*, 68–76 and E. F. Sutcliffe, "The General Council of the Qumran Community," *Biblica* 40 (1959), 971–983.

/43/ M. Sanhedrin 1:5–6.

/44/ J. M. Allegro, *DJD* V, 8. Cf. Schürer II, 187 n. 10. Allegro suggests a possible parallel in 4Q IsD, a *pesher* on Is. 54:11, 12, but this passage seems to refer to the twelve Israelites and three priests of DSD 8:1f. or to a group of twelve priests as in DSW 2:1–12 (cf. *HAQ*, 65) or to the advisors to the king in TS 57:11–15. Cf. Y. Yadin, *Megillat Ha-Miqdash* I, 266–268; Y. Yadin, "The Newly Published Pesharim of Isaiah," *IEJ* 9 (1959), 39–42; D. Flusser, "*Pesher Yesha'yahu We-Ra'ayon Shnem-'Asar Ha-Sheliḥim Be-Reshit Ha-Naṣrut*," *Eretz Israel* 8 (1966/7), 52–62; J. M. Baumgarten, "The Duodecimal Courts of Qumran, the Apocalypse, and the Sanhedrin," *JBL* 95 (1976), 59–78 (reprinted in his *Studies in Qumran Law* [1977], 145–171); Y. Yadin, "A Note on 4Q 159 (Ordinances)," *IEJ* 18 (1968), 251f. n. 4; J. Strugnell, "*Notes en marge du Volume V des* 'Discoveries in the Judaean Desert of Jordan,'" *RQ* 7 (1970), 195f.; and F. D. Weinert, "4Q 159: Legislation for an Essene Community outside of Qumran," *JSJ* 5 (1974), 179–207.

/45/ According to Allegro the position of this fragment is tentative. Since Yadin ("A Note on 4Q 159," 250) has omitted this fragment from consideration, apparently he considers it improperly placed.

/46/ Other restorations are with Allegro, *DJD* V, 8. This restoration, however, is tentatively proposed by me.

/47/ The meaning "case" is accepted by Yadin, 252 n. 5.

/48/ So Yadin, 252 n. 6. This is much more likely than "in a capital case," as the sect used *devar mawet* to indicate capital cases.

/49/ This expression occurs in regard to the *moshav ha-rabbim* in DSD 6:8–10 (see *HAQ*, 68). Cf. also DSD 9:7 referring to the priests (see *HAQ*, 70). Yadin (252 n. 7) translates "their ruling they shall seek," and compares Deut. 17:9ff.

/50/ Allegro compares Josh. 1:18. Note the use of *mrh* in a technical sense by the tannaim to refer to a member of the court who rejects its decision and gives legal rulings in accord with his own view.

/51/ It is impossible to know if the verb *yumat*, coming as it does immediately after a lacuna, should be interpreted as belonging to a preceding sentence or to the words that follow it.

/52/ Rabin to CDC 10:3 cites occurrences of *be-yad ramah* in DSD 5:12 and 8:22. In addition, this term occurs in DSD 8:17, 9:1; CDC 8:8, cf. 20:30 (*yarimu yad*). This term appears opposite *bi-shegagah* ("in error") and its synonyms. Schechter (to CDC 10:3) and Licht (to DSD 8:17) trace this usage to Num. 15:30 (where Targum Pseudo-Jonathan translates *bi-zedana'*, followed by Rashi). There the opposite (v. 27) is *bi-shegagah*. Rabin notes that Mishnaic Hebrew would use *be-mezid*. Qumran legal texts have an entire set of terms, often biblical in nature, whereas Mishnaic Hebrew had developed new usages (cf. Rabin, *QS*, 108). It is probable that this phenomenon is the result of the early date of the Qumran material and the importance which the Bible had for the sect. It must be considered, however, as part of the more general issue of the place of Qumran Hebrew in the dialectology of the period.

/53/ The reading of 1QS *hḥyd* is clearly to be emended to *hyḥd* (*ha-yaḥad*).

/54/ See *HAQ*, 66f.

/55/ *HAQ*, 70–75.

/56/ See above, n. 3.

/57/ *"Megillat milḥemet bene 'or,"* 588f.

/58/ Yadin, *War Scroll*, 53–57.

/59/ Schürer II (1979), 202, and M. Stern, *Greek and Latin Authors on the Jews and Judaism* I (1976), 26–31.

/60/ *Sifre* Deut. 153 (ed. Finkelstein, p. 206); cf. B. Yoma' 26a and Ginzberg, *Sect*, 48. See Maimonides, H. Sanhedrin 2:2.

/61/ The sources are conveniently assembled in "*Bet Din shel Kohanim*," *Enc. Tal.* 3, 181; cf. Z. Frankel, *Darkhe Ha-Mishnah* (1959), 62f.; J. Brüll, *Mevo' Ha-Mishnah* (1876), 52f.; and D. Tropper, *The Internal Administration of the Second Temple at Jerusalem* (Yeshiva University Doctoral Dissertation, 1970), 123–147.

/62/ *Ant.* 4, 8, 14 (214), Gk. ὑπηρέται paraphrasing Deut. 16:18. Cf. *Sifre* Deut. 15 (ed. Finkelstein, p. 25); Ginzberg, *Sect*, 48f.; and B. Yevamot 86b. (Note the citation there of a non-existent verse.)

/63/ *HAQ*, 44 and n. 144, 49–54.

/64/ *HAQ*, 22–32.

/65/ *Sect*, 47f.

/66/ Above, n. 1.

/67/ Cf. Maimonides, H. Sanhedrin 1:3–4 for a convenient summary, and Joseph Caro, *Kesef Mishnah* to 1:4.

/68/ On the *moshav ha-rabbim*, see *HAQ*, 68–72.

/69/ *Special Laws* IV, 55–56, translated by E. R. Goodenough, in *The Jurisprudence of the Jewish Courts in Egypt* (1968), 189.

/70/ Cited in Colson's note *ad loc.* (Vol. VIII, 42f. n. a). Cf. Belkin, *Philo and the Oral Law* (1940), 182.

/71/ *Special Laws* IV, 157ff.

/72/ *Special Laws* IV, 151–154, and Belkin, 182–4.

/73/ Belkin (184), however, cites *Sifre* Num. 95 and B. Sanhedrin 17a (*baraita'*) which states that "according to Tannaitic tradition, the members of the first Sanhedrin were appointed by lot" from a pre-selected pool.

/74/ Goodenough (189f.) notes that Philo's "discussion of the ideal judge is throughout Greek in inspiration." He sees it as derived from some "current Greek treatise on the judge." Indeed, the passage mentions the use of pebbles (cast into an urn) in connection with the judges' procedure. This indicates that there was more than one judge and that the method of voting was the common Greek one. Goodenough (192) correctly wonders if the pebble was used in Jewish courts or if this was simply copied by Philo from his source. The most logical answer is both. Indeed, the Jewish courts of Alexandria in his day must have been very much like those of the "Greeks" in external form. On the other hand, such practices may have also been described in his source, and for this reason he felt it appropriate to make use of them in describing the Torah's ideal judge.

/75/ *Sect*, 48.

/76/ In Charles, *APOT*, the phrase is translated "according to occasion" and compared to M. 'Avot 5:22.

/77/ See below, 37f.

/78/ On the progressive revelation of the law, see N. Wieder, *The Judean Scrolls and Karaism* (1962), 67–70, *HAQ*, 22–36, and Rabin to CDC 6:14. For the preposition *b*, cf. the phrases *shanah be-shanah* and *pa'am be-fa'am* (Wernberg-Møller to DSD 8:15). The sequence *k . . . b . . .* occurs in 1 Sam. 18:10; Num. 24:1; Jud. 16:20, 20:30f.; 1 Sam. 3:10, 20:25. I cannot locate an example of *l . . . b . . . .*

/79/ Taking *lamod* as an inf. of *lmd*. Cf. *havdel* in l. 20. Habermann saw it as an inf. of *mdd* (Licht). Wernberg-Møller, *ad loc.*, comments that "the phrase presupposes that the bulk of revelations was put down in writing and contained in a particular book." According to him (123) these revelations were contained in the *Sefer He-Hagu.*

/80/ *HAQ*, 33–36.

/81/ DSD 8:15–16. Cf. DSD 1:9 (*HAQ*, 27). On progressive revelation at Qumran, see *HAQ*, 22–36.

/82/ Restored with Licht.

/83/ So Licht, basing himself on context. H. N. Richardson, "Some Notes on 1QSa," *JBL* 76 (1957), 111 translated "pillars" missing the technical sense of this term.

/84/ Pp. 65–79.

/85/ Num. 1:3 and *passim*, 14:29, 26:2, 4; 2 Chron. 25:5; cf. 1 Chron. 27:23.

/86/ *War Scroll*, 77.

/87/ Num. 8:24.

/88/ *HAQ*, 68.

/89/ J. Neusner, *Fellowship in Judaism* (1963), 22–40, and Rabin, *QS*, 32–36. See below, 161–168.

/90/ T. Sheqalim 3:26 (cf. Lieberman, *TK*, *ad loc.*); *Sifre* Num. 62 (ed. Horovitz, p. 59); B. Ḥullin 24a (*baraita'*); *Be-Midbar Rabbah* 4:12.

/91/ *War Scroll*, 78.

/92/ See below, 34f.

/93/ Yadin, *War Scroll*, 78.

/94/ For sources and discussion, see L. Ginzberg, *The Legends of the Jews* (1968) V, 79 n. 22; 80 n. 24; 86 n. 37; 99 n. 73; 112f. n. 104; A. Altmann, "The Gnostic Background of the Rabbinic Adam Legends," *JQR* N.S. 35 (1944/5), 379–387, and R. Gordis, "The Knowledge of Good and Evil in the Old Testament and the Qumran Scrolls," *JBL* 76 (1957), 126–129.

/95/ Cf. Ginzberg, *Legends* V, 276 n. 36. On the notion that Abraham was the first to show signs of old age, see V, 258 n. 272.

/96/ Cf. Yadin, *War Scroll*, 72f.

/97/ That man's military prowess decreases with age is stated in *Mekhilta' De-Rabbi Ishmael* Shirah 4 (ed. Horovitz-Rabin, p. 130), and *Mekhilta' De-Rabbi*

Shim'on ben Yoḥai to Ex. 15:3 (ed. Epstein-Melamed, p. 81, ed. Hoffmann, p. 61). Cf. S. Kraus, *Paras Wa-Romi* (1948), 219.

/ 98/ To CDC 10:7.

/ 99/ Read *'et* (Schechter). Rabin's restoration to *br's*, based on DSD 6:14, is no more convincing, and, as he indicates, "excludes the otherwise attractive rendering 'who musters.'" *'Et* is used regularly in CDC. Cf. Kutscher, *Ha-Lashon*, 316 and G. W. Nebe, "*Der Gebrauch der sogennanten nota accusativi 'et in Damaskusschrift XV, 5.9 und 12*," *RQ* 8 (1973), 257–264.

/100/ The process of mustering is described several lines above on this same page. Apparently, the members were arranged in order and their names listed. On these lists, see *HAQ*, 66f. For the connection of this sectarian organization with military tactics, see Yadin, *War Scroll*, 60f.

/101/ On this official, see below, 95 and *HAQ*, 29 n. 51.

/102/ These are the sectarian communities scattered throughout the country. Cf. A. Rubinstein, "Urban Halakhah and Camp Rules in the 'Cairo Fragments of a Damascus Covenant,'" *Sefarad* 12 (1952), 283–296.

/103/ Note the differing ways of formulating the ages in these passages. The syntactic structure of these formulations requires a thorough study.

/104/ Part of the *pe'* of *u-mishpaṭ* is visible (Licht). The phrase *riv u-mishpaṭ* occurs also in CDC 14:12 where Rabin translates "litigation and judgment (or: ruling)." That passage is certainly a legal context. The expression occurs, however, in 1QSa 1:20 (as restored by Licht, but the restoration is definite) where it is clearly in a military context. Cf. Is. 3:13f., 34:8; Jer. 25:31; Ps. 35:1, 74:22; DSW 4:12; and DST 10:33f. From Yadin's reference (*War Scroll, ad loc.*) to our passage, it is apparent that he agrees with the interpretation presented here.

/105/ Cf. Num. 11:16; Josh. 22:21. The transition to the *sarim*, below in our passage, is based on Deut. 20:9 *sare ṣeva'ot be-rosh ha-'am* (so Licht). Note also the use of *le-hityaṣev ba-milḥamah* in l. 21 which confirms the military connotation of this verb.

/106/ Note the spelling with *waw*. This is probably a popular plural derived directly from the singular *rosh*. Cf. E. Qimron, *Diqduq Ha-Lashon Ha-'Ivrit shel Megillot Midbar Yehudah* (1976), p. 257 n. 45.

/107/ Or "clans," although the division according to numbers would favor the interpretation given above.

/108/ A similar list of officers appears below in 1:29–2:1. Cf. Ex. 18:21; Deut. 1:15 (Licht); and 1 Chron. 28:1. Licht is correct that the omission in our list of the Torah's *sare 'alafim* is a result of their designation here as the *roshe* (*sic*) *'alfe yisra'el*. On the system of organization, Licht compares DSD 2:21–3; CDC 13:1–2; 1 Macc. 3:55 (although some of the translations have obscured the literal meaning, "captains of thousands, and captains of hundreds, captains of fifties, and captains of tens," so S. Tedesche, *The First Book of Maccabees* [1950], commentary, *ad loc.*) and Yadin, *War Scroll*, 59–61.

/109/ Licht, *ad loc.*

/110/ It is true that the text of 1QSa mentions *shofeṭim we-shoṭerim* immediately after the mention of the officers of thousands, hundreds, fifties and tens. The author of the text naturally associated the *shofeṭim* as well, since they occur together with the *shoṭerim* in Deut. 16:18. Licht correctly notes that these *shofeṭim* are military officers, not judges, as can be shown from comparison with l. 24 in which we learn that they were Levites. These Levitical provosts (so Yadin) were responsible, according to the *War Scroll*, for supervising the mustering of the army. (On these provosts, see Yadin, *War Scroll*, 15f.) Yadin defines their duties as "dealing with conscription problems, matters of law and order, transmission of orders, and supervising their execution." They were between forty and fifty years old. The association of biblical *shofeṭim* with these provosts should not be surprising in light of the biblical usage of *shofeṭ* as a military leader. Cf. *HAQ*, 64 and the material cited there in n. 276.

/111/ Num. 4:3, 23, 30, 35, 39, and 47.

/112/ Cf. Rashi, *ad loc.*

/113/ B. ʿArakhin 19a.

/114/ Cf. Joshua Isaac ben Jehiel Shapira, *Noʿam Yerushalmi, ad loc.* See also *Shemot Rabbah* 1:30 and Ginzberg, *Sect*, 330.

/115/ See below, 55f.

/116/ *Sect*, 45f.

/117/ *Das Buch der Jubiläen und die Halacha* (1930), 14f.

/118/ *Sefer Ha-Miṣwot*, 22, 59, 131, 159.

/119/ Ṭur Ḥoshen Mishpaṭ 7.

/120/ 2 K. 22:1; 2 Chron. 34:1.

/121/ 2 K. 22:3. The literal meaning of the text is probably that the reform began in his eighteenth regnal year, rather than when he was eighteen. Indeed, 2 Chron. 34:3 specifically refers to the eighteenth year of his reign. The *ʾaggadah* assumed, however, that it referred to his being eighteen years old (cf. Rashi to B. Shabbat 56b).

/122/ Cf. Ginzberg, *Sect*, 331f.

/123/ So P. Sanhedrin 4:7 (ed. Krot. 9, 22b).

/124/ Menaḥem ben Solomon Ha-Meiri, *Bet Ha-Beḥirah Ha-Shalem ʿal Massekhet Sanhedrin*, ed. I. Ralbag (1970/1), *ad loc.*, and Meir ben Todros Ha-Levi Abulafia, *Sefer Ḥiddushe Ha-Ramah* (1970/1), *ad loc.*

/125/ Cf. M. Sanhedrin 4:1.

/126/ According to MS Munich it is an elder who was unable to have children (*she-loʾ hayah raʾui le-vanim*).

/127/ It is only by combining the two traditions we have discussed here that Maimonides is able to rule that one cannot be a judge if he is *either* a *zaqen* or childless. See H. Sanhedrin 2:3; Shegagot 13:1. As noted in the marginal note marked with asterisk to H. Shegagot 13:1, it is possible to read Maimonides here in line with his comment to M. Horayot 1:4 to the effect that only a *zaqen she-loʾ raʾah banim* is not considered a legitimate judge, yet H. Sanhedrin 2:3 confirms unquestionably the reading of the printed edition. Cf. Abraham ben Moses di-Boton's *Leḥem Mishneh* to H. Shegagot 13:1.

/128/ M. Sanhedrin 1:6, M. Yomaʾ 1:3, 5. It is suggested by David Pardo in his commentary, *Ḥasde Dawid*, to T. Sanhedrin 7:5 that the tannaitic traditions refer only to appointing an elder to the court. Nevertheless, if one reaches old age and is already serving, he is not retired. Contrast Ginzberg, *Sect*, 331f. who seems here to be caught up in a polemic.

/129/ Such headings are frequent in CDC. For a similar phrase, see Ben Sira 35:2 and 15:12.

/130/ Lit. "for him who gives least" (Rabin). This use of the *pi'el* is common in tannaitic texts. While *le-mu'at* appears in 13:1 and 1QSa 1:18, Rabin is correct that "the traces are not consistent with" this reading.

/131/ From Ezek. 16:49 where the prep. *b* does not appear. Cf. also Zech. 14:13. In light of our pl., *yaḥaziqu*, it is interesting that the versions to Ezek. 16:49 also have the plural (G. A. Cooke, *A Critical and Exegetical Commentary on the Book of Ezekiel* [1936], 179). This verse is quoted in the same form in CDC 6:21 to which Rabin notes that the Peshiṭta has *be-yad*. He suggests the possible influence of our author's favorite *heḥeziq b-*, "hold fast to."

/132/ Rabin takes *yigwa'* to mean "who dies." He explains that the funds are to be used for burial expenses. While Rabin is certainly right that this root can mean to die as in the series *gw'* . . . *mwt* . . . , burial expenses cannot have been appreciable in those days. (*Lewayat ha-met* in the prayerbook version of M. Pe'ah 1:1 [S. Baer, *Siddur 'Avodat Yisra'el*, 39] is a medieval addition.) Instead, we should take *gw'* in the sense of being about to die, as it appears in Num. 17:27; Ps. 88:16; and Ben Sira 48:5. (Cf. also Ben Sira 8:7, and M. H. Segal, *Sefer Ben Sira' Ha-Shalem* [1971/2], 33.)

/133/ So Schechter and Rabin. Cf. Gen. 4:12. Ginzberg translates "begs" basing himself on Ps. 59:16, where new JPS, however, has "They wander in search of food." Ben Sira 36:30 may confirm the suggestion of Schechter and Rabin that our text refers to a homeless (Ben Sira: wifeless) man. Cf. Aḥiqar 2:28 (Segal, *Ben Sira'*, 234).

/134/ To redeem him (Segal, Rabin). I have noted in *HAQ*, 105 n. 139 that CDC used both the biblical root *nkr* as well as the newer term *goy* to signify "non-Jew." Here we see both terms. This is probably an example of the phenomenon of two synonyms in construct with one another, so common at Qumran.

/135/ From the lexical point of view, *betulah* need not signify a virgin. See A. S. Hartom, J. J. Rabinowitz, "*Betulah, Betulim,*" *Enc. Bib.* 2, 383.

/136/ Heb. *go'el* appears here in the sense of close kinsman. Presumably close relatives ordinarily undertook to provide the dowry (Rabin). Cf. Ruth 2:21 (parallel to *qarov*). It should be noted that the use of *go'el* in Ruth is different from that in our text. In Ruth the "redeemer" is the closest relative charged with marrying the widow. Thus, it is a technical term in the "levirate" system presupposed by Ruth. The differences between this system and the legislation of Deut. 25:5–10 are readily apparent.

/137/ Cf. Gen. 24:43 and Ex. 2:8 where the girl is clearly unmarried.

/138/ Schechter's reference (followed by Segal) to Jer. 30:17 shows that *doresh* is one who has concern for or cares for. Cf. BDB, 205b for examples. We translate with RSV to Jer. 30:17. It is possible that the meaning of this word in our text is a suitor, as Rabin has taken it. The restoration of this line in M. H. Segal, "Notes on 'Fragments of a Zadokite Work,'" *JQR* N.S. 2 (1911/12), 139 cannot be accepted. Segal was prevented from seeing the manuscript by Schechter's agreement with the Cambridge University Library. The MS does not support his reading.

/139/ So Rabin, *ad loc.*

/140/ *Every Good Man*, 87.

/141/ Rabin, *ad loc.*

/142/ Cf. below, 174–176 nn. 16–18.

/143/ See S. W. Baron, *The Jewish Community* II (1945), 290–350.

/144/ *Special Laws* IV, 72–78.

/145/ On headings like this cf. *HAQ*, 82f.; and CDC 10:14; 14:10; and 16:10 (Ginzberg, *Sect*, 41).

/146/ From the exegesis of what follows as well as its approximate quotation (and exegesis?) in DSD 6:27f., it appears that this passage is a quotation from a non-biblical source. This quotation cannot be identified from any texts known to us. Perhaps a future discovery will provide a clue as to its identity. Rabin compares CDC 16:10.

/147/ The expression occurs in 1 Sam. 25:26, 31, 33 (where it is tantamount to bloodshed [Schechter]); Jud. 7:2; Job 40:14 (with *zeroa'*) in reference to men. That *yad* is not to be taken as the subject of the verb is shown from l. 10 where the subject is clearly masculine. Alternately, it is possible to emend to *hwšy'*[*h*] and to see *yad* as the subject. Cf. DSD 6:27 [*hw*]*šy'h*.

/148/ So Schechter, followed by Segal and Rabin. Rabin explains that this means who says, *mashbi'akha 'ani*, comparing M. Shevu'ot 8:2–3. Such an adjuration required a response by the adjured in order to be valid.

/149/ Cf. Lev. 14:7. For oaths in the street, see M. Shevu'ot 8:4; and B. Bava' Meṣi'a' 30b (Rabin). The latter is amoraic.

/150/ Schechter emended to *lifne*, and is followed by Wernberg-Møller, p.112. While I cannot find evidence for such a usage of *lifnim*, perhaps this form was synonymous with *lifne* at Qumran. *Lifnim m*(*in*) in Rabbinic sources means "inside of," not "before." Cf. CDC 15:3f. (Rabin).

/151/ We prefer Schechter's *ma'amaram* (cf. Est. 1:15; 2:20; 9:32 and the Aramaic Dan. 4:14; Ezra 6:9) to Rabin's admittedly "quite un-Hebrew" *me-'omram*. Our text uses *ma'amar* in the sense in which it is found in Esther. In Mishnaic Hebrew it is a technical term for the declaration with which a levirate marriage is accomplished as well as a term for the divine words with which the world was created. Rabin's interpretation was motivated by the lack of a preposition ("according to") in Schechter's reading. It is unlikely that the previous *lifnim* should apply to this noun as well as to *ha-shofeṭim*. We must assume either that a preposition is to be understood, or that one has been lost in transmission. Segal supplies the preposition *b*-, yet *k*- seems more appropriate (cf. Est. 3:4). Wernberg-Møller, p. 112, suggests comparison with DSD 6:25–27 (on which see below, 39f.) and therefore wishes to see *m'mrm* as parallel to DSD's *be-'amrot*, a strange *hif'il* of *mrh*, "to rebel" (see below n. 164). He then translates: "The man, who swears in the open field, and not before the judges, or (in any other way) rebels against them (i.e. the judges)—his hand has saved him." While this interpretation is clever, it neglects the radically different contexts of the two passages. CDC 9:8–10 clearly deals with oaths. These are nowhere mentioned in DSD 6:25–27 where respect and obedience to one's superiors are the subject of the text. The only common element is the quotation of the same pre-existent source. There is no reason, therefore, to regard a perfectly clear word, *ma'amaram*, as a strange *hif'il*. Even more damaging to his view is that *mrh* in the *hif'il* requires the preposition *'im* to indicate the victim of the rebellion (usually God in the Bible). An object clause never designates the one rebelled against.

/152/ Attention should be drawn to the fragment of this text found in cave 5 at Qumran (5Q 12, *DJD* III, 181).

יהיו נקן]
אשר אמר לוא ה]וכח
על השבועה אשר]
על פני השדה א]שר
ל]ו[ן וכול הא]ובד

While confirming the text found in the medieval Cairo *genizah* MS, the fragment indicates that material not present in the Cairo texts preceded that in our passage. This is confirmed, according to the editors of *DJD* III, by a manuscript of our text from cave 4 which has still not been published.

/153/ B. Bava' Qamma' 27b. Cf. S. Albeck, *Bate Ha-Din Bi-Yeme Ha-Talmud* (1980), 33–40.

/154/ Cf. T. Bava' Qamma' 10:16; P. Sanhedrin 8:3 (26b); and *Sifra'* Qedoshim, parashah 2 (ed. Weiss, 88c).

/155/ See Ṭur Ḥoshen Mishpaṭ 4 (Schechter).

/156/ The *waw* of *wa-'asher* is pleonastic (see R. J. Williams, *Hebrew Syntax: An Outline* [1976], p. 71, sec. 435). The use of *wa-'asher* to introduce a law occurs in Neh. 8:15 and 10:31. In both cases *wa-'asher* precedes a law which is part of a series. Similar usage occurs in DSD 5:10–16 and 9:16. Licht (*Serakhim*, 37 n. 16) correctly notes that this is not the usage encountered in our passage where *wa-'asher*, in introducing the clauses of the Penal Code, means "the one who" (Heb. *'ish 'asher*).

/157/ Wernberg-Møller states that in the parallel passage in CDC 14:21, the text reads *wa-'asher yedabber*. Actually the *resh* of *yedabber* is restored (so Rabin). CDC as it is preserved in the *genizah* MS could not have contained the entire Penal Code as the broken bottom of p. 14 makes clear. Further, p. 15 appears to continue with regulations found at the beginning of the code and then to turn to other matters. Yet assuming the parallel with our law, which appears certain, several possibilities suggest themselves. First, as Wernberg-Møller suggests, *yedabber* can be a variant for *yashiv*. In that case we would expect that the preposition *'el* would follow the verb as *'et* in DSD fits with *yashiv*, but not with *yedabber*. Yet a more likely suggestion is that CDC has the clauses reversed, so it read (approximately): *wa-'asher yedabber be-qoṣer 'apayyim we-heshiv 'et re'ehu bi-qeshi 'oref*. Alternately, perhaps the predicates remained the same and only the verbs were interchanged with the clauses as they now remain. Finally, it is possible that CDC simply omitted the first clause. Such possibilities are merely speculation. If the Qumran CDC material were completely published, it would be possible to make more valid assessments of the relationship of DSD and CDC.

/158/ The *hif'il* of *šwb* followed by *'et re'ekha* occurs in Job 35:4. This passage is lacking in the Qumran Job Targum. Cf. DSD 6:8–10 and *HAQ*, 68.

/159/ For the translation, see below, 106f. n. 61. The form *qeshi* occurs only in Deut. 9:27 (a construct). E. Ben-Yehudah, *Millon Ha-Lashon Ha-'Ivrit* (1959), lists *qeshi* as an independent noun whereas A. Even-Shoshan, *Ha-Millon He-Ḥadash* (1971) sees it as a construct of *qoshi*. *Qoshi 'oref* occurs in DSD 4:11. *'Oref qasheh* is found in DSD 5:5 and is restored by Licht in DSD 5:26. *Qeshi 'oref* is found as the interpretation of *qeshi* (Deut. 9:27) in *Midrash Tanḥuma'*, ed. Buber, Shelaḥ, p. 41a. This parallel is of little value for several reasons. First, the citation of Deut. 9:27 may have conditioned the form *qeshi*. Second, the *Tanḥuma' midrashim* are generally dated to the ninth or tenth century (M. D. Herr, "Ṭanḥuma' Yelammedenu," *EJ* 15 [1971], 795). Finally, the parallel in *Be-Midbar Rabbah*, ed. Vilna, 16:28 reads *qesheh* (*qšh*). This latter *midrash* is no earlier (M. D. Herr, "Numbers Rabbah," *EJ* 12 [1971], 1263f.).

/160/ *Qeṣor 'appayim* occurs also in DSD 4:10 where Licht remarks that it is the opposite of *'orekh 'appayim* (in line 3). He also refers to *qeṣar 'appayim* in Prov. 14:17. In v. 29 *qeṣar ruaḥ* appears as the opposite of *'erekh 'appayim*. Note also the further uses of the root *qṣr* with *ruaḥ* and *nefesh* in BDB, 894a. The alternation of the forms *qoṣer* (accent on first syllable) and *qeṣor* is discussed by Licht, *Serakhim*, 45f. See also E. Y. Kutscher, "*Le-Diyyuqah shel Leshon Megillat Yam Ha-Melaḥ*," *Leshonenu* 22 (1957/8), 102f.; Z. Ben Ḥayyim, "Traditions in the Hebrew Language, with Special Reference to the Dead Sea Scrolls," *Aspects of the Dead Sea Scrolls*, ed. C. Rabin, Y. Yadin (1958), 203; M. H. Goshen-Gottstein, "Linguistic Structure and Tradition in the Qumran Documents," *Aspects*, 110f.; and Qimron, pp. 118–121. Examples were already listed in Yalon, *MMY*, 73, first published as "*Megillat Sirkhe Ha-Yaḥad*," *KS* 28 (1951/2), 66. The suggestion of Kutscher and Ben Ḥayyim (contrast Goshen-Gottstein) that such words were pronounced with two ō (=*ḥolem*) vowels must be accepted. Such pronunciations have been amply documented from Greek transcriptions of Hebrew.

/161/ Only the tops of the letters *pr* are visible as the parchment is torn. Yet the reading is absolutely certain (Brownlee, Wernberg-Møller, and Licht).

/162/ While the MS clearly reads *yswd*, we follow Brownlee, Wernberg-Møller, and Licht in emending to *yswr*. For the *yissurim* and the root *ysr* at Qumran, see *HAQ*, 49–54, where it is noted (p. 49) that the sect regularly used *yissur*(*im*) as a substitute for the biblical noun *musar* (so also Brownlee to DSD 3:1). Note the *qal* of *pr'* with *musar* in Prov. 13:18 and 15:32 (Licht's reference to 15:13 is an error). Cf. Prov. 8:33. The *porea' musar* is contrasted with one who observes the reproof (instruction) he is given (*shomer tokhaḥat*) in Prov. 13:18. In addition, *pr'* appears with *'eṣah*, a synonym for *musar* (Prov. 1:25). This phraseology was especially popular in medieval Hebrew literature (see Ben-Yehudah VI, 5209a). Note CDC 8:8, *wa-yifre'u be-yad ramah*, translated by Rabin, "[They] rebelled high-handedly." Rabin calls attention to the Vulgate which (like the Jewish commentators) translates "*qui deserit disciplinam*." It should be noted that *yesod ha-yaḥad* is a possible reading in DSD 7:17, 18 and 8:10. It is possible that those passages caused the error here, if we do not emend elsewhere as well. Cf. *HAQ*, 46 n. 160 where the same confusion is discussed and an emendation is proposed.

/163/ Other than Zech. 13:7, this noun occurs only in Leviticus. The word is used only in connection with sexual, legal and commercial (not cultic) matters. Despite the widespread use of the noun in medieval Hebrew literature (Ben-Yehudah V, 4561af.), its occurrence (other than in quotations) in Rabbinic literature is extremely doubtful. The usage in T. Shevu'ot 3:6 (ed. Zuckermandel, p. 449) is simply a quotation, although it appears to us as direct speech. (Note that ed. Vilna and *Ḥasde Dawid read kofer* for *kiḥesh*. Cf. also S. Lieberman, *Tosefet Rishonim* II [1938], 177.) The amoraic usage in B. Shevu'ot 30a is called into serious question by the readings of MSS Munich, Florence, Alfasi, She'iltot, sec. Yitro (*DS*, *ad loc.*). At the very least, it is clear that *'amit* was not in use during the Rabbinic period.

/164/ The form is equivalent to *be-hamrot*, with confusion of *'alef* and *he'*. For the confusion of gutterals at Qumran, see Licht, *Serakhim*, 47, and Qimron, p. 83. We cannot agree with H. L. Ginsberg (in Brownlee, *ad loc.*) that this is merely a scribal error. In fact, it reflects a general breakdown of gutterals already found in the Qumran texts.

/165/ *Hif'il* of *mrh* followed by *'et pi* X occurs in Deut. 1:26, 43, 9:23; 1 Sam. 12:14 where X represents "the Lord." The only place in which X is a person is in Josh. 1:18. Apparently, this is why only this passage is cited by Licht. For *peh* in the meaning of a command, see BDB, 805a. 1 K. 13:21 defines *mrh* (*qal*) followed by *pi 'adonai* as "[You] had not kept the commandment which the Lord your God commanded you." It is difficult to see any difference between the *qal* and *hif'il* of this verb. While the *hif'il* of *mrh* is attested in Rabbinic literature, the usage with *'et pi* cannot be located. Note Ben Sira 39:31 in which the phrase occurs regarding God's command.

/166/ *Sc.* his fellow member of the sect.

/167/ On the purpose and nature of the sectarian rosters, see *HAQ*, 65–67. Cf. DSD 6:10f. and Licht, *Serakhim*, 130.

/168/ Licht, *Serakhim*, 44f. discusses the difficulty of determining if we have a Hebrew archaizing form *lifanehu* or an Aramaicized *lifanohi*. (*Waw* and *yod* are indistinguishable in the MS, and comparative evidence from other MSS is equivocal.) Licht has followed the *editio princeps* "because it is easier for the comtemporary reader" (45). Yalon, *MMY*, 72 favors the Aramaic *lifanohi*, cf. Kutscher, *Ha-Lashon*, 47, 161; Goshen-Gottstein, "Linguistic Structure," 116; and Yalon, 55f. See also Ges. 91l.

/169/ The restoration of [*hw*]*šy'h* follows Brownlee and Licht. *Lw'* is the normal spelling for the negative at Qumran. Yet here it signifies the preposition *l* + pronominal suffix, usually spelled *lw* (so Brownlee and Licht). Note that there are fifteen cases in the MT in which *lo'* has been written for *lo* (S. Frensdorff, *Sefer 'Okhlah We-'Okhlah* [1864], p. 98 no. 105). The opposite phenomenon is twice attested (Frensdorff, p. 99 list 106). Note also that Qumran and MT share the phenomenon of extra *'alef* at the ends of words (Frensdorff, p. 98, no. 104, and for the entire problem, Licht, *Serakhim*, 47). The *plene* spelling of the negative *lo'* is normal at Qumran (Qimron, p. 76f.). Further examples and explanation of our phenomenon at Qumran are found in Kutscher, *Ha-Lashon*, 129–131.

/170/ The scribe wrote *wn'n'š* and then erased the first *'ayin* rather than the second (Licht, Wernberg-Møller), apparently just a sloppy error. For this use of the *nif'al* of *'nš*, see below, 159–161.

/171/ Restored with Brownlee and Licht.

/172/ While Licht and Wernberg-Møller assume that there was a space (of nine letters, according to Wernberg-Møller) in the scroll before the next law (this is at the bottom of the column, and as usual damaged), Brownlee adds *wmwvdl* (*u-muvdal*), which would mean that in addition to being fined, the offender would be removed from the purity (on which see below, 165–168). One might object that in the law before this, the exclusion is mentioned before the fine. This objection is obviated by many laws to follow in which the fine precedes the instruction to remove the offender. See below, 177 n. 38 for this restoration. The question is further complicated by the need to understand the reason for the placing of the spaces in this and other Qumran scrolls. Cf. S. Talmon, "*Pisqah Be'emṣa' Pasuq* and 11QPs[a]," *Textus* 5 (1966), 11–21.

/173/ Cf. *HAQ*, 66f.

CHAPTER TWO
THE QUALIFICATIONS OF WITNESSES

1. *The Law of Witnesses*

The judges spoken of in the last chapter were not the only *personae* involved in the judicial process. While it was important to ensure that members of the judiciary met the requirements of the law, it was equally crucial that witnesses conformed to the rigid qualifications of the sectarian law. These qualifications are intended to ensure the reliability of the witness and include the requirement of membership in the sectarian community. The primary text for our inquiry will be CDC 9:23–10:3:

> **ואל יקובל עוד לשופטים להמית על פיהו אשר לא מלאו ימיו לעבור על הפקודים ירא את אל אל יאמן איש על רעהו לעד עובר דבר מן המצוה ביד רמה עד זכו לשוב**
>
> Let no witness/1/ be accepted by/2/ the judges to put (someone) to death by his testimony,/3/ whose days/4/ are not sufficient/5/ to pass among the mustered/6/ (and who is not)/7/ God-fearing./8/ Let no man be trusted/9/ against/10/ his neighbor as a witness, who violates any of the commandment(s)/11/ intentionally,/12/ until (his deeds) have been purified/13/ (sufficiently for him) to return./14/

The first part of this passage provides that in capital cases no one below the age of mustering and who is not "God-fearing" may serve as a witness. The second part of the text requires that no one who intentionally violates any of the commandments be accepted as a witness until his repentance is complete. Each of these aspects requires extensive clarification in order to understand the attitude of the sect towards the qualifications of witnesses. The scholarly controversy regarding the testimony of women at Qumran will also be treated in this chapter.

2. *Minimum Age of Witnesses*

In view of the fact that the manuscript reads *ʿod*, "still," and that the first part of the law mentions judges, it might be proposed that the text deals with the requirements for judges. Understood in this way, the translation would read: "Let there not be accepted any more as judges to put (someone) to death by his sentence. . . ."

This interpretation is not plausible, however. First, the law of judges is explicitly stated elsewhere in this document, and it is not characteristic of this text to repeat itself in such matters. Second, the law immediately preceding this one is the extensive law of testimony (CDC 9:17–22), and the second part of this passage also deals with witnesses. It would be hard to believe that a short passage regarding judges would have been sandwiched between material relating to witnesses. Third, the age of mustering mentioned here differs from the age elsewhere (CDC 10:6–9) established for judges. Even more telling, it is lower than that established for judges (age twenty-five) in CDC 10:6–9, a passage which applies to both capital and non-capital cases. Finally, in such a view it becomes difficult to integrate the word *'od*. At best, this statement would then have to be understood as an amendation to a previous law that had once allowed younger judges. Now, however, they would henceforth be prohibited—a strange statement, to say the least. It is therefore certain that this law deals with the ages of witnesses and that it must be emended accordingly.

The first requirement of the witness in capital cases is that he will have passed the age of mustering. Use of the phrase *la-'avor 'al ha-pequdim* proves unquestionably that the age being described is twenty, for this phrase in the Pentateuch always refers to age twenty (Ex. 30:14; 38:26)./15/ Twenty was the minimum age for military service in biblical times, according to Scriptural reports./16/ The sect did not envision military service to begin until twenty-five, and, indeed, this was the minimum age for service in the judiciary./17/ Even when the sect, by a somewhat farfetched exegesis, transformed the minimum age into twenty-five, they avoided using the clause *la-'avor 'al ha-pequdim* in this connection, since it could denote no age other than twenty./18/

That twenty is intended in CDC 9:23–10:3 is confirmed in 1QSa 1:9f:

> ו[בן] עשרים שנ[ה יעבור על ה]פקודים לבוא בגורל בתוך משפ[ח]תו ליחד בע[דת] קודש
>
> And when he is twenty year[s old he shall pass among the mu]stered to enter into full status/19/ along with/20/ his fam[il]y,/21/ to join/22/ the holy congre[gation.]/23/

But this passage confirming the age of twenty as the age of mustering raises another question. What was the mustering for if not for military purposes? There can be no question that the sect saw itself as preparing—or better, in a state of perpetual preparedness—for the final eschatological battle. For this reason, much of its organizational structure is built along military lines. Yet in the law before us, the sect's "peacetime" organization differed from its military structure. Even though twenty-five was established as the minimum age for military service, the traditional twenty was retained as the minimum age for full-fledged membership in the sect. The rights of testimony, voting in the sectarian assembly, and, as will be seen below, marriage were conferred with the attainment of this age. Mustering, then, referred to the system of governance and authority which the sect maintained in the present, pre-eschatological age.

The age of mustering is once again encountered in CDC 15:5f. where it is stated:

והבא בברית לכל ישראל לחוק עולם את בניהם אשר יגיעו לעבור
על הפקודים בשבועת הברית יקימו עליהם

And as to anyone who enters/24/ the covenant from among all Israel, as an eternal ordinance,/25/ their sons who reach the age of passing among the mustered shall take upon themselves/26/ the oath of the covenant./27/

This passage discusses the transition from the status of the child of a sectarian to that of an independent sectarian. At the age of twenty, which is known to be that at which mustering occurred, the sons of the members of the sect could themselves become members with full privileges, provided they swore the oath of the covenant in which they took upon themselves the obligation to follow both the sectarian interpretation of the Torah and the various ordinances of the group.

The question might arise as to whether this passage refers only to males, as it has been translated here, or to females as well. It will be seen below that the context of the passage quoted from the *Serekh Ha-'Edah* certainly favors understanding this law as referring only to males. Further, the mustering of the Pentateuch applied only to males,/28/ and it is most probable that this was the case at Qumran as well.

What was the position of women? It appears that the status of women in the sect (on which more will be said below) was determined only insofar as their husbands took on membership. Women whose husbands were part of the sect, and girls whose fathers were members, were considered members by virtue of this status.

Indeed, the same was the ruling of biblical law regarding the priest and his family, as to whether they could eat of the various priestly dues. The Torah specified (Num. 18:11f. and 18:25–32) that the household of the priest could share in the eating of the priestly dues (*terumot*). Further, even the slaves of a priest were to eat of these dues. But when a priest's daughter married a non-priest, her rights to these offerings ceased. If she were childless and, due to the death of her husband or divorce, she returned to live in her father's house, she again could partake of the *terumot* (Lev. 22:10–14).

Comparison to the laws of *terumot* is especially relevant since it is known that the sect, like the Pharisaic *ḥavurah*, endeavored to fulfill the purity laws relating to the eating of *terumah* by the priests even in eating their regular, everyday victuals. Tannaitic *halakhah* regarding the *ḥavurah* also dealt with the question of family members. It was only the male head of the household who became a *ḥaver*, and the rest of his family derived their status in turn from him. Once a man had accepted his obligations as a *ḥaver* before the members of the *ḥavurah*, probably represented by a court of three of its members, he then could represent the *ḥavurah* in "swearing in" his family./29/ On the other hand, if children were born to him once he had joined, they automatically received the status of *ḥaver*./30/ If a *ḥaver* married the daughter of an *'am ha-'areṣ*, however, she had to undertake her new status before the *ḥavurah* (or its three representatives)./31/ The only essential difference between this practice and that of the sect is that in the case of minors coming of age, the sect required an oath, whereas the *ḥavurah* of tannaitic sources required public acceptance of the regulations of the *ḥaverim*.

The phrase *be-tokh mishpaḥto* in our passage from 1QSa 1:9f. is susceptible to two interpretations. The first is that the twenty-year-old, still not married and not yet constituting an independent household, remains under the authority of his family, even when he attains independence within the sect, until such time as he should marry. After all, 1QSa 1:10f. (which will be discussed below) prescribes twenty as the minimum age for beginning family life.

Another possibility—and one which appears more attractive—is that from twenty, since it is expected that the young man will soon marry, he (and his family) will attain full status in the sect. The text would then be emphasizing that just as he, as the child of a (perhaps first-generation) sectarian, had automatically been able to join the sect without the need to pass through the novitiate, so the same privilege would be accorded to his family. Further, if he were to marry a woman whose family was not of the sect, she would automatically be granted the appropriate status upon their marriage. The parallels in biblical and tannaitic sources to this interpretation have already been treated.

J. Liver/32/ has noted that according to 4Q Ordinances 2:6–9 it was at the time of passing his first mustering that the now mature sectarian would give the half *sheqel*, as a once in a lifetime offering:

כסף ה[ע]רכים אשר נתנו איש כפר נפשו מחצית [השקל תרומה לאדני]
רק [פעם] אחת יתננו כל ימיו

As to the money of valuation which they gave, each as an atonement for himself, a half *sheqel* as an offering to the Lord, he shall give it only once in his entire lifetime.

While this passage could take us far afield in relation to the biblical exegesis behind it, it should be noted that the sect understood Ex. 30:11–16 to refer only to the first mustering at age twenty. Only the first time did the male have to offer the half *sheqel*.

3. *The Age of Twenty in Jewish Sources*

L. Ginzberg has argued that the minimum age of twenty for witnesses in capital cases is a reflection of early Jewish law according to which the age of legal majority was twenty, not thirteen as in later Jewish practice./33/ Whether this is correct or not, it is certainly true that the age of twenty plays a major role in Jewish legal sources.

Tannaitic *halakhah* assumed that majority took place at puberty. According to the House of Hillel, puberty was assumed to take place between the twelfth birthday and the twentieth for females and between the thirteenth and the twentieth for males. The House of Shammai took eighteen as the maximum. Rabbi Eliezer suggested a compromise, namely that eighteen be accepted for females and twenty for males./34/ Rabbi Judah the Prince is said to have accepted eighteen as the maximum./35/ To the tannaim, then, all laws involving active observance had to be undertaken at the age of thirteen and one day for boys and twelve and one day for girls./36/ This would ensure that no adult (beyond puberty) who was obligated to observe the commandments would delay beyond the required point.

On the other hand, the Rabbis believed that some did not reach puberty until twenty. Hence, it was not possible to be entirely certain of majority until twenty. Indeed, Rabbi Judah the Prince required a minimum age of twenty for partaking of sacrifices (*qodshe mizbeaḥ*), serving as precentor, and reciting the priestly blessing. This ruling is suggested by Ezra 3:8 which specifies that Levitical service was to begin at twenty./37/ Several amoraic passages state that the heavenly court does not punish anyone below the age of twenty./38/ Since below that age it is possible that physical majority has not been reached, the heavenly court gives the benefit of the doubt./39/

The Book of Jubilees 49:17 understands the obligation of eating the paschal lamb to begin at age twenty. C. Tchernowitz/40/ explains that the author was no doubt guided here by the use of *'ish* in Ex. 12:4 which he understood to refer only to one above twenty, basing himself on biblical precedent. Indeed, a somewhat damaged but still legible passage in TS 17:8 likewise fixes the start of the obligation to eat of the paschal lamb at twenty years of age. Rabbinic law,/41/ however, allowed a child to eat of the paschal lamb as soon as he could eat the required minimum./42/ Tannaitic tradition in B. Ḥullin 24b reports that the priests in the Temple imposed their own requirement that officiating priests be at least twenty years old. Such a practice may lie behind 2 Chron. 31:17. At the same time, it is known from *Ant.* 15, 3, 3 (51) and *War* 1, 22, 2 (437) that Aristobulus III was appointed by Herod as high priest at the age of seventeen.

Ginzberg and Rabin cite P. Sanhedrin 4:7 (ed. Krot. 4:9, 22b) which states that judges in capital cases must be at least twenty years old./43/ Yet this statement sheds little light on the requirements for witnesses. Due to the juxtaposition of the discussion of the disqualification of witnesses and judges in M. Sanhedrin 3:1, it could conceivably be possible to construct an analogy between the ages of judges and witnesses in Rabbinic tradition. However, such an analogy cannot be sustained for the Qumran materials, wherein there is evidence that the required age of judges was at least twenty-five./44/

The context in the Palestinian Talmud shows that the concern of the amoraim was to exclude one who fails to attain sexual maturity. Since at twenty one still might be unsure of sexual maturity (majority), such an age requirement is proposed. This amoraic statement specifically indicates that money matters (*dine mamonot*) are not covered by it.

Two statements of Anan ben David have been taken by Ginzberg to indicate that Anan understood the age of majority to be twenty./45/ In one passage Anan says that one who enters a synagogue inebriated and is above twenty is "guilty of a capital crime."/46/ Most probably this simply refers to his being guilty of an offense deserving death at the hands of Heaven, which, we have seen in the Talmudic view as well, begins only upon the age of twenty, when it can be assumed with certainty that physical majority has been reached.

It is also stated by Anan that contact with an unclean animal does not render a person impure unless he is at least twenty years old./47/ The actual nature of this contact is eating,/48/ as can be seen from Lev. 11:40 which Anan is here interpreting. The reason for the age of twenty is clear. Again, from this age maturity can be assumed, and, hence, responsibility for this offense. It is therefore not surprising that later Karaites do not adopt the view of Anan,/49/ as he never intended it as a definition of legal majority, only as the age for which a person was held responsible for his offense.

Philo adapts a series of three seven-year periods in which maturity gradually takes place. By seven a child has recognized reason and speech, by fourteen reproductive power, and by twenty-one completes his growth./50/ This clearly Hellenistic typology is simply too general to be understood as having any legal ramifications.

4. *Moral Qualifications for Witnesses*

The second qualification for a witness in a capital matter is that he be *yare' 'et 'el*, "God-fearing." While this term seems at best to be ambiguous, it specifies an exact requirement. In CDC 20:15–22 there appears a *pesher*-like passage which is based on Mal. 3:16–19. The phrase *yir'e 'adonai* in that passage is transformed, in order to avoid the use of the Tetragrammaton,/51/ into *yir'e* [*'el*]. From the context it is clear that the God-fearers of the *Zadokite Fragments* are the members of the sect./52/ If so, the second requirement of our passage is that the witness in capital matters be a member of the sect.

An important consideration is whether or not non-members of the sect would have been accepted as witnesses in monetary matters. Although there is no way of solving this problem on the basis of this passage, the strict regulations limiting financial contact between the sectarians and other Jews of Palestine/53/ make it doubtful that non-members of the sect could be accepted as witnesses in such cases. If so, why does this passage specify that witnesses in *capital* matters must be members of the sect? Such a provision would seem to imply that the testimony of non-members was accepted in financial matters. This contradiction is best resolved by the assumption that those who were in the various stages of the novitiate were permitted to serve as witnesses in financial matters, while only those who had been accepted as full-fledged members of the sect might testify in capital matters.

The third provision of this passage is that no one who has intentionally transgressed any of the commandments may serve as a witness until his deeds show evidence of repentance. It has been demonstrated elsewhere that *miṣwah* (commandment) is a technical term for the sect's law as derived through Scriptural exegesis./54/ No one who purposely violated any of the laws so derived might serve as a witness against a fellow member unless he had purified himself through repentance sufficiently to return to normal participation in the activites of the sect. It should be remembered that all intentional violators of sectarian law were forbidden certain regular functions of the sect for specified periods of time./55/

What if a member violated a clear law of the Torah, part of the *nigleh* ("revealed")?/56/ Should it be assumed that such a person could participate in legal proceedings as a witness against his fellow? Certainly not. It was an *a priori* assumption that a person who violated laws of the revealed Torah could not bear witness. After all, the entire framework of trust was based on allegiance to Scripture. One who through his actions showed disregard for the Law, could not possibly be trusted as a witness in the view of the sect.

Josephus, in his brief outline of the laws of the Torah, notes that no one should be accepted as a witness unless his testimony is confirmed by his past life./57/ In other words, witnesses are to be accepted only if they live in accordance with the Torah.

Rabin cites the tannaitic regulation excluding certain classes of transgressors from bearing witness./58/ Essentially, these exclusions cover only those about whom one has special reason to doubt their honesty. Most prominent are professional gamblers who have no other occupation. Yet this is not really a parallel to the sectarian law as the sect excluded *all* purposeful transgressors from testimony.

Since most cases tried involved laws contained in the *nigleh*, "revealed," known to all Israel, one might think that observance of the *nigleh* would qualify one as a witness in the sectarian court. This passage tells us that this is not so. One must also observe the *miṣwah*, equivalent to the *nistar* or "hidden" law, of which only the sect had the correct interpretation. The text excludes members who have gone astray. Once repentance was attained, however, the right to bear witness was recovered along with the other sectarian privileges.

Already in amoraic times there is evidence of a tendency to widen the tannaitic restrictions to exclude from testimony those who had violated the law./59/ Ultimately, medieval codification would rule that all purposeful violators of commandments would be excluded from serving as witnesses./60/ This is not the first time in which close parallels have been found between sectarian legal practice and post-Talmudic *halakhah*./61/ There is no way of telling if these result from parallel tendencies or from even indirect influence of some kind.

Tannaitic *halakhah* required definite proof that those disqualified from testifying had repented before they were once again allowed to bear witness.

The examples given in the Tosefta/62/ involve the offender's destroying the tools of the trade or crime which has disqualified him. For example, the professional gambler is expected to destroy his dice. Such an act unquestionably demonstrates his repentance.

Since the sect had a complex system for regulating the actions of its members, it is certain that they likewise would have waited for an offender to demonstrate through his actions that he had fully repented before his testimony would be accepted. After all, in Judaism repentance is not simply a feeling of contrition or even a decision to suspend transgression. It is a form of *action* whereby one shows his ability to desist./63/

5. *The Testimony of Women*

It is now time to turn to the controversial passage in 1QSa 1:9–11 which has been taken by some as indicating that women were admitted as witnesses in the legal system of the sect:/64/

> **ולוא [יקרב] א[ל] אשה לדעתה למשכבי זכר כי אם לפי מולואת לו**
> **עש[רים] שנה בדעתו [טוב] ורע ובכן תקבל להעיד עליו משפטות התורא**
> **ולה[תי]צב במשמע משפטים**

The first part of the passage may be translated as follows:

> He shall not [approach] a woman/65/ to have sexual relations with her/66/ until/67/ he reaches/68/ the age of twe[nty] years at which time he knows [good] and evil./69/

Considerable conflict, however, surrounds the text and translation of the second part of the passage. The first editor of the fragment, D. Barthélemy,/70/ understood the text to indicate that the women were entrusted with ensuring the faithfulness of their husbands to the sect's way of life. In accordance with this view, N. Richardson translated the second part:

> And at that time she will be received to bear witness of him (concerning) the judgment of the law and to take (her) pl[a]ce in proclaiming the ordinances./71/

J. M. Baumgarten/72/ has raised several objections to this interpretation of the text. First, he notes that the context is one which clearly refers to males. Second, he finds it difficult to understand how a wife's eligibility to testify could be tied to the age of her husband. Third, he cannot see how the authors of the document (which Richardson assumed to be "marrying Essenes"/73/) would have given women the "dominant function of participating in the judicial proceedings of the community and acting as witnesses against their husbands."/74/

In response to Richardson's claim that there is no biblical injunction against women's testimony and that there is no reason to force the Qumran documents to conform to other systems of Jewish law, Baumgarten notes that women's testimony was also inadmissible in Athenean and Roman law and that this was the "tenor of the times."/75/ Indeed, according to

Baumgarten, Josephus attributes the disqualification of women as witnesses to the law of Moses./76/ Accordingly, Baumgarten ememds *tqbl* to *yqbl* and *'lyw* to *'l py*. He then translates:

> And he shall be received to testify in accordance with the laws of the Torah and to take [his] place in hearing the judgments./77/

He interprets the latter part of the text to mean that twenty is the minimum age also for attending hearings in court. Such observation of judicial procedures, in his view, has a parallel in M. Sanhedrin 4:4 in which the students of the sages are pictured as sitting in front of the court during the sessions of the Sanhedrin.

6. *Twenty as the Age of Majority at Qumran*

While Baumgarten's emendations and interpretations of the passage are certainly attractive, two alternatives should be mentioned. Regarding the emendation of *'alaw* to *'al pi* it is also possible to retain the text as is and to understand the passage to indicate, as does Licht, that from age twenty it is possible for charges to be brought against him./78/ In other words, the liability to be tried would begin at twenty. This would fit well with the role of twenty as the final passage from minority to majority in various Jewish legal sources. Once he was definitely of majority, he could be punished according to the sect's view.

Licht's view may be supported by reference to CDC 15:12f.:/79/

> **וכאשר יקים אותו עליו לשוב אל תורת משה בכל לב ובכל נפש [נפרע]ים א[נו] ממנו אם ימ[ע]ל**

> But when he takes it upon himself/80/ (with an oath) to return to the Law of Moses/81/ with all (his) heart and with all (his) soul,/82/ w[e] may [exact] punishment/83/ from him should he trans[gre]ss./84/

This law, as restored above, refers to the newly recruited sectarian who is liable to punishment according to the sect's regulations only once he takes on the obligations in an oath. This oath takes place, according to the *Zadokite Fragments*, after examination by the *mevaqqer* (CDC 15:11).

The text discussed here is part of a larger unit, CDC 15:5–13, which concerns entry of new members into the sect. Whereas the first part discusses those born into the sect (ll. 5f.), the remainder of the text is devoted to outsiders seeking admission. The use of *we-khen* (l. 6) shows that the law for both groups is essentially the same./85/ In both cases, the oath taken is for the purpose of rendering the swearer liable to the sect's penal system. Indeed, the same technical use of the *hif'il* of *qwm* in the sense of "to take upon oneself an obligation by oath" is present in both texts. Yet it has already been shown that the oath for born members takes place at twenty, and it seems from the text now before us that this oath is for rendering them liable. If so, it would be logical to understand 1QSa 1:9–11 likewise to refer to the fact that the born sectarian, after reaching the age of twenty (and taking the oath described in CDC 15:5f.) would now be liable to be testified against, and thereafter, to be punished by the decree of the sectarian court.

An alternative can also be posed to Baumgarten's assumption that from twenty it was possible to join the students who assembled at the court. Licht has proposed that the reference here may be to some kind of periodic covenant renewal ceremony which the sect believed would occur in the end of days. Indeed, such a ceremony probably occurred in the life of the sect as a regular annual event./86/

In accord with Licht's view, then, the passage would be translated:

> And he shall be liable to testimony against him (regarding) the laws/87/ of the Torah/88/ and to take [his] place when the laws/89/ are proclaimed./90/

One other peculiarity of this passage must be discussed. It characterizes the age of twenty as that in which marriage and sexual relations are first permitted. Further, it says that this is the age of the knowledge of good and evil. The knowledge of good and evil as a biblical motif, especially in regard to the Garden of Eden story, has been the subject of extensive discussion. While G. W. Buchanan sees the motif as indicating maturity generally,/91/ R. Gordis has argued for taking this phrase as referring to sexual maturity./92/ While it is not in the domain of this study to determine the original meaning of this expression in the Hebrew Bible, it must be stated that Gordis is undoubtedly correct when he states that the passage under discussion here has adopted the very same interpretation as his. To the author of this Qumran document, knowledge of good and evil means sexual maturity, and when such knowledge comes at twenty, a man is ready to marry and begin sexual relations./93/

Why is twenty presented as the age of sexual readiness? It is undoubtedly the case that the sect, as did the tannaim later on, took the view that by twenty puberty certainly had occurred. They, therefore, were ensuring with this law that child marriage, at least for males, would not take place. This ruling may have been part of the sectarian tendency toward the regulation of sexual life. According to Josephus, the marrying Essenes allowed themselves sexual relations only to avoid the depopulation of the world./94/ According to the tannaitic sources, some groups of *ḥasidim* greatly minimized sexual life./95/ Some Essenes apparently took a negative view of sexual life as did some Christians later on./96/ Perhaps the sect shared these tendencies and wanted to ensure that male sectarians would not participate in sexual relations before it was definite that they had attained procreative ability. Hence, they did not allow relations until twenty.

This view is in marked contrast to that of the tannaim who permitted early marriages and who favored marriage at eighteen./97/ Further, the tannaim saw it as a transgression to delay marriage beyond twenty./98/

The connection of the marriage age and the ability to testify can now be understood. In both cases, the sect sought to be certain beyond any doubt that the candidate had physically reached the stage of majority. The only way to be certain, they believed, was to insist on the age of twenty, regarded as it was as the latest age of puberty normally possible.

7. *Summary*

According to sectarian law, the minimum age for witnesses was twenty, and this was also the age of mustering, and attainment of the rights of voting and marriage. Twenty was viewed in ancient Judaism as the age by which puberty, hence majority, was always completed in normal cases. At this age the children of sectarians became full-fledged members of the sect upon taking the oath of initiation. Families were accepted along with the husbands. The acceptance of the husband meant automatic status for the family within the sect. A twenty year old was required to donate the half-sheqel as a one-time offering. No one except a member of the sect could testify before the sectarian courts, nor could anyone who was known to intentionally violate a law derived by the sect through the medium of sectarian biblical exegesis. Despite claims to the contrary by some scholars, the testimony of women was not admitted at Qumran.

NOTES

/1/ Reading *ʿd* (*ʿed*) with Schechter and Rabin. The error can be explained as the result of the fact that the adverb "still" can be spelled *ʿwd* or *ʿd*. At some point in the transmission of the text, a scribe was confused and thought that the letters *ʿd* (which should have been read *ʿed*, "witness") represented the adverb. He therefore wrote it in the usual orthography. The possibility that we are dealing with the confusion of *waw* and *yod* at an early stage in transmission (Qumran manuscripts do not usually distinguish the two) must be rejected here as there is no attestation for "witness" spelled *plene*.

/2/ The *puʿal* of *qbl* does not occur in the Bible but is used in the participle in Rabbinic sources. The *piʿel* is followed by an infinitive in Est. 9:27 and 2 Chron. 29:16. The *piʿel* is followed by the preposition *l-* in 1 Chron. 21:11. With the exception of the *puʿal*, then, the language of our phrase can be attested in late biblical Hebrew. Cf. *ḥelqam loʾ yequbal lefanekha* in Rashi to Num. 16:15 (based on *Midrash Tanḥumaʾ* Koraḥ, sec. 6 (73b), ed. Buber, sec. 18 (45bf.); cf. *Be-Midbar Rabbah* 18:10, but the language of Rashi is not prefigured in these sources). The preposition is the *lamed* of reference, construed with passive verbs (BDB, 514a, sec. e).

/3/ Translating with new JPS to Deut. 17:6; 19:15. Num. 35:30 uses *le-fi* instead of *ʿal pi*. On the Qumran interpretation of these passages, see below, 74–78.

/4/ Perhaps "years." See BDB, 399b, sec. 6c.

/5/ Rabin notes that 1 Chron. 17:11 is the only use of *mlʾ* followed by the pl. of *yom* regarding age. 2 Sam. 7:12 contains the same text. Referring to CDC 10:6, regarding judges, Schechter, followed by Segal, assumed that this meant twenty-five. In light of the almost verbatim citation of Ex. 30:13f., this cannot be accepted. If we would say that the ages for judges and witnesses should be the same, then should we say that in accordance with the requirements for judges, one past the age of 60 cannot bear witness? Ginzberg, *Sect*, 396 n. 166 suggests an alternative explanation for *'asher lo' mal'u yamaw*—namely that the person has not completed the trial period for membership in the sect. If so, the entire passage would mean "who has not completed his trial period by which to become a full-fledged member of the sect." Such an explanation might be possible if this were the only text available. However, 1QSa 1:9f. (discussed presently), which was not available to Ginzberg, makes clear that the passage intends to specify an age limit.

/6/ The phrase is from Ex. 30:14 and appears as well in CDC 15:6. On the mustering procedure, see Yadin, *War Scroll*, 59–61 and *HAQ*, 66f. It was intended to facilitate preparing a roster of members and organizing the sect in military units.

/7/ Schecter supplied *lo'* here. It is unnecessary as the negative before *mal'u* extends to *yare' 'el* as well. Cf. Ginzberg, *Sect*, 46.

/8/ Cf. the quotation in CDC 20:19 (Ginzberg and Rabin). That "fear of God" constitutes a body of knowledge can be seen from 2 K. 17:28, 32, 34, 39, 41, as well as Ps. 19:10 (where emendation must be rejected). See also Pss. Sol. 2:37, 3:16, etc. as well as Ex. 18:21, in reference to judges (Rabin).

/9/ Segal takes this as *hof'al*, *yo'oman*. The *hof'al* does not occur in the Bible at all. In a *baraita'* in B. 'Avodah Zarah 16b, ed. Vilna, a *hof'al* is found, yet the marginal note, R. Ḥananel, and *DS* (*ad loc.*) suggest the possibility that this word is a corruption. Favoring this reading, however, is the rule of *lectio difficilior*. The parallel in T. Ḥullin 2:24 (ed. Zuckermandel) does not show a *hof'al*. (On this *baraita'*, see Z. W. Rabinowitz, *Sha'are Torat Bavel* [1961], 178.) The occurrence of a *hof'al* in the poetry of Yannai (Even-Shoshan, *s.v.*) is probably due to innovation based on the commonly used *hif'il*. It appears that we have little choice but to read our form as a *nif'al*, *ye'amen*. The *nif'al* of *'mn* followed by *'al* in the sense of being "reliable concerning" is frequent in Rabbinic literature (*e.g.* the *baraita'* just cited). P. Soṭah 2:5 (18b) is an explanation of the response *'amen*. This passage is the only case of a non-participial *nif'al* of *'mn* which could be located in Rabbinic literature. J. Levy, *Wörterbuch über die Talmudim und Midraschim* (1963), labels this a biblical usage. Interesting is the reading of MS Rome, *we-ye'amnu* (*wy'mnu*) *ha-devarim* where ed. Venice reads *ye'amnu* (*yy'mnu*) *ha-devarim* (S. Lieberman, *'Al Ha-Yerushalmi* [1929], 62). Perhaps all we have in the printed text is a slight misquotation of Gen. 42:20. If not, the scribe of MS Rome made his error under the influence of this verse which reads *we-ye'amnu* (*wy'mnu*) *divrekhem*. We must remember that while MS Rome preserves many valuable readings, it is replete with errors. Apparently, it was copied by a poor scribe from a good *Vorlage*. It is not surprising that our text, composed centuries before the tannaitic literature was redacted, still shows the use of *nif'al* imperfect of this root, a form not unusual in the Bible. Indeed, Ben Sira 36:21 and 50:24 preserve such forms. The *nif'al* of *'mn* occurs with *'ed* in Jer. 42:5 and Ps. 89:38. Rabin's translation, "be declared a reliable witness," presupposes the meaning of the *hif'il* in Rabbinic usage (so M. Jastrow, *Dictionary of Talmud Bavli*,

Yerushalmi, Midrashic Literature and Targumim [1950], *s.v.*). But we have seen that it is unlikely that our form is a *hof'al* serving as a passive of this Rabbinic sense.

/10/ The preposition *'al* is common after the *nif'al* of *'mn* in tannaitic usage (*e.g.* the *baraita'* discussed in the preceding note) to indicate concerning whom or what the person is reliable. For witnesses, cf. M. Sanhedrin 3:2. This usage does not occur in the Bible.

/11/ The usage *'br davar mi(n)* is found in DSD 8:22, on which see below, 169f. The root *'br* in the *qal*, followed by *miṣwah* (sing.) occurs only in Est. 3:3, referring to the command of an earthly king. The root occurs with the pl. *miṣwot*, the divine commandments, in Deut. 26:13 and 2 Chron. 24:20. In the former passage the preposition *min* precedes *miṣwot* as in our text. For *davar*, "anything," followed by *min*, meaning "any of," see Ex. 5:11, 9:4; Josh. 8:35, 11:15 (cf. DSD 8:17), 21:43; and Est. 6:10.

/12/ Cf. above, 44 n. 52.

/13/ Since, as Rabin notes, our clause is an elipsis of that in DSD 8:18, we ought to take the verb *zkw* as referring to the deeds of the transgressor. There is no way of knowing if our verb is to be derived from *zkh* or *zkk*. (But cf. A. M. Honeyman, "Isaiah I 16 *hizzakw*," *VT* 1 [1951], 63–65.) Only the third person, pl., perfect occurs for *zkk* in the Bible (Job 15:15, 25:5; Eccl. 4:7). But this need not be significant as there can be no doubt that Hebrew was a spoken language at Qumran and that the sectarians had the ability to fill out paradigms with forms not found in Scripture. From the Rabbinic dictionaries it would appear that *zkk* ceased to function as a verb by the tannaitic period, and *zkh* lost the meaning "to be pure." It is noteworthy that in discussing M. Menaḥot 8:5 in which the word *zakh*, "pure," appears (based on Ex. 27:20 which is quoted by the Mishnah), B. Menaḥot 86b found it necessary to quote a *baraita'* which defines *zakh* as *naqi*, "pure." (Cf. the parallel in *Sifra'* 'Emor, parashah 13:6.) Ginzberg (*Sect*, 47) suggests emendation to *'d ḥzrw bw lšwb* (*'ad ḥazero vo la-shuv*) which he translates, "until he gives up his sinful way of life to return to God," or to *'d znḥw* (*'ad zenaḥo*), "until he abandons." The need for these proposals is obviated by the explanation given above in this note.

/14/ The *qal* of *šwb* means much more than "to repent" at Qumran. (This was not realized by Schechter and Segal in their editions of CDC.) It is a technical term for joining the sect or for rejoining it after a period of suspension due to transgression. For this latter sense (in negative context) see DSD 8:23 and 9:1.

/15/ Cf. Num. 1:3; 1 Chron. 27:23.

/16/ Cf. de Vaux, *Ancient Israel* (1965) I, 225.

/17/ Above, 30–32.

/18/ So Licht.

/19/ So Licht. See his "*Ha-Munaḥ Goral Bi-Khetaveha shel Kat Midbar Yehudah*," *Bet Miqra'* 1 (1955/56), 90–99.

/20/ It is also possible to translate "among" or "in the midst of" (Richardson).

/21/ Licht (*Serakhim*, 247) attributes the mention of "families" here to the predilection of 1QSa to the restoration of biblical society in the end of days. Cf. Yadin, *War Scroll*, 49–53.

/22/ Cf. DSD 5:20 in which the phrase *'adat qodesh* appears in connection with *lhyḥd*. Our word is a *hif'il* with elided *he'* on which see Qimron, p. 148f.

/23/ The restoration of *'adat* is definite as half of the *dalet* is visible (Licht). Cf. DSD 5:20; 1QSa 1:20, 2:16 (as restored by Barthélemy, *DJD* I); CDC 20:2, and Rabin, *QS*, 37–52.

/24/ The use of *ha-ba'* as a technical term for joining the group also occurs in Rabbinic usage for both the *ḥavurah* and conversion (S. Lieberman, "The Discipline in the So-Called Dead Sea Manual of Discipline," *JBL* 71 (1952), 202, reprinted in his *Texts and Studies* (1974), p. 203. Cf. his *Greek in Jewish Palestine* (1965), 80.

/25/ Note the use of *plene* spelling for Masoretic *qameṣ qaṭan* in *ḥoq*. The phrase *ḥoq* (*ḥuqat*) *'olam* appears in Ex. 29:28; Lev. 6:11, 15, 7:34, 10:15, 24:9; Num. 18:8, 11, 19 in cultic context, often in association with *ben* in the pl., referring to the Sons of Aaron. Cf. also Ex. 12:24. In Jer. 5:22 the phrase means "a law of nature." Apparently, the phrase in our passage simply means that the process is to be repeated generation after generation.

/26/ On the *hif'il* of *qwm* followed by *'al* in the sense of "to take upon oneself an oath," see below 70f. n. 80.

/27/ Cf. CDC 15:6–11; DSD 6:13–15. Cf. *shevu'at 'issar* in DSD 5:8. Rabin compares the initiatory oaths of the Essenes in *War* 2, 8, 7 (139–143).

/28/ Num. 1:2.

/29/ T. Demai 2:14 (and Lieberman, *TK*, *ad loc.*), which mentions the full *ḥavurah*, and a *baraita'* in B. Bekhorot 30b which mentions the three representatives. Lieberman ("Discipline," 200 n. 15) assumes that the Babylonian recension is secondary and that the acceptance of *ḥaverut* took place before the entire *ḥavurah*. A. Oppenheimer (*The 'Am Ha-Aretz* [1977], 120 n. 7) takes the variation as the result of differing practices or date.

/30/ P. Demai 2:3 (23a); Lieberman, *TK*, to T. Demai 2:14.

/31/ T. Demai 2:16 (and Lieberman, *TK*, *ad loc.*). Cf. Oppenheimer, 139 and R. Sarason, *A History of the Mishnaic Law of Agriculture*, Part III, Vol. 1 (1979), 90–94.

/32/ "*Maḥaṣit Ha-Sheqel Bi-Megillot Midbar Yehudah*," *Tarbiz* 31 (1960/61), 18–22. Cf. his "*Parashat Maḥaṣit Ha-Sheqel*," *Y. Kaufmann Jubilee Volume* (1960/1), 54–67.

/33/ *Sect*, 45f., and 326–331.

/34/ For the definition of the physical symptoms of puberty, see M. Niddah 5:9, 6:11 (cf. M. Sanhedrin 8:1); and J. Preuss, *Biblical and Talmudic Medicine*, trans. and ed. by F. Rosner (1978), 128–130. Cf. also J. Neusner, *A History of the Mishnaic Law of Purities* (1974–80) XV, 88f., 93–95.

/35/ A *baraita'* in B. Niddah 47b. Cf. Tosafot, *ad loc.*, and a *baraita'* in B. Yevamot 80a.

/36/ Cf. M. 'Avot 5:21 (regarding males) and T. Niddah 6:2 (cf. B. Niddah 46a and S. Lieberman, *Tosefet Rishonim*, *ad loc.*).

/37/ T. Ḥagigah 1:3 and Lieberman, *TK*, *ad loc.*

/38/ P. Bikkurim 2:1 (64c); P. Sanhedrin 11:7 (30b); B. Shabbat 89b. Cf. *Bereshit Rabbah* 58:1 and *Tosefot Yom Ṭov* to M. Niddah 5:9.

/39/ Ginzberg, *Sect*, 45f. claims that "according to Talmudic law no one under twenty years of age may dispose of real estate (Bava Bathra 156a) which probably indicates that some business circles are often more conservative than judges." Actually, the source he cites allows the sale of real estate belonging to the young man. It only prohibits selling land he acquired as an inheritance from his father. Maimonides, H. Mekhirah 29:13, correctly comments that this law is designed to protect the young man from squandering his inheritance before becoming initiated into the management of financial affairs (*darkhe ha-'olam*). Cf. also B. Giṭṭin 65a.

/40/ *Toledot Ha-Halakhah* IV (1950), 372.

/41/ T. Ḥagigah 1:2; B. Sukkah 42b. The entire passage in B. Sukkah 42b is an amoraic recapitulation of the *baraita'* with interspersed amoraic comments. Note that the interpolation traces the source of this *halakhah* to Ex. 12:4.

/42/ Rabin (to CDC 10:1) also cites a regulation from Fetḥa Naghast, an Ethiopian law code, which requires witnesses to be twenty.

/43/ Ginzberg, *Sect*, 46; Rabin to CDC 10:1; cf. above, 36.

/44/ See above, 23.

/45/ *Sect*, 46.

/46/ Harkavy, 22. The translation is that of *Sect*, 46. Note that Anan saw all wine as forbidden to Karaites as a result of the destruction of the Temple.

/47/ *Sefer Ha-Miṣwot*, 38, 59, 131.

/48/ So Ginzberg.

/49/ Aaron ben Elijah of Nicomedia, *Gan 'Eden*, 172b; Hadassi, *'Eshkol Ha-Kofer*, 11d; Ginzberg, *Sect*, 149. But note that L. Nemoy, *Karaite Anthology* (1952), 31 states that Daniel al-Kumisi is said to have exempted men under twenty from religious ordinances.

/50/ *Allegorical Interpretation* I, 10, cited by Ginzberg, *Sect*, 149 n. 171.

/51/ On this phenomenon, see below, 136.

/52/ There is no possibility here of reference to the semi-proselytes known from other Second Temple sources.

/53/ DSD 5:14–17.

/54/ *HAQ*, 47–49.

/55/ DSD 8:17–9:2 and below, 165–168.

/56/ For this term, see *HAQ*, 22–32.

/57/ *Ant*. 4, 8, 15 (219).

/58/ M. Sanhedrin 3:3; M. Rosh Ha-Shanah 1:8; T. Sanhedrin 5:2, 5 of which Rabin cites only the first and last. On these traditions, see [Z. Frankel], "*Beitrage zur Sacherklärung der Mischnah*," *MGWJ* 20 (1871), 494–501. Note that repentance allowed the testimony of these transgressors to be accepted again (T. Sanhedrin 5:2; P. Rosh Ha-Shanah 1:7 [ed. Krot. 1:9, 57bf.]; P. Sanhedrin 3:5 [21a]; P. Shevu'ot 7:4 [37d]; B. Sanhedrin 25b).

/59/ B. Sanhedrin 26b.

/60/ Maimonides, H. 'Edut 12:1.

/61/ See below, 115f.

/62/ T. Sanhedrin 5:2.

/63/ B. Yoma' 86b and in the beautiful formulation of Maimonides, H. Teshuvah 2:1.

/64/ Restored with Licht.

/65/ For the use of *qrb* with *'ishah* in the sense of sexual relations, see Lev. 18:19. While later tradition took this as a general prohibition on contact, the original text clearly is meant to refer to sexual relations. The *lamed* of *'el* is partly visible.

/66/ Cf. Num. 31:17 (although following B. Yevamot 60b, Rashi takes this as meaning capable of sexual relations) and Jud. 21:11. Licht remarks that the terminology has been transferred from reference to the female to the male.

/67/ Licht notes the spelling *ky* (as in Masoretic Hebrew) and compares DSD 5:14 (*ki 'im* also).

/68/ Cf. Jer. 29:10 *le-fi melot*. On the spelling see DSD 6:18 (*mwl't*) and DSD 7:20 (*mlw't*). Cf. also Licht, *Serakhim*, 45f.

/69/ See Gen. 2:9; Deut. 1:39; Is. 7:15–16. This expression is discussed below, 64.

/70/ *DJD* I, 113.

/71/ Richardson, 113.

/72/ "On the Testimony of Women in 1QSa," *JBL* 76 (1957), 266–269, reprinted in his *Studies in Qumran Law*, 183–186.

/73/ Richardson, 119.

/74/ Baumgarten, 184. Baumgarten's statement regarding "Pharisaic law" that "even in cases where women are qualified [to testify], a person cannot testify against his relative," is somewhat difficult to understand since women's testimony is accepted in order to prove the death of her own husband and permit her remarriage, and this is the primary case in which female witnesses are accepted in Rabbinic *halakhah*. Cf. M. Yevamot 15:4; M. Soṭah 6:2.

/75/ Cf. also 1 Cor. 14:34–35; 1 Tim 3:11–12.

/76/ *Ant.* 4, 8, 15 (219). Cf. *Ant.* 4, 8, 4, (196–198). It is possible, however, that Josephus intentionally introduced some non-Scriptural laws into his account.

/77/ Baumgarten, 185.

/78/ *Serakhim*, 253f.

/79/ Discussed as well in *HAQ*, 29.

/80/ On the *hif'il* of *qwm* followed by *'al* in the sense of taking an oath, see DSD 5:8, 10; DST 14:15; CDC 16:7 and Nebe, 257–264. Ginzberg, *Sect*, 295 notes that this is not a biblical usage, and sees it as an Aramaism, meaning to "confirm under oath" or "swear." (When Ginzberg wrote, it was usual to consider cases of parallel usage in Aramaic and late biblical or post-biblical Hebrew to be the result of Aramaic influence. Today, scholarship is more circumspect and recognizes the frequency of common usages.) Ginzberg cites as examples M. Sanhedrin 7:6 which is a *pi'el*, however, and the fascinating case of the ancient *baraita'* in B. Qiddushin 66a. This is the famous story of Alexander Jannaeus and the Pharisees. Janneus is told in Ginzberg's translation, "Make them [the Pharisees] take a loyalty oath on the high priestly frontplate" (*haqem lahem ba-ṣiṣ*). Cf. *Shir Ha-Shirim Rabbah* 7:9 on the *ṣiṣ*.

/81/ A technical term for joining the sect. Cf. CDC 16:1f. Mal. 3:22 is the source of *torat mosheh*. On the sanctity of the Law of Moses, see below, 137f. Cf. 1 K. 2:3 *be-torat mosheh* followed by v. 4, *be-khol levavam u-ve-khol nafsham*.

/82/ Cf. Deut. 10:12, 11:13. If the source of the phrase were Deut. 6:5, we would expect reference to the *me'od*. That the sect had *me'od* in its text can be seen from Y. Yadin, *Tefillin from Qumran* (1969), slip no. 2, l. 24 opp. Plate XV; cf. slip no. 1, l. 19f., opp. Plate XIV (for Deut. 10:12). Deut. 11:13 was originally contained in slip no. 4 (Yadin, 14). See also 2 Chron. 15:12. Note that an exegesis of Deut. 6:5 lies behind DSD 5:8f.

/83/ Restored with Rabin who considers the restoration "somewhat uncertain." The same usage occurs in M. 'Avot 4:4. See Levy, *s.v.*

/84/ Only the top of the *lamed* is visible. In the Bible the verb refers primarily to marital infidelity or misappropriation of cultic property. There is in addition a third metaphorical sense of acting treacherously against God or justice. In tannaitic usage, only the sense of misappropriation of cultic or sacred property survives.

/85/ On *we-khen*, cf. Licht *ad loc.* and above, 11.

/86/ Licht, *Serakhim*, 63–65.

/87/ The pl. *mishpaṭot* is anomalous.

/88/ Licht compares other spellings with final *'alef* instead of *he'* in 1QSa 2:22; DSD 7:4, 10:1, 3:11.

/89/ On *mishpaṭim* as law derived through sectarian exegesis, see *HAQ*, 42–47.

/90/ S. Hoenig, "On the Age of Mature Responsibility in 1QSa," *JQR* 48 (1957/8), 373 translates as follows: "And thus it shall be accepted that the laws of the Torah forewarn him and that he is to stand in obedience to the laws and the fulfillment thereof," including the first two words of the next sentence with our passage. Baumgarten, however, shows without question the many linguistic and exegetical problems posed by this translation ("1QSa 1.11—Age of Testimony or Responsibility?" *JQR* 49 [1958/9], 157–160) and the attempts by S. Zeitlin, in an editorial note, *idem.* 160f. and Hoenig, "The Age of Twenty in Rabbinic Tradition and 1QSa," *JQR* 49 (1958/9), 209–214 do little to justify it. Hoenig, however, has assembled the most complete collection of material on the age of twenty in the Rabbinic tradition.

/91/ "The Old Testament Meaning of the Knowledge of Good and Evil," *JBL* 75 (1956), 114–120.

/92/ "The Knowledge of Good and Evil in the Old Testament and Qumran Scrolls," *JBL* 76 (1957), 123–138.

/93/ Licht, however, takes it to mean general maturity in our passage, despite the context, which clearly supports Gordis's view. See also P. Borger, "'At the Age of Twenty' in 1 Q Sa," *RQ* 3 (1961–62), 267–277.

/94/ *War* 2, 8, 12 (160–161). Cf. Schürer II, 570 n. 55 for bibliography.

/95/ B. Niddah 38a–b (*baraita'*).

/96/ Cf. 1 Cor. 7:1, 2, 6, 7, 9 (Gordis).

/97/ M. 'Avot 3:21. This passage is often taken as a later addition. Texts indicating earlier ages (Ginzberg, *Sect*, 328 n. 34) usually refer to contracting the marriage, rather than to the actual start of married life.

/98/ B. Qiddushin 29b.

CHAPTER THREE
THE LAW OF TESTIMONY

1. *Witnesses and their Testimony*

The Qumran law of testimony has been the subject of much debate in recent years. Discussion has revolved around several issues: the number of witnesses required by the Qumran legal system, the combination of testimony of single witnesses, and, finally, the question of whether parallels to the provisions of this passage do or do not exist in Rabbinic literature. The difficulty with this passage stems from what seems to be characteristic of the laws in the *Zadokite Fragments*. Often the text deals only with special cases while omitting the general rules. The text before us is based on presuppositions not stated, and it is to them that any analysis must turn.

CDC 9:16–23 is the basis for this discussion./1/

כל דבר אשר ימעל איש בתורה וראה רעיהו והוא אחד אם דבר מות
הוא וידיעהו לעיניו בהוכיח למבקר והמבקר יכתבהו בידו עד
עשותו עוד לפני אחד ושב והודיע למבקר אם ישוב וניתפש לפני
אחד שלם משפטו ואם שנים הם והם מעידים על דבר אחד והובדל
האיש מן הטהרה לבד אם נאמנים הם וביום ראות האיש יודיעה
למבקר ועל ההון יקבלו שני עידים נאמנים ועל אחד להבדיל
הטהרה

Regarding any case in which a man transgresses/2/ against the Torah,/3/ and his neighbor witnesses it,/4/ and he is the only witness: If it is a capital case,/5/ he (the witness) shall report it in his (the offender's) presence/6/ to the examiner (*mevaqqer*)/7/ with reproving (*be-hokheaḥ*)./8/ The examiner shall record it (the offense) with his (own) hand until (such time as) he (the offender) should repeat it (the offense) in the presence of one (witness). Again/9/ he (the witness) shall report (it) to the examiner. If he (the offender) should again be apprehended/10/ in the presence of one (witness) (i.e. a third time),/11/ his verdict is complete./12/ If, however, two witnesses testify to one/13/ case, he (the offender) shall only be removed from the pure food,/14/ provided they are reliable (witnesses)./15/ On the very day/16/ the person (the witness) shall see it, he shall report it to the examiner. Concerning property (cases), they may accept/17/ two reliable witnesses, and (rely) on a single (witness)/18/ only to remove (the offender) from the pure food.

This passage describes a procedure whereby the testimony of single witnesses to separate commissions of the same offense, duly recorded by the examiner, can be taken together to convict an offender. The passage assumes that three witnesses are required for capital convictions and two for convictions in financial matters. It requires the usual "reproof" which will be shown in the next chapter to be essential to all cases in the Qumran legal system. In cases in which only two witnesses testify regarding a capital matter or only one witness testifies regarding a financial matter, the offender is removed from the pure food, a punishment which is tantamount to reduction to the status of a novice in his first year./19/

2. *The Number of Witnesses Required*

M. Makkot 1:7 and 8 indicate/20/ that the tannaim interpreted the number "three" in Deut. 17:6 to denote an option of having more than two witnesses. The sages inferred by analogy that a group of more than two witnesses constituted a unit to be treated in the same way as a unit of two. Indeed, Deut. 17:6; Num. 35:30, and Deut. 19:15 made clear to the Rabbis that the Torah meant to exclude conviction in capital cases by one witness's testimony, and that testimony of two was sufficient for execution. The tannaitic conclusions based on the number "three" were in accord with the hermeneutical assumption that the Torah contained nothing superfluous and that every word had its purpose. Probably, the Rabbis knew that ancient procedure had required a minimum of two witnesses./21/

The sect had a slightly different view which can best be understood by allusion to the law of Sabbath limits./22/ CDC 10:21 states, "Let him not walk about outside his city MORE THAN A THOUSAND CUBITS."/23/ CDC 10:5–6 reads, "Let no man walk after an animal to pasture it outside of his city except two thousand cubits."/24/

These laws, although contradictory at first glance, are clearly the result of sectarian *midrash*. Ex. 16:29 was taken as referring not only to the desert period but to all time. The verse, however, did not define the limits of *taḥtaw* or *meqomo*. The process of *midrash* was used to define these terms. The sect, as did the tannaim later on, cited the description of the boundaries of the Levitical cities in Num. 35:2–5/25/ and used this definition of the city limits. A man was permitted to go as far as these limits on the Sabbath but no further.

Although both the sect and the Rabbis made use of the passage in Numbers, both had trouble interpreting it. The tannaim eventually decided that the "two thousand cubits" referred to the *teḥum shabbat* ("Sabbath limit"), while the other figure of "one thousand" referred to the Levitical pasture land (*migrash*)./26/ The sect seems to have concluded that there were *two* Sabbath limits, that of 1000 cubits beyond which a man could not walk, and the other, of 2000 cubits beyond which he could not go in pasturing his animals. In other words, a man was permitted to walk an additional thousand cubits to pasture his animals./27/

It would appear that from the point of view of hermeneutics, the sect maintained that in groups of numbers, each had to have its own significance.

In regard to the law of testimony, then, the same rule prevailed. If the Torah enjoined conviction by two or three witnesses, one could assume that two different cases were intended, one requiring three witnesses and the other requiring two. Since there is a basic distinction in Jewish law between matters involving capital punishment and those requiring financial sanctions, it is logical to assume that the intention was for capital crimes to require three witnesses and for monetary matters to require only two.

The Qumran and tannaitic materials share a principle in regard to their exegesis of the pertinent verses. They both assume that even though the verses apply literally to capital cases, they also teach the law of money matters; hence the Rabbis require two witnesses there also. The sect goes further in assigning each number ("two" and "three") to a specific case. This would appear to be the same process which guided the Qumran exegesis in the setting of Sabbath limits. Thus, the sect's requirement of three witnesses in capital cases in which Rabbinic law accepted two may be traced to a different exegetical approach to the pertinent biblical material./28/

Several passages in the New Testament paraphrase Deut. 19:15 and repeat the requirement of "two or three" witnesses (Matt. 18:16; 1 Tim. 5:19; Heb. 10:28; and 2 Cor. 13:1–3)./29/ Two other passages (Jn. 8:17; Rev. 11:3) reflect what was probably the regular practice of requiring two witnesses./30/

Josephus in *Life* 49 likewise mentions the necessity of testimony by "two or three" persons. In *Ant.* 4, 8, 15 (219), in which he is reviewing the law of the Pentateuch, he indicates that three witnesses are preferable to two. *Ant.* 8, 13, 8 (358) contains Josephus's version of the story of Naboth. While the Masoretic text (1 K. 21:10, 13) and Septuagint both mention two witnesses, Josephus has increased the number to three./31/ From this one can conclude that Josephus understood capital cases to require three witnesses (Naboth) and other matters to require only two. This would put him in complete agreement with the traditions of the Qumran sect.

In reference to the story of Naboth, L. Ginzberg has observed that the version of Josephus "presupposes the old Halakah according to which in cases involving capital punishment three witnesses (or to be more accurate, one accuser and two witnesses) are necessary."/32/ As evidence of this older practice, Ginzberg cites Test. Abraham A, 13 which requires that "every matter shall be established according to three witnesses."/33/ This passage seems at first glance to contradict the view that only two witnesses were required in non-capital judgments. It must be remembered, however, that the context here is the final judgment of souls, certainly a "capital" matter. It cannot be known if the requirement of three witnesses in capital cases is an "older *halakhah*," but it was definitely the law in certain circles. Remembering the sectarian connections of Josephus,/34/ one need not be surprised at his reflecting an old schismatic legal tradition.

There may be a remnant of the requirement of three witnesses for capital cases in tannaitic *halakhah*. M. Sanhedrin 8:4 contains the rule that the rebellious son (*ben sorer u-moreh*) must receive his warning (*hatra'-ah*)/35/ in the presence of three. The use of *bi-fene*, "in front of," would seem to indicate that these three are to serve as witnesses. Indeed, the expression *yiddon be-*, "should be judged by,"/36/ appears in the same *mishnah* to indicate the size of the court before which stripes are to be administered to him. Despite the Babylonian amoraic explanation to the effect that the warning must take place before only two witnesses and that three judges are required for administering the stripes,/37/ the plain meaning of the *mishnah* is that the boy is to be warned in front of three witnesses./38/ Even if the witnesses constituted a court, they were still functioning as witnesses./39/ Tannaitic tradition preserves a dispute as to whether this procedure ever led to an execution./40/ At most, this procedure must have been very rare, and its regulations may go back to very ancient traditions./41/

The matter of separation from the pure food as it relates to the law of testimony may now be examined. Whereas three witnesses were required for capital matters and two for others, it was possible with fewer witnesses to impose the lesser penalty of removal from the pure food. This sanction could be effected based on the testimony of only two in a capital matter and one in other matters./42/ It can be seen from our text that this testimony could even be the result of separate commissions of the same offense and was subject to the usual sectarian regulations for the admissibility of such combinations of testimony. The reason for which fewer witnesses were accepted for separation from the pure food is that this was simply a sectarian sanction and not conviction for violation of a biblical prescription. Whenever a person could be shown, even with a minimum of testimony, to have transgressed, he was prohibited from contact with the pure food. For, as will be shown, the sect fervently believed that transgression rendered the offender ritually impure. Hence, he had to be removed to prevent his rendering the food of the other members of the group ritually impure. Such a punishment would be tantamount to reduction to the novitiate, as new applicants to the sect were not admitted to the pure food until they passed an examination./43/

In light of the parallels for the Qumran requirement of three witnesses in capital cases, it is necessary to reexamine a passage from the *Temple Scroll* (TS 64:6–13):/44/

כי יהיה איש רכיל בעמו ומשלים את עמו לגוי נכר ועושה רעה בעמו
ותליתמה אותו על העץ וימת על פי שנים עדים ועל פי שלושה עדים
יומת והמה יתלו אותו העץ כי יהיה באיש חטא משפט מות ויברח
אל תוך הגואים ויקלל אש עמו ואת בני ישראל ותליתמה גם אותו
על העץ וימות ולוא תלין נבלתמה על העץ כי קבור תקברמה ביום
ההוא כי מקוללי אלוהים ואנשים תלוי על העץ ולוא תטמא את האדמה
אשר אנוכי נותן לכה נחלה

Yadin has offered the following translation:/45/

> If a man has informed/46/ against his people and has delivered/47/ his people up to a foreign nation/48/ and has done evil to his people, you shall hang him on the tree and he shall die. On the evidence of two witnesses and on the evidence of three witnesses he shall be put to death and they shall hang him on [?] the tree./49/ If a man has committed a crime/50/ punishable by death and has run away to the midst of the Gentiles/51/ and cursed/52/ his people and/53/ the children of Israel, you shall hang him also on a tree and he shall die; and you shall not leave their bodies upon the tree in the night but you shall bury them/54/ the same day, for the hanged upon the tree are cursed by God and men; and you shall not defile the land which I give you as an inheritance . . .

Yadin deals with this passage at length in his introductory volume./55/ While it is not necessary here to enter into all the details of the passage, it should be noted that he is certainly correct in seeing the text as referring to death by hanging./56/ Certainly, the two kinds of informers mentioned in this passage are, in the view of the author of the *Temple Scroll*, liable to death by some form of crucifixion. What is of concern here is the manner in which the criminal is convicted. The text clearly states that in this case, certainly a capital crime in the view of the *Temple Scroll*, either two or three witnesses suffice to carry out the execution of the informer.

This would seem to stand in direct contradiction to the conclusion reached from analysis of the law of testimony in the *Zadokite Fragments*. Yadin has avoided the problem by reading *aḥer* and explaining our text from the *Zadokite Fragments* in such a way as it is consistent with the *Temple Scroll*./57/ He sees the law before us as indicating that whereas two witnesses are usually sufficient in capital cases, three are required when the testimony is to be compounded from that of single witnesses to isolated violations of the same commandment./58/ The same view is taken by B. Jackson./59/ Yet the specific mention of two witnesses as sufficient for *financial matters* in our passage from the *Zadokite Fragments* renders it extremely difficult to deny that the passage requires three witnesses in capital matters, even if the witnesses testify to one offense.

If so, how can the *Temple Scroll* be explained? In the Introduction it has already been noted that there are many reasons to believe that the *Temple Scroll* should not be assumed to emanate from the same circles that produced the *Zadokite Fragments* and the *Megillat Ha-Serakhim*. This may simply be one of many cases in which these texts disagree or represent different traditions. Indeed, contradictions are to be noted between the various texts of the Qumran corpus. Such contradictions can represent differing origins, points of view, or stages of development, even among a unified corpus of texts.

It must be noted, though, that this passage from the *Temple Scroll* deals with the punishment of informers./60/ If the *Temple Scroll* is seen as an integral part of the literature of the Qumran sect, as proposed by Yadin, then it might still be possible to understand how the sect could require three witnesses in capital matters and two in the case of informers. The aberrations of *halakhah* which occurred in the Middle Ages in regard to the problem of informers/61/ should caution against expecting to find the same regulations for this crime as for others. It may be that whereas in regard to other capital crimes the sect required three witnesses, it was less rigorous here and executed informers on the testimony of only two. Such tendencies would be expected in a sectarian group which saw itself as fighting for its survival.

3. *Combination of Testimony*

B. Levine has advanced the suggestion that the sect determined that the combination of successive occurrences of an offense before a single witness constituted grounds for conviction by analogy with the *shor mu'ad* ("forewarned ox") of Ex. 21:29./62/ This is only a first step in understanding this regulation. The sect emphasized the end of this verse. After describing the process whereby an ox is stoned upon its third goring offense if it result in death, the verse concludes, "and also his master shall die." In the view of the sect, this was taken to mean: And also if his master should be warned twice (by one witness in front of the examiner) regarding the commission of capital crimes, he too (like the ox) shall be liable to capital punishment (upon a third offense).

The New Testament provides a parallel to the combination of testimony found at Qumran. 2 Cor. 13:1–2 implies that a single witness could reprove (warn) a transgressor on two occasions after which if he transgressed again in the presence of the witness, the offender was liable to punishment according to the law of Deut. 19:15./63/ A similar procedure may underlie the statement of Philo that Joseph required three separate signs to the effect that there was no enmity among his brothers./64/ The combination of testimony may have been more widespread than the sources would suggest./65/

The acceptance of cumulative testimony required a system for recording the offenses that had been witnessed. This posed no problem for the sect, dependent as it was on written records for the process of admitting new members and keeping its rosters./66/ Further, as described in the next chapter,/67/ the sect required a formal procedure of reproof for an offense before that offense could serve as the basis for trial and conviction. This process necessitated that witnesses to any offense reprove the culprit formally in the presence of witnesses and that this reproof be officially recorded by the examiner. Such records served a dual purpose. They certified that the offender had been previously reproved for committing the same offense, and, if the offense had been committed in front of a single witness, served as the basis for conviction if other single witnesses should later report the same offense.

Tannaitic exegesis also had to interpret the words "and also his master shall die" in Ex. 21:29. Even if owners of "forewarned oxen" may have at one time been held responsible even with their lives for their animals' actions, this was no longer the case in tannaitic times./68/ The Mishnah, therefore, derived from this last clause that just as the master, if he were to be executed, would be tried before a court of twenty-three (small Sanhedrin), so must the ox be tried before twenty-three judges./69/

In tannaitic literature also there are cases in which a man's fate is sealed after three offenses. T. Sanhedrin 12:7 provides that an offender who cannot be convicted for lack of his acknowledgement of warning (*hatra'ah*) be incarcerated after three offenses. A minority view of Abba Saul assigns the final penalty to the fourth occurrence. T. Sanhedrin 12:8 indicates that one who has been flagellated twice on the third occurrence of the same offense is put in a cell in which he is fed barley "until his stomach splits."/70/ Again, Abba Saul assigns the final penalty to the fourth occurrence. This legislation may be but a survival of a system of "cumulative conviction" once more widely used and reflected in the Qumran law of testimony./71/

It may be said, therefore, that the acceptance of cumulative testimony, like the requirement of three witnesses in capital cases, results from the biblical exegesis of the sect. This exegesis differed from that of the tannaim whose exegesis is often intended to justify traditional practice.

L. Ginzberg alludes to several parallels in his notes to this passage./72/ These passages, however, seem to be of doubtful relevance. M. Makkot 1:9 concerns the combination of the testimony of two sets of two witnesses each. B. Makkot 6b also cited by him deals with a case in which two witnesses see a crime but each is unaware of the other's existence. It is assumed that such testimony is not valid in capital cases, but one Babylonian amora/73/ accepts such testimony as valid in monetary cases. The final text mentioned by Ginzberg is B. Sanhedrin 30. This probably was meant as a reference to 30a./74/ Here we find the mid second century tanna, Rabbi Joshua ben Qorḥa, stating that if two witnesses observed the same crime "one after the other," i.e. they witnessed different parts of the crime, their testimony may be taken as valid. This passage, however, assumes that we deal with two witnesses to one crime, not to the testimony of single witnesses to the commission of the same crime on two occasions./75/

The issue of these alleged parallels between the combination of testimony of single witnesses in sectarian practice and the Pharisaic-rabbinic tradition has been discussed by J. Neusner./76/ According to Neusner, the central question is how these two traditions attempted to solve the problem of the crime committed before only one witness: "Pharisaic-rabbinic law proved unable to solve the problem without appealing to judgment after death; the rules of evidence in the *Damascus Document* IX, 17–22 supply a somewhat better solution."/77/ After a review of the various translations and of the so-called "parallels" adduced by L. Ginzberg,/78/ Neusner concludes that:

> The presupposition of all the material alluded to by Ginzberg's note is precisely the opposite of that in *Dam. Doc.* IX, 17–22. In other words not only does the law of

testimony of the *Dam. Doc. not* exhibit "substantial agreement" with that of the rabbinic traditions (as Ginzberg claimed, p. 293), but it is based on quite contrary principles./79/

Pharisaic-rabbinic *halakhah* does not even raise "the possibility that the testimony of single witnesses to two separate, but similar, crimes may be combined to establish the guilt and effect the punishment of the accused,"/80/ yet such combination seems to be the rule at Qumran. Neusner continues with a thoroughgoing synoptic analysis of the Pharisaic-rabbinic traditions which attempt to solve the problem of crimes committed before only one witness. He begins by stating that the concept behind the Qumran law of combination is "utterly alien to the rabbinic traditions before us."/81/ This last sentence can also stand as a summary of his conclusions./82/

B. Jackson/83/ maintains that M. Sanhedrin 9:5 is a legitimate parallel to the combination of testimony in the *Zadokite Fragments*. This *mishnah* refers to one who killed another person in the absence of witnesses (*she-lo' be-'edim*). Such a criminal is placed in the *kippah* ("vaulted chamber, prison") variously interpreted as execution or life imprisonment./84/ Certainly, the plain meaning of the *mishnah* implies nothing of the combination of testimony. The Babylonian amoraim/85/ attempted to explain how the identity of such a murderer would be known in the absence of witnesses. Among the answers they give is that *two* witnesses would have seen the crime but not at the same time or that the witnesses were not aware of each other's presence./86/ Again we deal here with two witnesses and not one. This is not the case of single witnesses and cannot be taken as parallel to the procedure described in the *Zadokite Fragments*.

Jackson/87/ has pointed to two tannaitic passages which, according to him, explicitly reject the combination of testimony. *Mekhilta' De-Rabbi Ishmael* Mishpaṭim 20/88/ discusses the possibility of convicting a man about whom one witness testifies that he worshipped the sun and a second witness testifies that he worshipped the moon. *Mekhilta' De-Rabbi Shim'on ben Yoḥai* to Ex. 23:7/89/ deals with the same question, but the examples it cites are different. It discusses the case of two witnesses testifying about the same individual's having violated the Sabbath, one claiming the accused gathered figs and the other that he gathered grapes. It likewise inquires about one accused by one witness of having gathered dark grapes and by another of having gathered light grapes.

It is Jackson's assumption that these passages refer to testimony to two independent commissions of the same offense. Hence, he sees them as evidence that these sources rejected combination of testimony./90/ These passages, however, may be explained differently. They may refer to a pair of witnesses who testify to one and the same act. The problem is that their testimony disagrees in one small detail. Despite their essential agreement in regard to the offense committed, tannaitic *halakhah* rejects their testimony, basing itself on Ex. 23:7. The minor imprecisions in their testimony are seen as casting doubt on their reliability as witnesses./91/ Indeed, it was exactly this kind of imprecision that allowed Daniel to expose the false testimony of the lecherous elders in the Apocryphal story of Susanna.

4. *Summary*

The Qumran sect required three witnesses for capital conviction and two in money matters. When less than the required witnesses were available, the culprit could be barred from contact with the pure food of the sect. In cases in which individual witnesses testified to offenses, these were recorded by the examiner. After the required number of times, three in capital cases and two in money matters, conviction was possible. Attempts to cite parallels to these procedures from the Rabbinic tradition have been less than successful. The Scriptural exegesis of the sect led it to conclusions which differ from those of the tannaim. While partial parallels can indeed be cited, they only heighten the impression that in regard to the law of testimony, the framers of the legislation recorded in the *Zadokite Fragments* reached substantially different conclusions from those of the tannaim.

NOTES

/1/ Cf. B. Levine, "Damascus Document IX, 17–22: A New Translation and Comments," *RQ* 8 (1973), 195f.

/2/ Note that this law follows immediately on CDC 9:13–16 which was based to a large extent on Lev. 5:20–26. Note *ma'alah ma'al* in v. 22. It may be, therefore, that the order of the laws here in CDC is conditioned by the appearance of this word in both places, although *m'l* does not appear in CDC 9:13–16. While the Bible normally uses this word to refer to trespass of sancta, J. Milgrom, *Cult and Conscience* (1976), 16–35 has shown how it can be transferred to oath violations already in the Bible. In our text, the term has been taken one step further. What greater sanctum was there for the sect than the Torah? The term *m'l* can therefore be used to refer to violation of the laws of the Torah.

/3/ It is probable here that Torah is to be taken as referring to Scripture since the Qumran sect did not hesitate to derive laws from the Prophets and the Writings as did the Talmudic tradition.

/4/ For *r'h* in the technical sense of witness, cf. Lev. 5:1.

/5/ Ginzberg, *Sect*, 44, rejects this translation since the opening line referred to *kol davar 'asher yim'al*. He therefore takes *'im* as "even if."

/6/ The preposition *l* + *'ayin* in the plural indicates "in the presence of" in biblical usage.

/7/ On this official, see below, 95f.

/8/ On this usage, see below, 90.

/9/ For this repetitive usage of *šwb*, see Ges. sec 120d and BDB, 998a.

/10/ The *nif'al* of *tfs* means to "be seized, arrested, caught" (BDB, *s.v.*). Cf. Jer. 38:23, 50:24; Ezek. 12:13, 17:20, 19:4, 8, 21:28, 29. These figurative usages are based on the legal usage of the term. Although it must have been commonly used in everyday legal language, the Bible records the legal usage only in Num. 5:13. *Sifre* Num. 7 (ed. Horovitz, p. 12) and the Targumim take *nitpasah* there to mean that "she was not raped." Rashi to Num. 5:13 in giving this interpretation cites the parallel use of *tfs* in Deut. 22:28. There the reference is clearly to rape. Ibn Ezra to Num. 5:13, however, understands *we-hi' lo' nitpasah* to indicate that she was not apprehended by witnesses so as to render her suspect. The root appears in tannaitic sources as *tfś* (with *samekh*) and is commonly used in the legal sense. See Jastrow, *s.v.* For the *Temple Scroll*'s adaptation of Deut. 22:28, see TS 66:8–11 and Yadin, *Megillat Ha-Miqdash* I, 281–284.

/11/ So Levine, "Damascus Document," 195f., and B. Jackson, *Essays in Jewish and Comparative Legal History* (1975), 171–175. On *davar* in the sense of "case," see B. Jackson, *Theft in Early Jewish Law* (1972), 241f. Ginzberg's interpretation that the offender must commit the offense only twice must be ruled out on syntactic grounds as was realized by Schechter. To solve this problem, Ginzberg rearranges the passage to accord with his view.

/12/ Cf. tannaitic *nigmar dino* (Rabin).

/13/ Levine reads *'eḥad* here. So M. H. Segal, "*Sefer Berit Dameseq*," *Ha-Shiloaḥ* 26 (1912), 498. Cf. his interpretation in "Notes," 135–136 which anticipates that of Levine. Ginzberg read *'aḥer* and understood "even if there are two witnesses, but their testimony refers to different things, the man shall be excluded only in respect to purity." That is, while cumulative testimony of two is accepted, it is valid only in cases in which the same crime has been witnessed by both.

/14/ On this term, see below, 162f.

/15/ See Is. 8:2; Jer. 42:5; Ps. 89:3 (cf. Ps. 19:8) for the use of *ne'eman* to describe a witness. This usage is continued in the Rabbinic texts. *Ne'eman* also appears as a term for reliability regarding the *ḥavurah* as described in tannaitic sources. See M. Demai 2:2 and T. Demai 2:2. Despite Lieberman's emendation of *ha-meqabbel* in the Tosefta to *u-meqabbel* (*TK*, *ad loc.*), the Mishnah still indicates that *ne'eman* is a lower status than *ḥaver*. Apparently it denoted a novice who, previous to acceptance as a *ḥaver*, had already begun to observe the obligations. Cf. Lieberman, *TK* to T. Demai 2:1, n. 2–3. Rabin, *QS*, 18, understands the *ne'eman* as a stage in the novitiate preparatory to becoming a *ḥaver*. Oppenheimer, 152–156, rejects the view that *ne'eman* is a stage in entrance to the status of *ḥaver* and argues that the *ne'eman* is simply one with whom, although he is not a *ḥaver*, unrestricted economic contact is permitted. But see J. Neusner, "HBR and N'MN," *RQ* 5 (1964–66), 119–122.

/16/ That the report, in the form of the sectarian procedure of "reproof," must take place on the day of the transgression is clear from numerous passages. See below, 91.

/17/ Notice the impersonal usage here, so familiar from the tannaitic legal corpus. The tannaim, however, use the participle for this purpose.

/18/ Perhaps read *we-'ed*. The error would be due to confusion with the line above.

/19/ Cf. below, 165.

/20/ Cf. *Midrash Tanna'im* to Deut. 17:6 (I, p. 101) and 19:15 (I, pp. 115–116); *Midrash Ha-Gadol*, Deut., pp. 383 and 437; and *Sifra'* Wa-Yiqra' Parashah 12:11 (ed. Weiss, p. 27a).

/21/ Cf. 1 K. 21:10, 13 which affords a glimpse of actual legal procedure in biblical times and Susanna 34ff. on which see C. Tchernowitz, *Toledot Ha-Halakhah* IV, 390–391. Cf. Jackson, *Essays*, 153–171. The sect would have noticed, no doubt, that the trial in 1 K. 21:10, 13, was hardly conducted according to the law.

/22/ Cf. J. Rosenthal, "*'Al Hishtalshelut Halakhah Be-Sefer Berit Dameseq*," in *Sefer Ha-Yovel Mugash Li-Khvod Ha-Rav Shim'on Federbush*, ed. J. L. Maimon (1960), 292–303, and the detailed discussion in *HAQ*, 91–98, 113–115.

/23/ After a large *'alef* through which the scribe has drawn a line to indicate erasure comes the last phrase in larger writing. It is in the same hand but apparently made with a larger pen (Rabin, *ad loc.*). Schechter (*ad loc.*) and Ginzberg, *Sect*, 59 read *'alpayim*, but this would make CDC 11:5–6 redundant. Cf. also B. 'Eruvin 51a. Further, the large writing of these words in the medieval MS can only have been to assure that a strange law would not be harmonized with prevailing Talmudic law.

/24/ See Yadin, *War Scroll*, 73–75, to which cf. his "The Temple Scroll," *New Directions in Biblical Archaeology*, ed. D. N. Freedman, J. Greenfield (1971), 163.

/25/ Note the parallels: Num. 35:4: . . . *ha-'ir wa-ḥuṣah 'elef 'ammah* . . . ; CDC 10:21: . . . *ḥuṣ le-'iro* . . . *'elef be-'ammah*; Num. 35:5: . . . *mi-ḥuṣ la-'ir* . . . *'alpayim be-'ammah* . . . ; CDC 11:5: . . . *ḥuṣ me-'iro* . . . *'alpayim be-'ammah.*

/26/ M. Sotah 5:3, but cf. the sources quoted in Albeck's *HWT*, *ad loc.*, which indicate that the Levitical pasturage was 2000 cubits. The square character of the *migrash* is certain (in accord with the view of the sages in M. 'Eruvin 14:8). Cf. Naḥmanides to Num. 35:2; S. D. Luzzatto, *Perush Shadal 'al Ḥamishah Ḥumshe Torah* (1965), 493–497; G. B. Gray, *A Critical and Exegetical Commentary on Numbers* (1956), 467–468; and N. H. Tur-Sinai, *Peshuto shel Miqra'* (1962–67) I, 196 (who reads *'alpayim* in v. 4 with LXX).

/27/ So Rabin, *ad loc.*, *QS*, 90–91, and Yadin, *War Scroll*, 74.

/28/ Cf. also A. Dupont-Sommer, *Les Écrits esséniens découvertes près de la mer morte* (1959), 165 n. 4. For other exegetical possibilities, see Ibn Ezra to Deut. 17:6 who obviously felt the difficulty of the text.

/29/ Cf. Matt. 18:20.

/30/ See H. van Vliet, *No Single Testimony, A Study of the Adoption of the Law of Deut. 19:15 par. into the New Testament* (1958), 2–6, 87–92.

/31/ Van Vliet, 26–30.

/32/ *Legends* VI, 312.

/33/ *Sect*, 120 n. 53, 396 n. 164; *Testament of Abraham*, trans. M. Stone (1972), 22–77; van Vliet, 49.

/34/ *Life* 2.

/35/ On *hatra'ah*, see below, 97f.

/36/ So MSS Kaufman, Paris, and Parma "C." Ed. Naples here has *niddon* which is the reading of the later editions. (After *yiddon* the scribe of MS Kaufman first wrote *'oto*. Realizing his error he placed a line above it to indicate erasure and continued with *be-'esrim*.)

/37/ B. Sanhedrin 71a and Rashi, *ad loc.*; Albeck, *HWT*, *Neziqin*, 451f.

/38/ Cf. J. N. Epstein, *Mavo' Le-Nusaḥ Ha-Mishnah* (1963/4) I, 377. Epstein compares T. Sanhedrin 11:7 in MS Vienna and *ed. princ. Sifre* Deut. 219 (ed. Finkelstein, p. 252) reads *niddon*. Finkelstein is probably correct in stating that the *Sifre* is here "copying" the Mishnah. In that case we can conclude that both *yiddon* and *niddon* are readings dating to Rabbinic times.

/39/ For a similar confusion between two witnesses or three judges, cf. B. Yevamot 47a–b, and my comments in "At the Crossroads: Tannaitic Perspectives on the Jewish-Christian Schism," *Jewish and Christian Self-Definition* II (1981), ed. E. P. Sanders, 341 n. 52.

/40/ Sanhedrin 71a. Cf. T. Sanhedrin 11:6 and *Ant.* 4, 8, 24 (260–265). On the rebellious son and his execution, see Testament of Solomon sec. 110–115 (trans. F. C. Conybeare, "The Testament of Solomon," *JQR* O.S. 11 [1899], 39f.). The assumption of the story is that if not for the imminent natural death of the boy, Solomon would have pronounced the death sentence in accord with Deut. 21:18–21. (Deut 21:18–21 is repeated with only minor variation from MT in TS 64:2–6.) The Testament of Solomon is a curious blend of Jewish, Christian, oriental and Hellenic motifs and is generally dated to between c. 100–c. 300 A.D. (J. Petroff, "Solomon, Testament of," *EJ* 15, 118f.). Note that according to *Ant.* 16, 11, 2 (365), Herod invoked this accusation against his sons at their trial. (*Ve-tafsu vo* of Deut. 21:19 is strangely interpreted there as "placed their hands on his head.") This claim, as well as the entire speech of Herod, is probably the composition of Josephus or his source, as it does not occur in *War* 1, 27, 3 (540). Further, the punishment of strangulation mentioned in *Ant.* 16, 11, 7 (394) and *War* 1, 27, 6 (551) would not accord with the punishment of stoning prescribed for the rebellious son in Deut. 21:21 (cf. M. Sanhedrin 8:4).

/41/ Cf. Targum Pseudo-Jonathan, Fragmentary Targum, and Neofiti Targum to Gen. 38:25 in which Tamar refers to the seal, "strings," and staff of Judah as three witnesses. Since the language is figurative, it is impossible to draw historical conclusions from this most interesting parallel. The law of *geṭ mequshar* which requires three witnesses (M. Bava' Batra' 10:2) is not related. The third witness is only necessary to make sure that each tie has a signature. It is true that a late amora tried to connect the three witnesses to Deut. 19:15 (B. Bava' Batra' 160b). More likely, though, it was the shape of the document and the method of tying which necessitated three witnesses. See "*Geṭ Mequshar*," *Enc. Tal.* 5, 717–727; Y. Yadin, *Bar-Kokhba* (1971), 229–231; and *DJD* II, 141, fig. 28. If this third signature had been derived from Scripture, the tannaitic disagreement about the qualification of the third witness (B. Giṭṭin 81b–82a) would have been impossible.

/42/ Ginzberg, *Sect*, 120, compares the (apparently) amoraic principle of *'ed 'eḥad ne'eman be-'issurin*, one witness suffices to certify that something is not forbidden (B. Giṭṭin 2b, 3a; B. Ḥullin 10b).

/43/ Cf. Jackson, *Essays*, 178f., and below, 161–165.

/44/ Appeared earlier in Y. Yadin, "Pesher Nahum (4Qp Nahum) Reconsidered," *IEJ* 21 (1971), 6–8. For a detailed comparison with the MT and versions, cf. Yadin, *Megillat Ha-Miqdash* II, *ad loc.*

/45/ "Pesher Nahum," 8. Note numbers have been inserted.

/46/ Cf. Lev. 19:16 and note the reading *'mk* in "many Samaritan MSS" (Yadin, *Megillat Ha-Miqdash, ad loc.*); Targumim to Lev. 19:16; and P. Pe'ah 1:1 (16a) (Yadin, "Pesher Nahum," 6).

/47/ On this usage cf. Ben-Yehudah, *s.v.*; Y. Yadin, "*Le-Hashlim,*" *Tarbiz* 40 (1970/1), 390; J. Schirmann, "*Teshuvah,*" *Tarbiz* 40 (1970/1), 391; and E. E. Urbach, "*Hashlamot Le-Hashlim,*" *Tarbiz* 40 (1970/1), 392. Cf. S. Lieberman's "Roman Legal Institutions in Early Rabbinics and in the Acta Martyrum," *JQR* N.S. 35 (1944/5), 50–52. This usage in Rabbinic literature is basically an Aramaism, and the *'af'el* of *šlm* is the regular translation for the *hif'il* of *sgr* in the Targumim. What is most interesting here is the preference for such a "Rabbinic" usage over the biblical Hebrew *hif'il* of *sgr* we would have expected. Cf. my "The *Temple Scroll,*" 148f.

/48/ Yadin compares the similar prohibitions in the Ein Gedi synagogue inscription (B. Mazar, "*Ketovet 'al Riṣpat Bet-Keneset Be-'Ein Gedi,*" *Tarbiz* 40 [1970/1], 20, lines 10–13). This Byzantine period inscription (p. 23) contains an imprecation against anyone who causes dissension, speaks evil of his fellows to the non-Jews, or reveals to them the "secret" (*razah*) of the city. For the *Sitz-im-Leben* of this inscription, see S. Lieberman, "*He'arah Muqdemet La-Ketovet Be-'Ein Gedi,*" *Tarbiz* 40 (1970/1), 24–26. E. E. Urbach, "*Ha-Sod She-bi-Khetovet 'Ein Gedi We-Noshah,*" *Tarbiz* 40 (1970/1), 27–30 discusses parallels to this imprecation from the Greco-Roman world and then suggests a possible connection with the Essenes who had inhabited Ein Gedi. The parallel he cites from *War* 2, 8, 8 (139–141) can also be augmented by the text under discussion from the TS as well as the material discussed below, 171f. from DSD 7:15–18. Cf. also J. Feliks, "*Le-'Inyan 'Hi Ganiv Ṣevuṭeh De-Ḥavreh' Bi-Fesefas 'Ein Gedi,*" *Tarbiz* 40 (1970/1), 256f. On *goy nekhar* cf. TS 57:11; CDC 14:15. Yadin notes that this is not a biblical phrase. Cf. *HAQ*, 104 n. 135 and 105 n. 139.

/49/ Cf. Deut. 17:6–7, 19:15. Yadin compares Est. 9:13.

/50/ The last letter was added above the line. Cf. TS 57:10. Yadin's claim that this is an error must be disputed. It may simply be evidence of phonetic spelling. This word is routinely spelled without the final *'alef* in the *Zohar*.

/51/ On the spelling see Kutscher, *Ha-Lashon*, 404f.

/52/ Cf. Deut. 21:23.

/53/ The *waw* of *we-'et* was added by the scribe after he had written *'amo 'et.*

/54/ The scribe or someone else erased the *he'*.

/55/ *Megillat Ha-Miqdash* I, 285–291.

/56/ On *teliyah* as a death penalty, cf. also Urbach, "*Bate-Din,*" 44f.; A. Schlesinger, *Kitve 'Akiva' Schlesinger*, (1962), 12–15; J. Heinemann, "*Targum Shemot* 22:4 *We-Ha-Halakhah Ha-Qedumah,*" *Tarbiz* 38 (1968/9), 295f.; and J. M. Baumgarten, "Does *tlh* in the Temple Scroll Refer to Crucifixion?" *JBL* 91 (1972), 472–481, reprinted in his *Studies in Qumran Law*, 172–182.

/57/ Referring to my article, "The Qumran Law of Testimony," *RQ* 8 (1975), 603, Yadin explains the difference between his view and mine as resulting from the difference of opinion regarding the reading of *'aḥer* vs. *'eḥad* (*Megillat Ha-Miqdash* I, 294). However, he does not take into account the sources cited here which lead to the conclusion that certain circles in the Second Temple period required three witnesses in capital cases.

/58/ Yadin, *Megillat Ha-Miqdash* I, 290f., has noted that the scribe substituted *we-'al pi* for *'o* in Deut. 19:16. He has explained this change as exegetical, intending to emphasize that the three witnesses are required in the special case of single witnesses to a succession of violations. It is more likely, however, that the author or some scribe simply confused this verse with the similar material in Deut. 17:6 and transferred the reading of that passage to this. If so, the change would not have any relevance to the discussion here.

/59/ "Damascus Document IX, 16–23 and Parallels," *RQ* 9 (1977–78), 446. Jackson's arguments are based on the CDC passage itself without recourse to TS.

/60/ Cf. CDC 9:1 and commentaries *ad loc.*; Z. Falk, "*Beḥuqey hagoyim*," 569; P. Winter, "Ṣadoqite Fragments IX, 1," 131–136; and Yadin, *Megillat Ha-Miqdash* I, 292.

/61/ For a survey, see H. Klatzkin, Y. Slutsky, H. Cohn, "Informers," *EJ* 8, 1364–73.

/62/ "Damascus Document," 196. In Rabbinic law this was a type of *ḥazaqah*. See "*Ḥazaqah* (E)," *Enc. Tal.* 13, 739–760. As mentioned in n. 13, Segal had already reached this conclusion. Cf. Jackson, *Essays*, 108–152; J. J. Finkelstein, "The Goring Ox," *Temple Law Quarterly* 46 (1973), 169–290; R. Yaron, "The Goring Ox in Near Eastern Laws," *ILR* 1 (1966), 396–406, reprinted in H. H. Cohn, *Jewish Law in Ancient and Modern Israel* (1971), 50–60.

/63/ M. Delcor, "Courts," 76. Cf. Jackson, *Essays*, 193–201.

/64/ *On Joseph*, 235, ed. Colson, p. 253. On the rejection of a single witness by Philo, cf. Goodenough, *Jurisprudence*, 188–189. On the function of witnesses, see his 184–186.

/65/ The fourteenth century Karaite, Aaron ben Elijah of Nicomedia, *Keter Torah* (1866/7) to Lev. 5:1 mentions the view that *we-hu' 'ed* indicates that even a singular witness should report his testimony to the judge, lest a second witness be found. But the author specified that only in the case in which a second witness is found does the testimony of the first have validity (*titqayyem 'eduto*). Ginzberg, *Sect*, 119f. claims that a similar derivation stands behind our passage from CDC. If so, however, we would expect the language of the passage to betray it. Lev. 5:1 does, however, serve as the basis of CDC 9:10–12 on which see below, 111–116.

/66/ Cf. *HAQ*, 66–67.

/67/ Below, 89–98.

/68/ M. Sanhedrin 1:4 (cf. Albeck's *HWT*, 442 and Targum Pseudo-Jonathan to Ex. 21:29.

/69/ The Mishnah reads: *ke-mitat ha-be'alim kakh mitat ha-shor*. The sect's conclusion may be paraphrased as the reverse: *ke-mitat ha-shor kakh mitat ha-be'alim*. Z. Frankel, *Ueber den Einfluss der Palastinischen Exegese auf die alexandrinische Hermeneutik* (1851), 93f. suggests that a similar view to that of the tannaim stands behind LXX προσαποθανεῖται. This peculiar verb occurs as well in Dio Cassius, *Roman History*, LIII, 9, where Cory translates "to give up my life." προσαπο- means "besides" or "with" in compound verbs. Frankel is certainly right in stating that this is not the normal verb to denote death by judicial execution. Cf. Jackson, *Essays*, 129f.

/70/ Cf. 1 K. 2:27 and R. de Vaux, *Ancient Israel* I, 160. For a possible reference to incarceration, see CDC 15:14–15 as restored by Rabin. S. Lieberman has dealt at length with this penalty. He sees the punishment as involving life imprisonment, taking the phrase "until his stomach splits" to mean forever ("*Perushim Ba-Mishnayyot*," *Tarbiz* 40 [1970/1], 10–13). Jackson, "Damascus Document," 447 likewise argues that this is not a capital sanction, comparing Is. 30:20, *leḥem ṣar u-mayim laḥaṣ*. M. Sanhedrin 9:5 contains a similar regulation, except that it is ambiguous as to whether the incarceration takes place after the second or third flagellation. It is usually explained as referring to the third occurrence, with our passage from the Tosefta. Cf. B. Sanhedrin 81b. Note the amora Rabbi Simeon ben Laqish's view that this procedure applies only in cases of repeated violation of an offense incurring *karet*. This interpretation is based on the assumption that we are dealing here with a form of death penalty. If so, this view was already in evidence in the early amoraic period. Maimonides, *Perush Ha-Mishnayyot* to Sanhedrin 9:5 and H. Sanhedrin 18:4, indicates that the several occurrences must be of the same offense. These sources are also discussed in N. L. Rabinovitch, "Damascus Document IX, 17–22 and Rabbinic Parallels," RQ 9 (1977–78), 113–116 and the response of J. Neusner, "Damascus Document IX, 17–22 and Irrelevant Parallels," *RQ* 9 (1977–78), 441–444.

/71/ Cf. Jackson, *Essays*, 187–193.

/72/ *Sect*, 44 n. 118. Cf. 119f.

/73/ Rav Naḥman, c. 300 A.D.

/74/ J. Neusner, "'By the Testimony of Two Witnesses' in the Damascus Document IX, 17–22 and in Pharisaic-Rabbinic Law," *RQ* 8 (1972–75), 204. Neusner also compares T. Sanhedrin 5:5.

/75/ Cf. Neusner, "Testimony," 202–204.

/76/ "Testimony," 197–217. He defines "Pharisaic-rabbinic" as "the later rabbinic traditions about the Pharisees" (197 n. 1).

/77/ Neusner, "Testimony," 197.

/78/ "*Eine unbekannte jüdische Sekte*," *MGWJ* 56 (1912), 298–300, cited in the translation of H. R. Moehring by Neusner, "Testimony," 200–201. See now *Sect*, 44.

/79/ Neusner, "Testimony," 204.

/80/ Neusner, "Testimony," 205. Note the amoraic discussion in B. Bava' Qamma' 70b; B. Bava' Batra' 56b; B. Sanhedrin 30b; P. Soṭah 1:1 (16c); P. Ketubot 2:4 (26c); P. Sanhedrin 3:9 (10, 21c); P. Shevu'ot 4:1 (35c) in which it is said that two witnesses, each testifying to the presence of a single (but different) hair do not render a girl legally of age.

/81/ "Testimony," 205.

/82/ It is necessary to note a difference between the methodology employed in this study and that of Prof. Neusner. He limits his citations from Rabbinic literature to those about the Pharisees, since he is inquiring into whether the law of the Qumran sect and that of the Pharisees are similar. We make use of tannaitic traditions also since it is our purpose to use comparisons as an aid in interpreting the law of Qumran but not to claim influence.

/83/ "Damascus Document," 448.

/84/ The translation is by Jastrow, *s.v.* See above, n. 70.

/85/ B. Sanhedrin 81b.

/86/ Cf. Rashi, *ad loc.* and Maimonides, H. Roṣeaḥ U-Shemirat Nefesh 4:8.

/87/ *Essays*, 183. Cf. "Damascus Document," 447f.

/88/ Ed. Horovitz-Rabin, p. 327. Jackson alludes to the possibility that the clause *shomea' 'ani . . .* might indicate that what was being raised was "a once-held view." He wisely suggests extreme caution here. In fact, this formula is used in the tannaitic *midrashim* for the purpose of introducing exegetical possibilities in contrast with those first asserted and later confirmed. These possibilities are always raised as a foil against which to prove the interpretation first advanced. As such, they serve a casuistic and didactic purpose. It is very doubtful that such a formulation would ever indicate an older halakhic view. Cf. Albeck, *Mavo' La-Talmudim*, 96–98.

/89/ Ed. Epstein-Melammed, p. 216.

/90/ Maimonides adopts the same interpretation of the passage from *Mekhilta' De-Rabbi Ishmael* in his H. Sanhedrin 20:1 (cf. Radbaz).

/91/ Cf. Maimonides, H. 'Edut 2:2.

CHAPTER FOUR
REPROOF AS A REQUISITE FOR PUNISHMENT

1. *The Law of Reproof*

The law of testimony, discussed in the last chapter, mentioned the process of reproof, a part of Qumran legal practice which, we will see, served a very similar function to that of the Rabbinic *hatra'ah* ("warning"). Reproof at Qumran was not simply a moral duty. Rather, it was a prerequisite for conviction for all offenses, and it had to be performed according to specific regulations. The requirement of reproof is exegetically derived in CDC 9:2–8:

ואשר אמר לא תקום ולא תטור את בני עמך וכל איש מביאו הברית
אשר יביא על רעהו דבר אשר לא בהוכח לפני עדים והביאו בחרון
אפו או ספר לזקניו להבזותו נוקם הוא ונוטר ואין כתוב כי אם
נוקם הוא לצריו ונוטר הוא לאויביו אם החריש לו מיום ליום
ובחרון אפו בו דבר בו בדבר מות ענה בו יען אשר לא הקים את
מצות אל אשר אמר לו הוכח תוכיח את רעיך ולא תשא עליו חטא

As to that/1/ which He said,/2/ "You shall not take vengeance or bear a grudge against your kinsfolk (Lev. 19:18),"/3/ any man from among those who have entered/4/ the covenant/5/ who shall bring a charge/6/ against his neighbor which is not with "reproof"/7/ before witnesses,/8/ or brings it/9/ (the charge)/10/ when he is angry (with him)/11/ or relates it to his (the accused's) elders/12/ to make them despise him,/13/ is taking vengeance and bearing a grudge./14/ Is it not written that/15/ only "He (God)/16/ takes vengeance/17/ on His adversaries and bears a grudge against His enemies/18/ (Nah. 1:2/19/)?" (But)/20/ if he kept silent about him/21/ from day to day,/22/ and accused him/23/ of a capital offense/24/ (only) when he was angry with him, his (the accused's) guilt is upon him/25/ (the accuser), since he did not/26/ fulfill the commandment/27/ of God/28/ who said to him,/29/ "You shall surely reprove your neighbor,/30/ lest you bear guilt/31/ because of him (Lev. 19:17)."

Lev. 19:18 has been interpreted here to mean that a member who sees an offense must immediately perform the required "reproof." If he does not, but later makes an accusation, he violates Lev. 19:18 by "bearing a grudge" and "taking vengeance." This law assumes that anyone who brings a charge without having first fulfilled this "reproof" before witnesses does so out of anger or to defame the accused among the members of the sect. To emphasize or prove that vengeance and grudges are forbidden by Lev. 19:18, the text quotes Nah. 1:2 which is taken to mean that *only* God may take vengeance or bear a grudge. Therefore, any individual who does so violates the divine Law.

A similar idea is found in the Fragmentary and Neofiti Targumim to Deut. 32:35. There God says that vengeance is His and that He Himself will exact punishment from the evildoers. Rom. 12:19, however, is a much closer parallel: "Beloved, never avenge yourselves, but leave it (Gk.: give place) to the wrath of God; for it is written, "Vengeance is mine, I will repay, says the Lord."/32/ This last sentence is obviously a paraphrase of Deut. 32:35.

The question may be raised as to why the author of the *Zadokite Fragments* derives his proof-text from Nah. 1:2 when a text in the Torah was available. The preference for halakhic derivations from the Torah over Prophets and Writings is a Rabbinic predisposition. It is certainly not part of the scheme of Qumran legal hermeneutics./33/ In addition, Ginzberg notes/34/ that both the Samaritan Pentateuch and Septuagint *Vorlage* of Deut. 32:35 read *le-yom naqam we-shillem*./35/ It is possible that the sect had this reading which does not lend itself to the derivation of this law./36/

Since this Qumran text begins with an exegesis of Lev. 19:18 and ends with the interpretation of the preceding verse, Lev. 19:17 (*hokheaḥ tokhiaḥ* . . .), there can be no question that the use of the verbal noun *hokheaḥ* in our Qumran passage means "with fulfillment of the commandment of reproof of Lev. 19:17" as interpreted by the sect. This technical, forensic use of the term is certainly to be understood here./37/ Other interpretations, such as "with proof," become impossible, since they do not fit the context of an exegesis of Lev. 19:17f. Nor is it possible that *be-hokheaḥ* refers to simple moral reproof, since the text requires that the reproof take place before witnesses. While the exact meaning of *hokheaḥ* may seem a minor philological point, it provides the key to the understanding of numerous passages in Qumran literature.

Rabin/38/ has called attention to a linguistic parallel in the tannaitic Hebrew of the Palestinian Talmud./39/ There *hokheaḥ* appears as a nominal substantive. Rabin translates the term as "material evidence" in one usage and "a black mark against someone" in the other. Ben Yehudah simply translates "proof, evidence." These definitions are not sufficient for the Qumran passage before us because of the exegetical context in which *hokheaḥ* appears here. That the root *ykḥ* is itself susceptible to other meanings is certainly true, but the Qumran usage clearly refers to the formal process of reproof.

The starting point for the second part of our text is Lev. 19:17, requiring reproof of one's neighbor and indicating that otherwise one would bear guilt for the transgression committed by him. Like the Vulgate, the sect understood the double verb (infinitive absolute followed by the finite verb) to indicate that the reproof had to take place in public. If one did not properly reprove his neighbor, conviction was impossible according to Qumran law.

But would the witness be in violation of the law if he did not report an offense? Legal exegesis was used by the sect to discover the answer, and

Num. 30:15 was applied to the exegesis of the quoted proof-text, Lev. 19:17. According to Num. 30:15, there is a specified time limit within which a husband may annul the vow of his wife. If he keeps silent, however, *mi-yom 'el yom*, "from one day to the next," and then annuls the vow at a later time, the annulment is not considered valid. If his wife then disregards the vow, he has caused her to transgress by convincing her that he had annulled the vow, and he bears her transgression. He himself now becomes guilty of not fulfilling the vow./40/

Regarding the time limit, it is not possible to determine from this passage if *mi-yom 'el yom* denoted a twenty-four hour period or extended only until sunset. Both possibilities have been raised by tannaitic exegesis to Num. 30:15./41/ Majority opinion among the tannaim, however, was to extend the "day" only up to sunset/42/ as did early Karaite law./43/

The view that sunset was the end of the time limit on reproof according to the sect is further supported by *ba-yom* in DSD 5:24–6:1 which will be discussed below, and by Eph. 4:26: "Do not let the sun go down on your anger." Heb. 3:13 derives the requirement that reproof take place on the day of the crime from Ps. 95:7 (Heb. *ha-yom*).

The sect drew an analogy from the case of vows to that of the accuser and his "reproof." They accepted the specified time limit as the same, and then reasoned that anyone who accuses his fellow after allowing the deadline to pass was himself guilty of the offense of the criminal. It may be that he was guilty only of future offenses done by the criminal, as his reproof would have prevented these offenses. But if the analogy is carried to its furthest, the sect considered the accuser to be guilty of the very crime for which he brought charges.

This law is similar to that of *'edim zomemim*, literally "conspiring witnesses," as found in Deut. 19:16–21. A witness who maliciously bears false testimony suffers the penalty he sought to inflict on the accused. The element common with our text is that in both cases improper testimony or accusation was given, and the consequences are the same. To some extent the sect shared the interpretation of Deut. 19:16–21 which served as the basis for the anonymous tanna of M. Makkot 1:6. This interpretation claimed that the conspiring witnesses were to be executed even if the one they accused was not, provided that a guilty verdict had been rendered against the falsely accused. The Sadducees, however, took the view that the conspiring witnesses were to be executed only if the accused was actually put to death./44/ Our law states that the accuser who neglects to perform reproof is guilty of the criminal's offense—apparently irrespective of whether any punishment came to the accused as a result of his testimony. This is certainly similar to the exegesis of Deut. 19:16–21 which was the basis of the anonymous tannaitic *mishnah*, rather than that ascribed to the Sadducees.

Yet despite this parallel, sectarian law did not prescribe that a witness who failed to offer reproof properly be punished according to the offense of the criminal he did not reprove. Rather, we shall see that sectarian law required a specific penalty for those failing to perform reproof, and this penalty was independent of the specific offense involved.

The words *bi-devar mawet*, "in a capital matter," pose great difficulty for the understanding of this passage. It is uncertain whether this phrase completes the preceding clause or is the beginning of the next. Does this phrase mean that this entire law applies only to capital offenses but to no others? Such a conclusion might be supported by the occurrence of this phrase in CDC 9:17 (the law of testimony)/45/ in which "reproof" is associated with capital offenses. However, CDC 9:22 shows that the same law applies in non-capital matters. *Bi-devar mawet* in our text may also mean that the accuser who oversteps the deadline on "reproof" has incurred the transgression *as if* it were a capital offense. If so, *devar mawet* is used metaphorically like the Rabbinic phrase *mitḥayyev be-nafsho*, "he is obligated for his own life."/46/

Ginzberg offers a clever interpretation of the phrase *bi-devar mawet*. According to him, *even* if it be a capital crime, the accuser is liable. In other words, the text has singled out the "worst case" as an example. But the real intent of the law is that whatever the offense of the accused, it is this crime for which the accuser is held responsible in the event that he does not follow the proper process of reproof./47/ Ginzberg's interpretation is in line with a method termed *revuta'*, used by the amoraim in interpreting tannaitic traditions./48/ However, unless we can prove that the authors of the Qumran texts made use of such means of legal formulation, it is not justified to apply this approach.

A problem arises as to whether the offender was tried for the very act for which he was reproved, or, perhaps, he was reproved on the first offense and tried only upon repetition of the crime. This last possibility seems probable and is suggested by a parallel in Matt. 18:15–17.

> If your brother sins against you, go and tell him his fault, between you and him alone. If he listens to you, you have gained your brother. But if he does not listen, take one or two others along with you, that every word may be confirmed by the evidence of two or three witnesses. If he refuses to listen to them, tell it to the church; and if he refuses to listen even to the church, let him be to you as a Gentile and a tax collector./49/

Yet nowhere except in the case of insufficient witnesses (CDC 9:16–23) do the Qumran materials explicitly indicate that the culprit cannot be tried for the same crime for which he is reproved.

2. *Reproof in Qumran Literature*

Another passage, CDC 7:2f., emphasizes that the omission of reproof is tantamount to the violation of the prohibition of bearing a grudge. The sectarian is required:

להוכיח איש את אחיהו כמצוה ולא לנטור מיום ליום

> To admonish each man his neighbor according to the commandment/50/ and not to bear a grudge from one day to the next. . . ./51/

This passage comes from the section of the *Zadokite Fragments* termed the Admonition by Rabin. In it the sectarian is encouraged to live a life of righteousness and piety./52/ The passage is part of a "chain of *lameds*"/53/ and stands between allusions to prohibitions of fornication and a requirement of separation from impurity. This clause is, no doubt, a reference to the full set of regulations regarding reproof required of the sectarian. One who did not reprove his neighbor in this formal sense was regarded as "bearing a grudge."

This passage is not simply a reference to the moral obligation of reproof as understood in the Rabbinic interpretation of Lev. 19:17. The second clause is worded so as to constitute a direct reference to the law of CDC 9:2–8. It is certain that *we-lo' li-neṭor mi-yom le-yom*, "not to bear a grudge from one day to the next," is an explicit allusion to the full explanation of the Qumran law of reproof as a requisite for punishment outlined in CDC 9:2–8.

If we bear in mind that this obligation of reproof was considered a biblical injunction by the sect, we can easily understand that they also would have prescribed the manner and spirit in which it was to be given. DSD 5:24–6:1 provides:

להוכיח איש את רעהו בא[מת] וענוה ואהבת חסד לאיש אל ידבר אליהו באף או בתלונה או בעורף [קשה או בקנאת] רוח רשע ואל ישנאהו [בער]ל[ת] לבבו כיא ביום יוכיחנו ולוא ישא עליו עוון

> To "reprove"/54/ each his neighbor/55/ in tru[th],/56/ humility, and lovingkindness/57/ to a man:/58/ Let him not speak to him/59/ in anger or complaint/60/ or stub[bornly or in jealousy]/61/ (caused) by an evil/62/ disposition. Let him not/63/ hate him intrac[tab]ly,/64/ for/65/ on that very day/66/ shall he "reprove" him, lest he bear guilt/67/ because of him.

This text is essentially a summary of the requirements of reproof. The only missing detail, the witnesses, is taken up in the next line, discussed separately below. The passage emphasizes the spirit of love in which reproof must be given. Otherwise, if one fails to reprove his fellow, he may come to hate him (and this is prohibited by the first half of Lev. 19:17). If he fails to perform the reproof on the very day of the offense, he bears the transgression.

The text is made up of a mosaic of verses. Interestingly, they are not the same verses from which the law was derived midrashically in the *Zadokite Fragments*. Yet clearly, the passage must be dependent on that exegesis as can be seen from the use of *ba-yom*, "on that very day."

There is only one way to account for the presence of *ba-yom* at the end of this statement and the requirement that this reproof be performed on the very day on which the offense is witnessed. It must be assumed that this passage makes direct reference to the exegesis of Lev. 19:17 in light of Num. 30:15 in which the phrase *mi-yom 'el yom* appears. It was this very exegesis which served as the basis of the sectarian process of reproof as outlined in CDC 9:2–8 and of the requirement that the reproof be performed on that very day. For these reasons there is no possibility of taking this passage as referring only to moral reproof. It must be taken as dealing with the legal procedure outlined above.

The main thrust of the passage is that the commandment of Lev. 19:17, that of reproof, must be understood in light of Mic. 6:8, on which the language of this text is based. This passage teaches that the reproof must be offered in love and kindness, not in anger or in a complaining tone. In other words, it is not enough to fulfill the letter of the requirements as to time, witnesses, etc., but the spirit in which the reproof is offered is also important.

The importance of reproof is stressed in Ben Sira 19:13–17./68/ Test. of Gad 6:3–7 may bear the message that reproof be given without anger. That reproof must be given in love is stressed in the New Testament (Gal. 6:1; 2 Thess. 3:15; 2 Tim. 3:23–25).

B. Shabbat 119b contains an aggadic passage attributed to a first generation Palestinian amora stating that the destruction of Jerusalem was caused by its citizens' not reproving one another. Such was the importance this amora ascribed to reproof.

3. *Reproof as a Legal Procedure*

The continuation of this last passage in DSD 6:1, as interpreted by Licht, clarifies the requirement of witnesses for the procedure of reproof.

וגמ אל יביא איש על רעהו דבר לפני הרבים אשר לוא בתוכחת לפני עדים

And also,/69/ let no one bring a charge/70/ against his neighbor/71/ before the assembly/72/ which is not with reproof/73/ before witnesses.

The importance of this passage is threefold. First, because of its obvious linguistic parallels with CDC 9:2–8, it shows that both documents discuss the same institution and have the same legal requirements in this matter. Therefore, it confirms again the general view that the *Zadokite Fragments* and the *Manual of Discipline* can be used to explicate each other.

Second, this text shows that the Qumran law required the reproof under discussion before charges are brought *in court*. This is because the assembly is here functioning in its capacity as the sect's highest court. This also makes it probable that the "elders" (*zeqenim*) of CDC 9:2–8 likewise constituted a court.

Third, and most important, however, is the clarification this passage provides regarding the requirement that witnesses (other than those who saw the offense) be present when the reproof is made. It is this requirement of witnesses which makes it certain that this text deals not with a simple moral obligation (as the obligation of reproof is understood in tannaitic sources and in the New Testament) but with a forensic procedure which must be executed in accord with specific legal norms.

The substitution of *tokhaḥat* for *hokheaḥ* in this law raises the alternate possibility that this text might refer to evidence in the legal sense. If so, the text would be translated: "And also, let no one bring a charge against his neighbor before the assembly which is not accompanied by evidence (having occurred) before witnesses." This law would then forbid bringing charges in the absence of adequate testimony. Such charges would amount to no more than slander and would, therefore, involve the violation of biblical law.

This interpretation, however, is somewhat difficult. In order to convey this meaning, the text could simply have stated either *be-tokhaḥat* or *lifne 'edim*. The presence of both phrases can be satisfactorily explained only by accepting the first interpretation presented here. Further, the use of *tokhaḥat* is limited exclusively to the sense of "reproof." Only in the medieval period does the word appear in the sense of "proof."/74/ The meaning "reproof" is encountered in DSH 5:10, DST 9:9 and 24./75/

Several significant facts about the procedure of reproof may be learned from the Qumran law of testimony (CDC 9:10–23)./76/ First, reproof is mentioned there as a regular part of the Qumran legal procedure. Second, this process must take place in the presence of the examiner and in the presence of the offender. Further, it is the responsibility of the examiner to keep records of these proceedings in his own hand. Presumably, these documents formed a part of the sect's legal and administrative archive, a body of materials which, surprisingly, did not form, as far as is known, any part of the hoard of manuscripts recovered from the Qumran caves. The presence of such legal, administrative, and financial documents in the material preserved from the Bar Kokhba caves makes the absence of such documents, explicitly referred to as they are, a mystery in regard to the Qumran sect.

The examiner (Heb. *mevaqqer*) was an administrative official of the sect whose responsibility fell into two areas, according to CDC 13:6–13. He functioned as both a spiritual leader of the "camp" or sectarian settlement, and also as the recorder of the sect's administrative documents./77/ The most logical explanation of his function in the process of reproof is that he was here, perhaps as always, combining both his areas of function. Of course, he would have to be present to record the formal act of reproof and the accompanying testimony, so that it would be available in the event of a further violation of the same commandment. At the same time, the act of reproof, even when the sect gave it a technical legal function, never lost its moral and ethical aspect. The offender was to be told in no uncertain terms, in front of witnesses, that his actions were not in consonance with the Torah and the sectarian interpretation thereof. He was to be warned to mend his ways and repent. Therefore, the examiner, charged with shepherding his flock, was to take part in this process.

The Qumran law of testimony may also be of importance for clarifying the number of witnesses required for reproof. Above,/78/ it was argued that Qumran law required three witnesses for capital matters and two for money matters. If so, it may be that the sect required that three witnesses be present for reproof in a capital matter and two in a financial matter.

4. *The Importance of Reproof*

Several passages emphasize the importance of this reproof procedure to the sect. Indeed, DSD 9:16–18 makes clear that this process was followed only in regard to members of the sect and not regarding outsiders:

> ואשר לוא להוכיח ולהתרובב עם אנשי השחת... ולהוכיח דעת אמת ומשפט צדק לבוחרי דרך
>
> And that/79/ he not reprove or litigate/80/ with/81/ the people of the pit . . . ,/82/ but to reprove with true knowledge and correct judgment those who have chosen/83/ the (correct) path.

It is most probable that the limitation of this procedure to members of the sect is simply a reflection of the fact that this process of reproof was not part of the legal system in the rest of Palestine. Rather, reproof as a forensic procedure was developed uniquely by the sect.

The significance of this procedure to the sect can be seen in two passages which indicate that those who neglected to perform this reproof were themselves to be punished. DSD 7:8f. reads:

> ואשר יטור לרעהו אשר לוא במשפט ונענש ששה חודשים (שנה אחת) וכן לנוקם לנפשו כול דבר
>
> And whoever bears a grudge/84/ against his neighbor/85/ which is not according to/86/ the regulation(s)/87/ shall be fined/88/ for six months (one year)./89/ And thus also for him who takes vengeance/90/ for himself/91/ (regarding) any matter./92/

This law provides that the punishment for violation of the law of reproof of CDC 9:2–8 is that the offender be deprived of one-fourth of his food ration for the specified period./93/ Licht understands DSD 7:8f. as referring to failure to perform moral reproof and compares the Rabbinic classification of *law she-'en bo ma'aseh*, a negative commandment the violation of which involves no action./94/ He did not realize that our law deals with one who not only bears rancour, but who brings an accusation for which the required formal reproof has never been offered before witnesses. Such a person violates the sectarian law by taking improper legal action. This understanding of the text is supported by a poorly preserved parallel in CDC 14:22:

> [ואשר יטור לרעהו אשר] לא במשפט [ונענש] שנה [אחת]

> [Whoever bears a grudge against his neighbor which] is not just [shall be punished] for [one] year./95/

As restored by Rabin, this text indicates that the period of punishment for the omission of reproof was to be "one year." If Rabin's restoration of this passage is correct, then the reading of one year in DSD 7:8f. should probably be preferred. On the other hand, it is possible that the two readings represent two stages in the development of the sect's law. In any case, on the scale of such fines, this is a serious offense.

If Rabin's restoration is accepted, then both the *Manual of Discipline* and the *Zadokite Fragments* clearly prescribe a punishment for one who witnesses an offense and fails to perform the required procedure of reproof. This should be no surprise if it is remembered that the sect, as the texts showed above, treated the omission of reproof on the part of a witness as tantamount to the commission of the crime he had witnessed.

5. *Reproof and the Rabbinic "Warning"*

The comparison with Rabbinic *hatra'ah*, "warning," can now be made. The Rabbinic institution of *hatra'ah* provided that no one might be convicted of an offense without first having been warned. The witnesses were required to explain formally to the transgressor the exact penalty for the offense he was about to commit. Only if he then answered in the affirmative, demonstrating his acceptance of their warning, could he be convicted of violating the law./96/ It is apparent that in the early tannaitic period, *hatra'ah* was required only for offenses incurring death penalties imposed by the court. Only later in the tannaitic period did *hatra'ah* begin to develop into a procedure for all offenses, even the simple negative commandments punishable by flogging./97/

In function, both of these procedures, Qumran's reproof and the Rabbinic warning, served the same purpose. Neither legal system was willing to convict a person until it was certain that he fully understood the nature of his offense and the required penalty. Only then could he be considered a purposeful offender. Further, both systems required that the witnesses to the crime play the main role in ensuring the understanding of the offender.

The differences, however, are great. The sect saw reproof as occurring after a first offense. Almost certainly, at least two occurrences of an offense were required for conviction in the sectarian system. For Rabbinic law, warning could take place, indeed, had to, before the very same offense for which a person could be tried. So only one offense was required. In fact, Rabbinic law would not have permitted the warning for a previous offense, even if performed after the fact, to suffice for a later violation. The Qumran procedure required the use of record keeping, since it was necessary to be able, at any time, to determine if the reproof had occurred for a previous violation of the same law./98/

How did it happen that the Qumran and Rabbinic procedures developed so differently in this case? This variation is the result of the differing tendencies of the two systems of law in regard to their derivation. Rabbinic law could make use of the oral Law and its inherent flexibility. One has only to look at the Rabbinic derivations of *hatra'ah* from Scripture to realize that they represent use of the technique called by the amoraim *'asmakhta*, the interpretation of biblical passages to lend support to previously existing legal procedures. In the case of the sect of Qumran, oral tradition was not a factor in the development of the legal system. Instead, the sect derived all laws from a close and, in their view, inspired reading of the text of the Bible. Hence, the sect had no choice but to appeal to Scripture. The biblical ideal of reproof was available, and through clever exegesis the sect was able to create the institution of reproof to solve the legal problem of ensuring that the accused fully understood the nature and consequences of his crime and therefore was to be considered a purposeful offender.

6. *Summary*

Qumran law required that an offender who was a member of the sect had to be formally reproved before he might be punished for a crime. Widespread references in the scrolls show that this was a cornerstone of the sect's legal system. The obligation to perform this reproof fell on witnesses to or victims of such offenses. Refusal to perform such reproof was considered to constitute the biblical offense of "bearing a grudge." In essence, conviction was only possible after multiple commission of the same offense. Only after reproof for the first offense could a transgressor be penalized for a subsequent violation. Reproof was a formal process which took place in front of witnesses and before the examiner. This official also recorded the fact of such reproof in the legal archive of the sect. Presumably, he also recorded who the witnesses were. Only in cases wherein such official records existed was it later possible to bring the violator to court. Reproof had to be performed on the very day on which the crime was witnessed, and it was considered so important a procedure, from both a legal and moral point of view, that failure to perform it brought heavy fines upon recalcitrant witnesses.

NOTES

/1/ The *waws* of *wa-'asher* and of *we-khol*, below, need not be translated. It is characteristic of Qumran Hebrew to use *waw* in such cases where English requires no conjunction. That *wa-'asher* is not the end of the preceding law but the beginning of the new one is pointed out by M. H. Segal, "Additional Notes on 'Fragments of a Zadokite Work,'" *JQR* N.S. 3 (1912–13), 310. Ginzberg, *Sect*, 38–40 takes this and the preceeding as one law. Cf. Licht, *Serakhim*, 36f.

/2/ The *mem* of *'amar* in the MS is written over a *shin* (Schechter, LVII, Ktav Reprint, 89) which was apparently written first as a result of dittography with *wa-'asher*. The phrase (*wa-*)*'asher 'amar* is frequently used at Qumran to indicate a biblical citation both in "halakhic" and *pesher* ("aggadic") contexts. Rabin discusses formulae for introducing quotations in *QS*, 96f. but for some reason omits this phrase.

/3/ So new JPS. RSV translates literally, "the sons of your own people." This verse is also intepreted in *Midrash Le-'Olam*, ed. A. Jellinek, *Bet Ha-Midrash*, pt. 3, p. 113. Cf. CDC 8:5f. = 19:18 where this verse is alluded to, and the sect's enemies are accused of violating this commandment.

/4/ Emending to *b'y* (*ba'e*) with Schechter, Segal, and Charles, *APOT* II, 823. The phrase *ba'e berit* occurs in CDC 2:2 (Rabin) and in DSD 2:18, and CDC 6:19 (cf. *HAQ*, 35f.) reads *ba'e ha-berit*. Rabin reads *bw'y* (*bo'e*, so Licht to DSD 6:1, *Serakhim*, 137), citing a rare Mishnaic participle form in M. H. Segal, *Diqduq Leshon Ha-Mishnah* (1935/6), 143. Such a form is unlikely as I cannot locate any other examples. S. Lieberman, "Discipline," 202, has pointed out that the same use of *bw'* (although without *berit*) is found in Rabbinic usage for conversion or entrance to the Pharisaic *ḥavurah*. For evidence, he refers to his *Greek*, 80, in which he cites P. Demai 2:3 (22d, bottom). The very same *baraita'* is found in T. Demai 2:13 and B. Bekhorot 30b. A similar usage in a *baraita'* appears in T. Demai 2:10 and B. Bekhorot 30b. This usage of *bw'* is, therefore, tannaitic. The connection of this Rabbinic usage with this Qumran expression is also made tentatively by Rabin, *QS*, 14 n. 7. Rabin, 15f., notes that "the teachers named in connection with various points of detail are all contemporaries of R. Meir, about A.D. 150." If we assume that the anonymous material is at least contemporary with the named, this would give a *terminus ante quem* for the *baraitot* of mid second century A.D. It is, however, possible that the material contains much more ancient technical linguistic usages of which this use of *bw'* is one.

/5/ I.e. those who have joined the sect. On the significance of *berit* at Qumran, see Licht, *Serakhim*, 51f. That the root *bw'* followed by the object *berit* signifies taking the oath required of new members of the sect is shown by Licht, *Serakhim*, 127f.

/6/ Schechter points out that *davar* in Deut 22:20 means "charge." Cf. Deut. 19:15 (Segal). So new JPS as well as in Deut. 22:14. Cf. S. D. Luzzatto, *Perush Shadal 'al Ḥamishah Ḥumshe Torah* (1965), to Deut. 22:14 who first proposes this interpretation and then in a note written later retracts it in favor of the Targumic view, and the long note in S. R. Driver, *A Critical and Exegetical Commentary on Deuteronomy* (1895), 254f. The *hif'il* of *bw'* followed by *davar* occurs in Ex. 18:22 in which *davar* means "legal case." For the use of *'al* in the sense of "against" see BDB, 757bf.

/7/ Vocalizing *be-hokheaḥ* (with Jastrow and Ben-Yehudah, *s.v.*). The infinitive absolute is here being used as a noun. Such substantive use may have been seen by the sect in Pr. 15:12 (cf. Ralbag) and Job 6:25. The derivation of this legal term from Lev. 19:17 will be discussed below. There is no reason to accept emendations such as those proposed in Charles, *APOT* II, 823. Segal's assertion that this means a charge which cannot be proven by witnesses reflects a lack of understanding of the formal nature of this "reproof" as a prerequisite for conviction.

/ 8/ This stipulation is probably derived from the use of the infinitive abstract and finite verb. Cf. the Vulgate's translation, "*Sed publice argue eum.*"

/ 9/ Schechter emends to *whkhw* (*we-hikahu*). This reading (also rejected by Ginzberg, *Sect*, 40) is certainly unfounded and is the result of his failure to understand the significance of this law. (Cf. Charles, *APOT* II, 823.)

/10/ So Ginzberg and Rabin. An alternate explanation suggested by Segal is that he brings the accused before the elders.

/11/ Cf. l. 6, *u-ve-ḥaron 'apo vo.*

/12/ The elders are those referred to as second to the priests in the *moshav ha-rabbim* (DSD 6:6–8). Presumably, they had some other functions in the conduct of the sect. Licht to DSD 6:8–10 notes that similar passages (CDC 14:3–6, discussed in *HAQ*, 66f., and DSD 2:19–21) have *lewiim* where DSD 6:6–8 has *zeqenim*. He also refers to DSW 13:1, *ziqne ha-serekh*. Since the sectarian group was organized militarily in preparation for the soon-to-dawn eschaton, it is necessary to look at the *War Scroll* as a possible source of data on the organization of the sect in "peacetime." "No doubt the frequent military term 'Men of the Serekh' (or 'elders of the Serekh') aroused associations with 'serekh of the community' || '*serekh* of God' as names of the sect" (Yadin, *War Scroll*, 150). Cf. the discussion of *serekh* as a legal term in *HAQ*, 60–68. The most obvious conclusion to be drawn from this text in DSW is that the elders are separate from the Levites, as both are mentioned together here (*ha-kohanim we-ha-lewiim we-khol ziqne ha-serekh*). Yadin to DSW 13:1 also suggests that the *ziqne ha-serekh* might be identical with the *sorekhe ha-maḥanot*, the "camp prefects" of DSW 7:1 "who are the oldest amongst all the men in the field." They were between fifty and sixty years of age (DSW 7:1). Yadin suggests that "it is probable that they were appointed to keep law and order and supervise the execution of orders while the soldiers were in camp and perhaps to guard the camps when the soldiers had left for the battlefield . . . the possibility cannot be ruled out that the camp prefects were also responsible for marking out the camp and assigning places to the different units. Thus they were administrative officials. . . . Equally, the possibility exists that they fulfilled these same tasks also in the settlements or 'camps' (CDC, vii, 6) of the sect in peace time" (Yadin, *War Scroll*, 151f.). If we accept the identification proposed by Yadin, these *sorekhe ha-maḥanot* are the *zeqenim* of our text in CDC. In view of their role in Qumran life, it would be natural for them to be given reports of misconduct on the part of sectarians.

/13/ The *hif'il* of *bzh* occurs only in Est. 1:17 where it is likewise followed by a direct object.

/14/ In other words, he is violating the commandment of Lev. 19:18 cited above in the text of CDC.

/15/ Cf. the tannaitic expression *'en ketiv kan 'ellah* (examples in W. Bacher, *'Erkhe Midrash* [1922/3] I, 61). This expression was used specifically when the language of the verse being explained was unusual (so Bacher). Cf. Rabin.

/16/ MT has the Tetragrammaton for which our text substitutes the pronoun *hu'* in line with the general tendency at Qumran to avoid the Tetragrammaton in non-biblical texts, on which see below, 136. This tendency was already noticed in the *Zadokite Fragments* by Ginzberg, *Sect*, 40. Cf. however, his 163 n. 34 and 188

n. 146. Segal, 392 n. 1, refers to a similar convention of the Samaritans who substitute *shema'* for the Tetragrammaton in their Torah scrolls. It is possible that *hu'* is actually a surrogate divine name. Such a usage is found in DSD 8:13 (spelled *hw'h'*, but note that MS e has *h'mt*), and Ḥ. Yalon has cited numerous examples from biblical and Rabbinic literature (*MMY*, 81 cited by Rabin, *ad loc.*). See also Ginzberg, *Sect*, 57 on M. Sukkah 4:5; and E. Katz, *Die Bedeutung des hapax legomenon der Qumraner Handschriften HUAHA* (1966), 15–17, 53–81. Rabin cites B. Shabbat 104a where we read, *he', waw, zeh shemo shel ha-qadosh barukh hu'*. The text is a third century amoraic alphabet *midrash*. *DS*, *ad loc.* indicates that some witnesses to the text omit this sentence. But in view of the alphabetic order of the material it is hard to understand this omission as anything but an error in transmission.

/17/ MT has the defective spelling *nqm*.

/18/ MT reads *l'ybyw*.

/19/ Note that this verse does not appear in the *Pesher Nahum*, nor in the Twelve Prophets Scroll found at Wadi Murabba'at, nor in the Greek text of the Twelve Prophets found at Naḥal Ḥever. This lacuna is due only to the state of preservation of the material and implies nothing regarding the biblical text. That our text in CDC is not a quotation from the missing section of *Pesher Nahum* becomes clear from the lack of the standard rubric, *pishro*, "its interpretation is." Nor can it be argued that the form of the material was changed when it was introduced into the text of CDC since the subject matter is legal and would never be expressed in a *pesher* text.

/20/ Rabin translates "namely." He views this text as a continuation of the previous law, explaining the meaning of the enemies against whom God will take vengeance. He is, however, unable to explain why Lev. 19:17 was used as the proof-text rather than the more obvious Lev. 5:1 (l. 7 n. 2).

/21/ Adapted from Num. 30:15 (Schechter). There is some question if this should be translated "about him" as above or "to him." The latter would mean that he did not make the legally required "reproof." It cannot be translated "about it (the crime)" for in Num. 30:5, 12, 15 the feminine *lah* no doubt refers to the wife, and not to the vow (as *neder* and *'issar* are both masculine nouns). RSV to Num. 30:15 translates "to her." So also Ehrlich to Num. 30:5. Some support for "to him" may come from the interpretation of *dabber bo*, on which see below, n. 23.

/22/ MT to Num. 30:15 reads *mi-yom 'el yom*, but Ps. 96:2 and Est. 3:7 read *mi-yom le-yom*. Cf. Ps. 19:3. CDC 7:2 has *mi-yom le-yom*.

/23/ Schechter translated "spake against him," Rabin, "spoke about him." In the Bible the *pi'el* of *dbr* followed by the preposition *b-* refers to God's (or a *mal'akh*'s) speaking with a person, or to speaking about a person (S. R. Driver, *Notes on the Hebrew Text and the Topography of the Books of Samuel* [1966], 357f.). In this text the latter meaning seems most logical and is supported by the fact that only men are mentioned; God is not involved. Biblical examples of this usage, found only in non-legal context, are Num. 12:1, 8, 21:5, 7; Ps. 50:20, 78:19; and Job 19:18. It is the legal context of our passage that recommends the translation "accused him" instead of the more literal "spoke against him."

/24/ See CDC 9:17 for this expression. Schechter takes *devar mawet* as being the end of the previous clause and "meaning perhaps that he accuses him of a capital offense." He also suggests that it might be possible to emend to *dbr 'mt* (*devar 'emet*), a true accusation. The law would then say that "even if it be true" (so Schechter), i.e. the offense, the accuser has still violated the law of Lev. 19:17. Segal explains the whole circumstance as referring to one who witnessed a transgression and did not offer reproof, and then later in anger accused his fellow of a capital matter. In other words, the accusation is false. But this does not seem to fit the context as we are clearly dealing with a true accusation which was not made at the proper time or in the proper legal forum.

/25/ Emending with Schechter, to *'wnw bw* (*'awono bo*). This emendation is supported by the use in Num. 30:16 of the expression *we-nasa' 'et 'awonah*. Perhaps *'awon* here means "punishment" (see BDB 731a–b for examples including Num. 30:16). Cf. *Sifre* Num. 156 (ed. Horovitz, p. 208), *we-nasa' 'et 'awonah, maggid ha-katuv she-hu' mukhnas taḥteha le-'awon*. Charles, however, rejects Schechter's emendation and translates, "He has testified against himself because he did not. . . ." Charles is certainly correct that the text can be so understood without emending, but since the wording is so dependent on Num. 30, the emendation would seem correct. In addition, *bo* does not mean "against himself." Such a meaning would require *be-nafsho* or *be-'aṣmo*. I. Robinson, "A Note on Damascus Document IX, 7," *RQ* 9 (1977–78), 237–240 compares Ruth 1:21 and translates, "God has decreed against him that he did not fulfill the command. . . ."

/26/ The phrase *ya'an 'asher lo'* occurs only in 1 Sam. 30:22; Jer. 25:8; Ezek. 12:12, 16:43; and Ps. 109:16.

/27/ The use of the *hif'il* of *qwm* followed by *miṣwah* occurs only in Jer. 35:16, referring to the Rekabites' allegiance to the commandment(s) of their father Jonathan. Our passage may be influenced again here by Num. 30:14f. where the *hif'il* of *qwm* occurs repeatedly and means "to uphold" in reference to the husband's validation of the vow. Throughout the chapter the root *qwm* in the *qal* is used for the notion that the vow "stands," i.e. is obligatory.

/28/ The phrase *miṣwat 'el* does not occur in the Bible. *Miṣwat 'adonai* is quite common. Ezra 10:3 contains *miṣwat 'elohenu*. The Qumran author probably made use of the biblical phrase but eliminated the Tetragrammaton. Cf. above, n. 16.

/29/ Or "about him." Both usages are attested in BDB, 56a.

/30/ The spelling *r'yk* is probably phonetic, the *yod* indicating the equivalent of Masoretic *segol*. For examples of apparent plurals of this type which are actually singular, see Ges. sec. 93ss. Cf. also 91k for the opposite confusion with our noun, *rea'*. MT has *'amitekha*. This is a case of synonymous variants. On the variety of expressions for "the other man" see M. Noth, *Leviticus* (1965), 141f. For confusions of this type in CDC see Rabin to CDC 6:20.

/31/ See n. 25.

/32/ So RSV.

/33/ Cf. Ginzberg, *Sect*, 41, and Rabin, *ad loc*. Rabbinic tradition has a definite aversion to deriving law from the prophets. Only in a small number of cases did the Rabbis do so (see Z. H. Chajes, *Torat Nevi'im* [1836], in *Kol Sifre MaHaRaṢ Chajes* [1958] I, 3–136 and E. E. Urbach, "*Halakhah U-Nevu'ah*," *Tarbiz* 18 [1946/7], 1–27). Note the amoraic rule *divre torah mi-divre qabbalah la' yalfinan* (B. Ḥagigah 10b [which refers only to *gezerah shawah*, as noted by Tosafot]; B. Bava' Qamma' 2b; cf. B. Niddah 23b). The halakhic *midrashim* in Ezra and Nehemiah, however, treat prophetic material as having legal authority. In this way Qumran literature is similar to the biblical *midrash* of the early Second Temple period. (For a detailed discussion see a still unpublished section of my Brandeis University dissertation, *Halakhah at Qumran* [1974], 159–180, and especially for use of the prophets, 168–170.) It is possible that the rise of Christianity and its use of the prophets may have conditioned the later Rabbinic aversion.

/34/ *Sect*, 41.

/35/ Cf. Driver, *Deuteronomy*, 374f.

/36/ Ginzberg and Rabin refer to B. Pesaḥim 113b in which there appears a statement that God hates one who bears witness alone against his neighbor followed by a Babylonian amoraic story of how someone received lashes for this offense. In the story, R. Papa takes Deut. 19:15, *lo' yaqum 'ed 'eḥad be-'ish*, to mean "A single witness is forbidden to testify against anyone." It is difficult to establish the attribution or dating of this first statement. (The statement is in Hebrew and continues a list of statements all beginning with "three.") The manuscripts, however, differ on the attribution of the earlier statements of this type on 113a. Possibilities there are the third century Palestinian R. Yoḥanan or his pupil, R. Joshua ben Levi, or, in the case of one statement, a tannaitic attribution. See *DS*, *ad loc.*, nn. *bet* and *gimel*. Whatever the case, the Aramaic story was cited as an explanation of a previously existing Hebrew statement. Papa is a fifth generation Babylonian amora who died in 375 (Strack, 132). However, this passage is irrelevant to our Qumran law since in CDC 9:16–23, discussed above, 73f., 78–81, the law specifically permits such testimony and keeps a record of it for cumulative conviction.

/37/ Cf. Gen. 21:25 which the sect no doubt took as "Abraham accused Abimelech" and the phrase *mokhiaḥ ba-sha'ar* (Amos 5:10; Is. 29:21) as well as the use of this root in connection with the root *ryb* (Hos. 4:4; Job 40:2). Of course, the forensic usage underlies many of the occurrences of the root *ykḥ* in Job. See I. L. Seeligmann, "*Zur Terminologie für das Gerichtsverfahren im Wortschatz des biblischen Hebräisch*," *Suppl. to VT* 16 (1967), 266–268.

/38/ *QS*, 32, 111.

/39/ P. Niddah 2:3 (50a) (cf. B. Niddah 16b *mokhiaḥ*); twice in P. Demai 2:1 (22c); P. Demai 3:4 (23c); and P. Sheqalim 8:1 (ed. Krot. 8:2, 51a).

/40/ For the law of annulment of a woman's vows by her husband or father, cf. CDC 16:10–12.

/41/ See *Sifre* Num. 156 (ed. Horovitz, p. 208) and the commentaries of D. Pardo, N. Z. J. Berlin, Hillel ben Eliakim, and Malbim, *ad loc.* and Luzzatto to Num. 30:15. Also T. Nedarim 6:1 (cf. Lieberman, *TK*, *ad loc.*); B. Nedarim 76a; P. Nedarim 10:10 (42a); and B. Shabbat 157a. The Targum Pseudo-Jonathan to Num. 30:15 is ambiguous on this matter (*mi-yoma' de-shama' le-yoma' ḥoran*), but Targum Neofiti translates: *yom batar yom*, "day after day." LXX has ἡμέραν ἐξ ἡμέρας.

/42/ Taught anonymously as the only view in M. Nedarim 10:8 and *Sifre Zuta'* 30:17 (ed. Horovitz, p. 329) and transmitted anonymously in *Sifre* Num. 150 (ed. Horovitz, p. 208).

/43/ Benjamin of Nahawend in Harkavy, 180, quoted from the commentary of Yeshua' ben Yehudah, MS St. Petersburg.

/44/ Cf. Albeck's *HWT, ad loc.* See also *Sifre* Deut. 190 (ed. Finkelstein, p. 231); A. Geiger, *Urschrift und Übersetzungen der Bibel in ihrer Abhängigkeit von der innern Entwicklung der Judenthums* (1857), 140; Z. Pineles, *Darkah shel Torah* (1861), no. 148 (p. 172f.); L. Finkelstein, *The Pharisees* (1962) I, 142–144; II, 696–698 and notes. Finkelstein neglects to say that the Pharisees are not mentioned in the tannaitic discussion of this issue. Neusner, *Rabbinic Traditions* I, 2 has made the same assumption. In fact, M. Makkot 1:6 explicitly mentions the Sadducees. The "Pharisaic" view is, however, given anonymously. Following the statement of the Sadducean view, the interlocutors of the Sadducees are introduced by either *'ameru lahem ḥakhamim* (MSS Kaufmann, De Rossi 138 and Paris) or *'ameru lahem* (*ed. princ.* and MS Munich). In both the Mishnah and *Sifre* versions the Sadducee clause appears, preceded by the syntactically strange *she-hare*, "for indeed." Since the *Sifre* version is preceded by *mi-kan 'ameru* and lacks the response of the interlocutors, it is clear that the *Sifre* text was based on a version of the mishnah which contained only the anonymous apodictic statement (*'en ha-'edim zomemin nehergin 'ad she-yiggamer ha-din*) and the view of the Sadducees. In other words, the response of the interlocutors in M. Makkot 1:6 is a later stage in the tradition added to the previous form of the statement. The response, then, postdates the statement of the Sadducean view and, therefore, it cannot be ascribed with any certainty to the Pharisees. Also to be considered here is the story of Shim'on ben Sheṭaḥ and Judah ben Ṭabbai, known in several versions. While the roles assigned to the characters interchange in the versions, this will not concern us. One of these two is said to have executed a single conspiring witness in a case in which the falsely accused had not been put to death. The version of T. Sanhedrin 6:6 (ed. Zuckermandel, p. 424) and *Midrash Tanna'im* to Deut. 19:18 (ed. Hoffmann, I, p. 117) ascribes the attitude of the Sadducees of M. Makkot 1:6 to the Boethusians. On the other hand, the version of B. Ḥagigah 16b and B. Makkot 5b ascribes this view to the Sadducees (as in M. Makkot 1:6). In P. Sanhedrin 6:3 (ed. Krot. 6:5, 23b) the opponents appear as "they." The earliest version of this story, however, in *Mekhilta' De-Rabbi Ishmael* Mishpaṭim 20 (ed. Horovitz-Rabin, p. 327), does not find it necessary to polemicize against an incorrect view. Subsequent versions added it as an explanation of the strange behavior of the obviously learned "Rabbi" who should have known the *halakhah.* The later versions, in adding this explanation, differed in ascribing the incorrect view to the Sadducees, Boethusians, or unidentified "they." What is most important here is that the earliest form of this narrative did not contain any reference to the Sadducean view of M. Makkot 1:6 and, therefore, this narrative cannot serve as a basis for ascribing the view of the sages (or of the anonymous interlocutor) to the early Pharisaic sages Shim'on ben Sheṭaḥ and Judah ben Ṭabbai. (For full analysis of these traditions, see Neusner, *Rabbinic Traditions* I, 86–89, 94f., 105f., 122–127, and "Testimony," 204–216.) Note that Josephus, *Ant.* 4, 8, 15 (219), seems to represent the Pharisaic view. The apocryphal Susanna (v. 61f.) relates the execution of two conspiring witnesses in a case in which the accused had *not* been executed. This again appears to represent the "Pharisaic" view although it could be argued that they would have been executed even if the accused had been also. On Susanna, see Tchernowitz, *Toledot Ha-Halakhah* IV, 389–393, who indicates that what is described in Susanna cannot be taken as parallel to the "Pharisaic" point of view at all, because of the many inconsistencies with it found in the story. See also Tchernowitz I, 330–339 for a discussion of *'edim zomemim*. His theory that whereas the Sadducees were interested in retribution against the conspiring witnesses, the "Pharisees" wanted to strengthen the authority of the courts and to uphold the ideal of truth in judgment, must be regarded as unproven. He correctly rejects the view of those who claim that earlier *halakhah* applied the law of *'edim zomemim* to what was later called *hakḥashah*, contradictory testimony by the two witnesses. The Karaite Aaron ben Elijah of Nicomedia (*Gan 'Eden*, 177c, 194d) indicates that the Karaites accepted the Sadducean view and gives two different explanations for the Scriptural derivation of the Karaite view.

/45/ See above, 73.

/46/ M. 'Avot 3:4, 3:7, 8. For a non-metaphorical usage, see M. Bava' Qamma' 3:10.

/47/ *Sect*, 41.

/48/ Levine, "Damascus Document," 196.

/49/ RSV.

/50/ This cannot be read as a passive participle *meṣuwweh* because it is parallel to *mishpaṭ* (l. 2, previous clause). For the connection of *miṣwah* and *mishpaṭ* at Qumran, see *HAQ*, 47f.

/51/ Ginzberg compares Num. 30:15. See above, 91.

/52/ The full passage has been used in determining the definition of *mishpaṭ* at Qumran. See *HAQ*, 46.

/53/ On this syntactic structure, see Licht, *Serakhim*, 35–37.

/54/ As there was no more space at the end of the line, the scribe wrote the *ḥet* above the *yod*. Wernberg-Møller translates, "They shall admonish," apparently taking this clause as part of a "chain of *lameds*." On this structure, see Licht, *Serakhim*, 35–37.

/55/ Wernberg-Møller notes that while the text clearly is an adaptation of Lev. 19:17, *rea'* appears for MT *'amit*. The same is the case in CDC 9:8 (above, 89 and n. 30). He then asks whether this is an indication of a "literary relationship" between the texts. The most logical explanation would be that both draw on a textual tradition in which *rea'* stood in the biblical text or that both tend to substitute more familiar for rarer words when adapting or citing biblical texts. This would be in line with the findings of Kutscher in regard to 1QIs[a]. On *'amit* see above, 52f. n. 163.

/56/ The top of the *taw* is clearly visible above a tear in the scroll. Restored with Brownlee, Wernberg-Møller, and Licht.

/57/ The phrase *'ahavat ḥesed* occurs in Micah 6:8 (on which see the comments below, and cf. Jer. 2:2) and in the daily prayer *Sim Shalom* in the Ashkenazic rite (Baer, 103, found already in the 11th century *Maḥazor Vitry*, compiled by Simḥah ben Samuel of Vitry [d. before 1105], a pupil of Rashi, p. 67). The other rites have *'ahavah wa-ḥesed*, a reading already found in the versions of Amram Gaon, Saadyah Gaon, and Maimonides, as well as in some *genizah* fragments of the Palestinian rite (J. Mann, "Genizah Fragments of the Palestinian Order of Service," *HUCA* 2 [1925], 320). Other *genizah* texts contain a shorter version omitting this phrase entirely. Cf.

A. L. Gordon, *Tiqqun Tefillah*, in *Siddur 'Oṣar Ha-Tefillot* I, *ad loc.* and I. Elbogen, *Ha-Tefillah Be-Yisra'el* (1972), 46. A *baraita'* (B. Megillah 17b–18a, with numerous amoraic insertions and explanatory glosses) mentions *Sim Shalom*. That some version of the benediction was recited in the Herodian Temple by the priests is evident from M. Tamid 5:1. (See Albeck's *HWT*, *ad loc.*) Cf. M. Rosh Ha-Shanah 4:5. Our translation assumes that the phrase is essentially a construct of two synonyms. Gordon (in his commentary on *Sim Shalom*, 182a) suggests that the phrase may refer to *'ahavat ḥinnam*, "unrequited love," to which he compares Hosea 14:5. Brownlee translates, "loving devotion," Wernberg-Møller, "affectionate love." *'Anawah* and *'ahavat ḥesed* also occur together in DSD 2:24 and 5:3f. (Wernberg-Møller). These passages are, like ours, exegeses of Mic. 6:8, on which see n. 58. Wernberg-Møller's restoration of this phrase in the damaged CDC 13:18 seems likely from the photographs. He is certainly correct that there is no *waw* after the *he'* of *'anawah*. The prefix *b-* which he reads before *'anawah* is questionable. The only traces that can be seen there appear to be those of the end of the preceding word.

/58/ This sentence is an exegesis of Mic. 6:8 except that it is directed toward man rather than God. Therefore, it is necessary for the author to replace *'im 'elohekha* with *la-'ish*. Licht notes that after *la-'ish* there is a space large enough for three words (so his textual note, two words according to his commentary). The space is not actually that large, but is large enough for seven letters or spaces judging from the line immediately above it. Licht suggests that the space may be the result of the scribe's omission of something unclear in his *Vorlage*. (Wernberg-Møller suggests that it may indicate that he was uncertain of his text.) Alternately, the word *la-'ish*, he says, may have been written in error and the space used to indicate its erasure or a need to recheck the text. He points to a similar phenomenon in 1QSa 1:27. A final suggestion of his is that the space was left as a result of an effort to indicate the beginning of a new subject as does the mark in the right-hand margin of the column.

/59/ The scroll reads *'lyhwhw*. The final *hw* is clearly the result of dittography. Brownlee emends to *'el 'aḥeyhu*, "to his brother." Wernberg-Møller suggests that this may be a dialectical form.

/60/ Licht notes the parallelism of *riv* and *telunah* in DST 5:30. Cf. also the verbal use in 5:25. Licht also notes the verb in DSD 7:17 (twice). Wernberg-Møller translates, "with a snarl," and notes that only the plural appears in the Hebrew Scriptures.

/61/ Restored with Licht, based on MS d: *btlwnh 'w bqn't rš'*. The literal meaning of the phrase is "stiffneckedly." Licht refers to DSD 6:26 where a punishment is indicated for one who answers a member of the sect stubbornly (*bi-qeshi 'oref*). In DSD 5:5 the sectarian is obligated to "circumcise through (or in) the community (his) 'uncircumcised' inclination and (his) stiff neck (*'orlat yeṣer wa-'oref qasheh*)." *'Orlat yeṣer* is an alternate form of the phrase *'orlat lev(av)* occurring in the list of characteristics of the *ruaḥ 'awlah*, "the spirit of iniquity." Note that like our passage, DSD 5:11 is based on Mic. 6:8 although it represents an inversion of all the positive qualities mentioned by the prophet. DSD 4:5f. is based on the positive exegesis of this verse. The phrase also occurs in DST fragment 12:4 followed by *li-demamah*. The poor state of preservation of this fragment makes it difficult to speculate on its meaning. In our passage in DSD Brownlee restores *qšh wkwbd lb 'w*. . . . The poor syntax of this reading, even in terms of Qumran literature, makes it extremely unlikely.

/62/ Note the use of the construct here. *Rš'* is probably to be taken as the noun *resha'*, rather than as an adjective, as *ruaḥ* is feminine in the Bible and Rabbinic literature. *Resha'* is the last element in the construct chain. This noun is quite common at Qumran. The phrase *ruaḥ resha'* is probably equivalent to the *ruaḥ 'awlah* of DSD 4:9. DSD 4:9–14 describes this "spirit" in detail. It is equivalent to the "spirit of darkness" (DSD 3:25) and as such represents everything to which the sect is opposed. Our translation, "disposition," is meant to reflect the idea that the *ruaḥ* in this context is an internal or "psychological" phenomenon.

/63/ Note the form of the statement, *'al* followed by the jussive. For a thorough discussion of this form in the Qumran Sabbath Code, see *HAQ*, 80–82.

/64/ Restoring with Licht. Brownlee restores: *b'wrlt* (*plene* spelling) and is followed by Wernberg-Møller. Brownlee correctly rejects the suggestion of S. Iwry that we read *bktly* as "the context requires an adversative reference to the heart." The alternatives also proposed by Iwry, *b'wlt* and *bkslt* are also unlikely. H. L. Ginsberg, "Heart," *EJ* 8 (1971), 8, writes: "That Israel's 'heart' is obstructed (older translations, regrettably, 'uncircumcised') signifies that it is religiously stubborn and intractable—cutting away the obstruction of Israel's 'heart' of course means making it religiously reasonable." The obstruction is the *'orlah*. While Ginsberg is no doubt correct in his explanation of the image, it is still probable that no listener or reader in ancient times would have failed to understand the implicit metaphor of circumcision as symbolic of the covenant. This imagery is certainly reflected in Deut. 10:16 (which, like our text, also mentions *'oref*) and Jer. 4:4 as well as in DSD 5:5: *la-mul ba-yaḥad 'orlat yeṣer*. . . . It is this line that serves as the basis of Licht's restoration. Note also DSH 11:13 *lo' mal 'et 'orlat libbo* (Brownlee). Note that Targs. Onkelos and Pseudo-Jonathan to Deut. 10:16 translate *'orlat levavekhem* as *ṭipshut libbekhon*. Neofiti Targum reads: *'orlat ṭipshut levavekhon*. It is possible that *'orlat* in Neofiti is an intrusion from the Hebrew text, a phenomenon often found in Targum manuscripts.

/65/ Kutscher, *Ha-Lashon*, 134–137, maintains that despite the spelling with *'alef*, the pronunciation was *ki*. Goshen-Gottstein, "Linguistic Structure," 112f. disposes amply of the theory that the spelling *ky'* indicates a pronunciation *kiya'*. Cf. Qimron, 69.

/66/ Note the medial *mem*. The scribe first wrote *bywmyw* and then erased (probably by scraping) the last two letters. Licht's suggestion (critical note and commentary) that the text might be read *be-yomo* (he cites Deut. 24:15) does not seem helpful in light of the derivation from Num. 30:15 discussed above. Better is his citation of Prov. 12:16 in which *ba-yom* means "at once" (so RSV). Wernberg-Møller reads the manuscript as *bywmwr* which he takes as equivalent to *bywm 'or*, which occurs in Amos 8:9. This reading is impossible as the last letter is clearly a *waw*. A *resh* would require the upward hook at its extreme left as can be seen from comparison with other words in the scroll.

/67/ MT has *ḥet'*. This is another case of synonymous variance. It cannot be determined, however, whether the variant arose in a biblical text or in the course of adapting the biblical material to our context.

/68/ Licht, Wernberg-Møller. Cf. the note in Charles, *APOT*, to Ben Sira 19:13.

/69/ Medial *mem* in final position. Cf. J. P. Siegel, "Final *mem* in Medial Position and Medial *mem* in Final Position in *11 Q Ps a*," *RQ* 7 (1969–71), 125–130.

/70/ For the *hif'il* of *bw'* + *davar* see CDC 9:2–8 and above, n. 6. Cf. the use of *davar* in DSD 6:12 as well. Licht cites the use of this word in DSD 6:24 (pl.), 8:17, 22 which represent a different usage.

/71/ Note that in CDC 9:2–8 the word order is different: *'ish . . . yavi' 'al re'ehu davar*. That the similar wording of these two passages is no accident is certain. But there is no way of knowing if one is dependent on the other or if they both arise from a common source.

/72/ This detail is lacking in the version of CDC 9:2–8, yet our passage makes clear that CDC 9:2–8 refers to bringing formal charges *before the assembly*. The full name of this assembly is *moshav ha-rabbim*. For a full discussion of this body, see *HAQ*, 68–75. The shortened form of the name, *rabbim*, is used often in Qumran literature. Here the assembly is serving as a court (Licht).

/73/ *Tokhaḥat* here replaces *hokheaḥ* of CDC. *Tokhaḥat* is a wisdom term and occurs in the Bible primarily in Proverbs. Cf. H. Burgmann, "*TWKḤT in 1Q p Hab V, 10, Ein Schlüsselwort mit verhängnisvollen historischen Konsequenzen*," *RQ* 10 (1980), 293–300.

/74/ Ben-Yehudah, *s.v.*

/75/ Cf. J. Licht, *Megillat Ha-Hadoyot* (1957), *ad loc.*

/76/ Above, 73.

/77/ See *HAQ*, 29 n. 51.

/78/ Pp. 74–78.

/79/ For the use of *'asher* at the beginning of ordinances at Qumran, see above, 11.

/80/ Licht notes that no parallel to this usage can be found. Nonetheless, the reflexive use of the root *ryb* must refer to litigation. For the roots *ykḥ* and *ryb* in proximity, see Hos. 4:4 and Mic. 6:2.

/81/ Note the medial *mem* in final position. On this phenomenon, see above, n. 69.

/82/ A designation for those outside the sect. See DSD 9:22, 10:19; CDC 6:15, 13:14. The scribe of MS d first wrote *hd't* and then corrected himself.

/83/ MS d *lbḥyry*.

/84/ The *resh* is suspended over an erasure. The reading is certain, however.

/85/ Based on Lev. 19:18 (19:8 in Licht's note is a typographical error). The exegesis on which this law is based is that found in CDC 9:2–8 on which see the comments above, 89–92. The substitution of *rea'* for *ben 'am* is a result both of the fluidity of these synonyms and the occurrence of *rea'* in the second half of the verse. Cf. above nn. 30, 55.

/86/ The *bet* is suspended above an erasure.

/87/ On *mishpaṭ*, see *HAQ*, 42–47. Wernberg-Møller compares the phrase *be-lo' mishpaṭ* in DSD 7:4 which is equivalent. He also notes the similar wording in Matt. 5:22. He is referring to the texts reading εἰκῇ, "without cause" (so note in RSV). (See

K. Aland, M. Black, B. Metzger, A. Wikgren, eds., *The Greek New Testament* [1966], p. 13.) There is no evidence, however, that Matthew is here referring to any legal procedure. Brownlee translated *'asher lo' be-mishpaṭ* as "who has not been convicted." In his note he compared l. 18 as well as *'asher lo' be-tokhaḥat* in DSD 6:1.

/88/ DSD 6:25 makes it clear that while under the fine a person's food rations were reduced by one-fourth. On these fines, see below, 159. The collective economic activity of the sect must have resulted in a greater than subsistence level income. Otherwise, such a fine would have been impossible to sustain.

/89/ The words in parentheses appear above the line as a correction. (The *shin* of *shishah* is dotted.) Licht suggests that the correction resulted from comparison with what he terms a similar offense in DSD 6:25–27. We, however, prefer to assume that the emendation was meant to bring this law into harmony with CDC 14:22 as restored by Rabin. (Cf. Rabin, *ad loc.* and Wernberg-Møller to our passage in DSD.)

/90/ Also based on Lev. 19:18.

/91/ Licht, in his comment to DSD 7:3, points out that Rabbinic usage would prefer here *le-'aṣemo*. He notes, however, Deut. 21:14 and Ben Sira 4:20, 22 (vss. 21, 23 in ed. Segal). Nevertheless, he suggests that this might be Aramaic influence.

/92/ Syntactically, *kol davar* functions as the direct object of the verb *nqm* in the *qal*. Similar usage occurs in Deut. 32:43 where *dam* serves as the direct object of *yiqqom*. Perhaps *davar* would be better translated in the forensic sense of "charge." See above, n. 6.

/93/ See n. 88.

/94/ For sources see I. Lampronti, *Paḥad Yiṣḥaq*, Part IV (1812/13), *Lamed*, p. 36.

/95/ Restored with Rabin, based on DSD 7:8f.

/96/ Cf. "*Hatra'ah*," *Enc. Tal.* 11, 291–314.

/97/ T. Sanhedrin 11:1 (cf. B. Sanhedrin 8b, 80b) *Mekhilta' De-Rabbi Ishmael* Mishpaṭim 4 (ed. Horovitz-Rabin, p. 261), dealing with *mitot bet din*, whereas the amoraic material in B. Sanhedrin 40b–41a presumes the need for *hatra'ah* also in cases of *malqut*.

/98/ Cf. Rabin, *QS*, 111, and Jackson, *Essays*, 175f. n. 6.

CHAPTER FIVE
THE RESTORATION OF LOST OR STOLEN PROPERTY

1. *The Oath of Adjuration*

The process of determining guilt or innocence, treated in the last few chapters, was certainly of great importance to the sect. Yet the sectarians were also concerned with seeing that owners of property be protected. In this respect, the *Zadokite Fragments* speak of procedures designed to effect the restoration of lost or stolen property. Because the sect saw the illegal alienation of property as affecting the cosmic order, it was concerned as well to ensure restoration, even when the owner could not be located or was unknown. These provisions will be considered in the order in which they appear in the *Zadokite Fragments*, beginning with the oath of adjuration described in CDC 9:10–12:

וכל האובד ולא נודע מי גנבו ממאד המחנה אשר גנב בו ישביע בעליו בשבועת האלה והשומע אם יודע הוא ולא יגיד ואשם

But/1/ anything which is missing/2/ and it is not known who stole it from the property/3/ of the camp/4/ in which it was stolen,/5/ its owner/6/ shall swear an oath of adjuration./7/ Whoever hears, if he knows and does not tell, is guilty./8/

This text enjoins a procedure whereby when something is missing from the property of the camp and it is suspected of having been stolen, the owner makes an oath adjuring anyone who knows where the object is, or who has taken it, to come forward. If anyone knows and remains silent, he is guilty not only of failing to observe the positive commandment of returning lost (or stolen) property,/9/ but also of violating this oath. The effect of the procedure would be to bring to light any information which might lead to the restoration of the property.

This law shows once again that the *Zadokite Fragments* envisage a society in which communal use of property never obliterates the concept of private ownership so clearly assumed in the biblical tradition and, indeed, in the ancient Near East. Nevertheless, the illegal appropriation of property was seen as a crime against the entire sect as they were now deprived of its use. It was the owner of the stolen property, however, who was required to pronounce the oath.

Lev. 5:1 served as the basis for this Qumran law. This passage prescribes that a person who does not come forward after hearing an oath of adjuration in a case in which he was a witness, or heard something or was otherwise able to give information, shall bear his transgression./10/ But the passage in no way makes clear the kind of oath of which it is speaking, nor the circumstances under which guilt is incurred. The sectarian law adds an introductory statement and adapts the language of Lev. 5:1 and, in so doing, specifies the details of the case. First, it is clear that this is an instance of theft for which no witnesses have come forward, Second, the oath deals with stolen property which has not been recovered./11/ Third, the one from whom the property has been stolen swears the oath.

Yet the sect goes further. Our Qumran law designates the oath by the term *shevu'at ha-'alah*, "an oath of adjuration." This construct is found only once in the Bible, in Num. 5:21, referring to the woman suspected of adultery (Heb. *soṭah*)./12/ Analysis of CDC 9:6–8 regarding "reproof" as a requisite for punishment in the law of the Dead Sea sect/13/ showed that its language connects the law of annulment of vows (Num. 30:2–17) with that of reproof (Lev. 19:17). The sect made an analogy between these two passages in order to fill in the details of the procedure of reproof not given in the Torah. This is a form of the type of exegesis called *midrash* by the Qumran sect./14/ This same kind of exegesis is evident in our law. In order to fill in the specifics of the law of Lev. 5:1, the sect made an analogy with the law of the woman suspected of adultery (Num. 5:11–31)./15/

It should be noted that CDC 9:13–16, the next law of the *Zadokite Fragments* (to be described presently), contains the law of the return of stolen property. This law is linguistically and conceptually based on Num. 5:5–10, which immediately precedes the law of the suspected adulteress. It is possible that the juxtaposition of passages in the Scriptures, similar to the Rabbinic *doreshim semukhin*,/16/ was a factor in Qumran legal exegesis. Yet further examples will have to be shown in Qumran literature before this principle can be accepted as operative.

Using Num. 5:11–31, the following details can be supplied concerning the oath procedure in this text. First, it is only because the owner claims that some (unidentified) member of the sect stole the property that the sectarians are adjured with the oath. (This is analagous to the suspicion and accusation by the husband.) It is doubtful that any cultic details such as those of Num. 5 would have been part of this rite, especially since the sect, despite arguments to the contrary, did not maintain a sacrificial cult at Qumran./17/ Further, the analogy need not be carried so far as to include every detail. The owner of the property would recite the oath at Qumran. This is clear although in the case of the adulterous woman, it was recited by the priest, not by the husband.

What was the nature of the "oath of adjuration?" In the case of the woman suspected of adultery, the oath (Num. 5:19–22) may be paraphrased as follows: If you are innocent of the alleged adultery, then you will be immune to the effects of the "water of bitterness that induces the spell."/18/

But if you are guilty, may the Lord make you a curse and imprecation among your people, may the water enter your body, and may the spell bring about its effects. The oath (*shevu'ah*) consisted of two parts. The first is the element of swearing, in this case that the woman did not commit adultery. The second is the *'alah*, the curse which will befall the woman if her oath is false./19/

The same scheme is to be applied in the case of the missing property. Those who are adjured by the oath are assenting not only to swearing that they do not know the location of the property, but also to the provision of the curse which will befall anyone who swears falsely. In view of the judicial function of the priesthood at Qumran, and the requirement that priests be part of the court, the oath was taken in the presence of a priest./20/

An extremely important question is how the sect could have considered the oath to have obligated the listeners when there is no indication of any response on their part. Here the parallel with Num. 5:22 supplies the answer. After hearing the imprecation or adjuration regarding the stolen property, those listening were required to respond *'amen 'amen*. No doubt the imprecation was of sufficient horror that no one would be willing to chance it for some stolen item. Therefore, the function of the oath would be the same as that of the case of suspected adultery. If any of the listeners were guilty, they would come forward. If they were not, the owner would go away certain that none of his fellow sectarians had stolen his property.

Jud. 17:1 provides interesting confirmation of the antiquity of this institution in Israel. It seems that Micaiah (Micah) had stolen 1100 pieces of silver from his mother. Not knowing who the thief was, she pronounced an oath of adjuration in his hearing, and he, therefore, was obligated to come forward and return the property./21/ As a sign that the curse should not apply to him, as he had heeded the conditions of the oath, she said, "Blessed be my son by the Lord."/22/ Y. Kaufmann's view that the money had only been borrowed by Micaiah/23/ is extremely unlikely in light of the conclusion of the story. His mother donated a portion of the money for her son to set up a cult place, but Micaiah loses "the graven image, the ephod, the teraphim, and the molten image (Jud. 18:18),"/24/ and his priest deserts him to minister to the Danites (Jud. 18). Clearly, the lesson of the story is that Micaiah was eventually robbed of the very same money which he had stolen from his mother./25/ Reference to this oath of adjuration appears to be made in Prov. 29:24/26/ and Zech. 5:1–4./27/

A parallel may perhaps be cited from the Middle Assyrian Laws (15–12 century B.C.). Section 47/28/ deals, among other things, with an eyewitness who made a statement and subsequently denied it. After investigation, an exorcist (*ašipu*) is brought who adjures the witness as follows:

> He (the King) will not absolve you from the oath (*mamitu*) which you were made to swear to the king and his son; it is in accordance with the wording of the tablet which you were made to swear to the king and his son that you are sworn.

Presumably, this adjuration was sufficient to cause the recalcitrant witness to testify./29/

Most probably, the tannaitic *shevu'at ha-'edut*, "the oath of testimony,"/30/ is historically related to the practice described in Lev. 5:1 and in our sectarian law./31/ Indeed, the *Sifra'* directly connects the *shevu'at ha-'edut* to Lev. 5:1./32/ The tannaim prescribed that if a litigant claimed that someone had testimony to give in a case regarding money or movable property,/33/ he could ask the recalcitrant witness to swear an oath that he had no relevant testimony. This oath was either sworn directly by the witness, or the litigant adjured the witness, and the witness responded *'amen*./34/ Such oaths might be taken in our out of court./35/ They were voluntary, and once taken, the oath absolved the witness from any further testimony. The Rabbis emphasized in several passages the obligation of an individual to testify if he possessed information relevant to the case./36/

While the tannaim required that the oath be taken by or administered only to those specifically claimed by the litigant to be witnesses in his case, it seems that the Qumran law envisioned the public recitation of the oath so as to obligate the entire community. Such an oath is invalid according M. Shevu'ot 4:10 which states that if one pronounces the *shevu'at ha-'edut* in a synagogue without intending specific witnesses, the oath is not binding./37/

While it is tempting to accept the tannaitic assumption that the *shevu'at ha-'edut* is derived from Lev. 5:1, whether historically or exegetically, consideration must also be given to a second possibility. It may be that the connection between Lev. 5:1 and the *shevu'at ha-'edut* is only the result of the tannaitic tendency to find biblical support for already existing laws./38/

It is still necessary to clarify the meaning of *we-'ashem*, "and he is guilty," in this text from the *Zadokite Fragments*. First, it should be noted that Lev. 5:1 reads, *we-nasa' 'awono*, "he shall bear his iniquity,"/39/ or "he is subject to punishment."/40/ In fact, examination of these terms in cultic, Priestly context shows them to be synonymous variants./41/ Perhaps *we-'ashem* was introduced into our passage under the influence of verses 2 and 3 and other occurrences in the same chapter of Leviticus. In any case, both phrases indicate an obligation to bring a sacrifice—which the tannaim later called the *qorban 'oleh we-yored*, the variable (literally "ascending and descending") offering./42/ This was a sacrifice that varied according to the economic status of the worshipper, allowing the less fortunate the opportunity to discharge his obligations within his means. The sect had withdrawn from participation in the Jerusalem sacrificial cult because of its disagreements with the priesthood./43/ This law, therefore, is probably an ideal prescription like so many laws found in Qumran literature as well as in the post-70 A.D. Rabbinic traditions. It is also possible that the sect believed that the penalty for this crime would be administered at the hands of heaven./44/ Parallels for such a view can be adduced from Rabbinic sources,/45/ despite the fact that the tannaitic *halakhah* viewed the violation of a *shevu'at ha-'edut* as entailing the bringing of the *qorban 'oleh we-yored*, the sacrifice described in Lev. 5:6–13.

Normally in biblical and Rabbinic law only unintentional transgressions could be expiated by bringing a sacrifice. Nevertheless, if an individual was adjured to testimony and swore falsely that he had nothing to testify, even intentionally, he was still obligated to offer the sacrifice. The tannaim understood this obligation to apply only in a case in which there were two witnesses to the oath./46/ The sect probably would have agreed with the tannaitic view that the bringing of a sacrifice was required only when there were at least two witnesses to the oath. After all, the sect did require two witnesses in financial matters./47/

2. *Medieval Parallels*

A well known medieval Jewish custom, which can be documented already in the Geonic period, allows a litigant to adjure anyone who has testimony on his behalf or who is in possession of his property to come forward and testify or return the property. Such adjurations (termed *ḥerem* in Hebrew) included awesome curses and were directed at the entire community, without specifying any particular party or parties. Many sources may be cited,/48/ but only two particular examples will be discussed here, since others have already alluded to them as subjects of comparison with this Qumran law.

Rabin calls attention to a medieval responsum/49/ which reports that after a shipwreck and subsequent looting, the communities (*ha-qehillot*) "made a decree with an adjuration and oath" (*gazeru gezerah ba-'alah u-va-shevu'ah*/50/) against anyone into whose hands the stolen property might come that he must return it to the owner. While the linguistic usage is similar to the text of the Dead Sea sect, the situation is somewhat different. In the responsum, the concern is not with requiring divulgence of the location of the property. The oath is taken to require *return* of the property. It serves to strengthen the commandment of *hashavat 'avedah*, "returning of lost property." The decree is by the communities; the owner is not involved. As the respondent explains, the practice is designed to avoid the receiver's claim that he is entitled to legal possession of the property/51/ and, hence, should be reimbursed. The communities' function here is based on the right of the court to annul ownership,/52/ in this case that of the receiver of stolen goods who claims he owns the property.

Following Ginzberg, Rabin also compares a similar practice mentioned by Maimonides./53/ According to Maimonides, the victim of theft can pronounce a ban (*ḥerem setam*/54/) against whoever removed the property from his house and does not admit it to the court. This practice has an important feature in common with the sectarian law in that it involves an oath made by the victim. It differs, though, in that Maimonides' ban affects only the thief, not a witness. The Qumran law under discussion, however, obligates *anyone* who knows about the missing property to come forward. It is interesting that the terms *ḥerem* and *'alah u-shevu'ah* seem to have been interchangeable in medieval *halakhah*, as they appear as synonymous variants in the responsum discussed here, and Maimonides uses *ḥerem* to describe his procedure.

Ginzberg maintains that this institution was already in existence in the amoraic period. He bases his conclusion on a story related in *Wa-Yiqra' Rabbah* 6:2 regarding the proclamation of such an oath in the synagogue by the *ḥazzan*./55/ While this is the reading of the printed edition, the manuscripts have the thief simply hear the coincidental reading of Lev. 5:1 from the Torah./56/ For this reason Ginzberg's early dating of this institution cannot be accepted.

V. Aptowitzer/57/ has noted the mention of similar oaths in Karaite *halakhah*. However, investigation of these sources shows that this procedure may be documented only beginning in the fourteenth century. It is well known that with time the Karaites began to accept more and more of the Rabbinic traditions./58/ Apparently, here also they were influenced by the medieval Rabbinite custom.

3. *Restoration in the Absence of an Owner*

Two forms of restoration of property are discussed explicitly in the *Zadokite Fragments*. The first is the case of one who wanted to make restitution, apparently after repentance, and could not locate the owner. Unless this offender was allowed to make restitution in some form, his atonement would have been impossible. Similar is the case of one who finds lost property and cannot fulfill the commandment of restoring it since he cannot locate or identify its rightful owner. Both of these cases are dealt with in CDC 9:13–16:

> כל אשם מושב אשר אין בעלים והתורה המישב לכהן והיה לו לבד
> מאיל האשם הכל וכן כל אבדה נ[מצ]את ואין לה בעלים והיתה
> לכהנים כי לא ידע מוציאה את משפטה אם לא נמצא לה בעלים הם
> ישמרו

> (Regarding) every amount to be repaid/59/ which does not have an owner,/60/ the one making restitution/61/ shall confess/62/ to the priest/63/ and everything/64/ shall be his (the priest's) except/65/ for the ram of the guilt-offering./66/ And likewise any lost object/67/ which has been found/68/ and has no owner shall go to/69/ the priests, for its finder/70/ does not know the regulation pertaining to it./71/ If no owner is found for it, they (the priests)/72/ shall guard it./73/

The problem of how to make restitution in cases in which the rightful owner of property cannot be located or identified is treated in the first part of this passage. The wording of this law shows unquestionably that it is based on Num. 5:6–8. The biblical passage begins by stating the general requirement of restitution in cases of unjust gain (*ma'al*). It then proceeds to discuss the specific problem of the case in which there is no one to whom to make restitution. Note that the Qumran law omits the general case, choosing only to discuss the specific problem. No doubt the Qumran sect saw no need to recapitulate the obligation of restitution, as biblical law was sufficiently clear in this regard.

Numbers, however, did not specify the offenses committed (*ḥaṭṭat*, *ma'al*) for which the principal plus a penalty of one-fifth and a sacrifice are required or to whom the confession is made. A clearer definition of the offenses involved can be gleaned from Lev. 5:21–26. Early biblical exegetes already recognized that Num. 5:6–8 and Lev. 5:21–26 described the same institution./74/ Modern biblical scholars have likewise seen these passages as parallel. The sect cannot have failed to notice the numerous linguistic affinities between these two passages. The influence of the latter passage on the Qumran law is probably to be seen in the words *'avedah ni*[*mṣ*]*et . . . moṣi'ah*. (The only other occurrence in the Bible of *'avedah* with the root *mṣ'* is in Deut. 22:3 which is discussed below.)

This Qumran law does not indicate the offenses for which one must make restitution. The parallel in Lev. 5:21–23 specifies the following offenses: "If anyone sins and commits a breach of faith against the Lord by deceiving his neighbor in a matter of deposit or security, or through robbery, or if he has oppressed his neighbor or has found what was lost and lied about it, swearing falsely. . . ."/75/ Certainly, these offenses are those for which the *Zadokite Fragments* prescribe restitution.

The violations alluded to in Lev. 5:21–23 have been studied by J. Milgrom./76/ His general thesis is that the *'asham* sacrifice, which he translates "reparation offering," is brought as a result of "sancta desecration." In the case of these two passages the sanctum desecrated is God's name in which an oath has been taken. Each of the offenses of Lev. 5:21–23 involves a false oath. Milgrom's translation embodies his interpretation: "When a person sins by committing a trespass against the Lord in that he has dissembled to his fellow in the matter of a deposit or investment or robbery; or having withheld from his fellow or having found a lost object he has dissembled about it; and he swears falsely about one of the things that man may do and sin thereby . . . (Lev. 5:21f.)."/77/ By "withholding" Milgrom refers to one who distrains property or illegally withholds wages.

We do not know if the sect looked upon all the offenses of Lev. 5:21f. as involving oath violations, even if Milgrom is correct that this is the actual meaning of the biblical text. Milgrom notes that Philo/78/ adopted the same interpretation. Indeed, Philo is here in accord with some tannaitic views./79/ Since, in previous studies, so many parallels between the law of Philo, the tannaim, and the Dead Sea Scrolls have been noted, it is probable that the Dead Sea sect would have regarded the offenses of Lev. 5:21f. as all involving false oaths.

It is now possible to define the expression *'asham mushav* as an amount repaid to make restitution for taking a false oath. The oath was sworn dishonestly in order to retain possession of a deposit, an investment, stolen property, withheld or distrained property, or a lost object. CDC 9:10–12, the law immediately preceeding this in the *Zadokite Fragments*,/80/ deals with the use of oaths of adjuration to recover stolen property. Indeed, line 8 contains the subject heading, *'al ha-shevu'ah*, "regarding the oath," which would seem to be additional confirmation for the view that the sect regarded all the offenses of Lev. 5:21f. as involving false oaths.

The sectarian law has replaced the words *we-'im 'en la-'ish go'el*, "If the man has no kinsman (lit. 'redeemer')"/81/ with *'asher 'en be'alim*, "which has no owner." The sect took the passage in Num. 5:8 to mean, "if the man (finder) has no redeemer (i.e. owner) to whom to make restitution. . . ." This constitutes a clever solution to a problem which plagued the Rabbis. Can it be possible for any Jew to have no relative? All Israel are in fact relatives. The tannaim concluded, therefore, that Num. 5:6–8 refers only to the convert who has died leaving no heirs./82/ In order to make possible expiation in such cases, say the Rabbis, the Torah specified return to the priest.

A further difficulty arises as to whether our passage from the *Zadokite Fragments* intends to say that the confession should be made to the priest. In accord with this view it may be translated: "the one making restitution shall confess to the priest." It is also possible to translate: "the one making restitution to the priest shall confess." In this case the confession would be private.

Confession was a normal part of the procedure for offering a sacrifice./83/ Since most sacrifices were offered on account of transgressions, confession was necessary if the offering was to bring about atonement. Talmudic law is usually understood as having required private confession. Indeed, many Rabbinic sources seem to oppose public confession of sins./84/ However, the detailed account of the sacrifices for the Day of Atonement found in the Mishnah, tractate Yoma', describes how the High Priest would make his confession, and the people would respond with a doxology./85/ Apparently, the confessional formula he recited was audible to those present. If so, it is possible that the formula was to be said aloud in connection with all sacrifices. The Talmudic passages which appear to oppose public confession would be protesting against the public specification of actual transgressions,/86/ not against the recital of formulary confessions such as those known from halakhic sources./87/ Indeed, such confessionary formulae appear in CDC 20:28–30 and DSD 1:24–2:1./88/ The confession recited in connection with the restitution of property must have been similar in form.

L. Ginzberg/89/ has cited a passage from *Midrash Tadshe'*/90/ which expresses the idea that confessions which accompanied expiatory sacrifices were made in the presence of the officiating priest. This passage may, therefore, be an accurate representation of Temple procedure in the Second Temple period. If so, Ginzberg/91/ would be right in pointing to the place of public confession in the Christian tradition and noting that this rite may have its origins in the procedure followed in the Temple.

The term *'eyl ha-'asham* ("ram of the guilt-offering") in the Qumran law replaces and is synonymous with *'eyl ha-kippurim* ("ram of expiation")/92/ of Num. 5:8. *'Eyl ha-'asham* is clearly a reflex of Lev. 5:25 which had so profound an influence on the sectarian explanation of Num. 5:6–8./93/

The sect took the view that even when the sacrifice could not be performed, the priest could be the agent for the return of the "amount repaid." Thus, although the sect had withdrawn from the Jerusalem cult and its sacrifices, the priests at Qumran did serve as agents for the return of ownerless property. The abstention from sacrificial offerings (of which there no longer can be any question) was regarded, however, as temporary—only until such time as the sect, in the end of days, would take control of the "new Jerusalem."/94/

Ginzberg claims that in this respect the sect is in agreement with the tannaitic *halakhah* that return of the money is not precluded by the absence of a simultaneous sacrificial offering./95/ Indeed, M. Bava' Qamma' 9:12 indicates that in the event the money was returned to the priest and the sacrifice not successfully offered, the act of restitution is considered valid, and the property is legally the possession of the priest.

On the other hand, Ginzberg has failed to distinguish the context of the tannaitic ruling from that of the sect. The tannaim applied the biblical verses only to the case of the restitution of the property of a proselyte. Further, their ruling here was applicable only after the fact (*be-di-'avad*), whereas the sect's law outlines the correct legal procedure (*le-khatḥillah*).

Indeed, Rabbinic *halakhah* did not face explicitly the question of how to deal with this law in the absence of a Temple. Medieval codes of Jewish law omit this topic entirely. The only exception is Maimonides/96/ who, as is well known, included in his *Mishneh Torah* even laws practicable only in Temple times. However, Maimonides in large part repeats the laws of the Mishnah without dealing with the issue posed by the destruction of the Temple. Apparently, he believed that this law applied only in Temple times.

Karaite law dealt with the matter explicitly. Some suggested giving the money to the poor, others to the synagogue, and a third view allowed the thief to keep it, assuming repentance (without restitution) to be sufficient to bring about expiation for the offense./97/

Neither the Karaites nor the Rabbinites, then, apportioned such property to the priests after the destruction of the Temple. Indeed, this is the general tendency regarding priestly dues and portions in the post-destruction period. Rather than allowing the priests to make use of them, these portions are by and large left unused, even though it remains forbidden for an Israelite to eat them. Apparently, the connection of the priest and Temple was such that in the absence of the Temple the priest lost the legal right to make use of his priestly portions.

The word *ha-kol* ("everything"), found in our text but in neither of the biblical antecedents, indicates, according to Ginzberg/98/ and Rabin,/99/ that the priest received not only the principal to be repaid but also the added fine of one-fifth. While no specific evidence can be marshalled for this assumption, it seems most reasonable. A similar view is taken by the tannaim in M. Bava' Qamma' 9:11. Ginzberg, however, notes that some Karaites allot to the priest only the principal and not the added fifth./100/

An interesting question is how the added fifth was to be calculated. Tannaitic sources are divided on the question. The dominant view, and that accepted as *halakhah* by the medieval authorities, provided that the added sum constitute one-fifth of the total. In other words, the quantity to be added was actually one-fourth of the principal. On the other hand, a minority view interpreted the text more literally and therefore required that one-fifth be added, so that the added sum would constitute only one-sixth of the total./101/

The content of the first clause may now be summarized. If a person makes a false oath regarding the cases listed in Lev. 5:21f. and must make restitution, but finds that it is impossible to locate or identify the owner, he makes restitution to the priest, confesses (perhaps in the presence of the priest), and gives the priest not only the principal but the added fifth as well. Num. 5:6–8 has clearly been interpreted by the sect in light of Lev. 5:21–26. The derivation of this law, then, is an example of legal *midrash*.

4. *Restoration of Lost Objects*

It is now time to turn to the second clause. Here the text singles out a lost object and indicates that if ownerless, it should be given to the priests who will keep watch over it, presumably until the owner is either located or comes to claim his property.

Above, the use of the root *mṣ'* with the noun *'avedah* in Lev. 5:22f. was noted. The only other occurrence of this combination is in Deut. 22:3 which deals with lost objects. A distinction must immediately be drawn. Whereas the law of Lev. 5:21–26 concerns one who took a false oath in order to retain lost property illegally, Deut. 22:1–3 deals simply with the obligation to return lost property and with, as well, the case of property whose owner cannot be identified or located. There is no question here of a false oath. Even so, the sect interpreted Deut. 22:1–3 in light of Num. 5:6–8. The two clauses of the Qumran text, then, are connected not only in content (the lost object) but also in exegetical derivation (Num. 5:6–8).

The sect has modified the law of Deut. 22:1–3 to accord with that of Num. 5:6–8. Whereas Deuteronomy envisaged the finder's taking the property to his house and keeping it with him until the owner might claim it, the sect assigned such property to the priests. The tannaim, however, understood the phrase *'el tokh betekha* (Deut. 22:2) to stipulate that the finder was to take the property into his own house, "and not into the house of another."/102/ Here the sect and the Rabbis are certainly in disagreement.

Further, this law gives an explanation of why the sect chose to assign the property to the priests—"for its finder does not know the regulation pertaining to it." The sect must have had a complex series of rules regarding the disposition of found property. The tannaim discuss in detail specific categories of found objects which require special attention./103/ Among them are: animals which must be fed, books, clothing, and household vessels of semiprecious and precious metals. The sect apparently was concerned that lay members would be unable to determine the proper care to be given to the objects they had found, and, hence, entrusted these items to the priests. As this is the only law economically favoring the priests of Qumran, it is unlikely that this prescription should be considered a result of priestly political power./104/

It is also possible that the sect, like Josephus (or his source) was concerned that through either inadvertence or temptation, the finder would fail to try to return the property to its original owner. It appears that according to Josephus an oath had to be taken by the finder to the effect that he had not appropriated the property of another./105/

How could the sect be so bold as to modify biblical legislation so substantially? Only one suggestion can be made. The sect interpreted *betekha* of Deut. 22:2 to mean the Temple. Ample justification for the use of *bayit* for the Temple, usually in the combinations *bet 'adonai* and *bet 'elohim*, can be cited from Scripture./106/ Nonetheless, such an interpretation of Deut. 22:2 would be quite radical in view of the following phrase, *we-hayah 'immekha*, "it shall remain with you."/107/ It is possible that the sect took the word *'immekha*, "with you," in a collective sense. As such, they would still be fulfilling the words of the Torah if the priests, as representatives of the community, were to hold the lost object. Having found support for the idea that the lost item be given to the sanctuary, it was only one short step for the Qumranites, who had themselves withdrawn from the Temple and its cult, to assign such a role to the priests.

It is doubtful that the sect actually derived this second clause from exegesis. Rather, the sectarians seems to have started with the idea that the lost property should be entrusted to the priests and perhaps used an exegesis of *bayit* to support this conclusion. Such a process would be an example of what the amoraim later called *'asmakhta'*, the finding of Scriptural support for previously held views.

Rabin draws attention to an important aspect of this law. According to tannaitic *halakhah* certain lost objects, lacking specific signs identifying them, can be claimed immediately by the finder. The finding of objects with distinctive signs must be announced publicly so that the owner may claim them./108/ The amoraim correctly realized that the basic factor operating here is a psychological one. They used the term *ye'ush*, "giving up hope," to describe the reaction of one who lost an object lacking a distinctive sign. On the other hand, they assumed that one who lost an object with a mark to distinguish it, would give up hope of recovering it much more slowly. The tannaitic law, as understood by the amoraim, assumed, therefore, that at the point at which the loser gave up hope of recovery, the object became ownerless (*hefqer*), and could be claimed by the finder. The sect, in requiring that all lost objects he kept indefinitely by the priests for safekeeping, seemed to lack this entire concept, considered by the amoraim to be biblical./109/

Rabin's analysis is supported by the use of the verb *šmr*, "to guard, watch," in the Qumran text. This verb, as used in biblical and Rabbinic legal contexts, denotes one who takes care of another's property and who, therefore, takes a degree of responsibility for it. The Mishnah classifies the various types of bailees (*shomerin*) and their degree of responsibility toward the owner./110/ These regulations are seen by the tannaim as deriving from Ex. 22:6–14. It is probable, therefore, that the use of this verb (*yishmero*) in our passage indicates that the priests at Qumran were to hold the object as bailees, until such time as a claim for repossession might arise.

Ginzberg has suggested the possibility that the clause *ki lo' . . . yishmero* which appears at the end of the text might be a later addition to the law./111/ As the text now stands, Ginzberg sees an inherent contradiction in it. Whereas *we-khen* ("and thus") at the beginning of the second part would normally mean that what follows is similar to or the same as that which precedes it, the text goes on to state a completely different ruling in the second part. Because of the use of *we-khen*, the reader would have expected that the law for the lost object in the second part would have been the same as that for the object dishonestly gained in the first part. Nevertheless, while the first part allows the priests to take full possession of the property, the second provides that they serve as bailees only. Therefore, theorizes Ginzberg, the law originally stated that the object was to become the possession of the priests in both cases. This he sees as the original Qumran ruling. At some point in the sect's history, the law was modified to render the priests simply guardians of the property of some unidentified owner. At this point, the final clause (*ki lo' . . . yishmero*) was added in accord with the new ruling.

This interpretation is ingenious and highlights an important issue in the study of these texts: the possibility that as in Rabbinic legal texts, there may be layers of development behind the material as it has come down to us. This possibility is especially to be reckoned with in the case of the *Zadokite Fragments*, known to us both from Qumran and the Cairo *genizah*. We have no way of tracing the literary history of the *genizah* recension and, until parallel passages are available from both corpuses, we cannot be sure to what extent medieval scribes may have altered the text.

In this particular law, it is probable, however, that *we-khen* is simply a reflex of Deut. 22:3 "*we-khen ta'aseh . . . we-khen ta'aseh . . . we-khen ta'aseh le-khol 'avedat 'aḥikha 'asher to'vad mi-mennu u-meṣa'tah.*" This verse has clearly left its imprint on the formulation of this law, and there is no reason not to credit the threefold appearance of *we-khen* in the verse with its occurrence in our passage.

Further, Ginzberg's theory would have the sect in its earlier stage permanently appropriate to the priests all lost property the owner of which could not be immediately located. While it was possible to see how Scriptural basis could be found for the storage of an item with the priests rather than with the finder, it is difficult to contemplate how the sect would have circumvented the injunction of Deut. 22:2 to keep the property only "until your brother requests it, at which time you shall return it to him."

The hermeneutical approach of our Qumran passage is very much akin to that of the tannaitic *gezerah shawah.* This exegetical device involves drawing an analogy between verses based on similar words or phrases. This method allowed our text to begin with Num. 5:6–8 which is interpreted in light of Lev. 5:21–26. It then proceeded to use the Numbers passage to explain and considerably modify Deut. 22:1–3. This series of legal *midrashim* is bolstered by the linguistic similarities in the verses. While the conclusions the sect reached from this exegesis were often at odds with those of the later Rabbis, the use of this exegetical method may be considered a basic point of similarity.

5. *Summary*

The Dead Sea sect interpreted the difficult Lev. 5:1 by drawing an analogy with the law of the suspected adulteress. This *midrash* supplied them with a procedure of adjuration for locating stolen property and, in most cases, identifying the thief. It seems from biblical and comparative evidence that the procedure which the sectarians followed was already known in the biblical period. By tannaitic times it had developed into the *shevu'at ha-'edut*, "the oath of testimony." In medieval times a procedure much closer to that of the sect is attested in the Jewish legal tradition. But, as is so often the case with Qumran traditions and their later counterparts, there is no way of knowing if there is any direct historical connection between them.

Num. 5:6–8 was understood by the sect in light of Lev. 5:21–26 to indicate that in cases in which through false oaths or dishonest practices a person had illegally retained possession of the property of another, restitution was required, even if the owner could not be located. In such cases, after confession of his transgression in the presence of the priest, the now penitent sectarian was to make restitution to the priest, who became the rightful owner of the restored property. On the other hand, Deut. 22:1–3 was interpreted in light of Num. 5:6–8 to require, in the case of lost property the owner of which cannot be found, that the priests be entrusted with the property as temporary bailees or guardians, to hold the property until such time as the owner shall claim it.

NOTES

/1/ *Waw* of opposition. CDC 9:8–10, discussed above, 38f., prohibited the taking of unauthorized oaths, "but," in the view of the sect, the oath described in our law is mandated by the Torah, and, hence, permitted.

/2/ On the use of this root in CDC 10:22f., see *HAQ*, 98 n. 91. There I translated the occurrence in our passage as "lost." I have corrected the translation to "missing" here because "lost" has the connotation of accidental misplacing whereas our law deals with theft. The use of the root *'bd*, "to be lost," is found in reference to property in Deut. 22:3; cf. 1 Sam. 9:3, 20; Jer. 50:6; Ezek. 34:4, 16; Ps. 119:176. In none of these passages, however, is the thing missing presumed or shown to have been stolen.

/3/ So Segal. Schechter had emended to *mi-mo'ed*, "from the Tent" of Meeting. Segal also notes that emending to *be-mo'ed* and taking this word with what follows, we could understand that the oath is to be taken in the "synagogue." (He cites Ps. 74:8; cf. Job 20:23 for *mo'ed* meaning synagogue. Neither passage is very convincing. M. Soṭah 9:15, *bet wa'ad*, is a *bet midrash* [So I. Lipschutz, *Tiferet Yisra'el*] as can be seen from M. 'Avot 1:4.) He would translate "then in the *Meeting-place* of the camp in which the theft has been committed. . . ." This explanation has the advantage of giving meaning to the otherwise difficult *'asher gunnav bo*. (Segal, *ad loc.* and "Notes," 135.) Ginzberg, *Sect*, 41, also rejects Schechter's emendation, noting that *mo'ed* cannot be used for *'ohel mo'ed* and that the latter phrase could not be used to mean anything other than what it means in the Bible. He states that the use of *me'od* for "property" is biblical and Rabbinic. It would be more correct to say that the Rabbis (see M. Berakhot 9:5) were aware of the biblical usage of *me'od* for "property." No such usage by the Rabbis themselves is attested in the lexica. For *me'od*, Rabin cites Deut. 6:5 as understood by Targumim, Peshiṭta (cf. to 2 K. 23:25), possibly LXX, M. Berakhot 9:5 (midrashic). So also Rashi. That Gk. δυνάμεώς in LXX to Deut. 6:5 can mean property (in the sense of possessions) is quite doubtful. The meaning, "property, quality," listed by H. Liddell and R. Scott, *A Greek-English Lexicon* (1968), is clearly irrelevant to our passage. Rabin is probably correct in noting that *mwdh* (MS f *m'dh*) should be understood as *me'odo*, "his power," in DSD 10:16. Licht gives this as a second interpretation of the text of 1QS and primary interpretation for the variant. Rabin feels that "power" must also be the meaning in CDC 12:10. Yet there *be-khol me'odo* might mean "at any cost" to the purchaser or "any of his property," i.e. the seller's. Ben Sira 7:30 is probably a reflex of the biblical use of *me'od*, "property."

/4/ This means the sectarian settlement and presumably refers to those scattered throughout the land, mentioned in CDC 12:24 (restored), 13:20, 14:3. See Rubinstein,

"Urban Halakhah," 283–296. According to Ginzberg, a second *ha-maḥaneh* has been omitted through haplography. The text would then mean, "If a man has lost something and does not know who has stolen it—the lost article—from the property of the camp, he shall adjure the camp . . ." (translation from *Sect*, 41). If this emendation were correct, we would require *'et* before the second *ha-maḥaneh* as it would be the direct object of the verb *yashbia'*. *'Et* could not be omitted in this case because the object precedes the verb.

/ 5/ *Pu'al*, third person, sing. Cf. Ex. 22:6 (and Job 4:12). This clause seems to be extraneous. Ginzberg, however, takes this as *ha-ganav*, "the thief," and would render (including his emendation discussed above, n. 4), "he shall adjure the camp in which the thief abides." While this view is attractive, it depends on his emendation which is itself highly speculative.

/ 6/ *Be'alim*, the pl., is used often in the Bible for an "owner." In Mishnaic Hebrew, the pl. is *required* for this meaning.

/ 7/ The phrase is from Num. 5:21. Cf. Dan. 9:11 and Neh. 10:30. Schechter's emendation to *yashmia'*, "he shall announce," is not acceptable in light of the biblical source of our phrase (cf. Segal). For the ancient versions and modern translations of this phrase, see H. C. Brichto, *The Problem of "Curse" in the Hebrew Bible* (1968), 50 n. 55. On the usage of the roots *'lh* and *šb'*, see Brichto, 22–71 and 215–218.

/ 8/ Taken from Lev. 5:1 (Schechter) which Targum Pseudo-Jonathan understood as a reference to false oaths (Rabin). Note that our text replaces *we-nasa' 'awono* of Lev. with *we-'ashem* (found in Lev. 5:2, 3). See below. The practice cited by Schechter from B. Bava' Meṣi'a' 28b deals with the obligation of the finder of a lost object to make known his find. In tannaitic times finds were announced first at the Temple and then, after 70 A.D. in synagogues and schools. In Jerusalem, finder and loser would meet at a special location called *'even ṭo'in* (so MS Munich, cf. *DS*, *ad loc.*).

/ 9/ Deut. 22:3.

/10/ So Rashi, Naḥmanides, following the Rabbinic tradition (for which see below, n. 26). The Targum Pseudo-Jonathan and Philo take this verse differently. Targum Pseudo-Jon. translates that if a person saw someone else, or otherwise knew that someone had violated an oath, and he does not come forward, he (the witness) is guilty of the transgression himself. Philo, *Special Laws* II, 26 (ed. Colson, 323) presents essentially the same law adding that the prospective witness is prevented from coming forward by friendship, shame, or fear. At first, Belkin, 152, states that "this law has no basis in the Bible." In citing the Rabbinic parallels to this view Belkin notes that the Rabbis derived their view from interpretation of Lev. 5:1. He then seems (153) to castigate B. Ritter (*Philo und die Halacha* [1879], 47f.) for his view that Philo based his statement on a misunderstanding of Lev. 5:1. It seems, then, that Belkin has come full circle and accepts the notion that Philo's law is a result of "midrashic" exegesis of Lev. 5:1. I. Heinemann, *Philons griechische und jüdische Bildung* (1962), 94, takes the view that this Philonic law is the result of the influence of the LXX to Lev. 5:1, and he notes that it is in contrast to the usual Rabbinic principle that sins of omission are not subject to judicial action. Colson, in his note to *Special Laws* II, 26, suggests that "Philo takes the Greek word for adjuration as = '(false) swearing.'" The analysis of Cohen, 748–750 reads too much into Philo's words. He sees Philo as referring specifically to one who hears another utter an oath to the effect that he has no relevant testimony when, in fact, he does. Yet Philo speaks only of one who hears a false oath and does not specify at all the kind or subject of the oath. It is apparent that this Philonic law is actually the result of interpretation of Lev. 5:1, as is found in the Targum Pseudo-Jonathan. Indeed, the same view is expressed in the 13–14th century Yemenite *Midrash Ha-Gadol* of David ben Amram Adani to Lev. 5:1 (ed. Steinsaltz, p. 109). It is not possible that Adani had even indirect access to the Philonic tradition, and so it appears that his interpretation is based on the Targum Pseudo-Jonathan. Targum Neofiti and some late Rabbinic sources take this verse as referring to one who hears another blaspheming and does not report it to the authorities. He is considered to bear the same guilt as the blasphemer (reading *ḥeruf* in Neofiti, rejecting the marginal reading which is probably the result of an effort to harmonize the text with that of Targum Pseudo-Jonathan). For the blasphemy motif, see also *Midrash Tanḥuma'* to Leviticus, 4b–5a, ed. Buber, 5a, sec. 14. Cf. also Cohen, 750f. (For the use of *ḥakham* in the sense of a single expert judge [*mumḥeh*] as used in *Tanḥuma'*, see T. Yevamot 4:7.) An additional case of being punished for knowing someone else violated an oath is found in *Pirqe Rabbi 'Eli'ezer* chap. 38 in regard to the story of Achan in Josh. 6–7 (assuming *ḥerem* and *shevu'ah* to be identical as the Rabbis do, on which see below). For the above views, see Ch. Albeck, "*Halakhah Ḥiṣonah Be-Targume 'Ereṣ Yisra'el U-Va-'Aggadah,*" *Sefer Ha-Yovel Le-Doqṭor Binyamin Menasheh Lewin Le-Yovelo Ha-Shishim*, ed. J. L. Fishman (1939), 97–99; and Belkin, 151–153. Noth, *Leviticus*, 44 suggests that the verse refers to one who hears someone unlawfully utter a curse and does not report it, and, therefore, incriminates himself. He seems to have been influenced by the above explanations. Luzzatto takes the verse as referring to one who swears falsely. He explains that such a person is referred to as "hearing" the oath since the person swearing would only answer *'amen* after the oath was recited by another. He compares Num. 5:22. This interpretation is impossible, however, as it would make this verse a repetition of Lev. 5:20–26 (the very same chapter) which deals with false oaths. Cf. also the analysis and comment on this verse in Brichto, 43. For a strange treatment, see A. Spiro, "A Law on the Sharing of Information," *PAAJR* 28 (1959), 95–101. Jackson, *Theft*, 220f. sees the original context of Lev. 5:1 as referring to the "unknown thief" and therefore interprets our passage as maintaining the "original significance" of Lev. 5:1.

/11/ Cohen, 747, takes the view that "theft was chosen as an example because it was not uncommon." From this, it can be deduced that he assumes that testimonial oaths, like the Rabbinic *shevu'at ha-'edut* (discussed below) were practiced at Qumran in other cases as well. There is no evidence for this, but some extension of the practice to other matters would seem likely. A fundamental question is whether the sect limited its use of oaths to money matters, like the tannaim, or if they extended it to all legal problems, as do the Karaites (on which see below).

/12/ On this law see M. Fishbane, "Accusations of Adultery: A Study of Law and Scribal Practice in Numbers 5:11–31," *HUCA* 45 (1974), 25–45.

/13/ See above, 91.

/14/ On *midrash* at Qumran, see *HAQ*, 54–60.

/15/ A similar analogy between Lev. 5:1 and the woman suspected of adultery is made in *Wa-Yiqra' Rabbah* 6:4, as a result of the connection between *qol 'alah*

(Lev. 5:1) and *shevu'at ha-'alah* (Num. 5:21). The statement is attributed to Rabbi Yose bar Ḥanina, a second generation Palestinian amora (H. Strack, *Introduction to the Talmud and Midrash* [1965], 123) from the second half of the third century. On his relationship to R. Yoḥanan, see "Yose bar Ḥanina," *EJ* 16 (1971), 850.

/16/ See Bacher, *'Erkhe Midrash* I, 91; II, 246f.

/17/ The debate revolves around the discovery at Qumran of animal bones deposited between large sherds or in jars. For detailed discussion see below, 200f.

/18/ So new JPS.

/19/ Brichto, 24f., 215. For the connection of the oath and curse in Rabbinic literature and in the Hellenistic world, see Lieberman, *Greek*, 121f. and Belkin, 146. The phrase *shevu'at ha-'alah* in Num. 5:21 served for the tannaim to indicate that all oaths had to include both the oath and curse (*'alah*). See *Sifre* Num. 14 and the sources in Lieberman. Lieberman also quotes some opinions to the effect that in the case of the woman suspected of adultery, a curse alone was valid. Cf. also Malbim to Lev. 5:1, and Cohen, 751 n. 72.

/20/ See above, 26–28.

/21/ So Ibn Ezra to Lev. 5:1; Rashi, Abravanel and Kimchi to Jud. 17:2; Burney and Moore to Jud. 17:2; and Cohen, 743. See also Brichto, 45 n. 44 for ancient and modern translations and the study of H. Gevaryahu, "*Bet Ha-'Elohim shel Mikhah Be-Har 'Efrayim U-Massa' Bene Dan*," *'Iyyunim Be-Sefer Shofeṭim* (1966), 547–584.

/22/ So RSV to Jud. 17:2. See Brichto, 45 and A. Ehrlich, *Mikra Ki-Pheschuto* (1899–1901), to Jud. 17:2. The words *we-'atah 'ashivenu lakh* in v. 3 logically belong after *'ani leqaḥtiw* of v. 2 and are part of Micaiah's admission and statement that he will return the money.

/23/ *Sefer Shofeṭim* (1968), 269.

/24/ So RSV.

/25/ So Gevaryahu, 547.

/26/ See Brichto, 43f. and n. 43. T. Bava' Qamma' 7:13 does refer to this verse in connection with the oath of testimony as does the parallel in *Mekhilta' De-Rabbi Ishmael* 13 (ed. Horovitz-Rabin, p. 295). Cf. also *Tanḥuma'* Lev. 7 (ed. Buber, p. 14) which also quotes this verse in connection with explaining Lev. 5:1 (all cited by Cohen, 747 n. 55).

/27/ See Brichto, 68f. and his nn. 80, 81.

/28/ *ANET*, 184. Cf. also G. R. Driver, J. C. Miles, *The Assyrian Laws* (1935), 128, 458, and the treatment of G. Cardascia, *Les Lois Assyriennes* (1969), 230–236.

/29/ Brichto, 42 n. 40 cites additional ancient Near Eastern parallels for the public proclamation. He acknowledges, however, that these cases do not involve imprecations. Much Greek material has been surveyed in Cohen, 745–750. These parallels, however, supply only an understanding of how Greek law saw the obligation of testimony and recalcitrant witnesses. This material does not, however, contribute to the understanding of our passage.

/30/ On this oath see Ch. Albeck, *Shishah Sidre Mishnah, Neziqin* (1959), 240, 242, and Cohen, 751–754. This oath is the topic of M., P., and B. Shevu'ot 4.

/31/ This is the view of Cohen, 751.

/32/ *Sifra'* Dibbura' De-Ḥovah (Wa-Yiqra', ed. Weiss, p. 22b). Cf. B. *Shevu'ot* 35a.

/33/ Cf. Cohen, 752f.

/34/ See Cohen, 751 n. 73 for classical parallels.

/35/ Cf. M. Shevu'ot 4:1.

/36/ T. Shevu'ot 3:2; B. Bava' Qamma' 56a; and Tosafot, *ad loc.* (and B. Epstein, *Torah Temimah* to Lev. 5:1, n. 27); *Sifra'* Qedoshim (ed. Weiss, p. 89a); B. Pesaḥim 113a (and *DS, ad loc.*); Cohen, 748; M. Sanhedrin 4:5. Note that T. Bava' Qamma' 3:4 emphasizes the application of this obligation to capital offenses as well. For medieval sources, see Cohen, 752 n. 75.

/37/ M. Shevu'ot 4:10; P. Shevu'ot 4:7 (ed. Krot. 4:10, 35d). Cf. Maimonides, H. Shevu'ot 9:9; and Albeck, *Neziqin*, 513 ("*Hashlamot We-Tiqqunim*" to M. Shevu'ot 4:10). The words *'ad she-yehe' mitkawwen lahem* in some Mishnah texts and in that of the Babylonian Talmud must be an explanatory gloss of later origin as they are omitted in ed. Naples, MS Kaufmann, MS Munich, ed. Lowe, and the Mishnah text in the Palestinian Talmud editions, MS Paris, MS Parma de Rossi 138, MS Parma de Rossi 984. MS Florence includes the clause *'ad she-yitkawwen lahem* in its Mishnah text. For other readings omitting the clause, see S. Adani, *Mele'khet Shelomoh, ad loc.* Our *mishnah* appears as well in *Sifra'* Ḥovah (ed. Weiss, p. 22b) and the reading in the printed texts as well as in MSS Vatican Assemani 66 (Finkelstein 99) and Vatican Ebr. 31 (Makor ed., p. 43, 22a in the penciled numbers on the MS) includes *'ad she-yehe' mitkawwen lahem.* It is common for material in the Mishnah or Tosefta to appear as well in the *Sifra'*. Epstein suggests that this relationship is due to the fact that the *Sifra'* emanates from the school of Rabbi Judah the Prince who carried on the traditions of Akiva. He specifically cites our *mishnah* as an example of this phenomenon. (Epstein, *Mavo' Le-Nusaḥ Ha-Mishnah* II, 728–731). If so, it is possible that the *Sifra'* here included a very early explanatory gloss on our *mishnah* which later entered into the text of the Mishnah. In studying Sifra' *Nega'im* and *Meṣora'*, however, Neusner, *Purities* VII, 4–7 (cf. 226–231) concludes that "both documents draw upon late first and second-century materials, which themselves attained the form now before us before inclusion in either compilation" (p. 7). If so, the explanatory gloss of which we have spoken would have already appeared in the version of the statement incorporated into the *Sifra'*.

/38/ We have noted (n. 37) that the *Sifra'* to Lev. 5:1 may be dependent on the Mishnah. This need not imply that the derivation of the law from Lev. 5:1 is also secondary. It may be that a law was derived from the Bible and then formulated as a *mishnah.* At a later stage that *mishnah* was adapted into the context of the tannaitic *midrashim.*

/39/ So RSV.

/40/ So new JPS. For this expression, see the detailed survey of Cohen, 740–744.

/41/ Noth, *Leviticus*, 44.

/42/ See Lev. 5:5–13; M. Shevu'ot 4:2; M. Horayot 2:7; M. Keritot 2:4. So Cohen, 744.

/43/ According to CDC 6:11–14 the sectarians agreed to abstain from entering the Temple (*ha-miqdash*) because of the priests' not following the proper specifications of the Law (*perush ha-torah*). This was apparently part of their oath of entrance to the sect.

/44/ Cf. *HAQ*, 78, 88.

/45/ T. Shevu'ot 3:1 (the view of R. Judah ben Bathyra); Belkin, 146 and n. 25; cf. Cohen, 743 and n. 37. D. Pardo, *Ḥasde Dawid, ad loc.* states that the view of R. Judah ben Bathyra is not found elsewhere [in Rabbinic literature]. He says that R. Judah disagrees with the Mishnaic view that obligates bringing a sacrifice for purposeful violations of the *shevu'at ha-'edut*. R. Judah thinks that the sacrifice is brought only for accidental violations (*shogeg*) and that in cases of purposeful violations the penalty is death at the hands of heaven (*mitah bi-yede shamayim*). Rabbi Judah ben Bathyra's view is in contrast to that of all tannaim and amoraim.

/46/ M. Shevu'ot 4:2, 3, 11. The reading *'amar li-shenayim* in *mishnah* 3 would seem to be a result of explanatory tendencies. Original is most probably the reading *la-'edim* of MSS Kaufmann, Paris, Parma de Rossi 138, Parma de Rossi 984, Florence, Munich, eds. Naples and Lowe, ed. Venice of the Palestinian Talmud, Alfasi, Rosh, as well as a *baraita'* in B. Shevu'ot 32a. Nevertheless, "two" are specifically mentioned in *mishnayot* 4 and 11 where all the above textual witnesses are in agreement.

/47/ See above, 74f.

/48/ See I. Agus, *Urban Civilization in Pre-Crusade Europe* (1965), 333 and *The Heroic Age of Franco-German Jewry* (1969), 252, 274 n. 210.

/49/ J. Müller, ed., *Teshuvot Ḥakhme Ṣorfat We-Lotir* (1880/1), no. 97, pp. 54b–55a. The responsum also appears with variations in Mordecai ben Hillel's *Sefer Mordekhai* to Bava' Meṣi'a' II (beg.) where it is signed by Gershom ben Judah (c. 960–1028).

/50/ Cf. the expression, *hiskimu we-heḥerimu be-'alah u-vi-shevu'ah* in a question addressed to Rabbi Isaac ben Sheshet, *She'elot U-Teshuvot Bar Sheshet*, no. 178. The case, however, is not parallel to ours.

/51/ As he saved it from the river. See B. Bava' Meṣi'a' 22b.

/52/ *Hefqer bet din hefqer*. See "*Hefqer Bet Din*," *Enc. Tal.* 10, 95–110.

/53/ H. Gezelah We-'Avedah 4:8. The commentary *Maggid Mishneh* of Joseph Caro says that this is "a geonic ordinance which is not mentioned in the Talmud." It seems that he is simply saying that since he knows of no reference to this practice in the Talmud, it *must* be geonic. This may be a conjecture, then, and not valuable in establishing the date of this practice (Ginzberg, *Sect*, 121 n. 59). Cf. also Joseph Caro, *Bet Yosef* to Ṭur Ḥoshen Mishpaṭ 28 (cited by Ginzberg as 18).

/54/ The tannaitic phrase *setam ḥaramin* (see concordances) refers to cultic donations and is not equivalent to Maimonides's *ḥerem setam*. Naḥmanides, in his "*Mishpaṭ Ha-Ḥerem*," ed. H. S. Shaanan, in *Ḥiddushe Ha-Ramban Le-Massekhet Shevu'ot*, ed. E. Lichtenstein (1976), 294 (cf. *Sefer Kol Bo*, 111a) writes, "The *ḥerem* mentioned in the words of the *'aggadot* and in passages in the Talmud is that the court bans (*maḥarimin*) something and says as follows (*bi-leshon zeh*): 'Whoever does such and such . . . will be under the ban (*ha-ḥerem*) or excommunicated (*muḥram*).' This language is simply called *ḥerem* (*setam niqra' ḥerem*)." See also *Ḥemdah Genuzah* No. 165, and Israel of Krems, *Haggahot Asheri* to B. Shevu'ot 4 (beg.). (On his authorship of this work, see E. E. Urbach, *Ba'ale Ha-Tosafot* [1980], 249, and Y. Dinari, "Israel of Krems," *EJ* 9, 1071f.)

/55/ *Sect*, 398–401.

/56/ See ed. Margaliot. The analysis of Cohen, 747, is unfortunately based only on the printed edition.

/57/ "Formularies of Decrees and Documents from a Gaonic Court," *JQR* N.S. 4 (1913/14), 46f.

/58/ Cf. Z. Ankori, *Karaites in Byzantium* (1959), 250–251.

/59/ Based on Num. 5:8. We translate with new JPS. RSV translates, "restitution for wrong;" NEB, "compensation payable."

/60/ See above, n. 6.

/61/ Heb. *ha-meshiv*. Schechter read *hmwšb* which he emended accordingly. In fact, the MS clearly reads *hmyšb*. Even Schechter's reading could be taken as *ha-moshiv*, resulting from confusion of the roots *šwb* and *yšb*. For such a case in the *hif'il*, see Ges. sec. 78b.

/62/ Emending with Schechter. The MS does, however, preserve a *resh*. For confirmation of the emendation, cf. Num. 5:7 as well as the similar wording in CDC 15:4.

/63/ Num. 5:7 does not specify to whom confession is made, nor does any other passage in the Bible containing the *hitpa'el* of *ydh*. Perhaps we should translate, "the one making restitution to the priest shall confess. . . ."

/64/ As Rabin notes, this includes the added fifth. See Num. 5:7; Lev. 5:24; M. Bava' Qamma' 9:11. It is difficult to explain the strange syntactic position of *ha-kol* or the space before it in the MS.

/65/ Heb. *levad* for MT *mi-levad* (Num. 5:8). Rabin understands this as "substitution of a less ambiguous word." It seems, though, that it might just be a case of synonymous variants in the sect's biblical text. *Mi-levad* occurs in CDC 5:5 and is explained in CDC 9:18 as meaning *ki-'im* in the language of the sect.

/66/ On *'eyl ha-'asham*, see below, 119.

/67/ Above, n. 2.

/68/ This form can be taken, with Rabin, as a perfect (*nimṣat*, see Segal, *Diqduq*, p. 150f.) or as a participle.

/69/ We do not translate "belong to" as the priests become only guardians (bailees) as indicated in the continuation.

/70/ Singular. For the *yod*, see Ges. sec. 93ss (Rabin). Rabin takes this as an "MH form after analogy of 3^{ae} infirmae."

/71/ For *mishpaṭ* in Qumran texts see *HAQ*, 42–47. In order to ensure proper observance of these laws, the article is entrusted to the priest(s).

/72/ So Segal.

/ 73/ On the technical uses of *šmr* in tannaitic usage, see below, 122.

/ 74/ *Sifre* Num. Naso' 2 (ed. Horovitz, p. 4).

/ 75/ So RSV, numbered as Lev. 6:2f.

/ 76/ *Cult and Conscience*, 84–128. Cf. Jackson, *Theft*, 171–180.

/ 77/ Milgrom, 84.

/ 78/ *Special Laws* I, 255; IV, 31–32 (cf. Belkin, 153–155).

/ 79/ M. Bava' Meṣi'a' 4:8; *Sifra'* Ḥovah parashah 13:8; and chapter 23.

/ 80/ See above, 111.

/ 81/ So new JPS.

/ 82/ M. Bava' Qamma' 9:11–12 and a *baraita'* in B. Bava' Qamma' 109a; *Sifre* Num. 4 (ed. Horovitz, p. 7); T. Bava' Qamma' 10:9; P. Bava' Qamma' 9:9 (7a).

/ 83/ T. Menaḥot 10:3 (cf. B. Yoma' 36a). Cf. "*Viddui*," *Enc. Tal.* 11, 418–421.

/ 84/ Ginzberg, *Sect*, 42f.

/ 85/ M. Yoma' 3:8, 4:2, 6:2.

/ 86/ Cf. the amoraic statement in B. Berakhot 34b and Rabbenu Nissim, *ad loc.*

/ 87/ Cf. the High Priest's confession for the Day of Atonement in M. Yoma' as well as the amoraic confessions in B. Yoma' 87b. See especially the confession of Ezra in Ez. 9:6–15.

/ 88/ See M. Weise, *Kultzeiten und kultischer Bundesschluss in der "Ordens-regel" vom Toten Meer* (1961), 75–82.

/ 89/ *Sect*, 42.

/ 90/ Chapter 18, ed. Epstein, *Mi-Qadmoniyyot Ha-Yehudim* (1956/7), 163 and Jellinek, pt. 3, p. 182f. Epstein sees this text as the composition of the eleventh century Rabbi Moses Ha-Darshan (p. 139). M. D. Herr, "Midrashim, Smaller," *EJ* 16, 1517 concludes that the text was composed at least by the time of Moses Ha-Darshan, rejecting Epstein's identification of the compiler. At all events, Epstein is correct that this text contains much Second Temple material, especially drawn from the Book of Jubilees.

/ 91/ *Sect*, 402.

/ 92/ So new JPS.

/ 93/ Cf. Rabin, *ad loc.* and Ginzberg, *Sect*, 43.

/ 94/ See below, 201.

/ 95/ *Sect*, 117.

/ 96/ H. Gezelah We-'Avedah 8:4–10.

/ 97/ Aaron ben Elijah of Nicomedia, *Gan 'Eden*, 193 b–c.

/ 98/ *Sect*, 43.

/ 99/ *Ad loc.*

/100/ Aaron ben Elijah of Nicomedia, *Keter Torah*, to Num. 5:8.

/101/ *Sifre* Num. 3 (ed. Horovitz, p. 6); B. Bava' Meṣi'a' 54b. Cf. T. Ma'aser Sheni 4:2 and Lieberman, *TK*, *ad loc.*

/102/ *Sifre* Deut. 223 (ed. Finkelstein, p. 256). Josephus paraphrases in accord with the tannaitic view in *Ant.* 4, 8, 29 (274). Cf. D. Goldenberg, "The Halakha in Josephus and in Tannaitic Literature," *JQR* (1976), 33–35.

/103/ M. Bava' Meṣi'a' 2:7–8.

/104/ On the position of the priests at Qumran, see *HAQ*, 70–75.

/105/ *Ant.* 4, 8, 29 (274).

/106/ BDB, 109a.

/107/ So new JPS.

/108/ This proclamation is also mentioned by Josephus in *Ant.* 4, 8, 29 (274). Cf. Goldenberg, 31f. Josephus's mention of the need to proclaim the place in which the object was found is parallel to the Rabbinic *siman* ("sign") although the Rabbis would have expected the loser to indicate the place in which it was lost as a *siman* that he was the owner. Cf. M. Bava' Meṣi'a' 2: 2–3; B. Bava' Meṣi'a' 22b (in the latest stratum of the amoraic material); T. Bava' Meṣi'a' 2:6; and H. Gezelah We-'Avedah 13:5.

/109/ P. Bava Meṣi'a' 2:1 (8b).

/110/ M. Bava' Meṣi'a' 7:8; M. Shevu'ot 8:1.

/111/ *Sect*, 43.

CHAPTER SIX
THE USE OF DIVINE NAMES

1. *The Tetragrammaton in Qumran Law*

Oaths served a definite legal purpose at Qumran in the adjudication of disputed cases and in the recovery of lost or stolen property. It is now appropriate to turn to the question of the nature of these oaths. In both the *Manual of Discipline* and the *Zadokite Fragments*, material can be found which expresses the attitude of the sect towards the use of divine names in the swearing of oaths, a practice common in Palestinian Judaism of this period. At the same time, the place of divine names in curses, the liturgy, and the reading of Scripture can also be determined.

Among the provisions of the sectarian Penal Code, DSD 6:27–7:2 rules:

> [וא]שר יזכיר דבר בשם הנכבד על כול ה[......] ואם קלל או
> להבעת מצרה או לכול דבר אשר לו........ הואה קורה בספר
> או מברך והבדילהו ולוא ישוב עוד על עצת היחד

Who]ever/1/ shall swear/2/ anything by the Honored Name/3/ for any[. . .]/4/ and if/5/ he pronounced a curse whether for fear/6/ of misfortune/7/ or for any (other) reason which he has . . ./8/ (or if)/9/ he is reading/10/ from Scripture/11/ or pronouncing a benediction,/12/ it (the sect) shall separate him, and he shall never return to the council/counsel of the community.

The text under discussion prohibits the use of the *shem ha-nikhbad* for certain purposes and prescribes permanent expulsion from the sect for violators of this prohibition. To understand this passage it is first necessary to clarify the meaning of the phrase, *ha-shem ha-nikhbad*.

This phrase appears in Deut. 28:58 in which it is identified with "the Lord your God." The same identification has been made by the Greek translator of Ben Sira 47:18./13/ *Ha-shem ha-nikhbad* appears in the Ashkenazic liturgy for the *'avodah* service on Yom Kippur in which *ha-shem ha-nikhbad we-ha-nora' meforash* is used instead of the Mishnah's *ha-shem ha-meforash*./14/ The Ashkenazic liturgy represents a tradition that *ha-shem ha-nikhbad* is identified with the Tetragrammaton. *(Ha-)shem ha-meforash* remains, however, in the version of Sa'adyah Gaon/15/ and the Yemenite *Tiklal*./16/ In view of these parallels, *ha-shem ha-nikhbad* in the *Manual of Discipline* must be interpreted as the Tetragrammaton.

No hesitation regarding the pronunciation of the Tetragrammaton is known from First Temple times. From its appearance in everyday matters in the Lakhish Letters,/17/ it can be assumed that it was a normal part of common speech, much as "God" is in modern English usage. L. Blau has shown that the avoidance of the use of the divine name is already in evidence in the later books of the Bible in which the Tetragrammaton is extremely rare./18/ Already by this time, *'adonai* was serving as a substitute for the Tetragrammaton. He concludes that the name was already not pronounced as written by 300 B.C. This tendency to avoid pronunciation of the Tetragrammaton is noticeable in Qumran biblical manuscripts and in the Masoretic text. In both corpora when the Tetragrammaton occurs, *'adonai* often appears before it. It was probably added at some point by a scribe to instruct the reader to substitute the surrogate name for the Tetragrammaton. Later, when this scribal phenomenon was no longer understood, the Tetragrammaton began to be read as *'elohim* in such cases, resulting in the ubiquitous *'adonai 'elohim* found so often in the Masoretic text of the prophets./19/

Philo understands Lev. 24:16 as prohibiting the pronunciation of the Tetragrammaton and stating that violators of this prohibition incur the death penalty./20/ This view may be based/21/ on the Septuagint's rendition of this verse which likewise takes it as a prohibition of the pronunciation of the Tetragrammaton./22/ Such an interpretation is also found in Targum Onkelos. Targum Pseudo-Jonathan, however, understands the verse to refer to one who pronounces the divine name in the course of blasphemy./23/

The avoidance of the pronunciation of the divine name is found as well in tannaitic *halakhah* which specifies that the Tetragrammaton be pronounced only in the priestly blessing in the Temple in Jerusalem. Otherwise, the substitute name, *'adonai*, was to be used./24/ T. Soṭah 13:8 indicates that at the death of Simeon the Just, the use of the Tetragrammaton in the priestly blessing was itself discontinued even in the Temple./25/ There is no way of confirming the accuracy of this tradition. What can be assumed, though, is that the tannaim at some point attributed the use of a surrogate, familiar to them from the last days of the Second Temple, to the period immediately following the death of this sage. He lived only shortly before the beginnings of the Qumran sect,/26/ so that tannaitic tradition considered the replacement of the Tetragrammaton with a surrogate as a priestly practice contemporary with the sect's early years.

M. Sanhedrin 10:1 attributes to the tanna Abba Saul (mid second century A.D.)/27/ the statement that one who pronounces the Tetragrammaton as written (*be-'otiyyotaw*) has no share in the world to come. Already by the time of this statement, the tannaim had prohibited the pronunciation of the Tetragrammaton. Abba Saul, however, went further than his colleagues when he added this offense to those resulting in forfeiture of one's portion in the world to come.

Babylonian amoraic texts indicate a hesitancy to teach the pronunciation of the divine name in study sessions./28/ A Babylonian amora suggests that in the world to come the Tetragrammaton will be pronounced as written./29/

An opposite tendency can be observed in M. Berakhot 9:5 in the view of some scholars. The Mishnah states that it was decreed that the divine name would be used in greeting one's fellow. It has been suggested by S. Lieberman that this was an emergency measure undertaken by the tannaim because of the excessive avoidance of the use of God's name by groups such as the Qumran sect./30/ The difficulty with this point of view is that this *mishnah* does not refer specifically to the use of the Tetragrammaton. It is probable that the name alluded to here is the surrogate, *'adonai*, which in early tannaitic times would have been pronounced without hesitation./31/ Even this name might have been introduced to dispel the view of "heretics" such as the Qumran sect./32/

The Greek church father, Theodoret (fifth century A.D.), reports that the Samaritans pronounced the Tetragrammaton as 'Ιαβέ./33/ It is possible that the use of the Tetragrammaton by them was limited to oaths. Indeed, the Palestinian Talmud notes that the Samaritans pronounced the Tetragrammaton when taking oaths./34/

The Arabic account of the fourteenth century Samaritan chronicler, Abu'l-Fatḥ ben Abī'l Ḥassan 'as-Sāmiri, regarding the Dosithean sect of the Samaritans relates that they refused to pronounce the Tetragrammaton as customary among the Samaritans and instead substituted *'elohim*./35/ Elsewhere he attributes the reverse position to the Dositheans and claims that they pronounced the Tetragrammaton while the "normative" Samaritans did not./36/ Further on, he says that the Samaritan "heretic" Shalīh ibn Ṭīrūn ibn Nīn "changed (= abolished) the reading of the Great Name by saying, 'one should recite only "Blessed be He."'"/37/ S. Isser argues that the Dositheans were a first century group of "Pharisaizing" Samaritans./38/ If so, it would follow that they abstained from pronouncing the Tetragrammaton and that the other Samaritans pronounced it as written. The contrary account, therefore, is mistaken.

The prohibition of the use of the Tetragrammaton found in the passage under discussion from the *Manual of Discipline* accords with the reverence it receives in regard to written documents at Qumran. In some non-biblical texts from Qumran the Tetragrammaton is written in palaeo-Hebrew script. Other divine names are written in palaeo-Hebrew script but with much less frequency./39/ Two basic theories have been offered for use of the palaeo-Hebrew script. M. H. Segal followed by S. Birnbaum/40/ suggested that this was a device to avoid the book's rendering the hands impure./41/ J. P. Siegal disputes this, and argues that the technique was used to highlight the special sanctity of this four-lettered divine name and to guarantee that it would not be erased accidentally./42/ Whichever explanation is accepted, this phenomenon demonstrates that a significant number of scribes whose work is represented at Qumran, or the traditions they inherited, regarded the Tetragrammaton as unique among the names and epithets of God.

Once this practice was established for the Tetragrammaton, it was extended by some scribes to other names of God as well. Indeed, there was a general tendency in Second Temple and tannaitic times to raise the level of sanctity of the divine names. Ultimately, substitute names were provided for those terms themselves originally surrogates./43/

Further evidence for the special sanctity of the Tetragrammaton at Qumran comes from the adaptation of biblical texts in sectarian literature. Sometimes direct Scriptural quotations are found with the Tetragrammaton in palaeo-Hebrew script. When biblical passages are being adapted or reworked, the *Manual of Discipline* on one occasion uses four dots to replace the Tetragrammaton (a practice found in other texts as well),/44/ and at another point uses the pronoun *hu'ah*./45/ The *Zadokite Fragments* often substitute *'el* for the Tetragrammaton, and all Qumran scrolls tend to use circumlocution to avoid the use of this divine name./46/

2. *Swearing of Oaths*

The *hif'il* of *zkr* followed by *be-shem* has been translated above as "to swear."/47/ This usage was adapted from the phraseology of the Bible by the author of DSD 6:27–7:2.

T. Nedarim 1:1 states that if one says *ba-shem*, this is considered a valid oath (*shevu'ah*)./48/ The subject of oaths and vows in Talmudic literature reflects the concerns of the common man rather than those of the houses of study./49/ It can be assumed that this phrase was in use as an oath formula, a fact which would strengthen the interpretation of swearing for the *hif'il* of *zkr* followed by *be-shem* in our text. S. Lieberman has noted that the *hif'il* of *zkr* itself can mean to swear in Rabbinic usage./50/

CDC 15:1–5 contains a regulation regarding oaths which goes much further than the law under discussion. The text picks up *in medias res* after a lacuna of one and one-third lines:/51/

> [יש]בע וגם באלף ולמד וגם באלף ודלת כי אם שבועת ה[סכ]ם באלות
> הברית ואת תורת משה אל יזכור כי בת.. ל פ[ ] ואם
> ישבע ועבר וחלל את השם ואם באלות הברית [נ]ש[בע לפני] השפטים
> אם עבר אשם והתודה והשיב ולא ישא [חטא ולא] ימות
>
> [he will s]wear and also by *'alef* and *lamed* and also by *'alef* and *dalet*/52/ except by an oath of ag[reem]ent/53/ by the curses of the covenant./54/ And he may not mention/55/ the Law of Moses for. . . . For if he were to swear and violate his oath, he would have profaned the Name. But if he [s]wore by the curses of the covenant [before] the judges,/56/ if he transgressed, he becomes guilty and confesses and makes restitution/57/ but will not bear [sin/58/ and will not] die.

Despite the difficulty of this fragmentary text, it can be deduced that the passage forbids swearing even by the names *'adonai* and *'elohim* (or *'el*?),/59/ and even by the Law of Moses. The only kind of oath permitted is by "the curses of the covenant."

The *'alot ha-berit* are the curses of Deut. 28:15–69 which are termed *divere ha-berit* in v. 69 and *'alot ha-berit* in Deut. 29:20./60/ M. Shevu'ot 4:13 and T. Shevu'ot 2:15 indicate that, indeed, the words of this passage were adapted in oath formulae, and that the Mishnah considered this passage to constitute the *'alot ha-berit*./61/

According to the *Zadokite Fragments*, one who swore by any divine name or the Torah and did not fulfill his oath would desecrate the name of God (since the Torah contains names of God). However, one who swore by "the curses of the covenant" would be a violator of an oath and guilty only of that crime. While violation of an oath was a serious offense, it in no way compared to profanation of God's name which was tantamount to blasphemy.

Indeed, a similar oath and the attendant imprecation is found in Jub. 9:14–15. Here Noah's sons apportioned the earth among their children in his presence, "and he bound them all by an oath, imprecating a curse on every one that sought to seize the portion which had not fallen (to him) by his lot." In order to indicate their acceptance of the oath, "they all said 'So be it; so be it.'"/62/

The prohibition of swearing by the Torah of Moses can be understood in two ways. It may be seen as resulting from a fear of accidentally blaspheming the name of Moses which was held in high respect. On the other hand, it can be simply an extension of the prohibition of oaths in the name of God. Since the Torah contains the name of God, an oath by it would be as binding as an oath by the divine name. Parallels can be cited for both approaches.

Regarding reverence for the name of Moses, Josephus records that the Essenes honored the name of the Lawgiver (Moses) second only to the honor they accorded to the name of God Himself. They condemned to death anyone who blasphemed the name of Moses./63/ The meaning of this text may be that, besides refraining from oaths in the name of God (on which see below), the Essenes even refused to use the name of Moses in oaths, since they believed it a capital offense to blaspheme his name. A false oath, even taken inadvertently, constituted such blasphemy.

M. Nedarim 1:2 and T. Nedarim 1:2, according to many manuscripts,/64/ mention an oath by *mohi*. This word *mohi* is understood by both Lieberman/65/ and Ginzberg/66/ as a form of the name Moses used in oaths. This word was recognized as a substitute form (*kinnui*) which rendered the oath valid. If so, there must have been at some point a common practice of taking oaths in the name of Moses.

On the other hand, it is also possible to cite parallels to the concept of an oath on the Torah and to assume that at issue here is the presence of divine names in the Torah. T. Shevu'ot 2:16 mentions an oath taken on the

Torah. There are variant readings of this passage, some declaring such oaths valid, and others asserting that they are not valid. Lieberman, following several quotations, accepts the reading declaring these oaths valid./67/ In any case, we have proof here that such oaths were in popular use in tannaitic times. The reading which declares an oath on the Torah valid agrees with the *Zadokite Fragments* in which divine punishment is meted out to the violator of this oath. Only if the oath were considered valid, could the swearer be liable to punishment. Indeed, comparison with the discussion of vows in B. Nedarim 14b makes it clear that the amoraim understood this issue as revolving about the divine names present in the scroll. An oath on the contents of the text (as opposed to the blank parchment) would constitute an oath on the divine names in it./68/

The Talmudic practice of holding the Torah while taking an oath/69/ is seen by Ginzberg/70/ as an oath by the Torah and parallel to CDC 15:1–5. In Talmudic times, however, oaths were still taken by divine names or substitutes./71/ If so, it must be assumed that the purpose of holding the Torah was to instill the gravity of the oath in the mind of the swearer. The oath, however, was not on the Torah.

Only in medieval times did holding the Torah become equivalent to swearing on it./72/ Ginzberg cites a responsum from the Cairo *genizah*, attributed to Sa'adyah or Hai Gaon, to the effect that an oath by the Torah cannot be absolved. Indeed, the responsum specifically says that an oath on any book *with the divine name in it* cannot be absolved. Ginzberg suggests that the purpose of this restriction was to discourage such oaths./73/

Even the use of substitutes for the divine name in oaths fell into disuse by the Geonic period. Instead, oaths were administered exactly as in this Qumran text—by the use of curses which the adjured was told would come upon him if he violated the oath. This development is no more than a continuation of the tendencies already observed in the Talmudic period to eliminate oaths by the divine name or even by substitute names. This tendency was much more pronounced in the sectarian groups during Second Temple times than among the Pharisaic predecessors of the tannaim.

Numerous sources indicate that sectarian groups in the Second Commonwealth were opposed to swearing or had hesitations about the use of the divine name for this purpose. As time passed, the Rabbinic leadership eventually took the same view, so that by the Geonic period, oaths by God, using any name, were no longer taken./74/

Joesephus relates that the Essenes would not swear by God. They considered taking an oath to be worse than perjury./75/ That they had no general prohibition on swearing is seen from their use of solemn oaths in the induction of new members into their sect./76/

Josephus tells us that the Pharisees and Essenes both refused to take an oath of allegiance to Herod, an ordeal from which he spared them./77/ Ginzberg assumes that this was because of the aversion of these groups to swearing in the name of God./78/ In his opinion, this is the only possible explanation for Herod's having excused them. If so, why did they not swear some other form of oath? It is most logical that they simply chanced a confrontation with Herod for religious and political reasons and were successful in refusing to swear allegiance. That the Pharisees were essentially opposed to his rule has been demonstrated conclusively by G. Alon./79/

Ginzberg suggests that the Essene aversion to swearing was only to oaths involving the name of God. Indeed, this is confirmed by Josephus's description of the use of oaths in the Essene initiation requirements./80/ These were oaths without divine names. Perhaps they contained curses such as are mentioned in our text from the *Zadokite Fragments*. Ginzberg rightly observes the difference between the Pharisees and the Essenes in this matter. The Pharisees would not take oaths in daily life but retained them for practical reasons in court procedure. The Essenes, being less practically inclined, completely rejected oaths by the name of God.

Philo states that the avoidance of oaths is the best of all courses, as taking oaths invariably raises questions about the credibility of the swearer./81/ Philo's discussion then turns to perjury./82/ Here again he suggests avoidance of oaths lest they accidentally turn out to be false and the divine name be profaned as a consequence. Elsewhere,/83/ Philo indicates his disapproval of oaths taken in the name of God. He suggests instead that, if necessary, the oath simply be either "by ———," with no reference after it, or in the name of "earth, sun, stars, heaven, the whole universe."/84/

Philo's disapproval of oaths by the name of God certainly goes hand in hand with his recognition of a view that perjury is punishable by death. He mentions a difference of opinion in this regard. Philo describes the stricter view which required the death penalty as that of "the better kind whose piety is extra-fervent." The lesser penalty of stripes is accepted by "those whose feelings of indignation are not so stern."/85/

This Philonic tradition has been the subject of a special study by B. Revel./86/ He sees Philo's view as resulting from the fact that false oaths are described as a profanation of God's name in Lev. 19:12, which may be paraphrased as follows: You may not swear falsely by My name, for if you do, you will be profaning it./87/ Philo, therefore, requires the death penalty for false oaths./88/ Rabbinic law likewise prescribed death for blasphemy (cursing God)./89/ The very same connection between false oaths and the profanation of God's name is made in our text from CDC 15:1–5. The sect, as did Philo, saw false oaths by the name of God as violating not only the Torah's prohibition of false oaths, but also that of profanation of the divine name. The very same connection is made in a midrashic passage in M. Sanhedrin 6:4.

Ben Sira 23:7–11 contains a poem against swearing oaths. This text clearly states that oaths are to be avoided lest one, through error or intention, swear falsely and incur liability for this transgression./90/

The New Testament contains an admonition against all swearing (Matt. 5:33–37; Ja. 5:12)./91/ In these passages it is clear that the primary concern is avoidance of the sin of perjury. Abstinence from all oaths would certainly prevent this transgression. Very similar in phraseology to the New Testament material is 2 En. 49:1–2 which forbids swearing by anything. On the other hand, it permits asseverative statements such as "I swear such and such."/92/

It was noted above that while the Pharisees may have avoided non-judicial oaths, there is no evidence that they avoided legally required oaths./93/ Tannaitic tradition knows of the use of the Tetragrammaton as well as the other names of God and various substitutes in oaths./94/ There can be no question that early tannaitic practice required that judicial oaths be taken by the Tetragrammaton./95/ On the other hand, the use of the Tetragrammaton in oath formulae was probably already discouraged by the end of the tannaitic period.

M. Giṭṭin 4:3 shows evidence of hesitation regarding the taking of oaths. Apparently, the tannaim feared the imposition of oaths in case they might lead to accidental violation./96/ The description of the oath process in T. Soṭah 7:2–4 includes stern warnings to the swearer about the serious consequences of a false oath. Even after he acknowledges the first warning, he is again told that he may not include in his mind any unstated conditions in an effort to deceive the court./97/ This procedure again reflects a fear of false oaths. For this reason the tannaim hesitated to impose judicial oaths. Ginzberg's suggestion that this hesitation was the result of Essene influence/98/ cannot be substantiated.

By amoraic times there were reservations about the use of the other divine names and even about oaths employing substitutes. The hesitation was clearly for fear of perjury which would be tantamount to blaspheming the name of God./99/ For this reason, the Geonim abolished the oaths in the name of God and substituted the use of curse formulae. The late midrashic sources cited by L. Ginzberg/100/ which oppose all swearing, even in court, reflect the same view as the Geonic traditions which have already been mentioned.

It is now time to place the two sectarian passages in their context in the history of Jewish law. In regard to oaths, the sectarians traveled the same path as did the Rabbinic tradition but so much more quickly. Initially, as reflected in the text from the *Manual of Discipline*, the sectarians limited the use of the Tetragrammaton as part of a general prohibition of its pronunciation which was motivated by its special sanctity. With time, for fear of the consequences of perjury, they prohibited as well the use of the other divine names and used only an oath based on imprecation. This is the view found in the *Zadokite Fragments* which, in the development of this particular law, reflects a later stage. The sectarians, then, arrived at the very same conclusion as the Rabbinic tradition, but they did so a millenium earlier.

Since we have already found elsewhere that the Dead Sea practice relating to the use of oaths of adjuration for the recovery of stolen property was the same as that of the later Geonim,/101/ the parallel that has been found here ought not surprise us.

3. *Pronouncing a Curse by the Divine Name*

Biblical Israel, like the ancient Near Eastern world in general, recognized the efficacy of curses./102/ Therefore, the Bible prohibited cursing of God, parents, judges, kings (Heb. *nasi'*), and the deaf./103/ The Rabbis extended these limitations only minimally./104/

That a strong magical tradition existed in the Hellenistic world is well known. The use of curses and spells for all kinds of reasons, including bringing harm to one's enemy or protecting oneself from danger, is well attested in the Greek magical papyri. The *Sefer Ha-Razim*, while a somewhat later text than the Dead Sea Scrolls,/105/ shows that such traditions penetrated Palestinian Judaism./106/ From DSD 6:27–7:2, it is apparent that such patterns were already emerging among the Judean populace when the sect was compiling its Penal Code. The absence of Greek vocabulary at Qumran or of any overt Hellenistic influence must be noted./107/ It is possible that this law is to some extent directed against practices identified with Hellenistic paganism by the sect, which, to their chagrin, were finding their way into Palestinian Jewish life./108/

A *baraita'* found in both the Babylonian and Palestinian Talmuds/109/ refers to the prohibition of cursing one's fellow by the divine name (*ba-shem*) as a negative commandment which occasions the punishment of flogging (*malqut*). In the amoraic discussion in the Palestinian Talmud it is proposed that this prohibition is derived from Deut. 28:58 in which Israel is commanded "to fear (*yr'*) this honored (*nikhbad*) and awe-inspiring name, (that of) the Lord your God."

The Palestinian Talmud/110/ contains a curious report to the effect that the third century Babylonian amora, Samuel, overheard a Persian curse his son by the Tetragrammaton. This imprecation resulted in the boy's death. Another version of this account appears in *Qohelet Rabbah*./111/ Here the story is told about a Persian woman who cursed her son with "one word" (*ḥada' millah*) of the Ineffable Name (*shem ha-meforash*). When Samuel heard, he said to prepare the burial shrouds. This "word" (*millah*) may be the name *yah* so well attested in the Babylonian Jewish Aramaic magic bowls./112/ In *Qohelet Rabbah* this story is preceded by a statement by the amora Rabbi Ze'era/113/ showing that even surrogate names (*kinnuyim*) were used for "killing one another." All these traditions show that in tannaitic and amoraic times such curses were known and forbidden by the Rabbinic tradition. Apparently, the sect reacted in the same way to such imprecations.

The curses of which our text from the *Manual of Discipline* speaks here are no doubt of the conditional kind. One person utters a curse against a second saying that if he (the second) does not do such and such, this curse will come upon him. Curses of this type were often used to force people to fulfill legal obligations or comply with one's will. In fact, the *'alot ha-berit*, "curses of the covenant," of Deut. 28:15–69 were of this conditional kind. This was also the case with the oath of adjuration intended to lead to the recovery of stolen property in CDC 9:11–12./114/

Often, curses which appear unconditional are in reality conditional. This is the case with the curse pronounced by the Levites in the blessing and curse ceremony of DSD 2:2–18. It is only the evil deeds of the accursed which have sealed his fate. True repentance and attachment to the sect would ensure that the conditions of the curse would not be fulfilled.

This Qumran text prohibited the use of the Tetragrammaton in curses. Since the efficacy of curses was dependent in the popular view on the invocation of a deity, anyone wishing to utter a curse would have wanted to use the divine name, hence the prohibition on its use in this context.

4. *Escape from Danger*

The Tetragrammaton might also be used to escape from danger or misfortune. Hai Goan (969–1038 A.D.) makes reference to such a practice in his famous responsum on magic./115/ His descriptions are paralleled in some late midrashic sources./116/ Our text (DSD 6:27–7:2) shows that this practice was truly much older. The fear of death and the feeling of urgency would have pressed the endangered individual to utter the Tetragrammaton hoping that God would save him.

Many examples of this kind of magic are present in the *Sefer Ha-Razim*/117/ and in the Hellenistic magical literature. These spells, in the name of the god or gods, were intended to provide salvation from some specific danger. The Aramaic Jewish magic bowls from late Talmudic and early Geonic Babylonia were similar in their intent except that they served primarily an apotropaic role, much as talismans did for many medieval Jews.

5. *Scriptural Readings and Benedictions*

The next category of use of the Tetragrammaton discussed in DSD 6:27–7:2 is that of reading from a canonical book (*sefer*). *Sefer* is a term for a biblical book, a meaning which appears already in Dan. 9:2./118/ The verb *qr'* (in our text with substitution of *he'* for *'alef*/119/) is a technical term for reading a canonical book, probably in public as part of the liturgy. This definition of *qr'* helps to explain that while the Rabbis prohibit the reading of *Ben Sira'*, they quote it so often themselves./120/ It was its public, liturgical reading which was prohibited. In the same way, our text refers to the public reading of Scripture in which the reader, either through a mistaken sense of reverence or through error, might pronounce the Tetragrammaton as written.

The public reading of Scripture was a regular part of the sectarian study sessions which all members were required to attend for one-third of each night of the year. The phrase *liqro' ba-sefer* appears in connection with these sessions in DSD 6:6–8./121/ It is no doubt to the recitation of the text at these sessions that the *Manual of Discipline* here refers. Unfortunately, nothing is known about the place of Scriptural readings in the liturgical life of the Qumran sect.

While there is a lack of sufficient information pertaining to the liturgical rites at Qumran, it is known that there was regular public recitation of benedictions, and evidence also points to recital of thrice daily prayers./122/ It is most probable that the Psalms Scroll (11QPs[a]) was a liturgical text, and that the Psalms played a prominent part in Qumran liturgy./123/ This is exactly what one would expect of a group whose origins were in the Temple priesthood./124/

It is certainly because of the priestly origin of the sect's leadership that the fear of accidental pronunciation of the Tetragrammaton in public reading of the Bible or recitation of liturgical texts was a matter of such great concern. After all, the Tetragrammaton had been pronounced on certain occasions in the Temple worship, and many of the members of the sect must have been familiar with its exact vocalization.

S. Lieberman points to T. Berakhot 7:6 which brands the use of *'el* or *'elohim* at the beginning and end of benedictions (in place of *'adonai*) as *derekh 'aḥeret*, literally, "another way," which Lieberman translates as "heterodoxy." In this connection, he calls attention to the avoidance of the divine name in the *Manual of Discipline* and the benediction formula *barukh 'atah 'eli* in DSD 11:15/125/ and so identifies the heterodoxy with our sect.

The *Thanksgiving Scroll* (*Hodayot*) calls into question this conclusion. Most of the hymns preserved in it begin with the formula *'odekhah 'adonai*. Several hymns begin *'odekhah 'eli*. However, there are also found *barukh 'atah 'adonai*, *barukh 'atah 'el*, and *barukh 'atah 'el ha-raḥamim*./126/ The sect used the surrogate *'adonai* in benediction formulae, even if they may have used *'el* occasionally.

It seems most likely that the lacuna in CDC 14:22–23 contained a regulation similar or parallel to that of DSD 6:27–7:2. This regulation would have prohibited the use of the Tetragrammaton for all the purposes mentioned in the *Manual of Discipline*. In regard to the attitude of the writer of the *Zadokite Fragments* to the use of surrogate names for curses and magic, it may be assumed that he would have prohibited them. Most likely, however, both the *Manual of Discipline* and the *Zadokite Fragments* would have agreed that surrogates might be used for prayer or the reading of Scripture. Indeed, *'adonai* and *'el* appear in the Thanksgiving Hymns (*Hodayot*).

Only in regard to the Tetragrammaton did pronunciation result in the expulsion of the member from the sect. This permanent expulsion is eloquent testimony to the gravity of this offense according to the *Manual of Discipline*.

Comparison of the punishments mentioned in the *Zadokite Fragments* and the *Manual of Discipline* points to the essential difference between the texts. The *Manual of Discipline* is concerned with sectarian regulations and the relationship of the transgressor to the sect. Hence, the *Manual of Discipline* imposes a sectarian sanction upon the offender. The *Zadokite Fragments* are concerned with the violations of the commandments of God and the effect of the transgression on the relationship between man and God. For this reason, the *Zadokite Fragments* speak of a biblical sanction. Certainly, hard and fast rules cannot be derived from these passages, but these laws reflect the general thrust of the two documents.

6. *Summary*

The study of these two texts has shown that the sect, like the Essenes, the New Testament, Philo, and the tannaim, was very hesitant about oaths. The Qumranites prohibited all oaths by the Tetragrammaton as well as those by other divine names or the Torah. Other uses of the Tetragrammaton for curses, magic, public reading of Scriptures, and recitation of benedictions were likewise prohibited. While the initial limitations on the use of the Tetragrammaton stemmed from the special sanctity of this name, the same status was eventually accorded to the other names in regard to oaths. Probably the use of these names in the liturgy led to a rise in their sanctity. It cannot be determined if further limitations were placed on the use of the other divine names, but it is relatively certain that their use was permitted in prayer and study. All oaths at Qumran, therefore, were taken on the "curses of the covenant." Divine names were not used in judicial oaths taken before the courts of Qumran or in the oaths of adjuration sworn to secure the return of lost or stolen property.

NOTES

/1/ Restored with Licht.

/2/ The *hif'il* of *zkr* with *shem* appears in Ex. 23:13, referring to the "name of other gods." This verse has been interpreted as a prohibition on swearing in their name by the Vulgate, Ibn Ezra, Cassuto, and *Mekhilta' De-Rabbi Ishmael* Mishpaṭim 20 (ed. Horovitz-Rabin, p. 332) where it is the first interpretation. A parallel appears in Hoffmann's edition of *Mekhilta' De-Rabbi Shim'on ben Yoḥai*, but it must be discounted as it does not appear in the *genizah* version published by Epstein. It was the *Midrash Ha-Gadol* (from which Hoffmann excerpted his *Mekhilta'* text) that took this interpretation from B. Sanhedrin 63b, where it refers to the words *lo' yishama' 'al pikha*, the latter part of the verse, and transferred it to this clause, citing it as an alternative interpretation. The *hif'il* of *zkr* appears with *be-shem* referring to a god in parallelism with the *hif'il* of *šb'*, "to swear," in Josh. 23:7. In Is. 48:1 a similar parallelism appears except that *be-shem* need not be repeated in the second clause and so appears only with *ha-nishba'im* despite the fact that it refers as well to *yazkiru*. It would seem from these parallelisms that the *hif'il* of *zkr* with *(be-)shem* may be interpreted as meaning "to swear." Indeed, this is the interpretation which served as the basis of the Vulgate to Josh. 23:7 (which either omitted the next verb or took this and the following verb as a hendiadys) and of Kimḥi to Isaiah. (*Hif'il* of *zkr* and *be-shem* also occurs in Am. 6:10 and Ps. 20:8). Cf. M. Greenberg, "The Hebrew Oath Particle *ḤAY/ḤE*," *JBL* 76 (1957), 35. For the use of Akkadian *zakāru* in the sense of "to declare under oath" see A. L. Oppenheim, ed., *The Assyrian Dictionary* (1961), vol. 21 (Z), s.v. *zakāru*. The G stem followed by *ina* is used in the sense of "to take an oath by" (16f.), and the Š stem (causative) is used for making others take an oath (21). *Zkr* meaning "remember" is a loan usage in Akkadian (22). The sect interpreted this expression to mean "swear." Note that Ben-Yehudah II, 1342a defines our expression as a synonym of the *hif'il* of *šb'*. Cf. also the use of *yazkir* (emending with Schechter and Rabin) in CDC 15:2 (see p. 136) and Lieberman, *Greek*, 34f. who likewise explains *mazkir* in T. 'Avodah Zarah 3:11 (so Zuckermandel and "*Nusḥa'ot Ketav Yad*" in ed. Vilna, as well as Ṭur Yoreh De'ah 124 [beg.], and J. Caro's *Bet Yosef, ad loc.* Note that Tosefta, *ed. princ.* reads *u-makkir*. Cf. Lieberman, *Tosefet Rishonim* II, p. 191).

/3/ So new JPS to Deut. 28:58, *ha-shem ha-nikhbad*, which indicates that our phrase must be vocalized *ba-shem ha-nikhbad*.

/4/ Licht suggests several conjectural restorations. The first is to restore *ha-[nora']* based on Deut. 28:58. This, unfortunately, makes little sense in context. Better, according to Licht, is the restoration *ha-[hawayah* (or *howeh*) *we-ha-niheyah]*, literally, "that [which is and is becoming]." See Licht's note to DSD 3:15. This is certainly a possible restoration here, as it makes sense in context, as Licht has stated. Licht's third possiblity, *ha-[hawayah we-nishba']*, does not seem to make sense at all. While Licht's second suggestion seems best, the space in the MS seems to be slightly too small for it. We therefore suggest restoring *h[wyh wnhyh]* (vocalized *hawayah we-niheyah*). Indeed, the trace to the left of the *he'* in the MS appears to be the top of a *waw*, confirming this reading. Due to the conjectural nature of the restoration, in order that our explanation of the passage should not appear to depend on it, we have relegated this reading to the notes and not included it in the text and translation.

/5/ *We-'im* frequently is used to introduce a subsidiary or alternate condition in Qumran literature. Cf. *we-'im bi-shegagah* in DSD 7:3 and above, 11.

/6/ *Nif'al* infinitive of the root *b't*.

/7/ The *mem* is causal (Williams, *Hebrew Syntax*, sec. 319). Wernberg-Møller points out that the passage "appears to be dependent" on Job 15:24. (This verse is not preserved in the Qumran Job Targum.)

/8/ Between *mi-ṣarah* and *hu'ah* there is a large erasure over which a second scribe has written *'o le-khol davar 'asher lo*. Space for approximately eight letters remains after *lo*. From the continuation, it is clear that something has been omitted before *hu'ah*.

/ 9/ Licht suggests that *we-'im* may have stood before *hu'ah* in the original but was erased in error.

/10/ Licht notes that *qoreh* is phonetic spelling for *qore'*. Similar confusion is found in 2 Sam. 1:6. See the many examples of confusion of final *'alef* and *he'* verbs in Ges. sec. 75nn–rr. In Mishnaic Hebrew most forms of final *'alef* verbs tended to assimilate to final *he'* forms but by no means was the process complete as it was in Aramaic (Segal, *Diqduq*, sec. 273). Cf. Qimron, p. 212.

/11/ For numerous examples of *qr'* in the *qal* with *sefer* as its direct object referring to the reading of a canonical text, see Ben-Yehudah VIII, 6129a–6130b. On *sefer* as a term for canonical books, see Dan. 9:2; N. M. Sarna, "Bible, the Canon, Text," *EJ* 4, 816; and for Rabbinic sources, Bacher, *'Erkhe Midrash*, I, 92; II, 247. See also DSD 6:6–8 (discussed in *HAQ*, 32f.).

/12/ Cf. DSD 6:3, 5 (a strange *hif'il*), 8; 1QSa 2:19f. (restored). Apparently the verb *brk* in the *pi'el* referred to benedictions before food as well as to the daily liturgy.

/13/ The Hebrew (MS B) *ba-shem ha-nikhbad* is translated ἐν ὀνόματι κυρίου τοῦ θεοῦ. (This passage is not preserved in the Ben Sira Scroll from Masada.)

/14/ *Maḥazor La-Yamin Ha-Nora'im*, ed. D. Goldschmidt (1970) II, 440, 441, 444. It is impossible to date this version of the *Seder 'Avodah* precisely. This phrase is not found in the Mishnah version (M. Yoma' 6:2). It should be noted that it is generally accepted that this clause in the Mishnah is a later addition based on the liturgy (Elijah Gaon to B. Yoma' 66a, and to 'Oraḥ Ḥayyim 621; *DS* to B. Yoma' 66a, note *qof*; Epstein, *Mavo' Le-Nusaḥ Ha-Mishnah* II, 971f.). This conclusion is based on manuscripts which either omit this clause entirely or differ as to its location. For the identification of *shem ha-meforash* with the Tetragrammaton, see Maimonides, H. Yesode Ha-Torah 6:2; H. Tefillah 14:10; and *Guide* I, 62.

/15/ *Siddur Rav Sa'adyah Ga'on*, ed. I. Davidson, S. Assaf, B. I. Joel (1941), 273, 274, 279 (*shem ha-meforash*). Note the reading of an Oxford fragment *'et qol shem ha-meforash* (273, n. 205).

/16/ *Tiklal Shivat Sion*, ed. J. Kafah (1951/2), 153, 154, 157 (all three have *'et shem ha-meforash*).

/17/ N. H. Torczyner, *Te'udot Lakhish* (1940), No. 2 (p. 26); No. 3 (p. 53); No. 4 (p. 106); No. 5 (p. 127); No. 6 (p. 138); No. 8 (p. 174); No. 9 (p. 176); No. 12 (p. 184); No. 21 (p. 217—restored).

/18/ "Tetragrammaton," *JE* 12, 118–120.

/19/ Cf. S. T. Byington, "*yhwh* and *'dny*," *JBL* 76 (1957), 58f.

/20/ *Life of Moses* II, 206. Cf. also *Life of Moses* II, 114. On the divine names in Philo, cf. Frankel, *Ueber den Einfluss*, 26–29.

/21/ So Heinemann, *Bildung*, 20.

/22/ ὀνομάζων δὲ τὸ ὄνομα κυρίου θανάτῳ θανατούσθω. Cf. the statement of Dio Cassius, *Roman History* XXXVII, 17 that the Jewish God is unnameable (ἄρρητον). Josephus, *Ant.* 2, 12, 4 (276) is likewise hesitant to discuss the divine name.

/23/ All these views are based on a definition of the root *nqb* in the sense of "to pronounce." Rashi, however, understands this verb to mean "to curse" and refers to Num. 23:8. The statement attributed to the Palestinian amora Rabbi Levi that one who pronounces the divine name is liable for the death penalty appears only in a late addition to the *Pesiqta' De-Rav Kahana'* (ed. Buber, p. 148a). This addition was made by the copyist of the Safed MS and apparently came from some "apocryphal" source.

/24/ M. Soṭah 7:6, *Sifre* Num. 39 (ed. Horovitz, p. 43); 43 (ed. Horovitz, p. 48); *Sifre Zuta'* to Num. 6:27 (ed. Horovitz, p. 250); and a *baraita'* in B. Soṭah 38a. The view of Hillel ben Eliakim that the substitutes are names such as *'el*, *'elohim*, or *ṣeva'ot* is rejected by Tosafot to B. Soṭah 38a. Tosafot and Moses David Abraham Treves Ashkenazi, *Toledot 'Adam* to *Sifre* Num. 39 (p. 73a) take the substitute to be *'adonai*, pronounced as written.

/25/ Cf. Lieberman, *TK*, *ad loc.*

/26/ This Simeon the Just is Simeon II who lived about 200 B.C. and is praised in Ben Sira 50:1–6. Cf. U. Rappoport, "Simeon the Just," *EJ* 14, 1566f. and G. F. Moore, "Simeon the Righteous," *Jewish Studies in Memory of Israel Abrahams* (1927), 348–364.

/27/ Strack, 116. On the possible existence of a Mishnah of Abba Saul which served as a source for the Mishnah, see I. Levi, *Über einige Fragmente aus der Mischna des Abba Saul* (1876), and J. N. Epstein, *Mevo'ot Le-Sifrut Ha-Tanna'im* (1957), 160–163. Note that the statement is attributed to Yohanan ben Nuri in *'Avot De-Rabbi Natan* Version A, 36 (ed. Schechter, 54b).

/28/ B. Pesaḥim 50a, B. Qiddushin 71a.

/29/ B. Pesaḥim 50a, which should be read with *Yalquṭ Shim'oni* to Ex. sec. 171 (marginal note in ed. Vilna).

/30/ "Light on the Cave Scrolls from Rabbinic Sources," *PAAJR* 20 (1951), 400 (cf. *TK* to T. Berakhot 6(7):20). Cf. also A. Marmorstein, *The Old Rabbinic Doctrine of God* (1968), 17–40. Lieberman also discusses the debate between the Pharisees and Hemerobaptists mentioned in T. Yadayim 2:9 (cf. M. Yadayim 4:8), from which one might draw the conclusion that the basis for hesitating to pronounce the Tetragrammaton was ritual purity. Nonetheless, the Dead Sea sect maintained high standards of ritual purity and still avoided the pronunciation of the Tetragrammaton. Cf. also G. Alon, *Meḥqarim Be-Toledot Yisra'el* I (1967), 204.

/31/ Cf. T. Berakhot 6(7):23–24. Indeed, Lieberman, *TK*, *ad loc.* seems to argue as well that the surrogate *'adonai* was instituted here rather than the Tetragrammaton. Albeck, *HWT* to M. Soṭah 7:6, following *'Arukh*, *s.v.* *'t* (cf. A. Kohut, *'Arukh Ha-Shalem* [1967], 281f.) and Maimonides to M. Berakhot 9:5, states that this refers to the use of a surrogate. These two medieval sources go so far as to suggest that *shalom*, taken by Jewish tradition as a name of God, was the surrogate in question. Cf. also Marmorstein, 104f.

/32/ Cf. the treatment of the passage by Alon, *Meḥqarim* I, 203–205 who sees it as directed against *ḥasidim* within the Pharisaic-rabbinic camp who chose to be more careful than required in abstaining from the use of the divine name. J. Mann, *Texts and Studies in Jewish History and Literature* I (1931), 580–583, 605f. discusses Hai Gaon's view that the use of the divine name in greetings was intended as an anti-Christian polemic.

/33/ W. Bacher, "Shem ha-Meforash," *JE* 11, 263.

/34/ P. Sanhedrin 10:1 (28b) referring to *kuta'e*.

/35/ S. J. Isser, *The Dositheans* (1976), 76.

/36/ Isser, 79.

/37/ Isser, 82.

/38/ Isser, 108f., 160–164.

/39/ See J. P. Siegel, "The Employment of Palaeo-Hebrew Characters for Divine Names at Qumran in the Light of Tannaitic Sources," *HUCA* 42 (1971), 159–165.

/40/ M. H. Segal, "*Le-Va'ayot shel Megillot Ha-Me'arot*," *Eretz Israel* 1 (1951), 39 n. 6; S. A. Birnbaum, *The Qumran (Dead Sea) Scrolls and Palaeography*, *BASOR Supplementary Studies* 13/14 (1952), 11–15, 25f.

/41/ Cf. M. Yadayim 4:5–6; T. Yadayim 2:13–14 and S. Leiman, *The Canonization of Hebrew Scripture* (1976), 102–120.

/42/ "Employment," 169–172.

/43/ Cf. J. Z. Lauterbach, "Substitutes for the Tetragrammaton," *PAAJR* 2 (1930–31), 43 n. 16; and Tosafot to B. 'Avodah Zarah 18a, s.v. *hogeh ha-shem.*

/44/ DSD 8:14. Cf. also 4Q Testimonia (*DJD* V, 57f.) and 4Q Tanḥumim (*DJD* V, 60–62).

/45/ DSD 8:13. See above, 100f. n. 16.

/46/ This was already noted for the *Zadokite Fragments* by I. Levi, "*Le Tétragramme et l'écrit Sadokite de Damas*," *REJ* 68 (1914), 119–124.

/47/ See above, n. 2.

/48/ T. Nedarim 1:1 states: *ha-'omer . . . ba-shem hare zo shevu'ah*, "If one says 'by the name' this is an oath." (The reading *ka-shem* in MS Vienna is clearly an error as Lieberman, *TK*, *ad loc.*, points out. His note in the critical apparatus to the effect that a *genizah* fragment reads *shevu'at* is somewhat unclear. Actually, this fragment [according to a photograph published in the *Tosefta'* volume] reads *shevu'at qorban . . .* , showing that the scribe [or his *Vorlage*] made a homoeoteleuton and combined ours with the following clause referring to *la-shem*.) Cf. Deut. 6:13, *u-vi-shemo tishave'a* "and swear only by His name" (so new JPS). Lieberman calls attention to the use in magical papyri of the words *βασυμμ* (*be-shem*) and *βασμα* (*bi-shema'*). Lieberman explains that the use of *ba-shem* is tantamount to saying *'ani nishba' ba-shem*, "I swear by the name." On the magical use of *ba-shem* in the Greek papyri, see also G. Alon, "*Ba-Shem*," *Meḥqarim* I, 194–198 and S. Lieberman, "Some Notes on Adjurations in Israel," *Texts and Studies* (1974), 21–25. Cf. also M. Yoma' 3:8, 4:2, 6:2; T. Kippurim 1:1; and Albeck's *HWT* to M. Yoma' 6:2.

/49/ Lieberman, *Greek*, 115–141. Cf. his "*Mashehu 'al Hashba'ot Be-Yisra'el*," *Tarbiz* 27 (1957/8), 183–189.

/50/ *Greek*, 34f., "*Mashehu*," 185.

/51/ The passage immediately preceding (CDC 14:18–22) is part of the abbreviated penal code discussed below, 156. This penal code began with the superscription in l. 18, and our passage seems to conclude it in the present recension.

/52/ Such abbreviations are found in M. Shevu'ot 4:13. The claim by N. H. Tur-Sinai, *Ha-Lashon We-Ha-Sefer* II (1959), 171f. that such names of letters were not even known to the tannaim is not substantiated by him.

/53/ Restored with Rabin. Other suggestions ignore the traces. Hence, Schechter's restoration *hbryt* cannot be accepted nor can Ginzberg's *shevu'ah ha-ketuvah be-'alot ha-berit* (*Sect*, 91). Cf. Deut. 29:20; 2 Chron. 34:24. Rabin explains the *shevu'at heskem* as equivalent to the Rabbinic *shevu'at hesset*, the "eliciting oath" in his translation. This oath is amoraic in date (Maimonides, H. Shevu'ot 11:7; H. To'en We-Nit'an 1:3) and in its primary source appears in the name of Rav Naḥman (B. Shevu'ot 40b; B. Bava' Meṣi'a' 5a, 6a). Cf. also Hagahot Maimuniyyot to H. Shevu'ot 11:7 and Radbaz, *ad loc.*

/54/ Cf. DSD 5:12 (É. Cothenet, "Le Document de Damas," in J. Carmignac, É. Cothenet, H. Lignée, *Les Textes de Qumran* (1963), *ad loc.*

/55/ Schechter emends to *yzkyr*.

/56/ On the requirement that oaths take place before the judges, see above, 38f. Schechter restored here *ywb' lpny* (*yuva' lifne*), but this reading does not take account of the *shin*.

/57/ Cf. Num. 5:7, *we-hitwaddu . . . we-heshiv.*

/58/ Or perhaps restore *'wn*? Cf. Ex. 28:43.

/59/ Note the prominence of *'el* in DST which might suggest that it is referred to here.

/60/ The attempt of Cothenet to identify the *'alot ha-berit* here with DSD 2:5–18 must therefore be rejected.

/61/ On the text of this *mishnah*, see *Shinuye Nusḥa'ot* in ed. Vilna, *Tosefot Yom Ṭov, Mele'khet Shelomoh*, and *DS* to B. Shevu'ot 35a, n. *kaf*. Rashi to B. Shevu'ot 35a interprets the *mishnah* likewise except that he assumes that the oath was taken during the coincidental reading of the words *yakekha . . .* (Deut. 28:27) in the synagogue. Cf. below, 116 for a similar phenomenon.

/62/ Trans. Charles, *APOT*. The original Hebrew text must have read *'amen 'amen*. Cf. Num. 5:22.

/63/ *War* 2, 8, 9 (145). Note that in the very same section Josephus discusses the justice and scrupulousness of the trials which the Essenes conducted. Hence, context may support the interpretation of Josephus we have proposed here.

/64/ See Lieberman, *TK*, *ad loc.* n. 11 for a full list of manuscripts. Note that this is the reading of Tosefta MS Vienna and is confirmed by quotation of the Mishnah in both the Babylonian and Palestinian Talmuds.

/65/ *TK*, *ad loc.*

/66/ *Sect*, 93 n. 324.

/67/ *Tosefet Rishonim* II, 176.

/68/ So Ran, *ad loc.* Note that both (pseudo-)Rashi and the Ran consider this vow (*neder*) by the Torah as equivalent to an oath (*shevu'ah*).

/69/ B. Shevu'ot 38b. The express mention of the Torah scroll comes in what appears to be a disjointed Hebrew statement following directly on the heels of an Aramaic dispute. Actually, this dispute was interpolated into the midst of the statement of Rabbi Judah. If so, the attribution would indicate that by the beginning of the amoraic period in Babylonia, such a practice was already considered normative in the case of the *shevu'at ha-dayyanim*, the judicial oath. This oath was used when the defendant admitted to part of the claim (*modeh be-miqṣat ha-ṭa'anah*). Note that while the printed editions quote the statement as attributed to Rabbi Judah in the name of Rav, manuscripts and medieval citations attribute the statement to Rabbi Judah himself (*DS*, *ad loc.*). Cf. also the aggadic reflection of this custom in the story of Zedekiah's loyalty oath to Nebuchadnezzar told in *Pesiqta' Rabbati* 26 (ed. Meir Ish Shalom, 129b). Nebuchadnezzar required Zedekiah to hold the Torah on his lap (*eṣel birkaw*) during the oath.

/70/ *Sect*, 93 n. 325.

/71/ So Maimonides, H. Shevu'ot 11:8. Note the comment of Joseph Caro, *Kesef Mishneh* to H. Shevu'ot 11:13 that Maimonides "recorded the law of the Gemara as is his custom."

/72/ Much material on this subject is contained in Cohen II, 710–733. Although he notes that oaths in Talmudic law are not required of witnesses, he nonetheless confuses judicial and testimonial oaths in the course of his discussion.

/73/ L. Ginzberg, *Geonica* (1909) II, 146, 152.

/74/ Cf. Abraham ben David, *Hassagot Ha-Rabad*, to Maimonides, H. Shevu'ot 11:13, who refers to the Geonic ordinance eliminating the use of the divine name. A more historical picture would see this decision as the result of a longstanding tendency observable in Rabbinic sources.

/75/ *War* 2, 8, 6 (135). The reason given by Josephus for their negative view of oaths is that "they say that one who is not believed without an appeal to God stands condemned already" (trans. Thackeray). This explanation is strangely reminiscent of Philo's view (on which see below, 137) and raises the possibility that Josephus here may have been influenced by Philo or by a common Hellenistic source. In any case, Josephus's reason cannot be accepted at face value as an accurate report of the reasoning of the Essenes.

/76/ *War* 2, 8, 7 (139–142).

/77/ *Ant.* 15, 10, 4 (368–371). Cf. *Ant.* 17, 2, 4 (41–42) from which we learn of an oath of loyalty not only to Herod but to Caesar (Augustus) as well. The latter passage numbers the Pharisees who were excused at 6000 and indicates that they had to pay a fine which was paid by the wife of Pheroras, Herod's brother. Schürer I (1973), 314 n. 94 takes the view that *Antiquities* speaks of two separate occasions on which such loyalty oaths were demanded. On the other hand, it is possible that we deal with one event, and that Josephus drew the two somewhat conflicting accounts from different sources. Indeed, A. Schalit, *Hordos Ha-Melekh* (1964), 163–165, sees the two passages as referring to one event. He dates the oath to 27 B.C. when such oaths were to be sworn to Augustus at the start of his reign and suggests that Herod took the opportunity to add himself to the oath. However, in the German revision of his work, *König Herodes* (1969), 316–321, he accepts the view that two oaths were sworn, one in 27 B.C. and one in 6 B.C.

/78/ *Sect*, 93 (continuation of n. 321).

/79/ *Meḥqarim* I, 38–42.

/80/ *War* 2, 8, 7 (139–142).

/81/ *Decalogue*, 84–86; cf. Belkin, 140–144. For Hellenistic influence on Philo's views regarding oaths, see J. Heinemann, "*Philos Lehre vom Eid*," *Judaica, Festschrift zu Hermann Cohens Siebzigstens Geburtstag* (1912), 109–118; and Goodenough, 41–44. Indeed, the Hellenistic world showed the same desire to avoid oaths by the name of the divinity for fear of the consequences of false oaths (cf. Lieberman, *Greek*, 124f.).

/82/ Cf. Goodenough, 174–183.

/83/ *Special Laws* II, 2–5.

/84/ Such oaths would be understood to mean: As surely as the earth exists, so shall I tell the truth and fulfill my word. Cf. Lieberman, *Greek*, 124f.

/85/ *Special Laws* II, 28, trans. Colson. Cf. Belkin, 144–150.

/86/ "*'Onesh Shevu'at Sheqer Le-Da'at Philon We-Ha-Rambam*," *Horeb* 2 (1934/5), 1–5. Cf. his *The Karaite Halakhah* (1913), 61f. As noted by Revel, Maimonides, H. Shevu'ot 12:1, 2 likewise takes the view that one who swears falsely simultaneously profanes (*ḥll*) the divine name. Cf. the objection of Abraham ben David, *Hassagot Ha-Rabad* (the authenticity of which is challenged by Shem Tov ben Abraham ibn Gaon, *Migdal 'Oz, ad loc.*) as well as in the response of Joseph Caro, *Kesef Mishneh* and Radbaz. Maimonides, however, places the punishment for this offense in a special category, *din shamayim*, because of its gravity. In his view, a punishment apparently different from *karet* will be administered at the hands of Heaven.

/87/ The comment of *Sifra'* Qedoshim, parashah 2:7 (ed. Weiss, p. 88c), *melammed she-shevu'at shaw ḥillul ha-shem*, seems only to repeat the verse. However, it is probably to be explained as based on the distinction drawn by some (see Targum Onkelos and Rashi to Ex. 20:7) between *shevu'at sheqer*, a false oath, and *shevu'at shaw*, an unnecessary oath. The statement of the *Sifra'* means that just as a false oath, explicitly mentioned in the verse, leads to profanation of the divine name, the same is the case when an unnecessary oath is taken.

/88/ *Special Laws* II, 28. Cf. *Life of Moses* II, 206 which seems to require the death penalty for blasphemy.

/89/ M. Sanhedrin 7:5 and B. Sanhedrin 56a. J. Milgrom, "The Concept of Ma'al in the Bible and the Ancient Near East," *JAOS* 96 (1976), 238 states that some Rabbinic views prescribe the death penalty for oath violation. The Rabbinic sources he cites, however, do not support his contention.

/90/ Cf. Ben Sira 27:14.

/91/ Cf. Matt. 23:16–22.

/92/ Contrast Test. Reuben 1:6 and 6:9 which contain an oath with the formula "I swear by God, the Lord of heaven."

/93/ Above, 138f.

/94/ M. Shevu'ot 4:13.

/95/ *Sifre* Num. 14 (ed. Horovitz, p. 19); *Mekhilta' De-Rabbi Ishmael* Mishpaṭim 16 (ed. Horovitz-Rabin, p. 303); and a *baraita'* in B. Shevu'ot 35b. Cf. Revel, "*'Onesh Shevu'at Sheqer*," 3f.

/ 96/ Cf. B. Giṭṭin 34b–35a; P. Giṭṭin 4:3 (45c).

/ 97/ Cf. Lieberman, *TK, ad loc.*

/ 98/ *Sect*, 406.

/ 99/ B. Bava' Batra' 32b–33a contains a story which indicates hesitation about oaths in the minds of some Babylonian Jews in the time of Abaye (third–fourth century A.D.).

/100/ *Sect*, 92f. n. 321.

/101/ See above, 115f.

/102/ J. Z. Lauterbach's view ("The Belief in the Power of the Word," *HUCA* 14 [1939], 287–302) that the power of the word is to be ascribed to the possibility that the angels might accidentally misinterpret man's words as those of the Deity (which he applies also to explain the Rabbis' hesitation about oaths, 300 n. 49) cannot be accepted. It results from the usual *Wissenschaft des Judentums* refusal to admit the possibility of a magical element in Judaism. Apparently, angels and their errors were more acceptable to Lauterbach than the power of the human utterance. Cf. also S. Blank, "The Curse, Blasphemy, the Spell and the Oath," *HUCA* 23, pt. 1 (1950–51), 73–83, 93–95.

/103/ Ex. 21:17, 22:27; Lev. 19:14, 20:9, 24:15.

/104/ For a survey and sources, see "Blessing and Cursing," *EJ* 4, 1086f.

/105/ The text should probably be dated to the amoraic period. Cf. *Sefer Ha-Razim*, ed. M. Margaliot (1966/7), 23–25, which includes a comment by E. S. Rosenthal.

/106/ Cf. Margaliot's list of "*baqashot*" on pp. 147f. The language of this text harks back to earlier magical traditions. See B. Levine, "The Language of the Magical Bowls," Appendix to J. Neusner, *A History of the Jews in Babylonia* V (1970), 343–375.

/107/ Contrast the view of M. Hengel, *Judaism and Hellenism* (1974) I, 218–247. His view is based on the identification of the Essenes with the authors of the scrolls and the assumption that Essenism was greatly influenced by Hellenistic civilization.

/108/ Cf. L. Blau, *Das altjüdische Zauberwesen* (1970), 123–137.

/109/ B. Temurah 3a; B. Makkot 16a; B. Shevu'ot 21a; P. Shevu'ot 3:10 (3:12, 35a).

/110/ P. Yoma' 3:7 (40d).

/111/ To Eccl. 3:11. Both versions are part of a series of traditions relating to the use and transmission of the *shem ha-meforash*. The *Qohelet Rabbah* version is rich in detail which might be explained as the result of secondary expansion. On the other hand, the Palestinian Talmud version seems at best to be a quick summary of a series of traditions. If so, the *Qohelet Rabbah* version would be primary, despite the late date of *Qohelet Rabbah*. (M. D. Herr, "Ecclesiastes Rabbah," *EJ* 6, 355 dates the final redaction of *Qohelet Rabbah* to not earlier than the eighth century C.E. and not later than the second half of the tenth century C.E.) In favor of the secondary nature of the *Qohelet Rabbah* version, however, is its reference to the use of only a part of the divine name for the imprecation. This might be the result of apologetic tendencies on the part of those who did not wish to allow that a Persian woman knew and could make use of the Tetragrammaton. A definite conclusion, then, is not possible.

/112/ If, on the other hand, the *shem ha-meforash* of the *Qohelet Rabbah* version was a reference to the forty-two letter divine name or to some other compound name, known to have existed in Jewish magical circles in Rabbinic and medieval times, the meaning of *ḥada' millah* would refer to one of the parts of the composite divine name. Cf. my study, "A Forty-two Letter Divine Name in the Aramaic Magic Bowls," *Bulletin of the Institute of Jewish Studies* 1 (1973), 97–102.

/113/ A third generation amora who immigrated from Babylonia to Palestine after studying in the Babylonian academies (Ch. Albeck, *Mavo' La-Talmudim*, 233–236).

/114/ See above, 111–115.

/115/ B. M. Lewin, ed., *'Oṣar Ha-Ge'onim* (1927/8–1942/3), Ḥagigah, p. 23; Qiddushin, p. 176; Eliezer Ashkenazi, *Ta'am Zeqenim* (1854), 57b; Judah ben Barzilai, *Perush Sefer Yeṣirah* (1885), 103–105; and L. Ginzberg, *Ginze Schechter* II (1929), 428 sec. 32. The text is discussed as well in my "Forty-two Letter Divine Name," 99f.

/116/ *Pesiqta' De-Rav Kahana'* (ed. Buber, 140a; ed. Mandelbaum I, 308).

/117/ Cf. the list of *baqashot* in *Sefer Ha-Razim*, ed. Margaliot, 147f.

/118/ See above, n. 11.

/119/ See above, n. 10.

/120/ Segal, *Ben Sira'*, 37–42.

/121/ Cf. *HAQ*, 32f., 45, 47.

/122/ S. Talmon, "*Maḥazor Ha-Berakhot shel Kat Midbar Yehudah*," *Tarbiz* 28 (1958/9), 1–20, slightly revised English translation, "The 'Manual of Benedictions' of the Sect of the Judaean Desert," *RQ* 2 (1959–60), 475–500. See also M. Weinfeld, "'*Iqbot shel Qedushat Yoṣer Bi-Megillot Qumran U-Ve-Sefer Ben Sira'*," *Tarbiz* 45 (1975/6), 15–26 and S. Talmon, "The Emergence of Institutionalized Prayer in Israel in the Light of the Qumran Literature," *Qumrân, Sa piété, sa théologie et son milieu*, ed. M. Delcor (1978), 265–284.

/123/ See M. Goshen-Gottstein, "The Psalms Scroll (11QPs^{a}), A Problem of Canon and Text," *Textus* 5 (1966), 22–33 and S. Talmon, "*Mizmorim Ḥiṣoniyyim Ba-Lashon Ha-'Ivrit Mi-Qumran*," *Tarbiz* 35 (1965/6), 215f.

/124/ Licht to our passage alludes to the blessings found in *Serekh Ha-Berakhot* (1QSb). Licht views these as being intended for recitation at some eschatological occasion (*Serakhim*, 274). He also refers to a liturgical text, 1Q34^{bis} (*DJD* I, 152–155), of which at least part was intended for the Day of Atonement. Certainly liturgical are the many hymns and prayers found in the *War Scroll* which Yadin has discussed in detail (*War Scroll*, 208–228). Numerous fragments scattered in *DJD* I and III may be liturgies or hymns. Of some relevance is J. Strugnell, "The Angelic Liturgy at Qumrân—4Q Serek Šîrôt 'Ôlat Haššabāt," *Suppl. to VT* 7 (1960), 318–345 and my "*Merkavah* Speculation at Qumran: The 4Q *Serekh Shirot 'Olat Ha-Shabbat*," *Mystics, Philosophers, and Politicians: Essays in Jewish Intellectual History in Honor of Alexander Altmann*, (1981), 15–47 as well as A. S. van der Woude, "*Ein neuer Segensspruch aus Qumran (11 Q Ber)*," *Bible und Qumran*

(Festschrift H. Bardke), ed. S. Wagner (1968), 253–258. The liturgy at Qumran is a subject deserving thorough study.

/125/ "Light on the Cave Scrolls," 395f., 400–402.

/126/ See Licht, *Megillat Ha-Hodayot*, 12–14.

CHAPTER SEVEN
THE SECTARIAN PENAL CODE

1. *Purpose of the Sectarian Penal Code*

It is widely recognized that the *Manual of Discipline* in its present form is a complete document made up of various regulations enacted by the sect. In the Introduction we have discussed a possible reconstruction of the literary history of this document./1/ In any case, the various building blocks making up the text as we have it were the creation of the sect, and these building blocks mirror different aspects of sectarian belief and practice as well as different periods in the history of the sect. The final redaction of the document must have been effected by the Qumran sect. It is therefore possible to assume that the redactor had a specific intention in mind when compiling this work, and that this intention was consistent with the needs of the sect to which he belonged.

The Penal Code under discussion here must, therefore, be understood from two points of view. First, it must be asked: How did this section originate, and what was its original form? And, second, the function of this material in the complete document as it now survives must be determined.

The code begins with a heading which sets it off from what precedes it (DSD 6:24):

ואלה הדברים אשר ישפטו בם במדרש יחד על פי הדברים

And these are the regulations/2/ by which they shall judge in the interpretation/3/ of the community/4/ according to the(se) cases./5/

Following this heading comes the list of offenses. These begin with *we-'im*, "and if," or *wa-'asher*, "the one who," and each is followed by its penalty./6/ This format is in striking contrast to the usual formulation of Qumran laws. Generally, such laws are in the form of apodictic statements. Often the reader is left to assume the consequences for violation of the particular regulations or to conclude that punishment was to be left "in the hands of Heaven," to borrow a Rabbinic phrase. On the other hand, the Penal Code of the *Manual of Discipline* is a series of casuistic laws, sharing the apodosis stating the duration of the penalty to be imposed. The uniqueness of this text is further highlighted by the apodictic formulation typical of the *Manual of Discipline* in its preceding sections.

At one time the *Zadokite Fragments* contained a list of offenses and punishments similar to that preserved in the *Manual of Discipline*. Indeed, remnants of this list are found in the manuscripts of the *Zadokite Fragments* discovered in the Cairo *genizah*./7/ J. T. Milik has announced the presence of a list of similar form to that of the *Manual of Discipline* in Qumran manuscripts of the *Zadokite Fragments*. According to his report, Milik's list is much more extensive and complete than that found in the Cairo manuscripts./8/ It may be, therefore, that the list incorporated in the *Manual of Discipline* represents some form of abridgment or summary of a much longer list which was in use among the members of the sect.

A major theme, if not *the* major theme, of the *Manual of Discipline* is entry into membership in the sect. Membership can be characterized as an obligation, taken on freely, to comply with the complex set of rules and regulations by which the sect lived. Now the list of selected offenses and punishments (DSD 6:24–7:25) occurs in the *Manual of Discipline* immediately after the description of the final stage of entry of the new member into the sect (DSD 6:21–23). Indeed, J. Pouilly,/9/ following J. Murphy-O'Connor,/10/ has placed the Penal Code of the *Manual of Discipline* in the third stage of the history of the Dead Sea sect./11/ This stage, in his view, was brought about by a substantial increase in the number of members in the sect. The sect had meanwhile become both institutionalized and democratized. It is difficult to escape the conclusion, therefore, that the rules numbered in our list are, in fact, connected with the ceremony of initiation into the sect. Our next task, though, will be to understand exactly how.

DSD 6:14 requires that before the final year of probation leading to full status, the applicant be taught all the laws of the sect (*mishpeṭe ha-yaḥad*)./12/ Such teaching occurred only after he had taken an oath "to return to truth and to turn aside from all iniquity" (DSD 6:15). Presumably, this was the formal oath required of those entering the sect. It is known from Josephus that similar oaths were required by the Essenes./13/ It is unlikely that all the intricacies of sectarian law could be taught even in a year, and it is further unlikely that in taking an oath, all matters of the sect's law could be mentioned. This list in the *Manual of Discipline*, then, served as an abridgment which presented a reasonable sample of the sectarian regulations in connection with the oath taken by the initiant.

A parallel practice may be cited from a somewhat later description of the conversion procedure of the tannaim./14/ The proselyte had to accept the entire Torah in order to become a Jew. Nonetheless, he could not be instructed in all of it immediately, and it was certainly impossible to catalogue all the commandments in the context of the conversion procedure. It was therefore required that as part of the ceremony some of the commandments of the Torah be made known, including some of the simpler and some of the more difficult to fulfill. (The terms for simpler and more difficult might also refer to the nature of the penalties imposed for the transgression.) In any case, laws of charity had to be included in the selection./15/

This parallel can help also to elucidate the nature of the selection. The passage from the *Manual of Discipline* includes both the most minor and the most major transgressions. The hierarchy of seriousness can be easily determined by the stringency of punishment which lasted from ten days to two years.

The order in which the transgressions are presented is also significant. The most serious offenses come at the beginning and at the end. This was, no doubt, to heighten the impression on the new member, so that he would understand the seriousness of that to which he was swearing.

The code of punishments, then, had a definite place in the initiation of new members. It served as a selection of sectarian laws of which the new member might be informed and to which he would assent by oath. Such a theory for the *Sitz-im-Leben* of this passage is consistent with the form of the passage, its relationship to other Qumran texts, and the selection of offenses.

But there is much more to be learned from this list of offenses. After all, if the list represents a selection to be used as part of the initiatory rites, then the process of selection must say something profound about the self-definition of the Qumran sect. Indeed, the manner in which one enters any social group is an important key to understanding the nature of that group. It will be seen that the list is as remarkable for what is omitted as for what is included.

The first law is certainly consistent with the use of this list in connection with initiation. It imposes a stiff penalty on anyone who lies regarding his personal property./16/ After all, all property had to be registered as part of the initiation process./17/ Although private ownership was maintained, all property had to be made available for communal use./18/ Following this is a regulation regarding the sectarian hierarchy, forbidding disrespectful answers to those of more senior rank,/19/ again a regulation essential for the new member. The list then continues by singling out an offense considered especially significant by the sect, the misuse of the divine name./20/

At this point come a number of laws regarding what the Rabbis later called "commandments between man and man." It is forbidden to speak angrily of the priests or to insult unjustly a fellow sectarian. Dishonesty and defrauding another member or the sect as a whole are likewise forbidden Holding a grudge and speaking offensively (or obscenely) are also prohibited.

This collection of offenses is clearly intended to facilitate life in a small, closed-in settlement such as that at Qumran./21/ Morally insensitive behavior exhibited in so densely populated and intensely intimate a society might lead to dangerous divisiveness. The new member must understand thoroughly that violations of the code in this area could not be countenanced.

Next the list turns to the conduct of the *moshav ha-rabbim*, the sectarian legislative and judicial assembly./22/ It is forbidden to interrupt, to fall asleep during, or to be absent from the meetings./23/ Expectorating is prohibited in this council, presumably since it was an act of utter disrespect and might communicate ritual impurity. At any rate, the new member is here reminded about the manner in which the sect will decide its law. While many other regulations appear in Qumran literature on this subject, the compiler of this code chose only a few to emphasize to the new member that he now owed allegiance, participation, and respect to the administrative and legal system of the group of which he was now a part.

Then follow laws of modesty and "good taste." It is forbidden to gesticulate in such a way as to allow the garment to shift immodestly. It is also forbidden to laugh aloud. The next set of rules regards the prohibition of gossip against an individual or against the sect as a whole.

The final regulations concern the prohibition of rebelliousness against the sect or against a member, presumably one ahead of the offender in rank. The text discusses the one who throws off the yoke of the sect altogether. If he is a recent member, he may repent and begin the initiation period anew, but if he has completed ten years, he may never again be admitted. The list of regulations, then, concludes by telling the new member about to be admitted that temporary or even permanent expulsion will result from his violation of the sect's laws./24/

It is not too difficult to understand the special significance of the material selected for inclusion in the list, but what has been excluded? It is significant that the major areas of sectarian law known from elsewhere in the Qumran corpus, including passages in the *Manual of Discipline*, the *Zadokite Fragments*, and other sectarian compositions, are omitted. Where is the Sabbath, and the laws of ritual purity and impurity? Where are the laws of sacrifice, marriage, and the calendar about which the sectarian texts polemicized so vehemently?

The answer can lie only in the nature of the process of entry into the sect. At the earliest stages of the novitiate, a would-be sectarian had to accept the Qumran interpretation of what the Rabbis later called *halakhah*. Thus, the new member had long ago conformed to the sect's views on ritual purity, Sabbath, marriage and the many other aspects of the law. Now, as he was embarking on his final probationary period and was soon to be welcomed into total membership in the sect, these sectarian interpretations of the law were already axiomatic. But the new status of the sectarian and his complete entry to the communal meals/25/ and to the *moshav ha-rabbim* necessitated that the sectarian regulations in this list be given particular prominence. The selection of these regulations, then, results not only from the general relationship of the list to the process of joining the sect, but, more specifically, to the use of this list as part of the last stages in the initiation rites.

It can now be understood that this code of punishments served a central role in the initiation process at Qumran. While it stresses certain regulations and omits others practiced by the sect, it is so composed specifically for use in the final stages of the initiation of new members. As such, the code probably constitutes a selection drawn by its compiler from a larger text. While this list remains valuable for our understanding of the law and organization of the Qumran sect, the purposes for which it was compiled and its place in the life of the sectarians must be borne in mind.

2. *Formulation of the Penalty Clauses*

The most serious problem posed by the sectarian Penal Code results from the inconsistency in the formulation of the penalty clause in each provision of the code. The first law contains a full statement of its penalty, and must, therefore, serve as the starting point for discussion of this problem. DSD 6:24 states:

> **אם ימצא בם איש אשר ישקר בהון והואה יודע ויבדילהו מתוך טהרת רבים שנה אחת ונענשו את רביעית לחמו**
>
> If there is found among them a man/26/ who lies/27/ regarding/28/ property/29/ knowingly,/30/ they/31/ shall separate him from the midst of/32/ the pure food of the assembly/33/ for one year, and he shall be fined/34/ one-fourth of his food (ration)./35/

Here a man who does not honestly reveal the extent of his property upon entry to the sect is punished in two ways—removal from the pure food of the sect, and the docking of one-fourth of his food rations for a specific length of time.

When the next provision (DSD 6:26f.) states its penalty as *we-ne'enash shanah 'aḥa[t]*, there is substantial difficulty in regard to whether this penalty refers only to the docking of rations, or if it also involves separation from the pure food. On the other hand, the parallel usage of the root *'nš* and its meaning in the sense of monetary fine, already attested in biblical usage, would favor the conclusion that the text intends here only the reduction of rations. It cannot be said that all fines included the separation from the pure food as the laws that follow are careful in distinguishing this detail./36/

The following table sums up the penalty clauses of the prescriptions of the Penal Code, omitting those dealing with expulsion and demotion which will be analyzed separately./37/

6:25	ויבדילהו מתוך טהרת רבים שנה אחת ונענשו את רביעית לחמו They shall separate him from the pure food of the community for one year, and he shall be fined one-fourth of his food ration.		
6:27	[ומובדל] [and he shall be separated]	שנה אחת one year	ונענש He shall be fined
7:2f.	ומובדל אל נפשו מן טהרת הרבים and he shall be separated unto himself from the pure food of the community.	שנה אחת one year	ונענש He shall be fined
7:3, 7:4, 7:5, 7:12, 7:18		ששה חודשים six months	ונענש He shall be fined
7:4f.	ומבדל and he shall be separated	שנה אחת one year	ונענש He shall be fined
7:6		שלשה חודשים three months	ונענש He shall be fined
7:8 (twice)		ששים יום sixty days	ונענש He shall be fined
7:9		שלושה חודשים three months	
7:9f.		עשרת ימים ten days	
7:10		שלושים יום thirty days	
7:11, 7:15		עשרת ימים ten days	ונענש He shall be fined
7:12, 7:13, 7:14, 7:15		שלושים יום thirty days	ונענש He shall be fined
7:16	מטהרת הרבים ונענש	שנה אחת	והבדילהו

He shall be separated for one year from the pure food of the community, and he shall be fined.

While the table points out some inconsistencies in the penalty clauses, it also reveals some regularities which shed light on the formulation of penalties. Separation from the pure food is normally associated with the one year punishment, and, as will be shown below, with that of two years. Therefore, it is probably intended as well by 6:27 which seems to require emendation to add *u-muvdal*./38/ Clearly, separation from the pure food is stated where it applies and is not to be understood elsewhere. *We-ne'enash* must be taken as referring only to the diminution of the food ration by one-fourth, and not to separation from the pure food./39/

Those offenses for which *we-ne'enash* does not occur and in which the text states only a duration for the penalty can refer only to the reduction of the food ration. First, none of these penalty clauses refers to periods of one or two years, and, elsewhere in the code, the removal from purity applies only to punishments of such duration. Second, the prescriptions which omit *we-ne'enash* occur between others in which *we-ne'enash* appears repeatedly. It is probable that the scribe (or redactor) of the code simply abbreviated occasionally, or accidentally omitted this word. Finally, the occurrence in DSD 7:16 of a totally different formulation shows how necessary it was to state explicitly separation from the pure food.

Once these regularities are noted, an important literary observation can be made. There is a general trend in this code to abbreviate progressively. The first prescription (DSD 6:25) states fully the separation from the pure food and then the docking of one-fourth of the food ration. The purity clause then appears in 7:2f. in its full form. In 7:4f. it begins to occur in an abbreviated form, until upon reaching 7:16 the scribe (or redactor) felt constrained to reformulate the entire matter, repeating the entire purity clause to avoid confusion.

The food ration clause also went through a similar transformation. At first it was explicitly stated that one-fourth of the food would be withheld. Then the scribe (or redactor) felt free to omit this detail, stating the exact duration and assuming the reader would understand what was intended. He then went even further and omitted *we-ne'enash*, assuming that the reader needed no further details other than the duration. Toward the end, he returned to the inclusion of *we-ne'enash*.

There is another possibility to be considered concerning the formulation of the Penal Code. It has been argued above that the sectarian Penal Code constitutes a literary unit which circulated independently and was then placed in the *Manual of Discipline* by its compiler. But perhaps the original unit was itself a composite of statements. Such a process is easily visible in the Mishnah, in which certain groups of independent statements which earlier compilers had grouped into literary units were included as is. In these cases, the redactor(s) retained the units as they were, and the disparate origin of the original statements can still be detected./40/ Such a possibility might apply here. While the exegesis presented above would remain valid for the finished product, it would lead to a conclusion that the varying types of formulations evident in the penalty clauses show that the code itself was compiled into its present recension from earlier short statements of a "*mishnah*-like" character.

3. *Ritual Purity and Impurity and the Admission Process*

In order to understand the meaning of the separation from the pure food, it is necessary to consider the process of admission to the sect as described in the *Manual of Discipline*. Like the Penal Code, these regulations are seen by Pouilly as part of the third stage in the history of the sect during which large numbers of new members were joining./41/ Our treatment of the initiation of sectarians will concentrate only on the way in which ritual purity and impurity are reflected in the admission process.

The first step towards entry into the sect was examination by the *paqid be-rosh ha-rabbim*, the "official at the head of the community." If this official approved the candidate, the novice took his admission oath and was then taught the sectarian regulations. Only then did the *moshav ha-rabbim*, the sectarian assembly, render a decision on him, presumably based upon his performance to date. If he passed this examination, he attained a partial status. Accordingly, DSD 6:16f. states:

ובקורבו לעצת היחד לוא יגע בטהרת הרבים עד אשר ידרושהו לרוחו ומעשו עד מולאת לו שנה תמימה

And when he draws near/42/ to the council of the community/43/ he shall not come in contact/44/ with the pure food of the community until they investigate him/45/ regarding his spirit and his deeds,/46/ until he completes/47/ one full year./48/

The novice, after a year in which he may not touch the pure food, is again examined by the *moshav ha-rabbim*. He is then elevated to a higher status in which his property is temporarily admitted into communal use. His property is registered officially, although full title remains his. Nonetheless, he is still not a full member, as DSD 6:20f. provides:

אל יגע במשקה הרבים עד מולאת לו שנה שנית בתוך אנשי היחד

Let him not come into contact with the liquid food of the community until he completes a second year among the members of the community.

After this second year he is again examined, a third time, by the *moshav ha-rabbim*. If he again passes (DSD 6:22):

יכתובהו בסרך תכונו בתוך אחיו לתורה ולמשפט ולטוהרה

They shall register/49/ him in the appropriate place/50/ in the list/51/ among his brothers,/52/ for Torah, judgment, and purity. . . ./53/

At this point he is finally a full member of the sect; his property is subject to communal use; and he takes his place in the sectarian assembly.

The stages of initiation regarding ritual purity may be summarized as follows: The recruit, even after his examination by the *paqid*, instruction in some sectarian teachings, and reexamination by the community, was considered ritually impure and was not permitted to come into contact with any of the sect's victuals. After his second public examination, he was allowed to touch only solid food for a year. Apparently, even after being permitted to come into contact with solid foods, he was still not considered entirely free of the danger of ritual impurity until he passed a final examination before the sectarian assembly. After this final examination a year later, he was allowed to touch even the liquid foods of the community. Only then was he a full member regarding *ṭohorah*, ritual purity.

The attempt by some scholars/54/ to understand *ṭohorah* as the purification ritual of the sect must be rejected. Indeed, the waters of purification, what the Rabbis called the *miqweh*, are explicitly mentioned in DSD

3:4f. where they are termed *mey niddah*/55/ or *mey raḥaṣ*./56/ That these are technical terms in the sect's biblicizing ritual and legal vocabulary can be shown beyond a doubt. CDC 10:12f. contains two occurrences of the expression *mey keli* which is likewise a technical term referring to water unfit for ritual purification. Separation from the *ṭohorah*, therefore, is not separation from purification in the ritual bath, but is, in fact, separation from the pure food of the sect.

The claim that *ṭohorah* refers to purification has been conditioned by the description of the Essenes given by Josephus, according to which upon completing the initial period of probation, the Essene novice is allowed "to share the purer kind of holy water."/57/ While it is indeed possible to take this phrase as referring to the admission of the novice to the ritual bath and attendant purification, it is also possible to take this "water" as similar to the *mashqeh* of the *Manual of Discipline*. Josephus would have mistaken the order and therefore placed the liquid before the solid food in describing the Essene initiation process./58/ If, on the other hand, the passage is taken as referring to purificatory rituals, it cannot be used to interpret *mashqeh* at Qumran. For the "water" of Josephus is opened to the novice at the beginning of his initiation, whereas *mashqeh* at Qumran is the last stage. Even if Josephus's "water" is the purificatory bath, the *mashqeh* of the sect remains the liquid food. As to when new members of the Qumran sect were admitted to the ritual bath we cannot say. It can be surmised that after the initial oaths, purificatory facilities were made available to the novices, even if these baths were perhaps separate from those of the full-fledged members.

The same school of thought which saw *ṭohorah* as the purificatory baths of the sect has claimed that the *mashqeh* is the banquet or communal meal of the sect./59/ This claim has been based on an understanding of this meal as sacral, a view argued against in this volume./60/ It must be said that the essential difference between the two roots for drinking in Hebrew, *šqh* and *šth*, is that the former is used in the context of providing or pouring water, even in terms of animals or irrigation;/61/ the latter is used for drinking at meals or at parties./62/ Hence, *mashqeh* is properly understood as a liquid, whereas *mishteh* is used for a party. This distinction is operative in both biblical and tannaitic Hebrew and should caution against the assertion that *mashqeh* refers to the banquet of the sect. In fact, DSD 6:4–5 and 1QSa 2:18 use the verb *šth* in reference to the sectarian communal meals.

G. Forkman has in this connection made the important observation that the *Zadokite Fragments* describe a process of admission which involves only the first two steps of the procedure described in the *Manual of Discipline*: examination by an official followed by the oath to join./63/ Based on this observation, he concludes that the *Zadokite Fragments* describe a community of novices./64/

Licht has examined these regulations of the *Manual of Discipline* in light of tannaitic traditions in a detailed appendix, and he has succeeded in providing a clear explanation of them. He notes that in tannaitic halakhic terminology, a *mashqeh* is a liquid fit for human consumption which may contract ritual impurity. Indeed, the sect used the term in the same manner. The *mashqeh ha-rabbim* is, therefore, any liquid used in the preparation of or served at the meals of the sect, mainly, in the view of Licht, the drinks consumed at the meals of the community.

Licht explains that according to tannaitic *halakhah*, purity regulations regarding the *mashqim*, liquids, are in some senses stricter than those regarding solid foods (*'okhelim*). The tannaim understood that even the smallest amount of liquid which is impure can render clothing, food and drink, or vessels impure. In the case of solid foods, there must be at least an amount the size of an egg in order to render anything impure. There is yet another stringency of liquids. Whereas solid foods are subject to a descending scale of impurity as the impurity is passed from item to item, liquids remain in the first state, which conveys the highest level of impurity, no matter how many times the impurity is transferred from liquid to liquid./65/

These two stringencies regarding liquids may indicate why the sectarian entry process was stricter regarding contact with the liquid than with the solid food. In order to understand fully the process of initiation, it must be remembered that one who eats or drinks impure food will himself become impure as a result, and that the impurity he contracts will be in the same degree as the food or drink consumed./66/

Based on all of these tannaitic regulations, Licht proposes a most attractive explanation for the process of initiation: One who is not a member is impure in the stage of *'av ha-tum'ah* (the highest stage except for a dead body which is *'avi 'avot ha-tum'ah*). During the first year the candidate is impure in the first degree. In his second year he is impure in the second degree, and only once he is fully accepted, can he be presumed to be pure.

Since the *'av ha-tum'ah* renders impure both solid foods and liquids, the candidate in his first year is (just like the non-member) forbidden to touch both liquid and solid food. Since in the second year he is considered impure only in the second degree, and can render impure only liquids, he is permitted to touch the *ṭohorat ha-rabbim*, the solid food of the community, but is still prohibited from touching the *mashqeh*, the liquid food. Only after becoming a full member is he assumed to be pure and is he permitted to touch both liquid and solid food./67/

While Licht's theory cannot be directly proven, it has the advantage of providing a reasonable explanation for the data presented in the texts and, as will be seen presently, also explains the process of removal from the pure food as a punishment. What emerges from Licht's proposal is a unique relationship between the processes of what the sect regarded as repentance through the joining of its ranks and ritual purification. This ritual purification was to the sectarians no more than a symptom of a spiritual purification. Indeed, the sect believed that no amount of lustrations and ablutions would render pure anyone who was a still unrepentant transgressor./68/ To the sect, then, ritual purity and impurity were symbolic manifestations of the moral and religious state of the individual./69/

4. *Ritual Purity and Impurity and the Penalties*

It is now time to assess properly the punishment of removal from the *ṭohorah*, the solid food of the sect. What this penalty meant for the sectarian was a return to the status of one who had passed the first examination by the *moshav ha-rabbim*. In order to regain his status in the sect, he had to complete again the full progression of initiatory stages. Only then would he again become a full member of the sect. In other words, removal from the purity constitutes demotion to the status of a first year novice.

That this interpretation is correct can be seen from two passages from the *Manual of Discipline*. The second to last provision of the Penal Code (the last is expulsion, and it will be dealt with below) is as follows (DSD 7:18–21):

והאיש אשר תזוע רוחו מיסוד היחד לבגוד באמת וללכת בשרירות לבו אם ישוב ונענש שתי שנים ברשונה לוא יגע בטהרת הרבים ובשנית לוא יגע משקה הרבים ואחר כול אנשי היחד ישב ובמלואת לו שנתים ימים ישאלו הרבים על דבריו ואם יקרבהו ונכתב בתכונו ואחר ישאל אל המשפט

And as to the man whose spirit shall turn aside/70/ from the teaching/71/ of the community, so that he rebels/72/ against the truth,/73/ and goes after the foolishness of his heart,/74/ if he repents, then he shall be punished for two years./75/ In the first,/76/ he may not come into contact with (even) the pure (solid) food of the community, and in the second,/77/ he may not come into contact (with) the liquid/78/ of the community. And he shall sit behind all the members of the sect./79/ And when he completes two years,/80/ the community shall be asked/81/ regarding his affairs./82/ If they bring him near,/83/ he shall be registered in his proper place/84/ and afterwards he may be asked/85/ regarding/86/ judgment./87/

In this passage the sectarian has transgressed to the extent that he is forced to repeat the initiation process. He must repent, for otherwise no hope of purification exists. If he does, he begins the process described above. He is readmitted to the various levels of purity at exactly the same stages as a new member. In short, he is sent back to the lowest grade and allowed to reenter the sect with the possibility of progressing through the ranks once again.

DSD 8:16–19 which was apparently drawn from another source by the compiler of the *Manual of Discipline* is a parallel to the last passage. Once again the process of readmission for a member who has strayed from the sectarian law is described here:

וכול איש מאנשי היחד ברית היחד אשר יסור מכול המצוה דבר ביד רמה אל יגע בטהרת אנשי הקודש ואל ידע בכול עצתם עד אשר יזכו מעשיו מכול עול להלך בתמים דרך וקרבהו בעצה על פי הרבים ואחר יכתב בתכונו וכמשפט הזה לכול הנוסף ליחד

> And any man from among the men of the covenant of the community,/88/ who turns aside at all/89/ from any commandment/90/ intentionally,/91/ shall not come in contact with (even) the pure (solid) food of the men of holiness. And let him not be aware of any of their counsel/92/ until his deeds be purified from all iniquity/93/ so that he walks/94/ on the perfect path./95/ Then they shall bring him near/96/ for counsel according to (the decision of) the community. And afterwards, he shall be registered in his proper place. And (it shall be) according to this regulation (for) everyone who joins the community./97/

Not only does this passage repeat the basic ideas of the previous quotation, but also it makes explicit the relationship between temporary expulsion and the process of entry into the ranks of the sect. The penitent sectarian is left with no choice but to tread his way once again through the long process of initiation.

That this passage is in fact drawn from another source is supported not only by literary considerations, but also by the existence of a fragment, 4QS^{e}, which is reported to contain a text of the *Manual of Discipline* omitting DSD 8:16–9:11. This fragment has been dated paleographically to an earlier date than the 1QS manuscript of the *Manual of Discipline*. At the very least, it may indicate the existence of a recension omitting this passage./98/ That the manuscript is earlier does not prove that it represents an earlier recension as 1QS could have been copied from an even earlier recension containing these regulations. The existence of this alternate recension, therefore, while of great importance, cannot lead in and of itself to conclusions regarding the history of the text of the *Manual of Discipline*./99/

This passage has also been treated by J. Pouilly in his discussion of the evolution of the penal legislation of the Qumran community./100/ He follows the approach of J. Murphy-O'Connor in regard to the historical evolution of the sect/101/ and within this framework sees the text under discussion as part of the second stage of development. Only in this stage does one find penal legislation for the first time./102/ Indeed, it was in his view the result of some limited experience with community life which led to the redaction of the rudimentary legislation found in DSD 8:10–12 and 8:16–9:2. He sees the text before us and the continuation in DSD 8:20–9:2 as having developed independently. Otherwise, he says, it would be necessary to conclude with G. Forkman/103/ that there is some contradiction here. Forkman suggests that we distinguish between the section concerning "a member of the covenant" (*'anshe ha-yaḥad*) and the other about "a member of the holy perfection" (*'anshe temim ha-qodesh*). He sees these as two distinct groups within the community./104/

Pouilly rightly objects to Forkman's distinction, but his own suggestion that *'anshe ha-yaḥad* was replaced at some point by the two new titles *'anshe ha-qodesh* (8:17, 23) and *'anshe ha-temim qodesh* (8:20) is speculative, to say the least./105/ Pouilly, therefore, suggests that these two texts are no more than successive stages of formulation of the very same law, the second (DSD 8:20–9:2) being in his view no more than a new redaction of the rule of "excommunication." Whereas the first deals with a period of temporary excommunication of duration to be determined in each case, the second is more severe and precise.

The truth is that this entire theory cannot stand. Even though there are literary reasons to believe that DSD 8:16–19 and DSD 8:20–9:2 may have originally been formulated separately, the proposal that the first is earlier and more lenient than the second cannot be supported by the text. The linchpin of Pouilly's theory is that both passages discuss the same sort of offenses. Actually, the first passage deals with offenses against the *miṣwah*, the sectarian legal principles derived through biblical exegesis, called the *nistar* in many passages. The second passage deals with laws explicitly stated in the Torah, elsewhere called the *nigleh*. This second class was regarded with much greater severity by the sect, just as the Rabbis somewhat later were stricter in regard to biblical injunctions than in regard to the Rabbinic ordinances.

It has already been shown that all one year punishments include both the reduction of food rations and the separation from the pure food. In light of the connection of the Penal Code with the process of sectarian initiation, and the conclusion that separation from the pure food constitutes a form of demotion to lower status, consideration must be given to the exact nature of separation from the purity for one year. Above, it was seen that a two year separation meant that the offender retraced his steps through the sectarian initiation process. It seems apparent, then, that in the second year of his separation it was only the *mashqeh*, the liquid food, with which he could not come into contact, whereas for the first year he was also prohibited from coming into contact with solid food. Now the same logic must be applied to the one year separation. If, indeed, the offender is simply being demoted to the status of one who has still not been completely accepted to sectarian life and who still has one year to go to complete his initiation process, then it would be expected that the one year separation from the "pure food" was actually separation only from the *mashqeh*. After all, new initiants were allowed to touch solid food during their last year of initiation. It was only the liquid food from which they were to be separated.

While this theory is extremely attractive in light of the connections of the purity and initiation aspects of sectarian life, it has one difficulty. It requires the assumption that *ṭohorah*, which above was shown to refer to solid food, as opposed to the *mashqeh*, or liquid foods of the sect, can also refer to *all* victuals. Indeed, such semantic range is possible and perhaps even usual. English "food" is sometimes to be distinguished from drink, but often includes it. The use of *ṭohorah* as a general term for pure food, both solid and liquid, appears in DSD 7:25 (the last provision of the Penal Code) where no one could possibly deny that both solid and liquid foods are included. It would therefore seem probable that the interpretation proposed here for the "pure food" of the one year punishment is correct, but it must be fully understood that absolute confirmation of this view is not available.

5. *Expulsion from the Sect*

Certain offenses were considered so heinous as to require permanent expulsion from the sect. The final provision of the Penal Code (DSD 7:22–25) specifies the conditions for unconditional and permanent expulsion from the sect:

> **וכול איש אשר יהיה בעצת היחד על מלואת עשר שנים ושבה רוחו לבגוד ביחד ויצא מלפני הרבים ללכת בשרירות לבו לוא ישוב אל עצת היחד עוד ואיש מאנשי היח[ד אשר ית[ערב עמו בטהרתו או בהונו אש[ר לוא בעצת[הרבים והיה משפטו כמוהו לש[לח הואה מאתם]**
>
> And any man who shall be (a member) of the council of the community long enough/106/ to have completed ten years,/107/ whose spirit backslides/108/ so as to rebel against the community, and who goes forth from before the community/109/ to follow the foolishness of his heart,/110/ shall not return to the council of the community ever again. And as to any member of the commun[ity who has] dealings/111/ with him regarding his pure food/112/ or his property wi[thout the consent] of the community, his verdict shall be like his (the one expelled) so that [he is]/113/ ex[pelled/114/ from them.]

This prescription concerns a veteran member who after ten full years backslides from the way of the sect. He is to be unconditionally and permanently expelled, and his former fellows are forbidden to deal with him in regard to pure food or financial matters./115/ Members who continue to be involved with him will be expelled from the sect as well.

This passage recalls Josephus's famous description of those expelled from the Essene sect. They were placed in a kind of ritual no man's land. They had taken oaths to observe purity laws and were now denied entry to the Essene fellowship, the only realistic vehicle for observing those laws. Hence, they are pictured by Josephus as virtually starving for lack of food. Often, he says, the Essenes would relent and readmit these unfortunates when they saw that they were at death's door, on the grounds that their suffering had atoned for their transgression./116/

What is important about this description is what it shows about the sincerity of those expelled. Even after expulsion, they still sought to observe the laws of ritual purity of food. The same is the case in the passage from the Penal Code of the *Manual of Discipline*. The former member is still trying to enlist his fellows in helping him to maintain the laws of purity as defined by the sect and as accepted by him in his oaths of initiation.

This description of final expulsion from the sect also brings to mind the tannaitic sources regarding excommunication. It must be remembered that excommunication in Talmudic sources does *not* constitute any kind of expulsion from the Jewish people. Indeed, the principle that no Jew could ever lose his status or his identity as a Jew was always part of the Jewish legal system./117/

The earliest tannaitic accounts of excommunication concern the *niddui*, a temporary ban of short duration. These bans are pronounced in order to maintain the authority of tannaitic *halakhah* as decided by the academies./118/ Only in amoraic times did the ban become a method for forcing recalcitrant members of the Jewish community to abide by the decisions of the Rabbinic courts. What is most interesting is that the tannaitic sources are narratives regarding the banning of some specific person, whereas legal statements regarding this procedure are absent in tannaitic literature. Only later in the amoraic period was this institution developed fully. This development took place in Babylonia where the struggle of the amoraim to establish and maintain their authority in the face of competing authority structures made the use of such procedures essential. The medieval *ḥerem* (excommunication) constituting severence from the Jewish community (such as that imposed on Baruch Spinoza) was probably evolved under the influence of Christian excommunication./119/

Apparently, the strict ruling of DSD 7:22–25 was reserved only for those who had been part of the sect for ten years. Others were always eligible to accept the sectarian penalties and repent of their transgressions. DSD 8:21–9:2 seems to bring together the entire procedure in a formulation which originated in a source different from that of the Penal Code./120/

כול איש מהמה אשר יעבר דבר מתורת מושה ביד רמה או ברמיה
ישלחהו מעצת היחד ולוא ישוב עוד ולוא יתערב איש מאנשי
הקודש בהונו ועם עצתו לכול דבר ואם בשגגה יעשה והובדל מן
הטהרה ומן העצה ודרשו המשפט אשר לוא ישפוט איש ולוא ישאל
על כול עצה שנתים ימים אם תתם דרכו במושב במדרש ובעצה [על
פי הרבי]ם אמ לוא שגג עוד עד מולאת לו שנתים ימים כיא על
שגגה אחת יענש שנתים ולעושה ביד רמה לוא ישוב עוד אך השוגג
יבחן שנתים ימים לתמים דרכו ועצתו על פי הרבים ואחר יכתוב
בתכונו ליחד קודש

As to any one of them/121/ who shall violate/122/ anything/123/ of the Torah of Moses/124/ intentionally,/125/ or dishonestly,/126/ they shall expel him from the council of the community and he may never return. No one of the men of holiness/127/ shall have dealings/128/ with him financially/129/ or in regard to his counsel/130/ on any matter./131/ And if he does (it)/132/ in error, he shall be separated (even) from the pure (solid food) and from counsel,/133/ and they shall exact punishment,/134/ that he not judge a(ny) man and that he not be asked for any counsel for the two years unless/135/ his way shall become perfect in/136/ the session, the exegesis,/137/ and the counsel/138/ [according to the communi]ty/139/ so that/140/ he has not erred again for two years./141/ For/142/ on account of one unintentional transgression he shall be punished/143/ for two years, whereas one who transgresses intentionally shall never return. However, the unintentional transgressor shall be examined for two years regarding the perfection of his path and his counsel, according to the community. Afterwards, he shall be inscribed/144/ in his proper place in the holy community.

While this text basically echoes the same principles already discussed, it is somewhat stricter in that it commands the immediate expulsion of anyone who violates a commandment intentionally. Only unintentional transgressors may repent. These two versions may represent different stages in the history of the sect./145/

A general statement on the subject of expulsion is also found in CDC 20:1–8:/146/

> וכן המשפט לכל באי עדת אנשי תמים הקדש ויקוץ מעשות
> פקודי ישרים הוא האיש הנתך בתוך כור בהופע מעשיו ישלח
> מעדה כמי שלא נפל גורלו בתוך למודי אל כפי מעלו יוכיחוהו
> אנשי דעות עד יום ישוב לעמד במעמד אנשי תמים קדש ובהופע
> מעשיו כפי מדרש התורה אשר יתהלכו בו אנשי תמים הקדש אל יאות
> איש עמו בהון ובעבודה כי ארורוהו כל קדושי עליון

> And this is the regulation/147/ regarding any of those who join/148/ the men of holy perfection/149/ and (then) loathe/150/ to carry out the commands of the upright/151/ (He is the man who is melted in the midst of a furnace.)/152/: When/153/ his deeds become apparent,/154/ he shall be dismissed/155/ from the congregation, like one whose lot had never fallen among/156/ the disciples of God./157/ According to/158/ his offense shall men of knowledge/159/ reprove him/160/ until the day when he will again stand/161/ in the formation/162/ of the men of holy perfection./163/ And until/164/ his deeds appear according to the interpretation of the Law/165/ by which the men of the holy perfection shall live, let no man agree/166/ with him in property or work,/167/ for all the holy ones of the Most High/168/ have placed a curse upon him./169/

This passage has been taken by J. Murphy-O'Connor as reflecting the second stage in the evolution of the *Manual of Discipline*. He sees this passage as an interpolation into the text surrounding it./170/ The text concerns a discouraged member of the sect whose attitude is eventually evidenced by infringement of the law. Other members of the community are enjoined from contact with him, in Murphy-O'Connor's opinion, "for fear that his discouragement might prove contagious." The text suggests "a continuous effort to revive the conscience and enthusiasm of the unfortunate delinquent." He sees the same tendency in DSD 8:17–19 and takes both texts as referring to the same procedure. (He theorizes that CDC 20:1–8 would have been composed after the death of the teacher of righteousness when the community was thrown into disarray leading to rebellion and defections./171/)

In this context the passage has been studied by J. Pouilly./172/ He sees the text as self-contradictory. He understands the first section (ll. 3b–4a) as indicating the expulsion of guilty sectarians. He sees the second section (4b–5) as referring to [temporary] "excommunication," while the final section (6–8a) again returns to the expelled member who has been cursed by the holy ones on high.

In order to deal with this apparent difficulty, he suggests restoring the text as follows:/173/

בהופע מעשיו כפי מעלו יוכיחוהו אנשי דעות עד יום ישוב לעמד
במעמד אנשי תמים קדש ובהופע מעשיו ישולח מעדה כמי שלא נפל
גורלו בתוך למודי אל כפי מדרש התורה אשר יתהלכו בו אנשי
תמים הקדש אל יאות איש עמו בהון ובעבודה כי ארורוהו כל קדושי
עליון

The text would then contain, in his restoration, two regulations: (1) the temporary separation of those who are guilty; they are to be reprimanded by the "men of knowledge" and reintegrated after changing their ways, and (2) the complete expulsion of one whose transgression is extremely grave or who refuses to mend his ways and the requirement that others break relations with him.

Pouilly sees here the same development which he found in DSD 8:16–24. He claims that the earlier, lenient first part (according to his restoration), involving only temporary exclusion, was replaced by a later and stricter regulation involving total expulsion./174/ Here again it must be objected that the distinctions he has drawn for DSD 8:16–19 and 8:21–9:2 are fallacious as these laws deal with different kinds of violations. The sections dealing with partial expulsion refer, like DSD 8:16–19, to the case of one who violates a sectarian ordinance derived through biblical exegesis. The more stringent expulsion is required for one who violates a law explicit in the Torah. There is no historical development visible in this passage from the *Zadokite Fragments*.

But is his restoration required? It is possible to interpret the entire text of CDC 20:1–8 as parallel to DSD 8:16–19. Its legal details would accord in every way to our passage. The strong language of our passage may be the result of the author's desire to stress the gravity of disobedience to the sect's regulations. The passage before us in CDC 20:1–8 would then refer only to one who had transgressed a sectarian ordinance derived by Scriptural exegesis. Such a person was demoted to the state of a novice (outside of the *'edah*) until such time as he was readmitted. Up to that point, his status was the same as that of those who were not members of the sect, and he was regarded by the sectarians as accursed.

Besides the general treatment of expulsion from the sect which has been analyzed above, the sectarian Penal Code singles out three specific offenses for expulsion from the sect. One of these, found in DSD 6:27–7:2 on the misuse of the divine name, is treated fully in Chapter VI. The other two should be noted here. They appear together in DSD 7:17f.:

ואיש ברבים ילך רכיל לשלח הואה מאתם ולוא ישוב עוד והאיש
אשר ילון על יסוד היחד ישלחהו ולוא ישוב

If anyone/175/ shall go about slandering/176/ the community/177/ he should be/178/ expelled/179/ from among them, and he may never return. And as to the man who complains regarding the foundation(s)/180/ of the community, they shall expel him, and he may not return.

These two provisions indicate a rather authoritarian aspect of the life of the sect. Indeed, any complaints or criticisms of the sect result in unconditional expulsion. While it is tempting to say that this refers to talebearing or expressing criticism to those outside the sect, this is highly doubtful. Other passages make very clear that the passing of information regarding the sect to those outside of it was forbidden. These provisions must, therefore, be explained otherwise.

From other passages it is known that criticism of the sect's leaders was forbidden and resulted in punishment. The relevant provision of the Penal Code, DSD 6:25–27, has already been discussed./181/ It requires that a punishment of one year be meted out to anyone who spoke against those above him in sectarian rank. DSD 7:2f. is a similar law regarding the priestly leader of the sect:

> ואם באחד מן הכוהנים הכתובים בספר דבר בחמה ונענש שנה אחת ומובדל אל נפשו מן טהרת הרבים ואם בשגגה דבר ונענש ששה חודשים
>
> If he spoke/182/ angrily against one of the priests registered in the book,/183/ he shall be punished/184/ for one year and separated unto himself/185/ from (even) the pure (solid) food of the community. But if he spoke unintentionally, he shall (only) be punished for six months.

The penalty for speaking out against the sect's leaders is here specified. Note that this penalty as well as that of DSD 6:25–27 is of no greater magnitude than those prescribed by the other provisions of the Penal Code.

If so, why so severe a penalty, total and final expulsion, for those who gossip against the community or against the "foundation(s)" of the sect? The answer lies in the nature of the sect. The sect is in essence a voluntary group of people bound together by common goals, aspirations, and beliefs. One who makes clear his total disdain for or rejection of the essential principles and teachings of the sect is now *ipso facto*, by his own actions, rendered impure in the first degree and simply cannot be considered a member. He himself does not identify with the sect, and, therefore, his expulsion is no more than a consequence of his own beliefs.

What must be noted here is the distinct contrast between this concept and that of membership in the Jewish people. Later tannaitic tradition takes the view that Jewish status can never be reversed even if the person in question strays totally from adherence to Judaism and worships other gods. The man is a transgressor, but he is still a Jew./186/ Most probably this concept originated much earlier in Jewish history. Even in the days of the polemics between the various groups of Jews in the Second Commonwealth (including the Dead Sea sect), the opponents are never read out of the Jewish people on doctrinal grounds.

The sect, no doubt, would have agreed with this concept, as they never accuse their opponents of having left the Jewish people. Transgressors they are, but Jews all the same./187/ But when it came to the sect itself, doctrine was a crucial issue. Those who did not accept its principles were therefore "impure" and could not be tolerated in the sectarian community.

Because of the sect's concept of determinism, it believed that it was predestined as to whether a person was to be among the Sons of Light (the sect) or Sons of Darkness (everyone else)./188/ For this reason, they had no hesitation about expelling a member who, as a result of his behavior, made it clear that he was predestined to be part of the camp of Belial. But there were also others whose infractions did not merit so extreme a punishment. They were members of the Sons of Light who had only temporarily strayed. Such people were to be punished with partial separation from the sect.

6. *Summary*

The Penal Code was one of the sources before the redactor of the *Manual of Discipline*. Originally, this code was composed to serve as a summary of sectarian offenses to be taught to the new member as part of the admission process. For this reason it contained mostly provisions relating to the sect's organization rather than its rituals. Penalties involved the reduction of food rations for a specified period, lasting from one month to two years. Penalties of one year also carried with them the prohibition of coming in contact with the pure liquid food of the sect, while those of two years included prohibitions regarding both liquid and solid food in the first year, and liquid alone in the second year. Some offenses were of such magnitude that they led to expulsion from the sect. These included intentional violation of a law of the Torah, and the total rejection of the teachings of the sect.

To a great extent, the sect defined itself as a group maintaining the ritual purity of its food. It was therefore appropriate that partial expulsion from the sect, as a result of violation of the ordinances, be expressed in the form of separation from the pure food. Indeed, the right to approach the pure food was a step in the process of being accepted as a full member of the sect.

But the exclusion from the pure food is even more. It is a consequence of the belief that the offender will defile it, for to the sect, ritual impurity goes hand in hand with moral impurity. A transgressor, by his very presence, brings ritual impurity. Purification can occur only when repentance has preceded it. The punishment of separation from the pure food, then, and his suspension from the *moshav ha-rabbim*, the sectarian legislative and judicial assembly, reduce the sectarian to the status of a novice. Once more he must complete the final stages of the novitiate before again taking his place at the table of the sect.

NOTES

/ 1/ See above, 4–6.

/ 2/ Cf. Ex. 21:1.

/ 3/ The words *bm bmdrš yḥd* are omitted in MS g. For alternate interpretations of this passage, see Wernberg-Møller, *ad loc.*

/ 4/ On *yaḥad* as a substantive name for the sect, see S. Talmon, "The Sectarian *yḥd*—a Biblical Noun," *VT* 3 (1953), 133–140.

/ 5/ On the use of *davar*, see above, 44 n. 47.

/ 6/ Cf. Licht, *Serakhim*, 157.

/ 7/ CDC 14:18–22.

/ 8/ *Ten Years*, 96.

/ 9/ *"L'évolution de la legislation penale dans la communauté de Qumran,"* *RB* 82 (1975), 538.

/10/ See above, 20 n. 4.

/11/ For a complete discussion, see above, 5.

/12/ On the significance of the term *mishpaṭ*, see *HAQ*, 42–47.

/13/ *War* 2, 8, 7 (139–142).

/14/ A *baraita'* in B. Yevamot 47a–b.

/15/ For a discussion of this passage, see my "At the Crossroads," 122f.

/16/ According to Licht, this law deals with an individual who conceals his property from the sect in order to avoid renouncing it (so also Pouilly, 541). This problem, he says, is liable to occur in a society which requires its members to surrender their property. This explanation is in line with Licht's approach to the property issue at Qumran. He claims that all private ownership was outlawed. Upon full admission to the sect, members surrendered all property and funds completely to the sect. The sect operated as a collective. Those texts which seem to indicate private ownership at Qumran are explained otherwise by Licht, although he admits fully the difficulties they pose (*Serakhim*, 10–13). Licht refers to the parallel from Acts 5:1–11. According to Acts 4:32 the members of the primitive church "had everything in common" (RSV). Vss. 35f. state that ". . . possessors of lands or houses sold them, and brought the proceeds of what was sold and laid it at the apostles' feet . . . ," for communal distribution. Acts 5:1–11 tells of how Ananias and his wife, Sapphira, attempted to retain a portion of the proceeds of the sale of their property, giving only a part to the Church. Peter accused them of lying. Each in turn fell dead after hearing Peter's accusation. Licht sees their death as a miraculous punishment. He compares our text, noting that the difference in the consequence of this offense stems from the nature of the texts. Acts surrounds the apostles with miracles, whereas "the *Manual of Discipline* is an actual code, intended, at least partly, for [actual] conditions" (my translation). See also M. Hengel, *Property and Riches in the Early Church* (1974), especially, 23–41. Hengel's treatment involves detailed discussion of the Hellenistic aspects of the early Christian attitude to property. It should be noted that no such influences are discernible at Qumran. Cf. S. E. Johnson, "The Dead Sea Manual of Discipline and the Jerusalem Church of Acts," *ZAW* N.F. 66 (1954), 108–109. This parallel shows only that in a situation in which a person must admit his holdings, he may choose to conceal some. Reasons can be varied. In the New Testament, the husband and wife wished to retain private possession of a part of their property. In the Qumran law, the violator wished to avoid recording his full possessions because he wished to pay less income tax (see above, 37f.) and to limit the community's ability to make *use* of his property. Wernberg-Møller offers a completely different interpretation of the passage. He understands our text to be dependent on Lev. 5:1 and to "deal with the case of a man who, testifying in money-matters, suppresses his knowledge and commits perjury." He specifically rejects the relevance of the passage in Acts 5:1–11. A. R. C. Leaney, *The Rule of Qumran and its Meaning* (1966), 200 accepts the view of Wernberg-Møller.

/17/ DSD 6:19f. This procedure took place only after the applicant had passed the initial test of the *paqid* and the first and second public examinations before the *rabbim*. As these examinations had to be separated by at least a year, the registration of property would not take place until the new member had been with the sect for at least a year. Even so, until the completion of a second year and the passing of a third and final examination, again before the *rabbim*, the property was not available for communal use. Only after this final examination could his property enter into communal use.

/18/ Rabin (*QS*, 22–31) reviews all the passages in CDC and DSD which give evidence for private ownership. He then concludes that what was communal was the disposal or use of property. The owners, however, retained the actual ownership. This view seems to accord best with the texts before us. Upon being accepted, the member's property was listed so that he could use it to pay fines, etc. or so that he could take it with him if he left the sect for any reason. Apparently, the sect was able to make use of and control the individual's property in accord with its policies. The passage under discussion here, then, must be taken to refer to an individual who lies about his property to the sect in order to prevent the sect's taking advantage of this property. In other words, he denies its existence to avoid sharing it and paying income tax on it. Some have argued that all references to private property are in CDC, whereas DSD legislates for a society based on communal ownership. This argument is falacious as references in the *Manual of Discipline* clearly refer to private ownership (Rabin, *QS*, 23–25). In CDC 14:20 there is a fragmentary text reading]בממון והוא יודע ומ[(cited by Licht in our passage). This is the reading of Rabin, but the last *mem* seems highly questionable on my photographs. Further, the reading of Rabin, [ ]ק[ ]ר[ ]א[, immediately before is highly doubtful. Rabin states that "the traces are not consistent with reading either *mĕshaqqer* (as in D.[DSD]) or *la-mĕvaqqer*." This may be part of a law identical to that of DSD which stood in CDC. This is supported by the variant of MS g to our passage: [*be*]-*mamon* (restored with Licht). If this is the case, it shows that the sect in both its main center and in its apparently far-flung settlements observed this same regulation and, therefore, that the economic character of the communities was at least similar in respect to communal use and private ownership. Wernberg-Møller to our passage assumes that the six days of CDC 14:21 belong to the penalty clause of CDC 14:20 which he restores as *'[š]r [š]q[r] bmmwn whw' ywd'*. He comments on the fact that DSD demands a one year punishment while CDC requires only six days. It is unlikely, then, that these two lines are to be connected. Rabin points out that no punishment in DSD is less than ten days. It should be noted that the sect was no doubt engaged in considerable agriculture. See W. Farmer, "The Economic Basis of the Qumran Community," *ThZ* 11 (1955), 295–308 and "A Postscript to 'The Economic Basis of the Qumran Community,'" *ThZ* 12 (1956), 56–58. Cf. also M. H. [Goshen]-Gottstein, "Anti-Essene Traits in the Dead Sea Scrolls," *VT* 4 (1954), 147.

/19/ On this law, see above, 39f.

/20/ See above, 133–144 for a detailed discussion of this law.

/21/ On the population of Qumran, see below, 209 n. 104.

/22/ See *HAQ*, 68–71.

/23/ This text is discussed in detail in *HAQ*, 69f.

/24/ On expulsion, see below 168–173. Cf. also the survey of offenses in Pouilly, 541–545. M. Weinfeld, "*Teguvot La-Ma'amarim*," *Shnaton* 1 (1975), 255–257 and "*Defusim*," 60–81, calls attention to many parallels between these regulations and those of the Hellenistic societies. It is difficult, however, to discern any direct influence from the material he has collected.

/25/ See below, 191–202.

/26/ Based on the wording of Deut. 17:2 (Licht). Note that MT reads *ki*. This is a case of either synonymous variance in the biblical text or adaptation by the sect. After all, *ki* can have several meanings (cf. the Rabbinic formulation in B. Rosh Ha-Shanah 3a; B. Ta'anit 9a; B. Giṭṭin 90a; and B. Shevu'ot 49b, all in the name of Resh [R. Simeon ben] Lakish, a third century Palestinian amora).

/27/ This is probably *pi'el* as the *qal* occurs only in Gen. 21:23, a passage with archaic flavor.

/28/ The use of the preposition *bet* with the verb *šqr* to indicate that about which one lies or is false is found in Ps. 44:18 and 89:34. This usage is found as well in Rabbinic texts (Ben-Yehudah, *s.v.*, p. 7449a) and in CDC 14:20 as restored in n. 18.

/29/ MS g reads [*b*]*mmwn*. *Hon* is primarily a wisdom term for wealth or property. Note the biblicizing tendency of Qumran terminology.

/30/ Cf. Lev. 5:3 and 4, *we-hu' yada'*. *We-hu'* functions here to introduce an adverbial clause. (For the form *hw'h* see Kutscher, "*Ha-Lashon*," 38, 46, especially 343–347 and 452; Goshen-Gottstein, "Linguistic Structure," 119; and for a detailed comparison with the Arabic dialects, S. Morag, "*Ha-Kinuyim Ha-'Aṣma'iyyim La-Nistar We-La-Nisteret Bi-Megillot Yam Ha-Melaḥ*," *Eretz Israel* 3 [1954], 166–169.) Brownlee translates, "and it became known." The pronoun would then refer to the lie (Heb. *sheqer*), and the verb would be passive. The parallel he cites is admittedly based on emendation. He also quotes H. L. Ginsberg's translation (in Brownlee), "and he (the Supervisor) knows it." The problem with this view is that the text mentions no official here, nor would it be necessary to mention the fact that the dishonesty became known, as otherwise, how could any action be taken by the sect?

/31/ Translating with Brownlee who notes that we are dealing with a plural verb written defectively. Ginsberg (see above, n. 30) refers this verb to the "Supervisor."

/32/ The *hif'il* of *bdl* normally governs the preposition *mi*(*n*). Num. 8:14 uses the preposition *mi-tokh*. Ehrlich, to Num. 18:14 explains that *mi-tokh* is used to indicate a partial separation, whereas *min* would indicate a complete one. Nevertheless, the use of the preposition *min* in a parallel passage in DSD 7:16 would indicate that this is an example of synonymous variance.

/33/ On this term see below, 162f.

/34/ For the extra *waw* on the end, cf. DSD 8:11 (and *HAQ*, 28 n. 48). The equivalence to *we-ne'enash* is certain in light of the occurrence of this form in successive lines of the Penal Code. While the form is that of the participle, we translate, "he shall" because the tense of the entire apodosis is determined by the imperfect (with future meaning) verb *wa-yavdiluhu*. For the use of *'et* here, cf. Deut. 22:19 (not exactly the same usage), and see Ges. sec. 121a and b, for the construction of passive verbs with *'et*. Ginsberg emends to *w'nšw*. Brownlee notes, however, that DSD never uses this verb in the active voice. He says that the final *waw* is to be deleted.

/35/ For *leḥem* in the general sense of food for humans, see BDB, 537a, sec. 2a, and Ben-Yehudah III, 2657b.

/36/ Cf. Forkman, 58 who reaches the same conclusion.

/37/ Note that the duration of "one month" alternately appears as "thirty days" (see the table, p. 160). This is in accord with the thirty day months which form the backbone of the sectarian calendar. See S. Talmon, "The Calendar Reckoning of the Sect from the Judaean Desert," *Aspects of the Dead Sea Scrolls*, ed. C. Rabin, Y. Yadin (1958), 178f.

/38/ While Wernberg-Møller and Licht see this law as involving only reduction of the food ration for one year, Brownlee correctly suggests that *u-muvdal* be restored in the space at the end of the provision (on which see Licht's textual notes *s.v. wa-'a]sher*). If so, the punishment would also include being excluded from the pure food (*ṭohorah*). Indeed, DSD 7:4–5 concerns an offense of similar character for which punishment includes removal from the pure food.

/39/ So Forkman, *Limits*, 57f.

/40/ Cf. Ch. Albeck, *Mavo' La-Mishnah* (1966/7), 88–98. While the methodological reservations expressed by G. Porton, "Ḥanokh Albeck on the Mishnah," *The Modern Study of the Mishnah*, ed. J. Neusner (1973), 218f. are valid to a great extent, and while the role of Rabbi Judah the Prince may have been less than that envisaged by Albeck, nevertheless, the evidence Albeck had collected supports the claim that as material was being redacted, some preexistent and previously redacted materials found their way into the larger document.

/41/ Pouilly, 538–540.

/42/ On *qrb* in the technical sense of joining the sect, cf. Lieberman, "Discipline," 199f. n. 8.

/43/ I.e. the sect.

/44/ The root *ng'* is used here as a technical term referring to contact by an agent of impurity with an item susceptible to impurity.

/45/ *Yidroshuhu*, a pl. form. Licht takes this as sing., referring either to the *mevaqqer* (whom he apparently identifies with the *paqid*) or as an impersonal usage. Wernberg-Møller takes this as sing. in his translation and then suggests the possibility of a pl. in his commentary.

/46/ A defective pl. form. See Licht, *Serakhim*, 47f.

/47/ The scribe of our MS alternates between the spellings *mwl't* (DSD 6:17, 18, 21; 8:26), *mlw't* (7:20, 22), and *mwlw't* (1QSa 1:10). Licht is no doubt correct that the word was pronounced *mulot*. Cf. *Serakhim*, 45.

/48/ Based on Lev. 25:30, *'ad melot lo shanah temimah*. (Licht, Wernberg-Møller). Wernberg-Møller suggests that the redemption of property in the walled city described in this passage served as the basis of the sect's law here. He claims that the walled city was taken as the sectarian community, and the dwelling house is equivalent to the novice. Only after a year is he regarded as belonging to the buyer (the sect) permanently; but for the first year he is still not really part of the community. While his analogy may have been the basis of the use of this verse in regard to sectarian initiation, the actual derivation of the initiation system will be shown here to depend on the laws of ritual purity as envisaged by the sect.

/49/ *Yikhtovuhu*, pl. or perhaps sing. to refer to the *mevaqqer* (Wernberg-Møller).

/50/ On *tikhon* (?) see Licht to DSD 5:3 and M. Z. Kaddari, "The Root TKN in the Qumran Texts," *RQ* 5 (1964–66), 219–224.

/51/ On this use of *serekh*, see *HAQ*, 64–67. These *serakhim* were the rosters of sectarians in order of their status in the sect.

/52/ The members of the sect.

/53/ The *plene* spelling is to indicate the equivalent of Masoretic *qameṣ qaṭan*.

/54/ Pouilly, 531, H. Huppenbauer, "*ṭhr und ṭhrh in der Sektenregel von Qumran*," *ThZ* 13 (1957), 350f.

/55/ Cf. Num. 19:9, 13, 20, 21 (twice); 31:23.

/56/ The noun *raḥaṣ* occurs in the Bible only in the phrase *sir raḥṣi*, "my wash basin" (Ps. 60:10; 108:10). The use of the verb *rḥṣ* with *ba-mayyim* in the sense of ritual purification through water is regular in biblical usage, particularly in Leviticus. Note also *šmn rḥṣ* in the Samaria Ostraca (H. Donner, W. Röllig, *Kanaanäische und Aramäische Inschriften* [1964], No. 18:6 and the comments in Vol. II, 184).

/57/ *War* 2, 8, 7 (138). Note that *Ant*. 3, 11, 1–5 (258–269) contains a survey of the purity laws of the Torah. The terminology used there for ritual immersion is totally different from that which appears in connection with the "holy water" of the Essenes. In *War* 2, 8, 5 (129) the terminology is again different.

/58/ So Neusner, *Purities*, pt. XXII, 45.

/59/ Forkman, *Limits*, 57.

/60/ Below, 191–197.

/61/ BDB, *s.v. šqh*.

/62/ BDB, *s.v. šth*.

/63/ *Limits*, 64.

/64/ Cf. *Limits*, 84 n. 101.

/65/ *Serakhim*, 299–303.

/66/ T. Ṭevul Yom 1:6; cf. M. Ṭevul Yom 2:2; T. Ṭevul Yom 1:3; Neusner, *Purities* XIX, 23f., 26f.; and Lieberman, *Tosefet Rishonim* IV, 162. For the text of T. Ṭevul Yom 1:6, see D. Pardo, *Ḥasde David, ad loc.*

/67/ Cf. Oppenheimer, 55–62 for a survey of purity regulations and Alon, *Meḥqarim* I, 158–169. Oppenheimer, 130f. makes the same proposal for the stages of entry to the Pharisaic *ḥavurah*. Cf. his discussion of the Dead Sea sect, 148–151. His protestations against facile comparison of these groups are to be taken most seriously. See also Forkman, *Limits*, 52–57 for a survey of the sect's entry procedures and ritual purity.

/68/ This connection is made explicit in DSD 3:4–12 (cf. Licht, *Serakhim*, 74–76). Cf. also Maimonides, H. Miqwa'ot 11:12 for a similar concept.

/69/ Cf. J. Neusner, *The Idea of Purity in Ancient Judaism* (1973), 50–54, and Huppenbauer, 350f. Much material is gathered regarding purity and impurity in Dead Sea texts by B. Sharvit, "*Ṭum'ah We-Ṭohorah le-fi Kat Midbar Yehudah*," *Bet Miqra'* 26 (1980/1), 18–27.

/70/ Licht compares the somewhat different use of this verb in Est. 5:9 and Eccl. 12:3 as well as M. 'Avot 5:22 (Aramaic). But in none of these cases is there any element of turning from the correct path to the incorrect. Wernberg-Møller translated "whose spirit swerves." He notes the use of Arabic "to deviate" and points, *e.g.*, to Quran 3:5 "concerning those in whose hearts there is deviation ( )."

/71/ The use of *yesod* here is difficult. Licht suggests four possibilities. (1) First is the view that it refers to the principles of the sect and its constitution. While this view is attractive, he notes that it is not possible to relate it to other usages in the language of the sect, since *yesode ha-berit* of CDC 10:6 is to be read *yissure ha-berit* (cf. *HAQ*, 52f.). (2) It is also possible that it is connected with the difficult phrases *le-yassed mosad 'emet* (DSD 5:5), and *li-yesod ruaḥ qodesh* (DSD 9:3), both of which present the activities of the sect as analogous to the construction of a building. [This building is most probably the Temple, as the sect saw itself as a substitute for the Jerusalem Temple which it believed had been profaned by improper practices.] (3) The third possibility (preferred by Licht) is to take *yesod* as equivalent to *sod*, in the sense of the community (cf. DSD 6:19). [The emendation to *sod* proposed by Wernberg-Møller for this and the preceding line 17 is unnecessary, even if his interpretation may be correct.] (4) The final proposal of Licht's is to emend *yswd* to *yswr* (*yissur*) which he takes in the sense of reproof or rebuke. In fact, *yissurim* are sectarian teachings derived from biblical exegesis (*HAQ*, 49–54). Pouilly (544) takes *yesod* to refer to dignitaries, or those responsible for the teachings of the sect. Our translation is meant to obviate the need for a decision in this matter, as it is expected that the publication of further texts will clarify this use of the root *ysd* and determine whether or not the text should be emended here.

/72/ Cf. CDC 1:12; 8:5; 19:17, 34; DSH 8:10 in which *wybgwd* is certainly to be read. Indeed, most of the *yod* is visible in the plates.

/73/ Licht notes that *'emet* here is probably a synonym for the Torah. He is probably correct that the reference here is to the legal principles of the sect, not to prohibitions explicitly stated in the Torah.

/74/ Cf. Deut. 29:18. Targum Onkelos translates *be-harhor libbi*, probably to be translated "according to the impure (sinful) thoughts of my heart." Targum Pseudo-Jonathan has *bi-teqof yiṣra' bisha' de-libbi*, "according to the strength of the evil inclination of my heart." These interpretations depend on the root of *sherirut*. Targum Onkelos takes it as *šwr*, "to see" (cf. Rashi, and Licht to DSD 1:6) while Targum

Pseudo-Jonathan takes it as *šrr*, "to be strong." (Neofiti MS 1 translates neutrally *maḥshevet libbeh.*) The Vulgate translated "*in pravitate cordis mei,*" somehow understanding *sherirut* to refer to transgression committed in private. LXX translates: *τῇ ἀποπλανήσει τῆς καρδίας μου*, "in the digression of my heart from the truth," or "in the deception of my heart." (Cf. Liddell and Scott, *s.v. ἀποπλᾰνάω*). See also M. Weinfeld, *Deuteronomy and the Deuteronomic School* (1972), 105f. and n. 5.

/75/ *We-ne'enash* here refers to the reduction of his food rations by one-fourth, as shown above.

/76/ Phonetic spelling omitting the *'alef*. Cf. Licht, *Serakhim*, 47 and Qimron, 56.

/77/ Before *u-va-shenit* there is a space large enough for two words, followed by four letters which were dotted to indicate erasure and then erased (Licht). Wernberg-Møller suggests that the "erasions [*sic*] and empty spaces suggest that the text before the scribe was illegible in parts." While this would seem to be the usual cause of such features in ancient manuscripts, Licht is certainly correct in asserting that there are no particular problems in understanding this passage as it stands.

/78/ Licht emends to *be-mashqeh*, as the preposition is required with the root *ng'*. He notes that the word *mashqeh* is suspended above an erasure. Wernberg-Møller states that the word *bb'yr* (*bi-ve'er*) "with the well," stood in the text before the erasure. Probably, when the scribe made the correction, he accidentally forgot to rewrite the preposition. Wernberg-Møller takes this reading as referring to the well from which the members drew their drinking water. The correction was to make clear, in his view, that it was the drinking water, and not the well itself, which was meant by the text. (On the figurative well of CDC 3:16 which symbolizes the Torah, see Wernberg-Møller's note to our passage.) Note that according to CDC 10:12f., a collection of (stagnant?) water less than the minimum permissible for ritual immersion (*dey mar'il*, on which see Lieberman, *Greek*, 135 n. 151) is itself subject to ritual impurity. Since a well would normally contain more than the minimum for immersion, it can be assumed that it would not be subject to ritual impurity. Hence, the reading *bi-ve'er* may have been corrected for "halakhic" reasons. On the other hand, Wernberg-Møller's view that the *mashqeh* is only the drinking water of the sect constitutes too narrow a definition in light of what is known from the parallel laws of purity of food in tannaitic sources.

/79/ This sentence indicates that the offender, although forbidden to participate in the deliberations of the *moshav ha-rabbim*, was still allowed to attend them. This was probably the case as well with the new member in the process of passing through the stages of initiation. Although forbidden to participate in the decision-making process, these people sat in the back, much as did the tannaitic disciples at the meetings of the Sanhedrin (M. Sanhedrin 4:4). Cf. Baumgarten, *Studies*, 164, and D. Goodblatt, *Rabbinic Instruction in Sassanian Babylonia* (1975), 252–259. That parallels exist between the study sessions of the Rabbis and the practices of the Qumran sect has been noted by Rabin, *QS*, 103–108. Licht asserts that from other texts it seems that all the other punishments mentioned in the Penal Code included deprivation of the right to be present at the *moshav ha-rabbim* because the offenders were seen as impure. This view, however, cannot be substantiated. On the contrary, his suggestion that we interpret the other passages in light of this one is correct.

Those deprived of the right to be part of the sect's *'eṣah*, "council/counsel," could be present but were not permitted to speak. This is logical since demotion renders the offender a first year initiant who has passed the examinations of the *paqid* and the *moshav ha-rabbim*. From this point, he attended the sessions, although only two years later, after successfully passing the series of examinations, was he permitted to give his own views and cast his vote.

/80/ For this use of *yamim*, see BDB 799b. For *shenatayim yamim*, see Gen. 41:1; 2 Sam. 13:23, 14:28; Jer. 28:3, 11.

/81/ *Nif'al* (so Brownlee, Wernberg-Møller, and Licht).

/82/ He is again examined, in the same way that a novice would be given his final examination.

/83/ As the root *qrb* in the *qal* means to join the sect, the *hif'il* means to "accept (someone) for membership."

/84/ On the sectarian rosters, see *HAQ*, 65–67.

/85/ *Nif'al*, cf. n. 81.

/86/ See BDB, 40 and 41 (n. 2) regarding the use of *'el* and *'al*. The claim of BDB that this is the result of scribal error in MT must be rejected as our passage and many others show that this was a matter of usage.

/87/ Or "regulation(s)."

/88/ Translating with MS d which omits the first occurrence of *ha-yaḥad*. Otherwise, it is possible that *'anshe ha-yaḥad* and *berit ha-yaḥad* in our text represent two different readings which have been conflated to produce the reading of MS 1QS. In such a case, we would say that MS d represented a later recension which had corrected the text appearing in 1QS to avoid the conflation, thus giving rise to what might be termed a "corrected conflated reading." Cf. *li-verit yaḥad* in DSD 3:11f.

/89/ For the *qal* of *swr* followed by *davar*, literally "in regard to anything," see Deut. 17:11. Cf. DSD 1:15 in which *davar* is not used. Note also Josh. 11:15 in which the *hif'il* of *swr* is followed by *davar mi-kol 'asher ṣiwwah*.

/90/ On *miṣwah* in the sense of a law derived through sectarian biblical exegesis, see *HAQ*, 47–49.

/91/ See above, 44 n. 52.

/92/ The passage would seem to indicate that he was not permitted to attend the sessions of the *moshav ha-rabbim*, even as an observer. On the other hand, see n. 79 for evidence that such offenders were permitted to attend. Two possible explanations can be offered. We can interpret this text to mean that he was not allowed to take an active part in the discussions. However, the use of *yd'* would seem to indicate that he could not even be present. If so, a better approach is to see this entire text as an alternate and somewhat stricter recension of the previous text, taken by the compiler from a different source. Whether an historical progression from stricter to more lenient or *vice versa* can be detected in sectarian law is a matter that requires careful study, not simply the assumption that the stricter is always older. This assumption has been transferred by some from the nineteenth century *Wissenschaft des Judentums* view of the history of Rabbinic *halakhah* to the scrolls, but its validity as a general principle has yet to be proven for either corpus.

/ 93/ Cf. CDC 10:3 and DSD 5:13f. (Wernberg-Møller); DSD 9:9 (Licht); and Ps. 119:9.

/ 94/ Note the form of *le-halekh* and cf. tannaitic Hebrew *le-lekh*.

/ 95/ *Temim derekh* is to be understood as if the order of the two elements of the construct were reversed.

/ 96/ See above, n. 83.

/ 97/ Licht correctly notes that this last clause means that the repentent member is to be treated as though a new applicant. (Contrast Wernberg-Møller.) Perhaps we should translate, "This regulation shall be just like that for anyone who is added to the community." The *nif'al* of *ysf* should be taken in the tolerative sense.

/ 98/ J. T. Milik, "(Review of) The Manual of Discipline by P. Wernberg-Møller," *RB* 67 (1960), 413; *Ten Years*, 123.

/ 99/ For this reason the conclusions of Forkman, *Limits*, 562 cannot be accepted.

/100/ Pp. 526–532.

/101/ See above, 4–6.

/102/ This stage is also characterized in his view by the replacement of the priests by the *rabbim* in matters of government of the sect.

/103/ *Limits*, 59.

/104/ *Limits*, 60, 66.

/105/ This explanation is dependent on his views on the history of the sect which themselves depend on such terminological distinctions. Hence, he falls victim to circular reasoning here.

/106/ Licht prefers to adopt the reading of MS e *'d* (*'ad*), apparently because of the parallel usage in 6:17, 20f., 8:26. The problem here is that *'ad mulot* (cf. above, nn. 47, 48) means "up to," which would indicate that our law deals with one who is a member in his first ten years. On the other hand, the context clearly requires the sense of "more than." For this reason, the reading *'al* is to be preferred. Wernberg-Møller points to Ps. 19:7, 48:11 and Job 37:3 in which *'al* means "as far as," but this is not really the same as "more than." The use of *'al* for "more than" does occur in CDC 10:21, on which see *HAQ*, 90–98.

/107/ Wernberg-Møller notes 1QSa 1:6–8 in which it is stated that for the first ten years of his life a child should be trained in the Bible and its sectarian interpretation. During this period he is part of the *ṭaf* (so Licht, Barthélemy read *bṭb*). Apparently, ten years had some significance for the sect, although the fact that no duties are specified for the ten year old makes it doubtful that any great importance should be attached to this period. Parenthetically, it should be noted that Barthélemy's translation, "*et qu'il progresse* . . ." (*DJD* I, 112), itself indicates the unlikely nature of his reading. His dismissal of the reading *ṭaf* in light of the poor state of the correction in the MS seems unnecessary. The attempt of Richardson, 111 to substantiate Barthélemy's reading by reference to *bṭb* in Nabatean and Palmyrene inscriptions is unconvincing.

/108/ For the combination of *šwb* and *bgd*, cf. CDC 19:34 (Wernberg-Møller). On *ruaḥ*, see J. Licht, "An Analysis of the Treatise on the Two Spirits in DSD," *Aspects of the Dead Sea Scrolls*, ed. C. Rabin, Y. Yadin (1958), 87–100.

/109/ Wernberg-Møller points to *wa-yeṣe mi-lifne* in Gen. 4:16 (cf. Lev. 9:24, 10:2). He is no doubt correct in stating that our author substituted *ha-rabbim*, the sect, for the Tetragrammaton in the biblical examples. Indeed, the sect saw itself as representative of the revealed will of God on earth. Rebellion against it was tantamount to rebellion against the Deity. What is most interesting is that the sect apparently saw Cain's leaving the presence of God in Gen. 4:16 as referring to his spiritual downfall. Cf. Nahmanides, *ad loc.*

/110/ See above, n. 74.

/111/ Cf. DSD 6:17, 22, 9:8 and CDC 11:4, on which see *HAQ*, 109 n. 167.

/112/ No doubt including the *mashqeh* as well.

/113/ On the long forms of the pronoun found at Qumran, see Qimron, 225–227.

/114/ A *nif'al* with elided *he'*, *lī-shalaḥ* equivalent to *le-hishalaḥ*.

/115/ After all, a nonmember of the sect (which this man now is) was assumed to be ritually impure and to transmit this impurity. Accordingly, DSD 5:16 prohibits eating the food of nonmembers. (*Ywkl* is derived from the root *'kl*, with the *'alef* elided.) DSD 5:16f. forbids doing business with nonmembers except in a cash transaction which did not come under the prohibition of *'al yit'arev*. Probably the prohibition was against entering into dealings in which property would be held in common. Cash transactions, therefore, may have been permitted, even with the former sectarian who had been expelled.

/116/ *War* 2, 8, 8 (143–144).

/117/ See my "At the Crossroads," 139–149.

/118/ Forkman, 92–98, who bases himself on an unpublished dissertation by C.-H. Hunzinger, *Die jüdische Bannpraxis in neutestamentlischen Zeitalter* (Göttingen, 1954), which is summarized in *ThLZ* 80 (1955), 114f.

/119/ For a parallel from the Greek world, see G. Blidstein, "'Atima: A Greek Parallel to Ezra X 8 and to the Post-biblical Exclusion from the Community," *VT* 24 (1974), 357–360.

/120/ Licht, *Serakhim*, 184 takes the view that this passage originated in the same source as DSD 8:16–19 (quoted above, 166) which immediately precedes it. He explains the long introduction to our passage (not quoted here, ll. 20f.) which clearly should appear at the beginning of a literary unit and not in the middle, as the result of a decision by the redactor to switch the order of the material to place the lesser case before the more serious. Hence, he reversed the order, and neglected to move the introduction as required by the new order. While it is possible that such a change of order occurred, it is equally possible that the redactor drew these two passages from different sources.

/121/ Wernberg-Møller notes that this is the only occurrence of this form in 1QS, although it is common in 1QIsa[a]. Cf. Qimron, 228.

/122/ It is difficult to see how the suggestion of Yalon, to understand this as a *hif'il*, can be seriously entertained (cf. Wernberg-Møller, *ad loc.*). The verb *'br* without *'et* in the sense of "violate a command, covenant" occurs in Deut. 17:2; Is. 24:5; Hos. 6:7, 8:1. (Cf. Ps. 148:6 and Job 14:5 where the object is *ḥoq*.) The root *'br* followed by the preposition *m(in)* occurs in Deut. 26:13.

/123/ For this use of *davar*, see above, n. 89.

/124/ The *plene* spelling *mwšh* occurs in DSD 1:3, 5:8, 8:15; DSW 10:6; DST 17:12. On *torat mosheh*, see DSD 5:8; CDC 15:2 (on which see above, 136); CDC 15:9, 12, 16:2. This phrase clearly refers to laws explicit in the Torah as opposed to those derived by the sect through their own "inspired" exegetical processes (so Licht, *Serakhim*, 183).

/125/ See above, 44 n. 52.

/126/ Licht takes *bi-remiyah* here to refer to private transgression and explains the passage "intentionally, whether in public or in private." *Be-yad ramah*, then, as he explains, functions here in the dual meaning of "intentionally" and "in public."

/127/ Cf. Ex. 22:30.

/128/ See above, n. 115.

/129/ The first *waw* of *be-hono* is suspended above the line.

/130/ For *hon* and *'eṣah* together, cf. DSD 6:22 (Wernberg-Møller).

/131/ Note that the connotation of *davar* here extends beyond the previous usage in this passage to include matters not of a legal nature.

/132/ Heb. *ya'aseh*, active, parallel to "who shall violate a word of the Law of Moses" (l. 22).

/133/ He is deprived of his right to participate in the community's legislative assembly, the *moshav ha-rabbim* (Licht to 8:18).

/134/ Licht's interpretation is undoubtedly influenced by the reading of MS d *u-min ha-mishpaṭ*. Wernberg-Møller suggests that *'asher lo'* introduces "a quotation from the community's code of law," and translates, "they shall study the rule (which runs). . . ." The reading of MS d, however, quoted in n. 141 below, obviates this clever interpretation.

/135/ Understanding *'im* as equivalent to the more usual *ki 'im*. This solves the problem raised in Wernberg-Møller's n. 69.

/136/ Licht's interpretation seems to require "according to." Cf. Wernberg-Møller, *ad loc.*

/137/ A reference to the sectarian legal exegesis. See *HAQ*, 54–60.

/138/ For this clause MS d reads *we-shav ba-midrash u-va-'eṣah.*

/139/ Restored with Licht and Wernberg-Møller. Cf. DSD 9:2. Licht notes that the tops of the letters *rby* are visible.

/140/ Medial *mem* in final position.

/141/ The entire preceding clause is preserved in MS d:
שנת[ים ימי]ם ושב במדרש ובעצה אם לא הלך עוד בשגגה עד מלאת לו שנתים

/142/ For this spelling of *ki*, see Kutscher, 16f., 134–136, and Qimron, 69.

/143/ His food ration shall be reduced by one-fourth. See above, 159.

/144/ Cf. DSD 8:16–19, above, 166.

/145/ Wernberg-Møller's attempt to explain this passage as based midrashically on Num. 15 is unconvincing in light of the absence of real reference to a two year period in that biblical passage.

/146/ On the literary structure of the passage, see Pouilly, 534f.

/147/ A common formula in the *Zadokite Fragments* (CDC 8:16, 24f.; 15:7; 16:12). It could not be located in any other Qumran text. Schechter and Rabin take *we-khen* as referring to the provisions of CDC 19:32–20:1.

/148/ See above, 68 n. 24.

/149/ Cf. CDC 7:5 (Rabin). Our translation is in accord with Segal to CDC 5:7 (8:22 in his numbering).

/150/ Schechter translated "cease" taking the form as derived from *qṣṣ*. He does, however, acknowledge the possibility of derivation from *qwṣ*. Schechter's view is tempting in light of the derivation of the noun *qeṣ* ("end") from *qṣṣ* (so BDB). Nevertheless, *qṣṣ* does not take prepositions as does *qwṣ*. Further, the use of *qṣṣ* as a verb meaning "cease" is otherwise unattested. Segal already rejected Schechter's derivation, preferring *qwṣ*. Rabin notes that while the verb takes the preposition *b-* in biblical Hebrew, *min* "appears occasionally" in Mishnaic Hebrew. Rabin's reference to B. Makkot 33b must be a typographical error for 23b (there is no 33b). If so, he is referring to M. Makkot 3:15. This reference, however, is of little value as the reading *qaṣah* seems very late. The reading *ḥatah* is found in MSS Kaufmann, Parma de Rossi 984 ("C"), 138, Munich, *ed. princ.* (Naples), and in the quotation in the Palestinian Talmud. In fact, the use of *min* with the verb *qwṣ* is highly questionable. The only example that could be located is *Sifra'* Qedoshim ('Arayot), ed. Weiss, 93b. This reading is supported by the commentary of R. Abraham b. David (Rabad). Nevertheless, MS Vatican Assemani 66, p. 412 reads: *qoweṭ* (*qwwṭ*) *mi-mezono*. A marginal reading has *bi-mezo*(*no*). The use of *bet*, confirmed by the MSS, is found in B. Niddah 31b; B. Bekhorot 37a; B. Megillah 28a. The interchangeability of the prepositions *bet* and *mem* which can be shown for Qumran Hebrew may have resulted in this phenomenon. See my "The Interchange of the Prepositions *bet* and *mem* in the Texts from Qumran," *Textus* 10 (1982), 37–43.

/151/ Rabin notes that *yesharim* is a designation for the sect in DSD 3:1 and 4:22. While Licht to the former passage suggests that this usage is conditioned by Ps. 107:42 and similar passages, our text would favor some kind of exegesis of Ps. 19:9. Alternately, it may be assumed that the author, as often, desired to omit the Tetragrammaton and neglected to alter the construct *piqqude* to the absolute *piqqudim*. Thus, we would translate, "the just commands," i.e. the Torah (Ps. 19:8).

/152/ This parenthetical statement seeks to indicate that a man who joins the sect and then refuses to follow its prescriptions is the subject of Ezek. 22:19–22. The application of prophetic material to the sect's own time and situation is typical of the *pesher* form of biblical exegesis. Here the message is that such a person will come to know the Lord, as God's wrath will be poured out upon him (v. 22). Perhaps the reference to Jerusalem in v. 19 meant to the sect that such a recalcitrant was really allied with the Jerusalem priesthood—the sect's mortal enemy.

/153/ The scribe first omitted the preposition *b* and began to write the *h* of *hwf*'. Realizing his error, he drew a line through the *h* and wrote *bhwf*'.

/154/ Schechter's suggested emendation to *be-hora*' ("deteriorate") makes no sense in light of l. 6 below, which he, however, misunderstood. Rabin goes to great lengths in explaining our form. He notes the medieval use of the *hif'il* of *yp*' for "to discover, examine" (Judah Ha-Levi, according to Ben-Yehudah, *s.v.*, IV, 2102), and suggests that we here have the passive (*hofʿal*) of this "transitive use." The *hofʿal* of this verb is nowhere attested. Yet it is not impossible to find otherwise unknown verbal usages of this sort at Qumran. Nevertheless, comparison with other occurrences of this verb at Qumran raises another possibility. In DST 5:32 there occurs *hwpyʿ* whereas in an almost identical parallel passage in DST 7:3 we find *hwpʿ* (cf. Licht; and M. Mansoor, *The Thanksgiving Hymns* [1961], to DST 5:32). Where we would expect *twpyʿ* in DST 4:23, we find *twpʿ*. Cf. also CDC 20:25f. and DST 11:26f. If there existed only the medieval copies of the *Zadokite Fragments*, the problem could be accounted for by supposing defective spellings of the *hifʿil* which resulted from the mistake of some scribe. The Qumran material makes this explanation impossible. Two suggestions can be made. It may be that at Qumran there was a *hofʿal* of this verb in use with the same meaning as the biblical *hifʿil*. Or it can be that under the influence of the final *ʿayin*, infinitive and imperfect forms existed in the *hifʿil* which omitted the *i* vowel, perhaps by analogy with the imperative singular masculine *hofaʿ*. It is not possible in light of the parallels to claim that the *hifʿil* was restricted to the transitive use "reveal" at Qumran and that the intransitive was then expressed in the *hofʿal*. (See Yadin's lexical note in *War Scroll*, 222f. n. 3.)

/155/ The Babylonian vocalization provided in the MS indicates a *puʿal*, *yeshullaḥ* (gemination of the middle consonant is not indicated here). We do not translate "sent away" or "banished" as it appears from the continuation that the dismissed member continued to live in proximity to the sect and might be reinstated when he had mended his ways.

/156/ Literally, "had not." The root *npl* in the *qal* followed by *goral* occurs in Ezek. 24:6; Jon. 1:7; 1 Chron. 26:14. In Prov. 1:14 there appears the *hifʿil* of *npl* with *goral* followed by the preposition *be-tokh*, "among." Cf. the *hifʿil* used in DST 7:34. See Licht, "*Ha-Munaḥ*," 90–99, especially 95–99 (on the use of *goral* to refer to the sect). Segal notes that *she-lo'* is the only use of the particle *she-* for *'asher* in these fragments.

/157/ From context this is clearly a term for the sect. The phrase is taken from Is. 54:13 which, however, has the Tetragrammaton (so 1QIs[a]). The sect substituted *'el* as part of its general tendency to avoid the Tetragrammaton in sectarian writings. New JPS translates, "disciples of the Lord." Cf. also John 6:45. The Targum to Is. 54:13 translates, "*'alefin be-'orayta' da'donai*," "learned in the Torah of the Lord."

/158/ In biblical usage, *ke-fi* has the connotation of describing quantity, as "in proportion to," "according to the number of" (BDB, 805b). This compound preposition seems to have fallen into disuse in the Talmudic period as the only uses listed in the concordances are citations of Lev. 25:52, *ke-fi shanaw*, dealing with *halakhot* derived from that passage. *Ke-fi* does occur in Ben Sira 6:8 (medieval MS A); cf. Segal, *Ben Sira*, 36.

/159/ *Deʿot* is a poetic, amplificative plural. It occurs in CDC 15:15 and DSD 3:15 (*'el ha-deʿot*, "the God of knowledge"). (Cf. Ges. sec. 124e and Driver, *Samuel*, 25.) It is uncertain if this is a reference to the entire sect or to some group within it, perhaps the *maskilim*. (On the *maskil* at Qumran, see *HAQ*, 25 n. 24 and the sources cited there.) Pouilly, 535, suggests that the *'anshe deʿot* are "a particular group, perfect in its knowledge of the law and most able to impart to the offenders the zeal to practice the observances." (p. 535, my translation). Schechter's reading *m'wt* (*me'uwwat*? Segal compares Eccl. 1:15) is clearly incorrect as can be seen from the photographs.

/160/ Schechter's *yzkyrwwhw* (*yazkirwehu*?) is also a misreading according to the photographs. Reproof at Qumran was more than a private affair. It was a formal warning and written recording of a man's offense, to some extent similar to the Rabbinic *hatra'ah*. See the detailed discussion of this reproof, above, 89–98. Note that the scribe first wrote the letters *yḥ*. Realizing his error, he crossed out the letters and continued writing the word correctly.

/161/ The imperfect of *šwb* followed by an infinitive construct (with *lamed*) with the meaning "to do something again" occurs in Deut. 30:9; Job 7:7; Ezra 9:14; and Neh. 9:28.

/162/ Hebrew *ma'amad* had various connotations for the sect. While in Rabbinic literature it can have the meaning of a group of Israelites who assemble to recite biblical passages while the priestly representatives of their town officiated in the Jerusalem Temple, this usage is not found at Qumran (against Rabin to our passage, with Wernberg-Møller, 56f. n. 55). This is despite the fact that the very same or similar institution is envisaged in DSW 2:4f. (Cf. *HAQ*, 78, where my use of the Rabbinic term *'anshe ma'amad* for the Qumran institution was somewhat imprecise.) Yadin has discussed the use of *ma'amad* at Qumran (*War Scroll*, 146, 206f.). He notes that the author of the *War Scroll* used *ma'amad* "to describe the position of the soldiers when they stand arrayed for combat" (146). He also observes that this term is used in regard to the annual mustering and covenant renewal (206f.) for the "body containing the priests, levites, and Israelites (each group according to its own subdivision)" (207). The *bet ma'amad* of DSD 2:19–24 is the correct position of each member in the formation (Licht, *ad loc.*). It is clear that the sect's religious and (even if imaginary) military life were very much intertwined (*War Scroll*, 59–61), a pattern very much a part of Israelite wilderness life, taken by the sect as a model for its own organization. See S. Talmon, "The 'Desert Motif' in the Bible and in Qumran Literature," *Biblical Motifs*, ed. A. Altmann (1966), 55–63.

/163/ Note the erasure of אשר אין גורלו בתוך א. This is presumed to be a dittography from l. 4. Pouilly (533) raises the possibility that *wbhwp' m'syw* of l. 6 should also be deleted. Presumably, the scribe either neglected to draw a line through it or simply did not recognize it as an error. In the end, however, Pouilly sees this suggestion as improbable.

/164/ The syntax necessitates the assumption that the preposition *bet* can have this meaning. Rabin's suggestion that the author forgot how he started the sentence seems less likely.

/165/ This phrase refers to the Torah as the sect had interpreted it and, therefore, to the laws derived through that interpretation. The punishment extends until the offender conforms to the sectarian law.

/166/ So Rabin. In his note, Schechter suggests "associate." Cf. 2 K. 12:9. This is the *nif'al* of the root *'wt*. Note that in Gen. 34:15, 22f. the party with whom the subject makes the agreement is preceded by the preposition *l-* whereas our passage uses *'im*.

/167/ Members of the sect may not hold property in common with the offender, nor may they enter into a partnership with him whereby they work together. That our text does not deal with a prohibition on buying from or hiring the offender is clear from a passage in DSD 5:14 which states regarding non-members of the sect: ואשר לוא ייחד עמו בעבודתו ובהונו . . ., "That he not enter into partnership with him regarding his work or his property. . . ." The use of the root *yḥd* in the *hitpa'el* makes clear that the text refers to a partnership (Licht, *ad loc.*). According to our law from the *Zadokite Fragments*, the offender is to be treated like a nonmember until he mends his ways and lives in accord with the sectarian interpretation of the Law.

/168/ This phrase is parallel to the Aramaic phrase in Dan. 7:18 *qaddishe 'elyonin*. (This passage does not appear in any published Daniel fragments from Qumran.) Despite the pl. *'elyonin* where we would expect the sing. *'elyon*, this is a reference to God, the Most High. The difficulty is in the meaning of *qedoshim*. Scholars are divided as to whether the Daniel passage refers to angels or men (J. Collins, "The Son of Man and the Saints of the Most High in the Book of Daniel," *JBL* 93 [1974], 50–53). While at Qumran *qedoshim* is usually an angelic designation (Yadin, *War Scroll*, 231 and my "*Merkavah* Speculation," commentary to Text A, l. 24. Note the parallels cited there from early Jewish mystical literature.), it may also refer to the members of the sect (Collins, 52 and n. 17. Segal took our paragraph to refer to the *ṣadiqim* of the sect.). In fact, in the military descriptions of the *War Scroll*, angels and men fight side by side (Yadin, *War Scroll*, 237). The sectarian saw himself as living in the company of angels. Perhaps, then, it is not necessary in our passage to try to decide between the two meanings. Indeed, this is the conclusion of Collins (66) in regard to the Daniel material.

/169/ The supralinear vocalization indicates *'ēreruhu*, a *pi'el* pl. perfect with a third person sing. objective pronominal suffix. The *pi'el* occurs only in Gen. 5:29 and in the phrase *ha-mayim ha-me'arerim* in Num. 5:18–27. New JPS translates the former "placed under a curse" and the latter "the water that induces the spell." Clearly the *pi'el* has the special nuance of inducing a spell or placing under a curse. This same usage appears in late midrashic and medieval Hebrew literature (Jastrow, Ben Yehudah, *s.v.*). It is probable that there are more examples of this phenomenon than have been recorded in the lexica, since in most forms, lack of vocalization makes it impossible to tell the *pi'el* from the more frequent *qal*. Only dictionaries based on good manuscripts will be able to isolate such examples. This clause probably alludes to the sect's annual convenant renewal ceremony in which, according to DSD 2:5–18, after the priests recited an adaptation and expansion of the priestly blessing (Num. 6:24–27), the Levites recite a series of corresponding curses (beginning with *'arur* and on the model of Deut. 27:15–26) regarding those in the lot of Belial—the enemies of the sect. This recitation is followed by the priests' and Levites' joining together for a final curse against anyone present who secretly intends to ignore the rules of the sect, following his own desires. He is to be cut off from the members of the sect and his lot cast with those cursed forever (*'arure 'olamim*). Our text in the *Zadokite Fragments* makes specific reference to this ceremony in which the sectarian who would go astray was put under this curse. Since the curse is conditional on his going astray, the *pi'el* usage is appropriate, for, as noted above, it refers to placing someone under a curse or spell.

/170/ "A Literary Analysis of Damascus Document XIX, 33–XX, 34," 553f. Cf. his "*La genèse littéraire*," 532f.

/171/ "A Literary Analysis," 554f.

/172/ Pp. 532–538.

/173/ P. 536. For the series of errors which in his view would have produced the text before us, see 536. *Bhwfṣ* in Pouilly's reconstructed text is certainly a typographical error for *bhwp'*.

/174/ Ll. 4b–5 correspond to DSD 8:16b–19. Ll. 3c–4a and 6–8a correspond to DSD 8:21–24a.

/175/ Wernberg-Møller emends *w'yš* to *w'm*. Rabin to CDC 10:13 suggests emending our passage to *w'yš 'šr brbym*. In fact, emendation is unnecessary here.

/176/ So Pouilly. Licht takes *yelekh rakhil* here to refer to one who divulges the secrets of the sect to a nonmember, in accord with Prov. 11:13 (cf. 20:19). But it is hard to believe that such vague terminology would be used to describe an offense outlined so explicitly elsewhere (DSD 4:6, 9:17; DST 5:25). Apparently, the root *rkl* fell into disuse by the tannaitic period. It is possible that Lev. 19:16, *lo' telekh rakhil be-'ammekha*, served as the basis of this provision. Whereas the Targumim take *be-'ammekha* as the object of the slander, Naḥmanides argues strongly that it refers to its occurrence in public. (His use of *ba-rabbim* is no more than coincidence, as *ba-rabbim* means "in public" in Rabbinic Hebrew.) The sect may have understood the commandment in both ways. Slander against one's fellow (in public) or against one's community is forbidden, hence, the two regulations of DSD 7:15–17. Although a *baraita'* in P. Pe'ah 1:1 (16a) explains Lev. 19:16 to refer to gossip, the dominant tannaitic view takes it to refer in some way to the misuse of judicial authority (*Sifra'* Qedoshim, chap. 4:5–7, ed. Weiss, p. 89a; B. Sanhedrin 31a. Cf. also B. Sanhedrin 30a [amoraic]). Note that a similar *baraita'* to that of P. Pe'ah 1:1 (16a) appears in B. Ketubot 46a in which the same *baraitot* are formulated so as to apply to the *moṣi' shem ra'*, the man who claims his bride was not a virgin.

/177/ That *ba-rabbim* designates the object of the slander is clear from comparison with the previous provision of the Penal Code, DSD 7:15f., where *be-re'ehu* designates the object of slander.

/178/ This use of the infinitive is also found in DSD 5:24 (quoted above, 93) and in DSD 9:1, *le-hamit hu'*. Cf. Licht, *Serakhim*, 34f.

/179/ *Nif'al* with the *he'* elided. For such forms, see Licht, *Serakhim*, 46.

/180/ See above, 52 n. 162.

/181/ Above, 39f.

/182/ Licht notes Num. 12:1 (cf. Ibn Ezra) in which the *pi'el* of *dbr* is followed by the preposition *b* indicating the object of criticism.

/183/ On this list, elsewhere called *serekh*, see *HAQ*, 65–67.

/184/ His food ration is to be reduced by one-fourth for the duration of his punishment.

/185/ Wernberg-Møller's translation (following Brownlee), "and shall be put in solitary confinement," is impossible in light of the analysis of the penalty clauses presented above. He has cited two parallels, but these are open to question. CDC 12:3–6 refers to some kind of supervision by the sect. After all, seven years of imprisonment would hardly have been a measure of repentance. CDC 13:4–6 refers to the quarantining of those afflicted with *nega'im*, diseases, as prescribed by Lev.

13:1–14:32. For this use of *'el nafsho*, cf. Deut. 21:14. Ben Sira 4:20, 22, cited by Licht, is not parallel to our usage.

/186/ See my "At the Crossroads," 139–146.

/187/ *Idem.*, 115f.

/188/ See Licht, "Two Spirits," 87–100 and P. Wernberg-Møller, "A Reconsideration of the Two Spirits in the Rule of the Community (1Q Serek III, 13–IV, 26)," *RQ* 3 (1961–62), 411–441.

CHAPTER EIGHT
THE COMMUNAL MEAL

1. *The Non-Sacral Nature of the Communal Meals*

Those who committed offenses against the sectarian law and way of life were in many cases punished by being excluded from the pure food of the sect. Exclusion from the pure food of the community meant that offenders were unable to eat everyday meals with their fellows at the same table, since violators of the law were regarded as sources of ritual impurity. Several passages in the scrolls mention the banquets of the sectarians. Ritual impurity was also cause for exclusion from these formal, communal meals. Mistaken impressions of the meaning of these meals and of their character have, in turn, led to a mistaken view of the sectarian Penal Code.

It is possible to grasp the importance to the sectarian of exclusion from the communal meals and the gravity of this penalty by establishing the links between these meals and the eschatological aspirations of the sect. Indeed, this penalty meant that the offender was now unable to participate in a central eschatological ritual of the sect. While deprived of the pure food, he was deprived of the right to prepare for the coming end of days.

Initial evidence of the banquet comes from the *Manual of Discipline*. DSD 6:2f. requires that wherever members of the group reside:

ויחד יואכלו ויחד יברכו ויחד יועצו

> Together they shall eat; together they shall bless; and together/1/ they shall take counsel./2/

While this passage clearly indicates that communal meals were to be a part of the activities of the sect, it gives no specific information regarding them. There is no mention here of how often such meals should occur or whether all or only some meals were to be taken communally./3/

Further, the actions described here—eating, blessing, and taking counsel—are independent of one another. The community had various gatherings to fulfill each purpose. Blessing was apparently part of a fixed regimen of daily prayers as has been demonstrated by S. Talmon./4/ The blessing in the passage under consideration does not refer to the blessings recited for eating food, but rather to the liturgical worship of the group./5/ Taking counsel occurred in the *moshav ha-rabbim*, the Qumran legislative and judicial assembly./6/ What, then, was the particular nature of the gathering at which the sectarians partook of a communal meal?

The text continues (ll. 3–4) by requiring that wherever there are ten members of the group, there must always be a priest. Members shall sit before him according to rank, and in this order shall they be asked for their counsel./7/ At this point comes the only direct mention of a meal in the *Manual of Discipline* (6:4–5):/8/

> והיה כיא יערוכו השולחן לאכול או התירוש לשתות הכוהן ישלח ידו לרשונה להברך בראשית הלחם או התירוש
>
> Whenever/9/ they arrange/10/ the table/11/ to eat or the wine/12/ to drink,/13/ the priest shall extend his hand/14/ first/15/ to bless/16/ the first/17/ (portion) of the bread/18/ or the wine./19/

Several details may be noted. First, the passage indicates no obligation that all meals be communal. Second, the priest receives this honored status because of his position, not because the meal is cultic. The Qumranites gave special status to the Zadokite priests among them./20/ Third, the mention of bread and wine does not indicate that the meal was of sacral character. Rather, the normal drink was a weak, diluted, and often unfermented grape wine, similar to modern grape juice. Bread was the staple food, and so it is represented in literary materials./21/

It must be emphasized that according to the reading of 1QS this passage does not refer to a meal or banquet at which both bread and wine are to be served, but rather to an occasion at which the table is set for bread *or* wine. What these occasions were is not specified, but they involved either food or drink.

Dominant scholarly opinion has tended to see these meals, on analogy with the Christian Eucharist, as sacral in character. This view is summarized well by B. Gärtner. He sees the sacral meal of bread and wine as central to Qumran fellowship, tracing its origins to the Temple and priestly traditions regarding the eating of sacrifices. Parallels may also be drawn, he notes, between the bread of the presence (*leḥem ha-panim*) and the Qumran "sacral meal." He goes so far as to suggest, following M. Black, that the meeting hall of the Qumran "monastery" "may have contained a table reminiscent of that on which the 'bread of Presence' was exhibited in the Temple." In this connection he also states that only those ritually pure could partake of the meals in the "Meeting hall." He correctly notes that not all of the meals of the community were eaten in this fashion. Nonetheless, he sees "the community's sacral meal" as being "an anticipation of the perfected ritual of the heavenly temple." Parallels from the meals of the Therapeutae and the Essenes, as described by Philo and Josephus respectively, are seen likewise to point "to the temple as the place of origin of their cultic meal."

Gärtner interprets in this context the purification rituals which, he claims, are in evidence in the water supply provided at one end of the "Meeting hall." Finally he concludes:

> The Qumran sacral meal may have been intended to replace the custom of the temple priests' eating the flesh of the sacrificial animals: the holy oblation must be eaten by the sanctified in a consecrated room—a situation emphasized by the rites of purification in connection with the meal. These rites may also have included the taking of a ritual bath, a condition likewise imposed on the temple priests./22/

Additional support for the view that the Qumran communal meal was sacral in character has been derived from comparision with the meals of the Therapeutae./23/ While this group, according to the description of Philo, is indeed in many ways similar to the Essenes as described in Philo and Josephus as well as to the sect whose literature was found at Qumran, there are also many differences./24/

In a recent paper, B. Bokser argues that Philo's account of the meals of the Therapeutae is conditioned by his "religio-sociological situation as well as his philosophical stance." In particular, the meals of the Therapeutae are seen as embodying characteristics which result from the "non-Jerusalem" setting./25/ In other words, the meal of the Therapeutae, according to Bokser, serves as a replacement for the Temple cult in which the Therapeutae did not participate. While Bokser does not discuss the reason for their nonparticipation, it can be presumed that it resulted from distance, as there is no evidence that the Therapeutae objected to the practices of the Jerusalem priesthood, as did the authors of the Dead Sea Scrolls.

In confirmation of his hypothesis, Bokser refers to the communal meals of the Qumran sectarians./26/ Bokser assumes that the purpose of the communal meals at Qumran was somehow sacral and that they were intended as a substitute for the sacrificial cult.

It is true that Philo's Therapeutae did celebrate their meals as a substitute for the Jerusalem cult. Yet this fact cannot be taken as evidence for the same phenomenon in the Qumran sect. Whereas the Therapeutae saw their meals as a substitute for the sacrificial service, it will be shown that no such point of view can be found in Qumran literature.

Y. Yadin has supported the claim that the communal meals at Qumran served as substitutes for the sacrifices in which the community did not participate by citing DSW 2:5–6. There, in sacrificial context, occur the words *'rk*, "to set out," and *shulḥan*, "table," used in the sense of "altar." These terms, as Yadin notes, also occur in the description of the communal meals at Qumran./27/ These linguistic parallels, however, do not prove Yadin's view. The use of eating and meal terminology in relation to sacrifices results from the concept found in the Bible and throughout the ancient Near East that sacrifices are a sort of meal, for or with the god(s)./28/ Hence, the cultic use of these terms. A glance at the lexica will reveal that these exact usages are common in the Bible, and no one would maintain that there took place communal meals as a substitute for the Temple cult in biblical times.

In actuality, none of the various aspects of the communal meals at Qumran necessitates understanding them as sacral meals. All the motifs—

purity, benedictions, bread and wine, and the role of the priest—can be explained against the background of contemporary Jewish ceremonial and ritual practice.

J. van der Ploeg has defined the sacral meal and discussed it in detail:/29/

> Since the essential act of a meal is the eating of the food, a meal can only be called sacred when the eating is a sacred act. This is normally the case when the food is sacred or when a sacred meaning is attached to it. In an article in the encyclopaedia, *Die Religion in Geschichte und Gegenwart* (2nd ed.),/30/ F. Pfister knows of four kinds of "cultic meals" (*kultische Mahlzeiten*): meals in which holy food is eaten; covenant meals; the meal of the sacrifice of communion; the meal offered exclusively to a god.

There simply is no evidence that the "meal" described in the Qumran passage cited above is a cultic or sacral meal. The purity of food and drink and the rituals associated with grace before and after meals were certainly widespread by this time, and in no way can it be said that every meal was sacral./31/

First and foremost among the so-called "sacral" ingredients in this meal is the aspect of the role of the priest./32/ It should therefore be explained that a tannaitic tradition of the House of Rabbi Ishmael contains a *baraita'* outlining privileges of this nature granted to the priests in recognition of their cultic status. The *baraita'*, basing itself in Lev. 21:8, states/33/ that a priest should be given the opportunity to be called to read the first portion of the Torah/34/ (which includes the recitation of the initial benediction), to pronounce the grace after meals first,/35/ and to receive first the best portion of food./36/ These procedures were probably ancient customs which showed no more than the deep reverence in which priest, Temple, and cult were held by the people. The demonstration of this respect in no way transformed the meal into a sacral occasion. On the contrary, if the meal were a sacral occasion, the privileges of the priest would be confined to areas in which *only* he might function. Rather, he is simply granted the opportunity to perform first rituals which each and every Jew present may fulfill.

The second motif usually seen as "sacral" is ritual purity. There is, of course, no question that the members of the sect ate their communal meals in a state of ritual purity. This concern is reflected in the process by which a person may join the sect.

DSD 6:13–23 contains prescriptions regarding the entrance of new members. These regulations, which have previously been discussed in detail,/37/ explain how the new recruit is progressively brought closer to complete membership. Part of this process relates to his coming into contact with the food and drink of the community. He is first allowed contact, after more than a year, with the pure solid food of the community (*ṭohorat ha-rabbim*). After a second year he is allowed contact with the liquid food (*mashqeh ha-rabbim*). This distinction between liquid and solid foods is similar to that of the tannaitic sources. Because liquids render foods susceptible to impurity, the regulations regarding the drink are stricter.

These purity laws, however, should not be confused with sacred meals. First, the laws of purity were to be observed by members at all times, whether they ate alone or communally. After all, these laws were the ancient heritage of the priesthood, and the Qumran sect, like the Pharisees, extended them to a wider circle of initiates. Second, purity of the food was an obligation which did not impart any sacral character to the act of eating. One might say that these purity laws were, from a functional point of view, similar to the laws of *kashrut*, although it must be emphasized that according to Jewish law they are two distinct entities.

Nor do the benedictions recited by the priest render the meal sacral. The tannaitic tradition mentioned above has been variously interpreted to indicate that the priest was entitled to the honor of reciting grace before and after the meal before the other participants./38/ In fact, such benedictions are a regular part of tannaitic tradition and are meant to emphasize man's dependence on the Creator for daily sustenance./39/ By early tannaitic times, blessings both before and after meals were most probably part of the *ḥavurah*. Indeed, the so-called *seder ha-se'udah*, the order of procedure for the formal dinner embedded in the Tosefta,/40/ is probably a reflection of the general dining patterns of Greco-Roman Palestine,/41/ somewhat refined by the tannaitic tradition. While there is no actual proof, it is extremely tempting to say that such procedures would have been followed by the members of the *ḥavurah*, at least in the last years of the Second Temple period./42/

In the tannaitic traditions such benedictions were part of all meals, whether formal or informal./43/ In fact, they had to be recited for anything eaten, and they bear no sacral connotations. In the same spirit are to be understood the benedictions mentioned in Josephus's description of the Essenes. There the priest says grace before and after the meal./44/ Josephus correctly interprets this practice in light of Palestinian Jewish custom of his day when he says that "at the beginning and at the close they do homage to God as the bountiful giver of life."/45/

Here again the non-sacral aspect of this grace must be emphasized. Indeed, despite the many assertions to the contrary, the entire description of the meal of the Essenes contains no sacral elements. Nowhere is it stated or even hinted that this meal was a replacement for the sacrificial cult or an imitation of Temple practice. On the contrary, the rules of purity and benedictions followed in it had a character and importance of their own. By this time they were totally divorced from the Temple context and part of the daily life of many pious Palestinian Jews of the time, whether Essenes, Pharisees, or members of the group whose texts were deposited at Qumran.

The passage before us refers to the eating of bread and the drinking of wine. The order in which these foods appear has caused some difficulty to scholars seeking to draw parallels with the Rabbinic tradition. Because of the prominence of the *qiddush* ("sanctification") prayer said over wine before the Sabbath evening/46/ and morning/47/ meals, questions have been raised regarding the order of the menu in our passage—with the bread preceding the wine. No such problem need be raised. The tannaitic passages regarding the procedure for the formal dinner, apparently concerning dinners not held on the Sabbath, describe as normal procedure the drinking of wine which was served during the meal. Such wine was brought to the table after the grace before meals had been said and the accompanying bread had been eaten./48/ This is no doubt the case in our text. The bread is that over which the grace before meals is said./49/ The wine is the wine served during the meal, and certainly not that used for the *qiddush* on Sabbath and festivals.

The meal discussed in the *Manual of Discipline* appears in the context of a discussion of the obligations of a group consisting of ten sectarians. It is certain from this passage and from the parallel to be discussed below that the procedure envisaged in the communal meal of Qumran requires a quorum of ten. Apparently, less than ten members (including among them a priest) did not constitute a quorum for such meals. Extremely important here is the parallel with the sectarian courts./50/ Ten judges constituted the court as described in CDC 10:4–10. Since the *Zadokite Fragments* legislate for groups of sectarians scattered in different places, termed "camps,"/51/ it seems that these courts would have been substitutes or agents of the *moshav ha-rabbim*, the full sectarian legislative and judicial assembly, which met regularly at Qumran. Whereas at Qumran cases would be tried before the *moshav ha-rabbim*, in the outlying sectarian communities the court of ten would try the case as a substitute for the assembly. Apparently, the same logic applied in the case of the communal meals. When there was a quorum of ten, the group could participate in the very same communal meals as those in the Qumran center./52/ Without such a quorum, the communal meals could not take place.

In an effort to find a parallel to this quorum of ten for the formal meal, Licht has drawn attention to a tannaitic tradition in T. Berakhot 5:23/53/ which provides that a group of ten men travelling along the road, even if eating from one loaf, should each recite the benedictions (meaning both before and after) individually. If this group reclines to eat in formal fashion, even if each individual eats from his own loaf, one recites the benedictions (and in this way the others fulfill their obligations). While the use of ten in this passage is interesting, it is doubtful if it has any relevance to the Qumran meal under consideration. The reference to ten in the Tosefta passage is probably to heighten the effect of the formulation. It says that even if there are as many as ten walking together (a ritual quorum), they still bless separately, so long as the formal act of reclining together is lacking. This is because only in such formal meals was the recital of benedictions delegated to one person.

A better parallel may be cited from M. Berakhot 7:3. This *mishnah* prescribes the various forms of the invitation to say grace (*zimmun*) recited when at least three adult males eat together. The text prescribes a version for three and one for ten. It then states that the law is the same for ten or ten myriads. In other words, ten is the dividing point. If there are more than ten, no matter how many people are actually present, the version for ten or more is employed. Paradoxically, the *mishnah* goes on to prescribe the versions for one hundred, one thousand, and ten thousand. The amoraim clearly understood the textual and halakhic problem posed by this *mishnah* and resolved it by attributing the first and second parts of the *mishnah* to two different tannaim./54/ From a literary point of view it is certain that the statement declaring the law to be the same for ten or ten myriads is an interpolation inserted into a previously existing tradition. If so, whoever formulated that insertion, either as a gloss or originally as an independent statement, saw ten, the ritual quorum, as the crucial matter here./55/ According to his view, only when ten were present, did the meal attain the true status of a formal, "public" meal requiring the expanded invitation to grace (*zimmun*). This tannaitic view, eventually adopted as the *halakhah*,/56/ shares its emphasis on the quorum of ten with the Qumran meal under discussion.

According to the parallel passage, 1QSa 2:11–22 (to be discussed below), after the benedictions on the bread are recited by the priest (and the Messiah of Israel at the eschatological banquet) each of the other guests, the members of the sect, is to recite his own benediction. Licht correctly notes that this is in direct opposition to the pattern found in the early tannaitic texts describing formal meals at which the grace is recited by one, thereby fulfilling the obligation of all./57/

In any case, it must be reemphasized that the recitation of benedictions before the meal and at its conclusion by a priest and the required ritual purity at the meal in no way rendered the meal sacral. Rather, these traditions were part of everyday life for the Jews of Palestine by this time and were observed by all the "sects" at every formal dinner or banquet regardless of its context. It can be expected that meals of groups, including family celebrations, the Passover Seder, and the meals of the Sabbaths and festivals, all followed these patterns in the Hasmonean and Herodian periods.

2. *The Messianic Banquet*

The key to understanding the function of the meal at Qumran is found in the *Serekh Ha-ʿEdah* (*Rule of the Community*). This text is a description of the days to come (*ʾaḥarit ha-yamim*), particularly of the Messianic banquet which will inaugurate this period./58/ The Dead Sea community believed that it was living on the verge of the days to come. The sectarians constituted their community as they believed Israel was to be constituted in the soon-to-dawn Messianic era. We might say that they lived with one foot in this world and one foot in the next. The Messianic banquet has so many features in common with the communal meal of the sect that one can only conclude that the function of the Qumran communal meals was to be what the Rabbis termed "a sample of the world to come."/59/ In other words, the significance of the communal meals was not sacral but rather related to Messianic expectations. The Qumranites did not act out a ritual as a substitute for a cult which they no longer practiced. Rather, they anticipated the great banquet to occur in the days to come./60/

1QSa 2:11–22 describes this banquet:/61/

> [מו]שב אנשי השם [קריאי] מועד לעצת היחד אם י[תוע]ד [בעת קץ] המשיח אתם
> יבוא [הכוהן ב]רואש כול עדת ישראל ו[כול אחיו בני] אהרון הכוהנים
> [קריאי] מועד אנושי השם וישבו ל[פניו איש] לפי כבודו ואחר [יבוא משי]ח
> ישראל וישבו לפניו ראשי [אלפי ישראל אי]ש לפי כבודו כ[מעמדו] במחניהם
> ובמסעיהם וכול ראשי [אבות העד]ה עם חכ[מיהם וידעיהם] ישבו לפניהם איש
> לפי כבודו [ואם לשולח]ן יחד יועד[ו לשים לחם ותי]רוש וערוך השולחן היחד
> [לאכול וה]תירוש לשתו[ת אל ישלח] איש את ידו ברשת הלחם ו[התירוש] לפני
> הכוהן כי[א הואה י]ברך את רשית הלחם והתירו[ש וישלח] ידו בלחם
> לפנים ואח[ר ישל]ח משיח ישראל ידיו בלחם [ואחר יבר]כו כול עדת היחד
> א[יש לפי] כבודו וכחוק הזה יעש[ו] לכול מע[רכת כי יו]עדו עד עשרא
> אנש[ים]

> [The ses]sion/62/ of the men of renown, [invited to] the feast/63/ for the council of the community when [at the end]/64/ (of days) the Messiah/65/ [shall assemble]/66/ with them. [The priest]/67/ shall enter [at] the head of all the congregation of Israel, and [all his brethren the sons of]/68/ Aaron, the priests, [who are invited] to the feast, the men of renown,/69/ and they shall sit be[fore him, each]/70/ according to his importance. Afterwards,/71/ [the Messiah] of Israel [shall enter]/72/ and the heads/73/ of the [thousands of Israel]/74/ shall sit before him [ea]ch according to his importance, according to [his station] in their encampments and their journeys./75/ And all of the heads of the [households of the congrega]tion,/76/ [their] sag[es and wise men,]/77/ shall sit before them, each according to his importance. [When they] mee[t/78/ at the] communal/79/ [tab]le,/80/ [to set out bread and wi]ne,/81/ and the communal table is arranged [to eat and]/82/ to dri[nk] wine, [no] one [shall extend] his hand to the first (portion) of the bread and [the wine] before/83/ the priest. Fo[r he shall] bless/84/ the first (portion)/85/ of the bread and the win[e and shall extend]/86/ his hand to the bread first./87/ Afterwa[rds,] the Messiah of Israel [shall exten]d his hands to the bread. [Afterwards,] all of the congregation of the community [shall ble]ss, ea[ch according to] his importance./88/ [They] shall act/89/ according to this statute whenever (the meal) is ar[ranged,]/90/ when as many as ten/91/ [meet] together.

From this passage the Messianic overtones of the Qumran communal meal are apparent. The Dead Sea community structured its life in "the present" in consonance with its view of the days to come. Accordingly, in such anticipation, they ate communal meals on some kind of regular basis, thus acting out the future Messianic banquet. While the Messianic banquet of Rabbinic sources was to be a one-time affair inaugurating the Messianic era,/92/ the Dead Sea community looked forward to a regular series of such banquets to be held in the days to come./93/

The banquet described in our text is presided over by the two Messianic figures expected by the Dead Sea community./94/ These were the priest, under whose administration and direction the cult would be restored in the

"New Jerusalem," and the Davidic Messiah who would serve as the temporal and military leader. In keeping with the importance of the priesthood at Qumran, and the emphasis placed upon the restoration of a purified cult in the days to come, the priestly "Messiah" is given the higher position.

What does this description of the banquet add to that outlined in DSD 6:4–5? First, both appear to be preceded by a meeting of the *moshav ha-rabbim*. Although not explicitly stated, it can be suggested that the communal meals of the sect normally took place in connection with meetings of the *moshav ha-rabbim*. The one priest of the former passage has here been augmented by the full complement of priestly members of the sect as well as the Davidic Messiah. The Messiah appears here as temporal leader, alongside the chief priest, clearly identical with the priestly "Messiah" expected by the sect. The Davidic Messiah is accompanied by the chiefs of the clans of Israel. Both priestly and temporal leaders sit in order of their rank. While this detail does not appear in the first description, it should be assumed that seating was also in accord with rank at the communal meals of the sect.

Note that the eschatological banquet is to be eaten seated, as opposed to the tannaitic usage of reclining at formal meals. Indeed, reclining was the Greco-Roman pattern, whereas the biblical tradition was one of sitting. The Messianic banquet, in keeping with the approach of the sect, would embody the traditions of Israel, not those of the Hellenistic pagans.

In both passages the two foods mentioned are bread and wine. While these probably do not constitute the entire menu, they are singled out since the benediction over the bread exempted the other foods as well, with the exception of the wine brought during the meal which required its own benediction. Whereas the communal meal of the sect in the manuscripts before us required *either* bread or wine, the Messianic banquet would involve both. In both passages the priest would recite the benediction first, and receive the first portion of the bread and wine. Regarding the Messianic banquet, it is stated that all others present would recite the benedictions in order of their rank after the priest (priestly Messiah). While this detail is omitted in the passage regarding the regular meal of the sect, it must have been the practice. Finally, both meals require the quorum of at least ten.

It is known from the *Manual of Discipline* that only full members of the sect not under any penalty could participate in these meals. Those outside the sect or those who suffered temporary demotion as a consequence of their transgressions were seen as ritually impure. After all, to the sectarians ritual impurity was a direct consequence of transgression of the divine law or its sectarian interpretation./95/

Needless to say, such a requirement of absolute ritual purity would have been expected for the Messianic banquet as well. Further, 1QS 2:3–9 indicates that those with physical imperfections were to be excluded from the "congregation" in the end of days. This attitude regarding ritual purity at the communal meals reveals the link between these meals and the Messianic expectations of the sect. The ultimate perfection of the Messianic era would be the realization of the sect's constant striving for total ritual purity. Thus, the communal meals establish a link between the sectarian observance in this world and those observances in the age to come through the crucial element of ritual purity. Total ritual purity may be seen as a catalyst which turns the ordinary communal meal into a foretaste of the great Messianic banquet at the end of days.

That the meal before us is not sacral, even while Messianic, is proven beyond a doubt. Its rituals in no way attempt to imitate or substitute for the Temple cult. On the contrary, they are simply those ritual aspects of the laws pertaining to meals observed by many Jews of the time. In the sectarian view these rituals would certainly continue in the end of days when they would be observed in complete perfection.

Simultaneously, the Jerusalem cult would be reconstituted in the Temple and conducted in accord with sectarian teachings under control of Zadokite priests. Thus, it cannot be maintained that the eschatological meal was intended as a substitute for the Temple, as the sect would certainly return to the mainstream of Temple worship in the end of days. The communal meals were not sacral substitutes for the Jerusalem-centered cult but a form of preparation for the soon-to-dawn eschaton and for the Messianic banquet to occur in the end of days. This banquet itself, arranged according to the customs of the communal meal of the present age, would not replace the Temple cult but would complement it in the age of Messianic perfection.

3. *Archaeological Evidence of the Communal Meal*

For the Dead Sea group we are fortunate in having not only the written remains in the form of the scrolls, but also the archaeological materials which shed so much light on life at Qumran. Archaeologists have established beyond a doubt that those who hid the scrolls in the caves are the same as those who inhabited the ruins at Qumran. It can, therefore, be established that here existed facilities for communal meals, and that remains of such meals may be found, whereas there is no evidence for a sacrificial cult.

Already during period Ib of Qumran's occupation, extending approximately from the reign of John Hyrcanus (135–104 B.C.)/96/ until the earthquake of 31 B.C.,/97/ the largest room of the Qumran buildings was a hall 22 m. long and 4.5 m. wide. The existence of a system for washing and draining the floor of this room has led scholars to the conclusion that it served as a dining facility and was used for the eating of communal meals. In an adjoining room were found some one thousand pottery vessels. These had been stacked according to type./98/ R. de Vaux has concluded that this was a storage room for the vessels used in the dining room./99/

In addition, one kitchen with several fireplaces was unearthed./100/ The kitchen, pottery storeroom, and dining hall continued in use during period II,/101/ which, according to de Vaux, lasted from the outset of the reign of Herod Archelaus (between 4 and 1 B.C.)/102/ to the Great Revolt against Rome. R. de Vaux has taken the view that Qumran was destroyed in June of 68 A.D. by the Romans./103/ He estimates that the group using these facilities "would not have numbered many more than two hundred members."/104/

Connected with the problem of meals at Qumran is the finding (primarily from period Ib) of deposits of animal bones buried between or around the buildings, placed in large sherds of pitchers or pots or in intact jars with their lids on./105/ These deposits are usually flush with the ground level. Examination of the bones shows that no deposit contained an entire skeleton. The bones had been taken apart and the flesh had been removed before burial. Many contain bones from a single animal, and the remainder represent two, three, or four animals. Animals included are: adult sheep, adult goats, lambs or kids, calves, cows, or oxen./106/

Many scholars have sought to explain these bones as either the remains of sacrifices or sacral meals. Without question they are bones of animals used for food. It has been determined that the meat was generally boiled and less often roasted. R. de Vaux states that the careful burials indicate a "religious preoccupation."/107/ He is hesitant to conclude that these animals are the remains of sacrificial rites. First, he says, no altar or cult place has been found at Qumran./108/ Second, we may add, the texts from Qumran make plain the community's view regarding sacrifice. They abstained from Temple offerings because of what they saw as the impurity of the cult as it was conducted by the Jerusalem establishment./109/ In the Messianic era the Qumranites would return victoriously to the "New Jerusalem" where they would reconstitute the cult according to their views and with their own priestly Messiah at its head./110/ There is no room in such a schema for sacrifice at Qumran./111/

Numerous attempts have been made to explain the reason for the burial of these bones./112/ None of these is satisfactory inasmuch as there is no literary evidence for the burial of bones in any Jewish sacrificial or religious rite./113/ Further, the archaeological parallels which have been cited are of questionable relevance. While it is possible that these bones are the remains of communal meals, their burial in the dining hall cannot be explained. There is no choice but to admit that until further discoveries, no satisfactory explanation can be offered. At all events, archaeological evidence shows that the facilities for communal meals were present at Qumran and that for some reason the remains of these meals were buried beneath the dining room.

4. *Summary*

The communal meal of the Dead Sea community was related to Messianic yearnings and expectations. In no way was it an attempt to replace the cult from which the group had withdrawn. As a matter of fact, the restored cult of the days to come is not mentioned in connection with the Messianic banquet. Both were to occur in the future age, but were separate motifs. Communal meals occurred, but there is no way of knowing how often. Archaeological evidence leads to the conclusion that the Qumran buildings were the site of these gatherings, and one can conjecture that the final Messianic banquet was to occur in the "New Jerusalem." The meals at Qumran, then, are not to be considered along with the meals of the Therapeutae and the Passover Seder. The latter two were replacements for the sacrificial cult and the result of the socio-religious framework in which these groups lived. The communal meals at Qumran were rather connected with the future expectations of the community and stemmed from the deep Messianic consciousness of this group.

The punishment of separation from the pure food of the sect meant that the offender could not partake of the communal meals. He was deprived of the opportunity to enact in the present age the Messianic banquet which would occur at the end of days. His offense had rendered him ritually impure, and his impurity had, in turn, led to his being considered unworthy of sharing in the coming age. Only repentance and the completion of his period of punishment would allow him to return to the full regimen of sectarian life and its attendant preparation for the soon-to-dawn eschaton.

NOTES

/ 1/ Licht and Carmignac, *ad loc.*, note that the scribe first began to write *lh*, erased it, and wrote *wyḥd*.

/ 2/ A reference to the holding of sessions similar to those of the *moshav ha-rabbim*, the sectarian legislative and judicial assembly.

/ 3/ Note that according to Philo and Josephus, the Essenes ate communal meals twice daily. See J. van der Ploeg, "The Meals of the Essenes," *JSS* 2 (1957), 167f. According to the texts now available, the Dead Sea communal meals do not include silence or require special clothing as do the Essene meals. The requirement of ritual purity, however, is common to both the Essenes of Philo and Josephus and to the sect of Qumran. See van der Ploeg, 168f.

/ 4/ See above, 143f. and 153 nn. 121–123.

/ 5/ Licht, *ad loc.*

/ 6/ For a thorough analysis, see *HAQ*, 68–75.

/ 7/ On this passage, see *HAQ*, 71.

/ 8/ We omit the dittography in this passage with the various editors. For commentary, see the notes of Licht and Wernberg-Møller, *ad loc.* Cf. also H. Ringgren, *The Faith of Qumran* (1963), 217–220.

/ 9/ On this form of *ki*, see above, 107 n. 65.

/10/ Pausal form in medial position. Cf. Licht, *Serakhim*, 46, and Qimron, p. 155.

/11/ Cf. Is. 65:11; Prov. 9:2 (Licht). Note the mention of wine in the latter passage and its implicit reference in the former. The space in the middle of *ha-shulḥan* in 1QS is the result of an imperfection in the parchment (Licht).

/12/ Licht cites P. Nedarim 7:1 (40b bottom), which discusses the definition of *tirosh*. The text states that *tirosh* in biblical Hebrew meant wine, while it implies that it means grape juice (unfermented) in Rabbinic Hebrew. Licht assumes that the text of DSD is in biblical Hebrew and understands *tirosh* here as wine.

/13/ That this root refers simply to drinking, and has no banqueting connotation, is shown above, 163.

/14/ Perhaps "hands," assuming a defective spelling. For such spellings, cf. Qimron, p. 231f. and Licht, *Serakhim*, 47f. Cf. T. Berakhot 5:7 according to *ed. princ.* and parallels cited by Lieberman, *TK*, *ad loc.* in which *posheṭ yado* is used in the same sense of taking food.

/15/ Phonetic spelling. Cf. Licht, *Serakhim*, 47 and Qimron, p. 56.

/16/ *Hif'il* usage in this meaning is unattested (Licht). Much less likely is the assumption that this is a *nif'al* which would require the translation, "to be blessed with . . ."

/17/ The word *bereshit* may be taken as either an adverb modifying the verb *yishlaḥ* (he should take his bread or wine first) or a noun meaning the first portion, as translated here. Cf. Wernberg-Møller.

/18/ The translation "food" would obscure the fact that bread, as the staple of the diet, was always blessed at the beginning of meals according to Jewish practice. This blessing exempted all other foods.

/19/ 1QS continues with a repetition of the last clause, *li-shetot ha-kohen . . . we-ha-tirosh*. The note of Milik, "(Review of) Manual," 413 on the reading of MS d is ambiguous, hence the confusion between P. Guilbert, "*Le plan*," 323–344 and Licht, *ad loc.*

/20/ Cf. *HAQ*, 71–75.

/21/ Licht to DSD 6:4–6.

/22/ *The Temple and the Community in Qumran and the New Testament* (1965), 10–13. Cf. M. Delcor, "*Repas cultuels Esséniens et Thérapeutes, Thiases et Ḥaburoth*," *RQ* 6 (1967), 401–425 who argues that the meals of the sect substituted for the cult and were seen by the sectarians as cultic acts. He bases his view on his interpretation of texts from Josephus's description of the Essenes and thereby confuses the issue.

/23/ Gärtner, 11f.

/24/ Schürer II (1979), 593–597. Cf. J. M. Baumgarten, "4Q Halakah[a] 5, the Law of Ḥadash, and the Pentecontad Calendar," *JJS* 27 (1976), 39–41 who suggests a calendric parallel between the Therapeutae and the Qumran community. Some differences regarding the meals are as follows: The Therapeutae did not serve wine or grape juice, but water (*Contemplative Life*, 73). They prohibited the drinking of wine (74) or eating of meat (73) (contrast also the Essenes of Josephus). The Scriptural study practiced by the Therapeutae (76–78) was not part of the Qumran meal, nor were the hymns (80). There is no mention of grace in the account of the Therapeutae.

/25/ B. Bokser, "Philo's Description of Jewish Practices," *Protocol of the Thirtieth Colloquy: 5 June 1977* (Berkeley: Center for Hermeneutical Studies, 1977), 1–11.

/26/ Bokser also refers to the Passover Seder. There can be no question that the Passover Seder, as it occurred after the destruction of the Second Temple in 70 A.D., served as a replacement for the paschal sacrifice and the attendant ritual. It seems probable, however, that the break caused by the destruction was not as sudden as Bokser would have us believe. The shift from sacrifice to prayer had been the result of a long process which was only completed by the destruction. This is not to say that the Jews would have abandoned their ancestral cult had the Temple not been destroyed by the Romans, only that the destruction hastened and intensified a process already occurring in the history of Judaism. Those who, like the Therapeutae, were separated by distance from the Temple in Jerusalem, must have celebrated the Passover before 70 A.D. in much the same manner as it was celebrated after 70 A.D. They gathered to eat of the unleavened bread and bitter herbs as well as to retell the story of the exodus and to recite hymns of praise to God. Cf. J. Neusner, "Emergent Rabbinic Judaism in a Time of Crisis," *Judaism* 21 (1979), 313–327, reprinted in his *Early Rabbinic Judaism* (1975), 34–49.

/27/ *War Scroll*, 200.

/28/ This theme is discussed repeatedly in W. R. Smith, *The Religion of the Semites* (1972). Although the lectures making up this book were delivered in 1888–91, this observation remains valid.

/29/ "The Meals of the Essenes," 164–166. The quotation is from p. 165.

/30/ III (1929), cols. 854f.

/31/ Note van der Ploeg's conclusion, "that the writings of Philo and Josephus . . . do not give us sufficient arguments to say that the Essenes had sacred meals. They only speak of their common, communal meals, and it would have been very strange indeed if all of these had been sacred; this would have been an exception to the rule observed everywhere, that true meals are only sacred in certain circumstances" (171). A similar view is espoused by M. Smith, "God's Begetting the Messiah in 1 Q Sa," *NTS* 5 (1958/9), 219.

/32/ For the role of the priest in the Hellenistic cultic banquets (thiases), cf. Delcor, "*Repas*," 410–412.

/33/ B. Giṭṭin 59b; B. Nedarim 62a–b; B. Horayot 12b; B. Mo'ed Qaṭan 28b. The *baraita'*, according to its attribution, should be dated to the latter half of the second century A.D. Tosafot to B. Ḥullin 87a asserts that Lev. 21:8 serves here only as an *'asmakhta'*, meaning that the precedence of the priest is only a Rabbinical ordinance. On the other hand, Abraham Abele ben Ḥayyim Ha-Levi Gombiner, *Magen 'Avraham* to *Shulḥan 'Arukh* 'Oraḥ Ḥayyim 201, paragraph 4 says that it is a biblical ordinance (*de-'orayta'*) and notes that it appears in Maimonides' *Sefer Ha-Miṣvot* (*'Aseh* no. 32, ed. H. Heller [1979/80], 45).

/34/ So pseudo-Rashi to B. Mo'ed Qaṭan 28b; pseudo-Rashi and Ran to B. Nedarim 62b; and pseudo-Rashi to B. Horayot 12b. Rashi to B. Giṭṭin 59b, however, takes *li-fetoaḥ rishon* in a wider sense and sees it as indicating that the priest should take precedence in regard to any honor. Whether it is the reading of the Torah or the study session (*yeshivah*), he should be called upon first. Cf. the statement of the amora Rabbi Joshua ben Levi in P. Berakhot 5:4 (ed. Krot. 5:5, 9d) and P. Giṭṭin 5:9 (47b) the context of which shows that it refers to the priest's precedence in the reading of the Torah.

/35/ Hebrew *u-levarekh rishon*. So pseudo-Rashi to B. Mo'ed Qaṭan 28b. Pseudo-Rashi to B. Horayot 12b understands this as referring to recitation of the *zimmun*, the invitation to say grace after meals, recited when at least three males have eaten together. Pseudo-Rashi to B. Nedarim 62a, however, sees the reference here as being to the grace both before and after the meal, giving precedence to the priest in both.

/36/ So Rashi to B. Giṭṭin 59b, and Ran to B. Nedarim 62b. (Pseudo-Rashi's interpretation to B. Nedarim 62b would make sense only if the *baraita'* applied to the high priest.) Among the examples of the application of this principle, Tosafot to B. Giṭṭin 59b, *s.v. we-liṭṭol*, mentions *ḥaverim* eating a meal (*se'udah*) together.

/37/ Above, 161–165.

/38/ See above, n. 35.

/39/ T. Berakhot 4:1.

/40/ T. Berakhot 4:8. Note the lengthy advice on eating and drinking in Ben Sira 31:12–32:13.

/41/ So Lieberman, *TK, ad loc.*

/42/ J. M. Baumgarten, "Qumran Studies," *JBL* 77 (1958), 251, notes that there is no evidence that the *ḥavurah* had communal meals.

/43/ M. Berakhot 6–7. Grace before meals is presumed in Matt. 14:19.

/44/ Thackeray's translation of *τροφῆς* as "meat" is too narrow. A better translation would be "food" or "meal" (cf. Liddell and Scott, *s.v.*).

/45/ *War* 2, 8, 5 (131), trans. Thackeray.

/46/ Already presumed in a dispute of the House of Hillel and the House of Shammai recorded in M. Berakhot 8:1.

/47/ *Mekhilta' De-Rabbi Ishmael* Yitro 7 (ed. Horovitz-Rabin, p. 229); *Mekhilta' De-Rabbi Shim'on ben Yoḥai* to Ex. 20:8 (ed. Epstein-Melammed, p. 149); *baraita'* and amoraic discussion in B. Pesaḥim 106a.

/48/ M. Berakhot 6:6; T. Berakhot 4:8 (*seder ha-se'udah*), 10.

/49/ Loaves were specifically provided for that purpose in the Essene meal. See Josephus, *War* 2, 8, 5 (130).

/50/ Above, 24–26.

/51/ CDC 7:6; 12:22; 13:20; 14:3; 14:9.

/52/ Delcor, "*Repas*," 412, notes the absence of this meal in the *Zadokite Fragments*. As noted in the introduction, the contrast between CDC and DSD is one of emphasis and balance. There is no reason to doubt the relevance of the material in DSD to both the main center at Qumran and the outlying settlements of sectarians.

/53/ Lieberman, *TK, ad loc.* follows P. Berakhot 7:4 (ed. Krot. 7:5, 11c) and explains the passage as referring only to *zimmun*. It must be remembered that when *zimmun* was recited, only the *mezammen* recited the blessings which followed, while the others responded *'amen*.

/54/ B. Berakhot 50a; P. Berakhot 7:3 (11c).

/55/ At least this is the explanation of Rabbi Akiva in the latter part of M. Berakhot 7:3. If Rabbi Akiva and Rabbi Yose the Galilean were really the originators of the points of view described in the anonymous first part of the *mishnah*, we would have expected a clear statement of the opposing points of view. Rather, the anonymous section should here be seen as being an earlier tradition to which the explanations were appended. Cf. also M. Megillah 4:3. Epstein, *Mavo' Le-Nusaḥ Ha-Mishnah* I, 430f. notes that "the law is the same for ten or ten myriads" is an addition to the *mishnah* which was not present in the Palestinian Talmud and in the *She'iltot*. He sees this line as having been added to the Babylonian Talmud's *mishnah* text some time before its final redaction. Cf. Epstein's "*Seride She'iltot*," *Tarbiz* 8 (1936/7), 24. On the other hand, Ch. Albeck, *HWT, ad loc.*, sees this line as an ancient *halakhah* and claims that the statement applies only to the use of *nevarekh* (rather than *barekhu*) which is used for all groups from ten up. Cf. also B. Bokser, "A Minor for *Zimmun* (Y. Ber. 7:2, 11c) and Recensions of Yerushalmi," *AJSR* 4 (1979), 1–25; G. Porton, *The Traditions of Rabbi Ishmael* I (1976), 13–15; and J. N. Lightstone, *Yose the Galilean*, I (1979), 11–13.

/56/ Decided by the Babylonian amora Rava', B. Berakhot 50a, and P. Berakhot 7:3 (11c).

/57/ For grace before meals, see M. Berakhot 6:6 which specifically states that in informal meals (at which the guests sit) the grace before meals is recited individually, whereas at formal meals (at which the guests recline) the grace before meals is recited by one on behalf of all. According to Tosafot to B. Berakhot 42a this *mishnah* applies as well to grace after meals.

/58/ M. Smith ingeniously theorizes, "God's Begetting the Messiah," 221–223, that 1QSa 2:11f. represents a judicial session at which priestly instruction regarding the laws of blemishes was given but which is not Messianic. His suggestion cannot be accepted as the continuation of the text seems to militate against Smith's approach.

/59/ The phrase appears in B. Bava' Batra' 16a, 17a.

/60/ L. F. Hartman, "Eschatology," *EJ* 6, 879 has recognized that the communal meals of Qumran prefigured the Messianic banquet, but he termed these meals "cultic" nonetheless. We emphasize again that the adherence to laws of ritual purity and the recitation of grace do not make the meal itself "cultic" in any way. Cf. also M. Burrows, *The Dead Sea Scrolls* (1968), 237, 265.

/61/ Restorations are with Licht. For other restorations, notes, and commentary, see *DJD* I, 117f.; J. Carmignac, É. Cothenet, H. Lignée, *Les textes de Qumrân* II (1963), 24–27; Richardson, 116–118, 121–123; E. F. Sutcliffe, "The Rule of the Congregation (1QSa), II, 11–12: Text and Meaning," *RQ* 2 (1959–60), 541–547; Y. Yadin, "A Crucial Passage in the Dead Sea Scrolls," *JBL* 78 (1959), 238–241; M. Smith, "God's Begetting the Messiah," 218–224; J. F. Priest, "The Messiah and the Meal in 1QSa," *JBL* 82 (1963), 95–100; R. Gordis, "The 'Begotten' Messiah in the Qumran Scrolls," *VT* 7 (1957), 191–194; and K. G. Kuhn, "The Lord's Supper and the Communal Meal at Qumran," *The Scrolls and the New Testament*, ed. K. Stendahl (1958), 70–72.

/62/ Barthélemy and Sutcliffe restore [*zh mw*]*šb* (*zeh moshav*) which, as Licht notes, is too large for the space. J. Carmignac, "*Quelques détails de lecture*," *RQ* 4

(1963–64), 85 and commentary, *ad loc.*, also notes that the space is too small. He restores *lmw[šb]*, taking the first sentence of our text as belonging to the previous paragraph. He begins our passage with *'im* (l. 11). Nonetheless, Licht has shown that it is still preferable to take this clause as the heading for what follows.

/63/ Translating with Cross, *Ancient Library*, 87 and n. 65. *Qeri'e mo'ed 'anshe shem* appears in Num. 16:2 as a description of the princes of the congregation who joined Koraḥ, Dathan, Abiram, and On in their rebellion against Moses and Aaron.

/64/ On the significance of *qeṣ* at Qumran, see Yalon, *MMY*, 77.

/65/ Here referring to the Messiah of Israel. On the two Messiahs, see below n. 94.

/66/ Accepting the restoration of Licht. For the proposed restorations, see Licht, 267–269 and Cross, 87–88, n. 67. The numerous textual problems and restorations in this entire passage in no way affect the basic conclusions reached below. Note, however, that P. Skehan, "Two Books on Qumran Studies," *CBQ* 21 (1959), 74 calls "on the testimony of a half-dozen witnesses, including Allegro, Cross, Strugnell, and the writer [Skehan], as of the summer of 1955," to the effect that the text "contains *yôlîd*." Even if this is correct, however, we would suggest emendation in accord with Licht's reading.

/67/ Barthélemy, *DJD* I, restored *'a[vot bene]*. See Licht, *Serakhim*, 267 for other restorations. To be added to his list is the suggestion of Sutcliffe, *[gm hw' b]rw'š*, which is rendered unlikely by the continuation of the passage.

/68/ Restored with Licht (following traces) who compares DSW 15:4. Licht also suggests restoring *we-no'adu 'elaw*, but it is difficult to see how this would connect with the continuation of the text. Perhaps he meant to suggest *we-no'adu 'elaw bene*. While such a restoration would make sense, it would be too long for the space available. Barthélemy restored *'avot bene*. Carmignac, "*Quelques détails*," 85f., and commentary, *ad loc.*, apparently prefers *'eḥaw bene* ('[*ḥyw bny*]), and compares 1 Chron. 16:39; Neh. 3:1; and DSW 13:1, 15:4.

/69/ The form *'enoshe* (also in 1:28) is a construct of *'enosh*, here substituted for the biblical *'anshe* encountered in l. 11. The *waw* is serving for Masoretic *qameṣ qaṭan*. *'Anshe ha-shem* (with the definite article) occurs in Gen. 6:4. Rashi's comment to this verse raises the possibility that our passage here may refer to those whose names appear in the official roster of the members of the sect. Cf. Targum Pseudo-Jonathan to Num. 16:2, *mefarshin bi-shemahan*. On the sectarian rosters, see *HAQ*, 66f.

/70/ For the restoration, cf. ll. 15–17 and 1:18.

/71/ The adverbial usage is noted by Licht.

/72/ Barthélemy restored *ye[shev mash]iaḥ*. The *yod* is suspended above the line.

/73/ The *yod* is suspended above the line.

/74/ Part of the *'alef* of *'alefe* is visible. Cf. 1:14 (Licht). Carmignac restores *šbṭy ysr'l* with 1 Sam. 15:17.

/75/ Barthélemy emends to *u-ve-ma'asehem*. Licht and Carmignac note the mention of the system of encampment and march in Num. 9:15–10:34. The organization of Israel in the desert period greatly influenced the sect and its view of the Messianic era. See Yadin, *War Scroll*, 38–64 and Talmon, "The 'Desert Motif,'" 55–63. The

Therapeutae also sat in order of importance according to Philo, *Contemplative Life* 67. Cf. also Matt. 23:6 and Luke 14:7–11 on the "place of honor" at the table (Carmignac).

/76/ Traces of the first and last letters are visible. Cf. 1:24f. which is also partly restored.

/77/ Restored with Licht who notes that half of the first *mem* is visible and compares 1:28. Barthélemy restored *ḥakhem[e 'adat ha-qodesh]*. On Licht's restoration, cf. Deut. 1:13 which requires that our text as restored be vocalized *wi-yedu'im*. While Rashi, Ibn Ezra, and Ramban all take *yedu'im* to refer to men of reputation, we have translated here in accord with Targum Pseudo-Jonathan *mare mandde'a'*, men of knowledge.

/78/ *Nif'al* of *y'd*, "to meet at an appointed place" (BDB, *s.v.*).

/79/ Taking *yaḥad* here as a designation of the sect. Alternately, one can translate, "[at the tab]le together."

/80/ Part of the *ḥet* is visible.

/81/ Barthélemy restored *['o li-shetot ha-t]irosh*.

/82/ Barthélemy restored *[u-masokh ha-]tirosh*. Cf. Prov. 9:2.

/83/ Written over an erasure.

/84/ Barthélemy restores *ky' [hw' m]brk*.

/85/ Cf. above, n. 17.

/86/ Barthélemy restores *wšlḥ*.

/87/ Cf. Ruth 4:7. Licht notes that in this and other biblical texts the word does not make reference to any specific time. A usage closer to that of our text is found in Ben Sira 4:17; 11:8; 37:8. DSD 6:5 (above, 192) uses *la-rishonah* in the same sense.

/88/ Licht observes that each would recite his own benediction, a practice in opposition to that of the tannaim.

/89/ Barthélemy and Licht suggest that the *waw* may have been suspended above the line.

/90/ Barthélemy compares DSD 10:14.

/91/ For the spelling with final *'alef*, cf. *tora'* in 1:11 (above, 62), and Licht's note, *ad loc.*

/92/ On this banquet, see Ginzberg, *Legends* I, 27–28; V, 43–46, n. 127, and G. F. Moore, *Judaism* (1971) II, 363f. Note that most of the sources cited are considerably later than the Qumran corpus. The numerous Apocryphal and pseudepigraphical references to this banquet are conveniently listed in Charles, *APOT* II, 859, *s.v.* "Messianic banquet." There can be no question that this idea was widespread when the Qumran texts were composed.

/93/ Priest, 97.

/94/ See the sources cited in *HAQ*, 51 n. 202 as well as R. E. Brown, "The Messianism of Qumran," *CBQ* 19 (1957), 163–175; K. G. Kuhn, "The Two Messiahs of Aaron and Israel," *The Scrolls and the New Testament*, ed. K. Stendahl, 54–64; and Priest, "The Messiah and the Meal," 95–100.

/ 95/ See above, 164f.

/ 96/ R. de Vaux, *Archaeology and the Dead Sea Scrolls*, 19. E. M. Laperrousaz, *Qoumrân, l'établissement Essénien des bords de la Mer Morte* (1976), 29–33 has discussed in detail de Vaux's dating of the end of period Ia and the beginning of period Ib. He shows that de Vaux has vacillated through the years as to the exact dates and criticizes his evaluation of the numismatic evidence. Laperrousaz concludes (33) that it is impossible on archaeological grounds precisely to place period Ia within the last century of the Hellenistic period of Palestine. By this he means (cf. 33, n. 2) that period Ia might be fixed anywhere from 163–63 B.C. Hence, he is unable to suggest an exact date within the Hasmonean period for the onset of period Ib (38).

/ 97/ R. de Vaux, 20–21. Laperrousaz, basing himself on detailed numismatic study, would date the end of period Ib to between 67 and 63 B.C. It is quite clear from the discussion (Laperrousaz, 38–45) that the evidence is susceptible to various interpretations. There can be no question, however, that this period ceased at least by the earthquake of 31 B.C.

/ 98/ See de Vaux's Plates Xa and Xb.

/ 99/ Pp. 11–12. Cf. Laperrousaz, 35–36. He notes that the pottery in question has been attributed to period II by J. T. Milik on the basis of palaeographic evidence.

/100/ R. de Vaux, 7, 10.

/101/ Laperrousaz, 47.

/102/ Laperrousaz, 50–56, fixes the beginning of period IIa during the reign of Herod the Great (37–4 B.C.). He suggests a second abandonment of the site which would, according to him, have resulted probably from the transformation of Judea into a procuratorial province in 6 A.D. This second abandonment is purely hypothetical and rests on insufficient evidence.

/103/ Pp. 33–41, followed by Laperrousaz, 56–58.

/104/ P. 86. Laperrousaz, 99–109 makes a detailed study of this question. He concludes that 300–350 people would have lived at Qumran during period Ib, and perhaps 350–400 would have occupied Qumran and Ein Feshka during periods IIa and IIb of Qumran (109). R. de Vaux's figure is not far removed from those of Milik (150–200) and Farmer ("a few hundred regular members") (de Vaux, 86 n. 1). We must also bear in mind that Laperrousaz is the first to take so seriously the facilities at Ein Feshka, as evidenced by his devoting pp. 63–90 of his study to this site.

/105/ See de Vaux's Plates XIa and XIb.

/106/ For detailed accounts of the finds, see Laperrousaz, 215–218 and Jean L.-Duhaime, "Remarques sur les dépôts d'ossements d'animaux à Qumran," *RQ* 9 (1977), 245–247.

/107/ P. 14.

/108/ Pp. 12–14.

/109/ See J. M. Baumgarten, "Sacrifice and Worship among the Jewish Sectarians of the Dead Sea (Qumran) Scrolls," *HTR* 46 (1953), 141–157; *HAQ*, 78; Cross, *Ancient Library*, 101–103; Ginzberg, *Sect*, 117, 281, 384–386; van der Ploeg, "The Meals of the Essenes," 172; and J. Nolland, "A Misleading Statement of the Essene Attitude to the Temple," *RQ* 9 (1977–78), 555–562.

/110/ The "New Jerusalem" is the theme of several Aramaic texts from Qumran on which see *DJD* I, 134–35; III, 84–89, 184–193. Cultic ceremonies would form part of the final battle described in the *War Scroll*. For a thorough analysis, see Yadin, *War Scroll*, 198–228. On the *Temple Scroll*, see above, 13f.

/111/ Cross reaches the opposite conclusion, though with some hesitation (*Ancient Library*, 102). He bases his opinion on the animal bones, but does not deal with the objections raised here. J. van der Ploeg, "The Meals of the Essenes," 170 discusses the attitude to sacrifice of the Essenes of Philo and Josephus. He takes the view that while the Essenes did not sacrifice in the Temple, they replaced the sacrificial cult with nonsacrificial ceremonies of their own. See also J. Bowman, "Did the Qumran Sect Burn the Red Heifer?" *RQ* 1 (1958), 73–84 and G. Klinzing, *Die Umdeutung des Kultus in der Qumrangemeinde und im Neuen Testament* (1971), 20–49.

/112/ A thorough survey is given in de Vaux, 14–16, n. 3. See also Laperrousaz, 211–215; L.-Duhaime, 249–251; and most recently, E. M. Laperrousaz, "*A propos des depôts d'ossements d'animaux trouvés a Qoumrân*," *RQ* (1978), 569–573.

/113/ The *Temple Scroll* contains no reference to this or any similar practice among its detailed prescriptions for the sacrificial offerings.

CONCLUSION
LAW AND COMMUNITY IN THE DEAD SEA SCROLLS

1. *The Sectarian Legal System*

The legal enactments of any society represent a response to both the self-definition of the group and the wider societal context in which it and its institutions developed. The Qumran sect defined itself by its unique beliefs, its singular approach to Jewish law, and its opposition to certain practices of all other Jews. From the close study of the laws and regulations of the sect, we have been able to learn much about the way the sect viewed itself and the nature of the society which it sought to construct, a society which constituted a sanctuary from the evils which surrounded its members and which would ready them for the soon-to-dawn eschaton.

Let us first recapitulate the basic elements of the Qumran legal system. We have seen that the functions of the *moshav ha-rabbim* of Qumran were fulfilled in the other sectarian settlements by courts of ten. In all sectarian courts, judges had to be trained in Scripture and its sectarian interpretation and had to conform to specific age requirements. Witnesses had to be members of the sect, and over twenty years old for capital matters. Whereas two witnesses were sufficient for financial matters, capital matters required three witnesses. The testimony of fewer witnesses sufficed for the imposition of sectarian sanctions even when the testimony was insufficient for conviction.

It was possible to make use of the cumulative testimony of single witnesses to successive commissions of the same crime, provided that the offense was duly recorded. All trials had to be preceded by the required formal reproof in the presence of witnesses before conviction was possible. In cases in which property was lost or stolen, laws provided for the use of oaths of adjuration to aid in the return of the missing items. When illegally gained property was to be returned but the owner was absent, it could be returned to the priests. If no one claimed lost property, it was to be entrusted to the priests for safekeeping.

A complex set of penalties was developed by the sect for various offenses against the sectarian regulations. These penalties were based on fines, separation from the pure food of the sect, and, for the more serious offenses, expulsion from the sect.

2. *Scriptural Authority and Sectarian Law*

The study of the various systems of Jewish law cannot be limited solely to the content of the laws contained in the various sources but must also consider the question of how the laws are derived, or, more specifically, how the legislators related to the Hebrew Bible which served as the ultimate basis for the development of the Jewish tradition in all its manifestations. An investigation of the legal and exegetical terminology of the scrolls was undertaken in *The Halakhah at Qumran* with specific reference to the contents of Jewish law later defined as *halakhah*. This term includes the unique combination of Jewish religious, civil, and criminal law which may best be seen as an attempt to actualize the laws of the Torah in changing circumstances. It was established in this previous volume that sectarian law was derived through what the sect regarded as inspired biblical exegesis. Oral traditions played no part in the development and transmission of sectarian law.

Taking this study one step further, the Qumran Sabbath Code was investigated in the attempt to test these conclusions. Study of the Sabbath Code clearly showed that Scriptural exegesis served as the basis of the sectarian law. In the present study, the chapters dealing with the Code of Court Procedure from the *Zadokite Fragments* have likewise confirmed this hypothesis. These laws were unquestionably shown to be derived through sectarian *midrash* exegesis.

Continuing the investigation of Qumran legal materials in this volume, the scope was widened considerably to include some of the sectarian organizational regulations, specifically the Penal Code of the *Manual of Discipline*. By the term organizational regulations we mean to describe the manifold rules of entry into the sect and the conduct of sectarian affairs. Put another way, this material consists of rules and regulations which do not belong to the category termed *halakhah* by Rabbinic Judaism. Rather, they were peculiar to this and similar sectarian groups. Such regulations were no doubt enacted to facilitate the actualization of the life of Torah, although the content of these regulations appears in many cases to have no basis in Scripture. Whereas the sect depended totally on Scriptural interpretation for the derivation of its "halakhic" laws, sectarian organizational regulations appear to have been conceived simply to facilitate the conduct of sectarian life. Of course, these nonscriptural laws were ultimately intended to fulfill the ideals which the sect perceived inherent in the Bible, and it was in order to actualize these precepts that the sect was founded.

3. *The Agenda of the Sectarian Codes*

In order to understand the legislation before us, which is indeed the sum total of available Qumran material on the subjects discussed, it is necessary to ask why the sectarian legislators included certain topics in their writings and excluded others. Indeed, these questions ought to be asked of all the legal materials in the Dead Sea corpus.

J. Neusner, in a study of the Mishnaic system of law in the order *Neziqin*, roughly parallel in subject matter to the material under study in this volume, has observed that the material can be separated into two major categories: One contains provisions for the "normal conduct of civil society—commerce, trade, real estate, . . . damages by chattels and persons. . . ." The second part concerns "the institutions governing the normal conduct of civil society, that is, courts of administration, and the penalties at the disposal of the government for the enforcement of the law."/1/ The former material is found primarily in the Mishnaic tractates Bava' Qamma', Bava' Meṣi'a', and Bava' Batra' and the latter in Sanhedrin and Makkot.

It is clear from even a cursory look at the detailed outline of the Mishnaic material which Neusner has presented/2/ that our texts from Qumran do not treat very much of the first category, but treat primarily the second. Many areas mentioned by the Torah and taken up as well in the Mishnah, among the most obvious the matter of bailees, are omitted altogether by the sectarian corpus. How is this to be explained? We would submit that the laws assembled in the sectarian documents are those for which, in the view of the Dead Sea sect, Scripture itself is insufficient. Therefore, a sectarian interpretation or *midrash* is necessary in order to understand the text. In cases in which the sect regarded the Bible as self-sufficient, laws were not formulated in the sectarian codes. Sectarian organizational regulations, independent of any biblical basis, had to be specifically formulated.

This conclusion may be rephrased using the terminology of the sect. Those laws found in the *nigleh* ("revealed") and hence known to all Israel are not usually stated in the texts of the sect. Those of the *nistar* ("hidden"), the correct interpretations of which are the possession of the sect alone and which were derived through inspired exegesis at the sectarian study sessions,/3/ are formulated in the sectarian codes (*serakhim*)/4/ and find their way into the texts before us. Alongside these, lacking Scriptural authority, organizational regulations had to be listed in the codes of the sect.

The study presented here has been based on two complementary sectarian texts: The *Zadokite Fragments*, containing a Code of Court Procedure, and the *Manual of Discipline* with its Penal Code. We have interpreted these two documents as complementary, although the differing perspectives of the two texts have been duly noted in the Introduction. Indeed, the *Zadokite Fragments*, concerned with the life of the sectarian outside the main center at Qumran and with the details of Jewish law, emphasized primarily the nature of the court system and the laws of testimony and procedure. It is the *Manual of Discipline*, concerned as it is with the definition of the members of the sect and their qualifications, entry, expulsion, and status within the sect, which describes the sectarian penalties. Such a distinction is natural, given the varying emphases of the texts before us.

What is most significant, though, is the intersection of the materials, showing the interdependence and unity of the corpus. This is especially observable in regard to the role of purity and impurity and separation from the pure food in the penalties of the sect. Whereas this foundation of sectarian law is spelled out in detail only in the Penal Code of the *Manual of Discipline*, it is taken for granted in the law of testimony of the *Zadokite Fragments*. Similarly, the general statements regarding the prohibited uses of the Tetragrammaton in the Penal Code of the *Manual of Discipline* go hand in hand with the similar proscriptions regarding the divine names and their usage in the oaths of the *Zadokite Fragments*. At one point, both texts have been observed to quote from an otherwise unknown but common source containing legal maxims of some kind.

There can be no question, then, that the relationship between the *Manual of Discipline* and the *Zadokite Fragments* presumed in this study, and proven by many other similarities and parallels, is again confirmed. Students of Qumran literature ought certainly to continue to investigate these texts in tandem, paying due respect, however, to their differing perspectives.

4. *Private Property*

The laws we have investigated will also help in the clarification of several issues surrounding the nature of the Qumran sect and its social character. In this respect, the question of private property has been extremely important. On the basis of descriptions of the Essenes and the early Christian church, dominant scholarly opinion has seen the sectarians as practicing community of goods. However, the legal system investigated here testifies otherwise. From the material before us it is certain that among members distant from the Qumran center, property was surrendered by the members of the sect for communal use, but private ownership remained in force. Otherwise, how can we explain subjects treated in the *Zadokite Fragments* such as the detailed system for dealing with the recovery of lost or stolen property and restitution of lost objects, laws which specifically mention "owners," the existence of an income tax, or the fact that there were some more needy than others among the members of the sect? From the laws regarding entry into the sect and from the Penal Code of the *Manual of Discipline* it seems that communal use of property is envisaged. Nonetheless, the concept of private ownership remained in force even at the center at Qumran.

5. *Marriage*

The common theory that the sectarians represented in the Qumran scrolls were celibate is supported primarily by sources describing the Essenes. These statements are then used as the basis upon which the Qumran scrolls are interpreted. We have already noted our reservations about this methodology in the Introduction. The texts we have investigated here have made clear, even though not directly referring to this issue, that the Qumran materials assume a society in which marriage, childbearing, and family life are expected and normal. Explicitly stated in the *Zadokite Fragments*, this assumption certainly applies to the sectarians outside the main center at Qumran. But was the sect at Qumran celibate? Here we are justified in making use of the picture of the ideal society of the future eschatological age described in the *Rule of the Congregation*. This text certainly assumes normal family life as part of its vision of the end of days. Based on this text, we may conclude that those in the Qumran community likewise were not celibate. That there may have been celibate sectarians at this period is possible, but they are not reflected in the Qumran materials before us.

6. *The Priesthood*

In our study of the court system, we saw that the priests and Levites occupied a central place in the hierarchy. Indeed, the sectarian texts uniformly accord the Zadokite priests a position of superiority in the conduct of the sect's affairs. At the same time, J. Murphy-O'Connor has convincingly shown in his analysis of the history of the *Manual of Discipline*,/5/ that by the completion of the sectarian corpus as we have it, this role had become more and more ceremonial, or formalistic, with the increasing democratization of the sect. This tendency is observable in the court system where priests and Levites constitute a minority of the court of ten, and in which the lay *mevaqqer*, examiner, takes a leading administrative role.

The superior role of priests and Levites is logical since the sect was founded and originally led by Zadokite priests. They had formed the sect in protest over the usurpation of their rightful place in the Jerusalem Temple, either immediately before or, most likely, in the aftermath of the Hasmonean revolt. With time, the sect attracted more and more laymen who gradually took a greater role, so that the courts and administrative system came to embody a "coalition," and the actual leadership gradually passed to laymen. Since the sect saw itself as a replacement Temple, seeking to achieve the purity and sanctification of the cult through the medium of sectarian life and observance, it was natural that the formal conduct of the sect's affairs continued to be controlled by the Zadokite priests. They were the legitimate leaders to be entrusted with the conduct of the sacred cult in Jerusalem, now being defiled, in the view of the sect, by others unworthy of their position.

7. *Ritual Purity and Impurity*

While the subject of ritual purity and impurity in the Qumran texts requires a fully detailed study of its own, something of an outline already emerges from the material studied here. The very fact that so much of this topic found its way into a study of the courts, court procedure, testimony and penal law is itself indicative of the overarching importance of this aspect of Qumran teaching. Indeed, we found that the basis of the complex system of the sectarian novitiate and entry of new members into the sect was the concept that those outside of the sect were ritually impure while the new member gradually became less and less impure through the initiation process until he was permitted contact with the victuals of the sect. At the same time, one who transgressed was to be removed from the pure food under certain circumstances, since his transgression rendered him impure. At the root of the matter is the idea that ritual impurity and subsequent purification are the function not of physical phenomena, but of sin and atonement.

Since the sect was a fellowship to ensure the actualization of the way of the Torah in the immediately pre-Messianic age, and since, as such, it was necessary to create by means of the sect a substitute for the sacrificial cult, entrance to the sect was limited to those who were ritually pure. Members who transgressed were accordingly defined and dealt with as temporarily impure. Certain transgressions resulted in expulsion from the sect, since the transgressor was regarded as no longer capable of repentance and purification. Thus was ensured the purity of the sect as a sanctuary of separateness which prepared its members for the eschaton. The eschaton itself was to be celebrated in absolute purity. Here the world of the present merges with that of the future. The insistence on purification in this world is also a preparation for the age to come. Hence, communal meals, eschatological in nature, were to be eaten only in absolute purity. Sinners were to be excluded, as they would be excluded from the banquet and community of the future age. Purity and impurity, then, defined the inner and outer limits of the sect in the present as they would in the Messianic age.

8. *The Organic Character of Sectarian Law*

The very fact that court procedure, testimony, purity and impurity, admission to the sect, oaths, divine names, penal code, communal meals and a host of other matters all had to be analyzed together because of the interlocking nature of their subject matter speaks eloquently of the organic character of sectarian law. Like Jewish law in all its manifestations, the areas of law can be distinguished for convenience or codification, but in reality the total system as a unity functions together, constituting a whole which is greater than the sum of its parts. Further, the system functions such that no ingredient can be removed without upsetting a delicate and perhaps previously imperceptible balance. This is the systemic nature of Judaism, and the Qumran sectarian legal traditions and way of life certainly fit this model.

Indeed, this organic character does not apply only to the legal system. We have seen the strong links between the legal system and the theological and doctrinal underpinnings of which it is only an outward expression. We have observed time and again how the laws of the sect were particularly appropriate to the kind of society the sectarians sought to create and to the self-image they sought to express in their way of life. The Jews of Qumran, as did all observing Jews through the ages, believed that observance of the law was only the outward expression of something much deeper, of a view of God, the world, and the Jewish people and of the inexorable march which would ultimately lead to the perfection of the world in the end of days.

NOTES

/1/ J. Neusner, "The Description of Formative Judaism: The Social Perspective of the Mishnah's System of Civil Law and Government," *AJSR* 5 (1980), 65.

/2/ "Description," 68–73. Cf. his "Scriptural, Essenic, and Mishnaic Approaches to Civil Law and Government: Some Comparative Remarks," *HTR* (1981), 419–434.

/3/ See *HAQ*, 22–32.

/4/ See *HAQ*, 60–68.

/5/ See above, 5.

BIBLIOGRAPHY

Aaron ben Elijah of Nicomedia, *Gan 'Eden*, Israel: Council of Karaites in Israel, 1972.

———, *Keter Torah*, Eupatoria: A. Firkovich, 1866/7.

Abraham ben David, Commentary to *Sifra'*, in *Sifra' De-Ve Rav*, ed. I. H. Weiss.

———, *Hassagot Ha-Rabad*, in Maimonides, M., *Mishneh Torah*, ed. Vilna.

Abraham ben Moses di-Boton, *Leḥem Mishneh*, in Maimonides, M., *Mishneh Torah*, ed. Vilna.

Abraham Ibn Ezra, *Perushe Ha-Torah*, ed. A. Weiser, 3 vols., Jerusalem: Mosad Harav Kook, 1976.

Abravanel, Isaac, *Perush 'al Nevi'im Rishonim*, Jerusalem: Torah We-Da'at, 1954/5.

Abulafia, Meir ben Todros Ha-Levi, *Sefer Ḥiddushe Ha-Ramah*, New York: Sifre Qodesh, 1970/1.

[Adani, David ben Amram], *Midrash Ha-Gadol, Sefer Wa-Yiqra'*, ed. E. N. Rabinowitz, New York: Jewish Theological Seminary, 1932.

———, *Midrash Ha-Gadol, Sefer Wa-Yiqra'*, ed. A. Steinsaltz, Jerusalem: Mosad Harav Kook, 1975.

Adani, Solomon, *Mele'khet Shelomoh*, in *Mishnah*, ed. Vilna.

Agus, I., *The Heroic Age of Franco-German Jewry*, New York: Yeshiva University Press, 1969.

———, *Urban Civilization in Pre-Crusade Europe*, 2 vols., Leiden: E. J. Brill, 1965.

Aland, K., Black, M., Metzger, B., Wikgren, A., eds., *The Greek New Testament*, London: United Bible Societies, 1966.

Albeck, Ch., *Das Buch der Jubiläen und die Halacha*, Berlin, 1930.

———, "*Halakhah Ḥiṣonah Be-Targume 'Ereṣ Yisra'el U-Va-'Aggadah*," *Sefer Ha-Yovel Le-Doqṭor Binyamin Menasheh Lewin Le-Yovelo Ha-Shishim*, ed. J. L. Fishman, Jerusalem: Mosad Harav Kook, 1939, 93–104.

———, *Mavo' La-Mishnah*, Jerusalem: Mosad Bialik, Tel Aviv: Dvir, 1966/7.

———, *Mavo' La-Talmudim*, Tel Aviv: Dvir, 1969.

———, ed., *Shishah Sidre Mishnah*, 6 vols., Jerusalem and Tel Aviv: Mosad Bialik and Dvir, 1957–59.

Albeck, S., *Bate Ha-Din Bi-Yeme Ha-Talmud*, Ramat Gan: Bar-Ilan University Press, 1980.

Alfasi, Isaac, *Hilkhot Rav 'Alfas*, ed. N. Sachs, 2 vols., Jerusalem: Mosad Harav Kook, 1968/9.

Allegro, J. M., *Qumrân Cave 4, Discoveries in the Judaean Desert* V, Oxford: Clarendon Press, 1968.

Alon, G., *Meḥqarim Be-Toledot Yisra'el*, 2 vols., Tel Aviv: Ha-Kibbutz Ha-Meuchad, 1967, 1970.

Altmann, A., ed., *Biblical Motifs*, Cambridge, MA: Harvard University Press, 1966.

———, "The Gnostic Background of the Rabbinic Adam Legends," *JQR* N. S. 35 (1944/5), 371–391.

Anan ben David, *Sefer Ha-Miṣwot*, in A. Harkavy, *Mi-Sifre Ha-Miṣwot Ha-Rishonim Li-Vene Miqra'* (Zikkaron La-Rishonim VIII), St. Petersburg, 1903.

Ankori, Z., *Karaites in Byzantium*, New York and Jerusalem: Columbia University Press, 1959.

Aptowitzer, V., "Formularies of Decrees and Documents from a Gaonic Court," *JQR* N.S. 4 (1913/4), 23–51.

Asher ben Yeḥiel, Commentary to *Mishnah Seder Ṭohorot*, in *Babylonian Talmud*, ed. Vilna.

Ashkenazi, Eliezer, *Ṭa'am Zeqenim*, Frankfurt am Main: I. Kaufmann, 1854.

Ashkenazi, Moses David Abraham Treves, *Perush Toledot 'Adam* (on the *Sifre*), 2 vols., Jerusalem: Mosad Harav Kook, 1972, 1974.

'Avot de Rabbi Natan, ed. S. Schechter, New York: P. Feldheim, 1967.

Babylonian Talmud, Codex Florence (Florence National Library II i 7–9), 3 vols., Jerusalem: Makor, 1972.

———, Codex Munich (95), 3 vols., Jerusalem: Sefer, 1971.

———, ed. Venice, 12 vols., 1520–1523.

———, ed. Vilna (with commentaries and Alfasi), 20 vols., New York: Otzar Hasefarim, 1964.

———, Tractate Soṭah, ed. A. Liss, 2 vols., Jerusalem: Institute for the Complete Israeli Talmud, 1977, 1979.

Bacher, W., *'Erkhe Midrash*, trans. A. Rabinowitz, 2 vols., Tel Aviv: 1822/3.

———, "Shem Ha-Meforash," *JE* 11, 262–264.

Baer, S., *Siddur 'Avodat Yisra'el*, Tel Aviv, 1956/7.

Baillet, M., Milik, J. T., de Vaux, R., *Les 'Petites Grottes' de Qumrân, Discoveries in the Judaean Desert of Jordan* III, 2 pts., Oxford: Clarendon Press, 1962.

Baron, S. W., *The Jewish Community*, 3 vols., Philadelphia: Jewish Publication Society, 1942–45.

Barthélemy, D., Milik, J. T., *et al.*, *Qumran Cave I, Discoveries in the Judaean Desert* I, Oxford: Clarendon Press, 1955.

Baumgarten, J. M., "Does *tlh* in the Temple Scroll Refer to Crucifixion?" *JBL* 91 (1972), 472–481.

———, "The Duodecimal Courts of Qumran, the Apocalypse, and the Sanhedrin," *JBL* 95 (1976), 59–78.

———, "4Q Halakha^{a} 5, the Law of Ḥadash, and the Pentacontad Calendar," *JJS* 27 (1976), 36–46.

———, "1QSa 1.11—Age of Testimony or Responsibility?" *JQR* 49 (1958/9), 157–160, with an editorial comment by S. Zeitlin, 160f.

———, "Qumran Studies," *JBL* 77 (1958), 249–257.

———, "Sacrifice and Worship among the Jewish Sectarians of the Dead Sea (Qumran) Scrolls," *HTR* 46 (1953), 141–157.

———, *Studies in Qumran Law*, Leiden: E. J. Brill, 1977.

———, "The Unwritten Law in the Pre-Rabbinic Period," *JSJ* 3 (1972), 7–29.

Belkin, S., *Philo and the Oral Law*, Cambridge, MA: Harvard University Press, 1940.

Be-Midbar Rabbah, in *Midrash Rabbah*, ed. Vilna.

Ben Ḥayyim, Z., "Traditions in the Hebrew Language, with Special Reference to the Dead Sea Scrolls," *Aspects of the Dead Sea Scrolls* (Scripta Hierosolymitana IV), ed. C. Rabin, Y. Yadin, Jerusalem: Magnes Press, 1958, 200–214.

Benjamin of Nahawend, *Mas'at Binyamin*, in Aaron ben Joseph, *Mivḥar Yesharim*, Eupatoria, 1834/5.

Ben-Yehudah, E., *Millon Ha-Lashon Ha-'Ivrit*, 8 vols., London, New York: Thomas Yoseloff, 1959.

Bereshit Rabba', ed. J. Theodor, Ch. Albeck, 3 vols., Jerusalem: Wahrmann, 1965.

Bertinoro, Obadiah, Commentary on the *Mishnah*, in *Mishnah*, ed. Vilna.

Biblica Sacra iuxta Vulgatam Clementinam, ed. A. Colunga, L. Turrado, Madrid: Biblioteca de autores Christianos, 1965.

Birnbaum, S. A., *The Qumran (Dead Sea) Scrolls and Palaeography*, *BASOR* Supplementary Studies 13/14, New Haven: American Schools of Oriental Research, 1952.

Blank, S., "The Curse, Blasphemy, the Spell, and the Oath," *HUCA* 23, pt. 1 (1950–51), 73–95.

Blau, L., *Das altjüdische Zauberwesen*, Farnborough: Gregg International, 1970.

———, "Tetragrammaton," *JE* 12, 118–120.

Blidstein, G., "'Atima: A Greek Parallel to Ezra X 8 and to the Post-biblical Exclusion from the Community," *VT* 24 (1974), 357–360.

Bokser, B., "A Minor for *Zimmun* (Y. Ber. 7:2, 11c) and Recensions of Yerushalmi," *AJSR* 4 (1979), 1–25.

———, "Philo's Description of Jewish Practices," *Protocol of the Thirtieth Colloquy: 5 June 1977*, Berkeley: Center for Hermeneutical Studies, 1977.

Borger, P., "'At the Age of Twenty' in 1 Q Sa," *RQ* 3 (1961–62), 267–277.

Bowman, J., "Did the Qumran Sect Burn the Red Heifer?" *RQ* 1 (1958), 73–84.

Brichto, H. C., *The Problem of "Curse" in the Hebrew Bible*, Philadelphia: Society for Biblical Literature, 1963.

Brown, F., Driver, S., Briggs, C., *A Hebrew and English Lexicon of the Old Testament*, Oxford: University Press, 1966.

Brown, R. E., "The Messianism of Qumran," *CBQ* 19 (1957), 53–82.

Brownlee, W. H., *The Dead Sea Manual of Discipline*, *BASOR* Supplementary Studies 10–12, New Haven: American Schools of Oriental Research, 1951.

Brüll, J., *Mevo' Ha-Mishnah*, 2 vols., Frankfurt, 1875/6, 1885/6.

Buchanan, G. W., "The Old Testament Meaning of the Knowledge of Good and Evil," *JBL* 75 (1976), 114–120.

Büchler, A., "Schechter's 'Jewish Sectaries,'" *JQR* N.S. 3 (1912/3), 429–485.

Burgmann, H., "*TWKḤT in 1 Q p Hab V, 10, ein Schlüsselwort mit verhängnisvollen historischen Konsequenzen*," *RQ* 10 (1980), 293–300.

Burney, C., *The Book of Judges and Notes on the Hebrew Text of the Book of Kings*, with "Prolegomenon" by W. F. Albright, New York: Ktav, 1970.

Burrows, M., *The Dead Sea Scrolls*, New York: Viking Press, 1965.

———, ed., *The Dead Sea Scrolls of St. Mark's Monastery*, vol. I, New Haven: American Schools of Oriental Research, 1950.

———, with Trever, J., Brownlee, W. H., *The Dead Sea Scrolls of St. Mark's Monastery, Vol. II, Fascicle 2; Plates and Transcription of the Manual of Discipline*, New Haven: American Schools of Oriental Research, 1951.

Byington, S. T., "*yhwh* and *'dny*," *JBL* 76 (1957), 58f.

Carmignac, J., "*Quelques détails de lecture*," *RQ* 4 (1963–64), 83–96.

———, Guilbert, P., *Les textes de Qumrân*, Vol. I, Paris: Letouzey et Ané, 1961.

———, Cothenet, É., Lignée, H., *Les textes de Qumrân*, Vol. II, Paris: Letouzey et Ané, 1963.

Caro, J., *Bet Yosef*, in Jacob ben Asher, *'Arba'ah Ṭurim*.

———, *Kesef Mishneh*, in Maimonides, M., *Mishneh Torah*, ed. Vilna.

———, *Maggid Mishneh*, in Maimonides, M., *Mishneh Torah*, ed. Vilna.

———, *Shulḥan 'Arukh*, 10 vols., New York: M. P. Press, 1967.

Cassuto, U., *Perush 'al Sefer Shemot*, Jerusalem: Magnes Press, 1969.

Chajes, Z. H., *Torat Nevi'im*, in *Kol Sifre MaHaRaṢ Chajes*, 2 vols., Jerusalem: Divre Ḥakhamim, 1958.

Charles, R. H., *The Apocrypha and Pseudepigrapha of the Old Testament*, 2 vols., Oxford: Clarendon Press, 1913.

———, *The Ethiopic Version of the Hebrew Book of Jubilees*, Oxford: Clarendon Press, 1895.

Charlesworth, J. H., "The Origin and Subsequent History of the Authors of the Dead Sea Scrolls: Four Transitional Phases among the Qumran Essenes," *RQ* 10 (1980), 213–233.

Cohen, B., *Jewish and Roman Law*, 2 vols., New York: Jewish Theological Seminary, 1966.

Collins, J., "The Son of Man and the Saints of the Most High in the Book of Daniel," *JBL* 93 (1974), 50–66.

Conybeare, F. C., "The Testament of Solomon," *JQR* O.S. 11 (1899), 1–45.

Cooke, G. A., *A Critical and Exegetical Commentary on the Book of Ezekiel*, Edinburgh: T. and T. Clark, 1936.

Cross, F. M., *The Ancient Library at Qumran*, Garden City, NY: Doubleday, 1961.

———, "The Development of the Jewish Scripts," *The Bible and the Ancient Near East*, ed. G. E. Wright, Garden City, NY: Doubleday, 1961, 133–202.

David ben Solomon ibn Abi Zimra, Commentary to M. Maimonides, *Mishneh Torah*, ed. Vilna.

Delcor, M., "*Contribution à l'étude de la législation des sectaries de Damas et de Qumran*," *RB* 61 (1954), 533–553; 62 (1955), 62–75.

———, "The Courts of the Church of Corinth and the Courts of Qumran," *Paul and Qumran*, ed. J. Murphy-O'Connor, Chicago: Priory Press, 1968, 69–84.

———, "*Repas cultuels Esséniens et Thérapeutes, Thiases et Ḥaburoth*," *RQ* 6 (1967–69), 401–425.

———,"*Les tribunaux de l'église de Corinthe et les tribunaux de Qumrân*," *Studiorum paulinorum congressus internationalis catholicus* (1961), 535–548.

Dinari, Y., "Israel of Krems," *EJ* 9, 1071f.

Dio Cassius, *Roman History*, trans. E. Cary, ed. H. Foster, 9 vols., Cambridge, MA: Harvard University Press, London: William Heinemann, 1968–1970.

Donner, H., Röllig, W., *Kanaanäische und Aramäische Inschriften*, 3 vols., Wiesbaden: Otto Harrassowitz, 1964.

Driver, G. R., Miles, S. R., *The Assyrian Laws*, Oxford: University Press, 1935.

Driver, S. R., *A Critical and Exegetical Commentary on Deuteronomy*, Edinburgh: T. and T. Clark, 1895.

———, *Notes on the Hebrew Text and the Topography of the Books of Samuel*, Oxford: Clarendon Press, 1966.

Dupont-Sommer, A., *Les écrits esséniens découverts près de la Mer Morte*, Paris: Payot, 1959.

Elbogen, I., *Ha-Tefillah Be-Yisra'el*, Tel Aviv: Dvir, 1972.

Elijah Gaon, *Be'ur Ha-Gera'*, in Caro, J., *Shulḥan 'Arukh*.

———, *Haggahot Ha-Gera'*, in *Babylonian Talmud*, ed. Vilna.

Encyclopaedia Biblica, Vols. 1–7, Jerusalem: Mosad Bialik, 1965–76.

Encyclopaedia Judaica, 16 vols., Jerusalem: Keter, 1971–72.

Encyclopaedia Talmudit, Vols. 1–15, Jerusalem: Talmudic Encyclopedia, 1951–76.

Engel, J., *Gilyone Ha-Shas*, 3 vols., Vienna: 1924–37.

Epstein, A., *Mi-Qadmoniyyot Ha-Yehudim*, Jerusalem: Mosad Harav Kook, 1956/7.

Epstein, B., *Torah Temimah*, 5 vols., Tel Aviv: Am Olam, Or Torah, 1955/6.

Epstein, J. N., *Mavo' Le-Nusaḥ Ha-Mishnah*, 2 vols., Jerusalem and Tel Aviv: Magnes Press, 1963/4.

———, *Mevo'ot Le-Sifrut Ha-Tanna'im*, Jerusalem: Magnes Press, 1957.

———, "*Seride She'iltot*," *Tarbiz* 8 (1936/7), 5–54.

Even-Shoshan, A., *Ha-Millon He-Ḥadash*, 7 vols., Jerusalem: Kiryat Sepher, 1971.

Falk, Z., "*Beḥuqey hagoyim* in Damascus Document IX, 1," *RQ* 6 (1967–69), 569.

Farmer, W., "The Economic Basis of the Qumran Community," *ThZ* 11 (1955), 295–308.

———, "A Postscript to 'The Economic Basis of the Qumran Community,'" *ThZ* 12 (1956), 56–58.

Feldblum, M., *Diqduqe Soferim, Massekhet Giṭṭin*, New York: Horeb, Yeshiva University, 1966.

Feliks, J., "*Le-'Inyan 'Hi Ganiv Ṣevuṭeh De-Ḥavreh' Bi-Fesefas 'Ein Gedi*," *Tarbiz* 40 (1970/1), 256f.

Finkelstein, J. J., "The Goring Ox," *Temple Law Quarterly* 46 (1973), 169–290.

Finkelstein, L., *The Pharisees*, 2 vols., Philadelphia: Jewish Publication Society, 1962.

Fishbane, M., "Accusations of Adultery: A Study of Law and Scribal Practice in Numbers 5:11–31," *HUCA* 45 (1974), 25–45.

Fitzmyer, J., "The Qumran Scrolls, the Ebionites, and Their Literature," *The Scrolls and the New Testament*, ed. K. Stendahl, London: SCM Press, 1958, 208–231.

Flusser, D., "*Pesher Yesha'yahu We-Ra'ayon Shnem 'Asar Ha-Sheliḥim Be-Reshit Ha-Naṣrut*," *Eretz Israel* 8 (1966/7), 52–62.

Forkman, G., *The Limits of the Religious Community*, Lund: CWK Gleerup, 1972.
Fragmentary Targum, see *Targum Yerushalmi La-Torah.*
[Frankel, Z.,] "*Beitrage zur Sacherklärung der Mischnah,*" *MGWJ* 20 (1871), 228–232, 264–271, 494–501, 530–542.
Frankel, Z., *Darkhe Ha-Mishnah*, Tel Aviv: Sinai, 1959.
__________, *Ueber den Einfluss des palästinischen Exegese auf die alexandrinische Hermeneutik*, Leipzig: J. A. Barth, 1851.
Frensdorff, S., *Sefer 'Okhlah We-'Okhlah*, Hanover: Hahn'sche Hofbuchhandlung, 1864.
Gärtner, B., *The Temple and the Community in Qumran and the New Testament*, Cambridge: University Press, 1965.
Geiger, A., *Urschrift und Übersetzungen der Bibel in ihrer Abhängigkeit von der innern Entwicklung der Judenthums*, Breslau: Julius Hainauer, 1857.
Gevaryahu, H., "*Bet Ha-'Elohim shel Mikhah Be-Har 'Efrayim U-Massa' Bene Dan,*" *'Iyyunim Be-Sefer Shofeṭim*, Jerusalem: Kiryat Sepher, 1966, 547–584.
Ginsberg, H. L., "Heart," *EJ* 8 (1971), 7f.
Ginzberg, L., *Geonica*, 2 vols., New York: Jewish Theological Seminary, 1909.
__________, *Ginze Schechter* II, New York: Jewish Theological Seminary, 1929.
__________, *The Legends of the Jews*, 7 vols., Philadelphia: Jewish Publication Society, 1968.
__________, "*Eine unbekannte jüdische Sekte,*" *MGWJ* 55 (1911), 666–698; 56 (1912), 33–48, 285–307, 417–448, 546–566, 664–689; 57 (1913), 153–167, 284–308, 394–418, 666–696; 58 (1914), 16–48, 143–177, 395–429.
__________, *Eine unbekannte jüdische Sekte*, Hildesheim, New York: Georg Olms, 1972.
__________, *An Unknown Jewish Sect*, New York: Jewish Theological Seminary, 1976.
Goldenberg, D., "The Halakha in Josephus and in Tannaitic Literature," *JQR* 67 (1977), 30–43.
Goldschmidt, D., ed., *Maḥazor La-Yamim Ha-Nora'im*, 2 vols., Jerusalem: Koren, New York: Leo Baeck Institute, 1970.
Gombiner, Abraham Abele ben Ḥayyim Ha-Levi, *Magen 'Avraham*, in Caro, J., *Shulḥan 'Arukh.*
Goodblatt, D., *Rabbinic Instruction in Sassanian Babylonia*, Leiden: E. J. Brill, 1975.
Goodenough, E., *The Jurisprudence of the Jewish Courts in Egypt*, Amsterdam: Philo Press, 1968.
Gordis, R., "The 'Begotten' Messiah in the Qumran Scrolls," *VT* 7 (1957), 191–194.
__________, "The Knowledge of Good and Evil in the Old Testament and Qumran Scrolls," *JBL* 76 (1957), 123–138.
Gordon, A. L., *Tiqqun Tefillah*, in *Siddur 'Oṣar Ha-Tefillot*, 2 vols., Jerusalem: Nehora' De-'Orayta', 1959/60.
[Goshen-]Gottstein, M. H., "Anti-Essene Traits in the Dead Sea Scrolls," *VT* 4 (1954), 141–147.
Goshen-Gottstein, M. H., "Linguistic Structure and Tradition in the Qumran Documents," *Aspects of the Dead Sea Scrolls* (Scripta Hierosolymitana IV), ed. C. Rabin, Y. Yadin, Jerusalem: Magnes Press, 1958, 101–137.
__________, "The Psalms Scroll (11QPs^{a}), A Problem of Canon and Text," *Textus* 5 (1966), 22–23.
Gray, G. B., *A Critical and Exegetical Commentary on Numbers*, Edinburgh: T. and T. Clark, 1956.
Greenberg, M., "The Hebrew Oath Particle *ḤAY/ḤE,*" *JBL* 76 (1957), 34–39.
Gruber, M., *Aspects of Non-verbal Communication in the Ancient Near East*, 2 vols., Rome: Biblical Institute Press, 1980.
Guilbert, P., "*Le plan de la 'Règle de la Communauté,'*" *RQ* 1 (1958–59), 323–344.
Habermann, A. M., *Megillot Midbar Yehudah*, Israel: Machbaroth Lesifruth, 1959.
Hadassi, Y., *'Eshkol Ha-Kofer*, Farnborough: Gregg International, 1971.
Harkavy, A., *Mi-Sifre Ha-Miṣwot Ha-Rishonim Li-Vene Miqra'* (Zikkaron La-Rishonim VIII), St. Petersburg, 1903.

Hartman, L. F., "Eschatology," *EJ* 6, 860–879.

Hartom, A. S., Rabinowitz, J. J., "*Betulah, Betulim,*" *Enc. Bib.* 2, 381–384.

Heinemann, I., *Philons griechische und jüdische Bildung*, Hildesheim: Georg Olms, 1962.

Heinemann, J., "*Philos Lehre vom Eid,*" *Judaica, Festschrift zu Hermann Cohens siebzigstens Geburtstag*, Berlin: Bruno Cassirer, 1912, 109–118.

__________, "*Targum Shemot 22:4 We-Ha-Halakhah Ha-Qedumah,*" *Tarbiz* 38 (1968/9), 294–296.

Heller, Yom Ṭov Lipmann, *Tosefot Yom Ṭov*, in *Mishnah*, ed. Vilna.

Hengel, M., *Judaism and Hellenism*, 2 vols., London: SCM Press, 1974.

__________, *Property and Riches in the Early Church*, trans. J. Bowden, Philadelphia: Fortress Press, 1974.

Herr, M. D., "Ecclesiastes Rabbah," *EJ* 6, 355.

__________, "Midrashim, Smaller," *EJ* 16, 1515–1518.

__________, "Numbers Rabbah," *EJ* 12 (1971), 1261–1263.

__________, "*Ha-Reṣef She-Be-Shalshelet Mesiratah shel Ha-Torah,*" *Sefer Zikkaron Le-Yitzhak Baer*, ed. H. Beinart, S. Ettinger, M. Stern, Jerusalem: Historical Society of Israel, 1980, 43–56.

__________, "Tanḥuma' Yelammedenu," *EJ* 15, 794–796.

Hillel ben Eliakim, Commentary on the *Sifre*, ed. S. Koleditzky, Jerusalem: 1947/8.

Hoenig, S., "The Age of Twenty in Rabbinic Tradition and 1QSa," *JQR* 49 (1958/9), 209–214.

__________, "On the Age of Mature Responsibility in 1QSa," *JQR* 48 (1957/8), 371–375.

The Holy Bible, Oxford Annotated Bible, Revised Standard Version, ed. H. G. May, B. M. Metzger, New York: Oxford University Press, 1962.

Honeyman, A. M., "Isaiah I 16 *hizzaku,*" *VT* 1 (1951), 63–65.

Hunzinger, C.-H., *Die jüdische Bannpraxis in neutestamentlischen Zeitalter*, doctoral dissertation, Göttingen, 1954.

Huppenbauer, H., "*ṭhr und ṭhrh in der Sektenregel von Qumran,*" *ThZ* 13 (1957), 350f.

Hurwitz, A., "*Le-Shimmusho shel Ha-Munaḥ 'Edah Be-Sifrut Ha-Miqra'it,*" *Tarbiz* 40 (1970/1), 261–267.

Isaac bar Sheshet, *She'elot U-Teshuvot Bar Sheshet*, Jerusalem, 1974/5.

Israel of Krems, *Haggahot Asheri*, in *Babylonian Talmud*, ed. Vilna.

Isser, S. J., *The Dositheans*, Leiden: E. J. Brill, 1976.

Jackson, B., "Damascus Document IX, 16–23 and Parallels," *RQ* 9 (1977–78), 445–450.

__________, *Essays in Jewish and Comparative Legal History*, Leiden: E. J. Brill, 1975.

__________, *Theft in Early Jewish Law*, Oxford: Clarendon Press, 1972.

Jacob ben Asher, *'Arba'ah Ṭurim*, 7 vols., New York: M. P. Press, 1968, 1975.

Jastrow, M., *Dictionary of Talmud Bavli, Yerushalmi, Midrashic Literature and Targumim*, 2 vols., New York: Pardes, 1950.

Jellinek, A., *Bet Ha-Midrash*, 2 vols. (6 parts), Jerusalem: Wahrmann, 1967.

Johnson, S. E., "The Dead Sea Manual of Discipline and the Jerusalem Church of Acts," *ZAW* N.F. 66 (1954), 106–120.

Judah ben Barzilai, *Perush Sefer Yeṣirah*, ed. S. Halberstam, Berlin: Itzkowitzki, 1884/5.

Kaddari, M. Z., "The Root *TKN* in the Qumran Texts," *RQ* 5 (1964–66), 219–224.

Kahana, A., ed., *Ha-Sefarim Ha-Ḥiṣonim*, 2 vols., Jerusalem: Makor, 1969/70.

Katsch, A. I., ed., *Ginze Mishnah*, Jerusalem: Mosad Harav Kook, 1970.

Katz, E., *Die Bedeutung des hapax legomenon der Qumraner Handschriften HUAHA*, Bratislava, 1966.

Kaufmann, Y., *Sefer Shofeṭim*, Jerusalem: Kiryat Sepher, 1968.

Kautzsch, E., ed., *Gesenius' Hebrew Grammar*, trans. A. E. Cowley, Oxford: University Press, 1910.

Kimbrough, S. T., "The Concept of Sabbath at Qumran," *RQ* 5 (1964–66), 482–502.

Klatzkin, H., Slutsky, Y., Cohn, H., "Informers," *EJ* 8, 1364–1373.

Klinzing, G., *Die Umdeutung des Kultus in der Qumrangemeinde und im Neuen Testament*, Göttingen: Vandenhoeck and Ruprecht, 1971.

Kohut, A., *'Arukh Ha-Shalem*, 9 vols., Israel: Makor, 1967.

Kraus, S., *Paras Wa-Romi*, Jerusalem: Mosad Harav Kook, 1947/8.

Kuhn, K. G., "The Lord's Supper and the Communal Meal at Qumran," *The Scrolls and the New Testament*, ed. K. Stendahl, London: SCM Press, 1958, 65–93.

____________, "The Two Messiahs of Aaron and Israel," *The Scrolls and the New Testament*, ed. K. Stendahl, London: SCM Press, 1958, 54–64.

Kutscher, E. Y., *"Le-Diyyuqah shel Leshon Megillot Yam Ha-Melaḥ,"* *Leshonenu* 22 (1957/8), 89–100.

____________, *Ha-Lashon We-Ha-Reqa' Ha-Leshoni shel Megillat Yisha'yahu Ha-Shelemah Mi-Megillot Yam Ha-Melaḥ*, Jerusalem: Magnes Press, 1959.

Lampronti, I., *Paḥad Yiṣḥaq* IV, Reggio: Tipografia della Societa, 1812/3.

Laperrousaz, E. M., *"A propos de dépôts d'ossements d'animaux trouvés à Qoumrân,"* *RQ* 9 (1977–78), 569–573.

____________, *Qoumrân, l'établissement Essénien des bords de la Mer Morte*, Paris: A. & J. Picard, 1976.

Lauterbach, J. Z., "The Belief in the Power of the Word," *HUCA* 14 (1939), 287–302.

____________, "Substitutes for the Tetragrammaton," *PAAJR* 2 (1930–31), 39–67.

L.-Duhaime, J., *"Remarques sur les dépôts d'ossements d'animaux à Qumran,"* *RQ* 9 (1977–78), 245–251.

Leaney, A. R. C., *The Rule of Qumran and its Meaning*, Philadelphia: Westminster Press, 1966.

Leiman, S., *The Canonization of Hebrew Scripture*, Hamden, CT: The Connecticut Academy of Arts and Sciences, 1976.

Levi, I., *"Le Tétragramme et l'écrit Sadokite de Damas,"* *REJ* 68 (1914), 119–121.

____________, *Über einige Fragmente aus der Mischna des Abba Saul*, Berichte der Hochschule für die Wissenschaft des Judentums in Berlin, 1876.

Levi ben Gershon, Commentary on Proverbs, in *Ketuvim*, New York: Schocken Books, 1946.

Levine, B., "Damascus Document IX, 17–22: A New Translation and Comments," *RQ* 8 (1973), 195f.

____________, "The Language of the Magical Bowls," Appendix to J. Neusner, *A History of the Jews in Babylonia* V, Leiden: E. J. Brill, 1970, 343–375.

____________, "The Temple Scroll: Aspects of its Historical Provenance and Literary Character," *BASOR* 232 (1978), 5–23.

Levy, J., *Wörterbuch über die Talmudim und Midraschim*, 4 vols., Darmstadt: Wissenschaftliche Buchgesellschaft, 1963.

Lewin, B. M., *'Oṣar Ha-Ge'onim*, 13 vols., Haifa, Jerusalem, 1927/8–1942/3.

Licht, J., "An Analysis of the Treatise on the Two Spirits in DSD," *Aspects of the Dead Sea Scrolls* (Scripta Hierosolymitana IV), ed. C. Rabin, Y. Yadin, Jerusalem: Magnes Press, 1958, 87–100.

____________, *Megillat Ha-Hodayot*, Jerusalem: Mosad Bialik, 1957.

____________, *Megillat Ha-Serakhim*, Jerusalem: Mosad Bialik, 1965.

____________, *"Ha-Munaḥ Goral Bi-Khetaveha shel Kat Midbar Yehudah,"* *Bet Miqra'* 1 (1955/6), 90–99.

Liddell, H., Scott, R., *A Greek-English Lexicon*, revised and augmented by H. Stuart Jones, R. McKenzie, with a Supplement, Oxford: University Press, 1968.

Lieberman, S., *'Al Ha-Yerushalmi*, Jerusalem: Darom, 1929.

____________, "The Discipline in the So-Called Dead Sea Manual of Discipline," *JBL* 71 (1952), 199–206.

____________, *Greek in Jewish Palestine*, New York: P. Feldheim, 1965.

____________, *"He'arah Muqdemet La-Ketovet Be-'Ein Gedi,"* *Tarbiz* 40 (1970/1), 24–26.

———, *Hellenism in Jewish Palestine*, New York: Jewish Theological Seminary, 1962.
———, "Light on the Cave Scrolls from Rabbinic Sources," *PAAJR* 20 (1951), 395–404.
———, "*Mashehu 'al Hashba'ot Be-Yisra'el*," *Tarbiz* 27 (1957/8), 183–189.
———, "*Perushim Ba-Mishnayot*," *Tarbiz* 40 (1970/1), 9–17.
———, "Roman Legal Institutions in Early Rabbinics and in the Acta Martyrum," *JQR* N.S. 35 (1944/5), 1–57.
———, *Texts and Studies*, New York: Ktav, 1974.
———, *Tosefta' Ki-Fshutah*, New York: Jewish Theological Seminary, 1955–.
———, *Tosefet Rishonim*, vols. I–III, Jerusalem: Bamberger and Wahrmann, 1937–9; vol. IV, Jerusalem: Mosad Harav Kook, 1939.
Lightstone, J. N., *Yose the Galilean* I, Leiden: E. J. Brill, 1979.
Lipschutz, I., *Tiferet Yisra'el*, in *Mishnah*, ed. Vilna.
Liver, J., "*Maḥaṣit Ha-Sheqel Bi-Megillot Kat Midbar Yehudah*," *Tarbiz* 31 (1960/1), 18–22.
———, "*Parashat Maḥaṣit Ha-Sheqel*," *Y. Kaufmann Jubilee Volume*, ed. M. Haran, Jerusalem: Magnes Press, 1960/1, 54–67.
Loewenstamm, S., "*Karet*," *Enc. Bib.* 4, 330–332.
Luria, David, Commentary to *Pirqe Rabbi 'Eli'ezer*, ed. Warsaw, 1851/2.
Luzzatto, S. D., *Perush Shadal 'al Ḥamishah Ḥumshe Torah*, ed. P. Schlesinger, Tel Aviv: Dvir, 1965.
Maimonides, M., *The Guide of the Perplexed*, trans. S. Pines, Chicago: University of Chicago Press, 1963.
———, *Mishneh Torah*, ed. Vilna, reprinted (with additions), 5 vols., Jerusalem: Pardes, 1955.
———, *Perush Ha-Mishnayot*, in *Mishnah*, Codex Parma "C," ed. Naples, and *Babylonian Talmud*, ed. Vilna.
———, *Sefer Ha-Miṣwot*, ed. H. Heller, Jerusalem: Mosad Harav Kook, 1979/80.
Malbim, M., *'Oṣar Ha-Perushim*, 4 vols., Israel: Mefarshe Ha-Tanakh, n.d.
Mann, J., "Genizah Fragments of the Palestinian Order of Service," *HUCA* 2 (1925), 269–338.
———, *Texts and Studies in Jewish History and Literature* I, Cincinnati: Hebrew Union College Press, 1931.
Mansoor, M., *The Thanksgiving Hymns*, Grand Rapids, MI: Eerdmans, 1961.
Marmorstein, A., *The Doctrine of Merits in Old Rabbinical Literature* and *The Old Rabbinic Doctrine of God*, 3 vols. in 1, New York: Ktav, 1968.
May, H. G., Metzger, B. M., eds., *The Oxford Annotated Bible*, Revised Standard Version, New York: Oxford University Press, 1962.
Mazar, B., "*Ketovet 'al Riṣpat Bet-Keneset Be-'Ein Gedi*," *Tarbiz* 40 (1970/1), 18–23.
Meiri, Menaḥem ben Solomon Ha-, *Bet Ha-Beḥirah Ha-Shalem 'al Massekhet Sanhedrin*, ed. I. Ralbag, Jerusalem: Harry Fischel Institute, 1970/1.
Mekhilta' De-Rabbi Ishmael with *Birkat Ha-Neṣiv* by N.Z.J. Berlin, Jerusalem: Committee for the Publication of the Manuscripts of the Netziv of Volozin, 1970.
Mekhilta' De-Rabbi Ishmael, ed. M. Friedmann (Ish Shalom), Vienna, 1869/70.
Mekhilta' De-Rabbi Ishmael, ed. H. S. Horovitz, I. A. Rabin, Jerusalem: Bamberger and Wahrmann, 1960.
Mekhilta' De-Rabbi Shim'on ben Yoḥai, ed J. N. Epstein, E. Z. Melamed, Jerusalem: Mekize Nirdamim, 1955.
Mekhilta' De-Rabbi Shim'on ben Yoḥai, ed D. Hoffmann, Frankfurt a. M.: J. Kaufmann, 1905.
Midrash Ha-Gadol. See Adani, David ben Amram.
Midrash Le-'Olam, ed. A. Jellinek, *Bet Ha-Midrash*, Jerusalem: Wahrmann, 1967, part 3, 109–120.
Midrash Rabbah, ed. Vilna, 2 vols., New York: Grossman, 1952.
Midrash Tadshe', in A. Epstein, *Mi-Qadmoniyyot Ha-Yehudim*, Jerusalem: Mosad Harav Kook, 1956/57, 130–171.

Midrash Tadshe', in A. Jellinek, *Bet Ha-Midrash*, Jerusalem: Wahrmann, 1967, part 3, 164–193.

Midrash Tanḥuma', with commentary by Ḥanokh Zundel ben Joseph, Vilna, 1833.

Midrash Tanḥuma', ed. S. Buber, New York: Sefer, 1946.

Midrash Tanna'im, ed. D. Hoffmann, Berlin: Itzkowski, 1909.

Midrash Tehillim, ed. S. Buber, Vilna: Romm, 1891.

Midrash Wa-Yiqra' Rabbah, ed. M. Margaliot, 5 vols. in 3, Jerusalem: Wahrmann, 1972.

Milgrom, J., "The Concept of Ma'al in the Bible and the Ancient Near East," *JAOS* 96 (1976), 236–247.

____________, *Cult and Conscience*, Leiden: E. J. Brill, 1976.

____________, "'Sabbath' and 'Temple City' in the Temple Scroll," *BASOR* 232 (1978), 25–27.

Milik, J. T., *Dix ans de découvertes dans le désert de Juda*, Paris: Les Éditions du Cerf, 1957.

____________, "The Manual of Discipline by P. Wernberg-Møller," (review) *RB* 67 (1960), 410–416.

____________, "*Megillat milḥemet bene 'or bivene ḥošek* by Y. Yadin," (review) *RB* 64 (1957), 585–593.

____________, *Ten Years of Discovery in the Wilderness of Judaea*, trans. J. Strugnell, Naperville, IL: Alec R. Allenson, 1959.

Mishnah, Codex Jerusalem Heb 4° 1336, Neziqin, Qodashim, Ṭohorot (Yemenite vocalization), Introduction by S. Morag, 2 vols., Jerusalem: Makor, 1970.

Mishnah, Codex Kaufmann, 2 vols., Jerusalem: Sifriyat Meqorot, 1967/8.

Mishnah, Codex Paris 328–329, Introduction by M. Bar-Asher, 3 vols., Jerusalem: Makor, 1973.

Mishnah, Codex Parma, De Rossi 138, 2 vols., Jerusalem: Kedem, 1970.

Mishnah, Codex Parma "B," De Rossi 497, Seder Ṭohorot, Introduction by M. Bar-Asher, Jerusalem: Makor, 1971.

Mishnah, Codex Parma "C," De Rossi 984, Sedarim Nashim, Neziqin, Jerusalem: Makor, 1971.

Mishnah, ed. Ch. Albeck, with vocalization by H. Yalon, 6 vols., Jerusalem, Tel Aviv: Mosad Bialik and Dvir, 1957–9.

Mishnah, genizah fragments. See Katsch, A.I.

Mishnah, ed. W. H. Lowe (*The Mishnah on which the Palestinian Talmud Rests*), 2 vols., Cambridge: University Press, 1883.

Mishnah, ed. Vilna, 12 vols., New York: Pardes, 1952/3.

Mishnah 'im Perush Ha-Rambam, ed. princ. Naples, 1492, Introduction by A. M. Habermann, 2 vols., Jerusalem: Sifriyat Meqorot, 1969/70.

Moore, G. F., *A Critical and Exegetical Commentary on Judges*, Edinburgh: T. and T. Clark, 1895.

____________, *Judaism*, 2 vols., New York: Schocken, 1971.

____________, "Simeon the Righteous," *Jewish Studies in Memory of Israel Abrahams*, New York: Press of the Jewish Institute of Religion, 1927, 348–364.

Morag, S., "*Ha-Kinuyim Ha-'Aṣma'iyyim La-Nistar We-La-Nisteret Bi-Megillot Yam Ha-Melaḥ*" *Eretz Israel* 3 (1954), 166–169.

Mordecai ben Hillel, *Sefer Mordekhai*, in *Babylonian Talmud*, ed. Vilna.

Müller, J., *Teshuvot Ḥakhme Ṣorfat We-Lotir*, Vienna, 1880/1.

Murphy-O'Connor, J., "The Critique of the Princes of Judah," *RB* 79 (1972), 200–216.

____________, "The Essenes and their History," *RB* 81 (1974), 215–244.

____________, "The Essenes in Palestine," *BA* 40 (1977), 100–124.

____________, "An Essene Missionary Document? CD II, 14–VI, 1," *RB* 77 (1970), 201–229.

____________, "*La genèse littéraire de la Règle de la Communauté*," *RB* 76 (1969), 528–549.

____________, "A Literary Analysis of Damascus Document VI, 2–VIII, 3," *RB* 78 (1971), 210–232.

____________, "A Literary Analysis of Damascus Document XIX, 33–XX, 34," *RB* 79 (1972), 544–564.

Naḥmanides, M., "*Mishpaṭ Ha-Ḥerem*," in *Sefer Kol Bo*, New York: Shulsinger, 1845/6 (*sic*).
———, "*Mishpaṭ Ha-Ḥerem*," ed. H. S. Shaanan, in *Ḥiddushe Ha-Ramban Le-Massekhet Shevu'ot*, ed. E. Lichtenstein, Jerusalem: Makhon Ha-Talmud Ha-Yisra'eli Ha-Shalem, 1976.
———, *Perushe Ha-Torah*, ed. C. Chavel, 2 vols., Jerusalem: Mosad Harav Kook, 1959.
Nebe, G. W., "*Der Gebrauch der sogennanten nota accusativi 'et in Damaskusschrift XV, 5.9 und 12*," *RQ* 8 (1972–75), 257–264.
Nemoy, L., "Anan ben David," *EJ* 2, 919–922.
———, *Karaite Anthology*, New Haven: Yale University Press, 1952.
Neusner, J., "By the Testimony of Two Witnesses in the Damascus Document IX, 17–22 and in Pharisaic-Rabbinic Law," *RQ* 8 (1972–75), 197–217.
———, "Damascus Document IX, 17–22 and Irrelevant Parallels," *RQ* 9 (1977–78), 441–444.
———, "The Description of Formative Judaism: The Social Perspective of the Mishnah's System of Civil Law and Government," *AJSR* 5 (1980), 63–79.
———, *Early Rabbinic Judaism*, Leiden: E. J. Brill, 1975.
———, "Emergent Rabbinic Judaism in a Time of Crisis," *Judaism* 21 (1979), 313–327.
———, *Fellowship in Judaism*, London: Vallentine and Mitchell, 1963.
———, "ḤBR and N'MN," *RQ* 5 (1964–66), 119–122.
———, *A History of the Jews in Babylonia*, 5 vols., Leiden: E. J. Brill, 1965–70.
———, *A History of the Mishnaic Law of Purities*, 22 vols., Leiden: E. J. Brill, 1974–80.
———, *The Idea of Purity in Ancient Judaism*, Leiden: E. J. Brill, 1973.
———, ed., *The Modern Study of the Mishnah*, Leiden: E. J. Brill, 1973.
———, "Oral Tradition and Oral Torah, Defining the Problematic," *Studies in Jewish Folklore*, ed. F. Talmage, Cambridge, MA: Association for Jewish Studies, 1980, 251–271.
———, "Rabbinic Traditions about the Pharisees before A.D. 70: The Problem of Oral Tradition," *JJS* 22 (1971), 1–18.
———, *The Rabbinic Traditions about the Pharisees before 70*, 3 vols., Leiden: E. J. Brill, 1971.
———, "Scriptural, Essenic, and Mishnaic Approaches to Civil Law and Government: Some Comparative Remarks," *HTR* 74 (1981), 419–434.
New English Bible, 3 vols., Oxford: University Press, Cambridge: University Press, 1961–70.
Nissim ben Jacob, Commentary to the Babylonian Talmud, in *Babylonian Talmud*, ed. Vilna.
Nissim ben Reuben Gerondi, Commentary to Nedarim, in *Babylonian Talmud*, ed. Vilna.
Nolland, J., "A Misleading Statement of the Essene Attitude to the Temple," *RQ* 9 (1977–78), 555–562.
Noth, M., *Leviticus*, trans. J. E. Anderson, Philadelphia: Westminster Press, 1965.
Oppenheim, A. L., ed., *The Assyrian Dictionary*, vol. 21 (Z), Chicago: The Oriental Institute, 1961.
Oppenheimer, A., *The 'Am Ha-Aretz*, Leiden: E. J. Brill, 1977.
Palestinian Talmud, ed. Krotoschin, Jerusalem: Torah La-'Am, 1959/60.
Palestinian Talmud, ed. Zhitomir (with commentaries), Jerusalem: Bene Ma'arav, 1979/80.
The Palestinian Targum to the Pentateuch, Codex Vatican (Neofiti 1), 2 vols., Jerusalem: Makor, 1970.
Pardo, D., Commentary on *Sifre De-Ve Rav*, 2 vols., Salonika, 1799.
———, *Ḥasde Dawid*, 5 vols., I, Leghorn, 1776; II, Leghorn, 1789/90; III, Jerusalem, 1889/90; IV, Jerusalem, 1970; V, Jerusalem, 1971.
Pesiqta' Rabbati, ed. Meir Ish Shalom, Vienna, 1880.
Pesiqta' De-Rav Kahana', ed. S. Buber, Lyck: Mekize Nirdamim, 1868.
Pesiqta' De-Rav Kahana', ed. B. Mandelbaum, 2 vols., New York: Jewish Theological Seminary, 1962.

Petroff, J., "Solomon, Testament of," *EJ* 15, 118f.

Philo [Works], ed., trans., F. H. Colson, G. H. Whitaker, R. Marcus, 10 vols. + 2 supplementary vols., Cambridge, MA: Harvard University Press, 1929–53.

Pineles, Z., *Darkah shel Torah*, Vienna: Friedr. Förster & Brüder, 1861.

Pirqe Rabbi 'Eli'ezer, with commentary by David Luria, Warsaw, 1851/2.

Ploeg, J. van der, "The Meals of the Essenes," *JSS* 2 (1957), 163–175.

Porton, G., "Hanokh Albeck on the Mishnah," *The Modern Study of the Mishnah*, ed. J. Neusner, Leiden: E. J. Brill, 1973, 209–224.

————, *The Traditions of Rabbi Ishmael*, 3 vols., Leiden: E. J. Brill, 1976–79.

Pouilly, J., "*L'évolution de la législation pénale dans la communauté de Qumrân*," *RB* 82 (1975), 522–551.

Poznanski, S., "*Anan et ses écrits*," *REJ* 44 (1902), 161–187; 45 (1902), 50–69.

Preuss, J., *Biblical and Talmudic Medicine*, trans. and ed. F. Rosner, New York, London: Sanhedrin Press, 1978.

Priest, J. F., "The Messiah and the Meal in 1QSa," *JBL* 82 (1963), 95–100.

Pritchard, J., ed., *Ancient Near Eastern Texts*, Princeton: Princeton University Press, 1969.

Qimron, E., *Diqduq Ha-Lashon Ha-'Ivrit shel Megillot Midbar Yehudah*, Hebrew University Doctoral Dissertation, Jerusalem, 1976.

Rabad. See Abraham ben David.

Rabbinovicz, R. N., *Diqduqe Soferim*, 15 vols., New York, Jerusalem, and Montreal, 1959/60.

Rabin, C., *Qumran Studies*, Oxford: University Press, 1957.

————, *The Zadokite Documents*, Oxford: University Press, 1954.

Rabinovitch, N. L., "Damascus Document IX, 17–22 and Rabbinic Parallels," *RQ* 9 (1977–78), 113–116.

Rabinowitz, I., "The Meaning and Date of 'Damascus' Document IX, 1," *RQ* 6 (1967–69), 433–435.

Rabinowitz, Z. W., *Sha'are Torat Bavel*, Jerusalem: Jewish Theological Seminary, 1961.

Radbaz. See David ben Solomon ibn Abi Zimra.

Ralbag. See Levi ben Gershon.

Ramah. See Abulafia, Meir ben Todros Ha-Levi.

Ran. See Nissim ben Reuben Gerondi.

Rappoport, U., "Simeon the Just," *EJ* 14, 1566f.

Rashi. See Solomon ben Isaac.

Revel, B., "*'Onesh Shevu'at Sheqer Le-Da'at Philon We-Ha-Rambam*," *Horeb* 2 (1934/5), 1–5.

————, *The Karaite Halakah*, Philadelphia: Dropsie College, 1913.

Richardson, H. N., "Some Notes on 1QSa," *JBL* 76 (1957), 108–122.

Ringgren, H., *The Faith of Qumran*, Philadelphia: Fortress Press, 1963.

Ritter, B., *Philo und die Halacha*, Leipzig: J. C. Hinrichs'sche Buchhandlung, 1879.

Robinson, I., "A Note on Damascus Document IX, 7," *RQ* 9 (1977–78), 237–240.

Rosenthal, J., "*'Al Hishtalshelut Halakhah Be-Sefer Berit Dameseq*," *Sefer Ha-Yovel Mugash Li-Khvod Ha-Rav Shim'on Federbush*, ed. J. L. Maimon, Jerusalem: Mosad Harav Kook, 1960, 293–303.

Rosh. See Asher ben Yeḥiel.

Rubinstein, A., "Urban Halakhah and Camp Rules in the 'Cairo Fragments of a Damascus Covenant,'" *Sefarad* 12 (1952), 283–296.

Sa'adyah ben Joseph Gaon, *Siddur Rav Sa'adyah Ga'on*, ed. I. Davidson, S. Assaf, B. I. Joel, Jerusalem: Mekize Nirdamim, 1970.

Sanders, J. A., *The Dead Sea Psalms Scroll*, Ithaca, NY: Cornell University Press, 1967.

————, *The Psalms Scroll of Qumran Cave 11, Discoveries in the Judaean Desert* IV, Oxford: Clarendon Press, 1965.

Sarason, R., *A History of the Mishnaic Law of Agriculture* Part III, Vol. 1, Leiden: E. J. Brill, 1979.

Sarna, N. M., "Bible, the Canon, Text," *EJ* 4, 816–836.

Schalit, A., *Hordos Ha-Melekh*, Jerusalem: Mosad Bialik, 1964.

____________, *König Herodes*, Berlin: Walter de Gruyter and Co., 1969.

Schechter, S., *Documents of Jewish Sectaries*, 2 vols. in 1, with "Prolegomenon" by J. A. Fitzmyer, New York: Ktav, 1970.

Schiffman, L. H., "At the Crossroads: Tannaitic Perspectives on the Jewish-Christian Schism," *Jewish and Christian Self-Definition* II, ed. E. P. Sanders, London: SCM Press, 1981, 115–156, 338–352.

____________, "Communal Meals at Qumran," *RQ* 10 (1979), 45–56.

____________, "A Forty-two Letter Divine Name in the Aramaic Magic Bowls," *Bulletin of the Institute of Jewish Studies* 1 (1973), 97–102.

____________, *The Halakhah at Qumran*, 2 vols., Brandeis University Doctoral Dissertation, Waltham, MA, 1974.

____________, *The Halakhah at Qumran*, Leiden: E. J. Brill, 1975.

____________, "The Interchange of the Prepositions *bet* and *mem* in the Texts from Qumran," *Textus* 10 (1982), 37–43.

____________, "Jewish Sectarianism in Second Temple Times," *Great Schisms in Jewish History*, ed. R. Jospe, S. Wagner, New York: Center for Judaic Studies and Ktav, 1981, 1–46.

____________, "*Merkavah* Speculation at Qumran: The 4Q *Serekh Shirot 'Olat Ha-Shabbat*," *Mystics, Philosophers, and Politicians: Essays in Jewish Intellectual History in Honor of Alexander Altmann*, ed. J. Reinharz, D. Swetschinski, Durham, NC: Duke University Press, 1981, 15–47.

____________, "The Qumran Law of Testimony," *RQ* 8 (1972–75), 603–612.

____________, "The *Temple Scroll* in Literary and Philological Perspective," *Approaches to Ancient Judaism* II, ed. W. S. Green, Brown Judaic Studies 9, 1980, 143–155.

Schirmann, J., "*Teshuvah*," *Tarbiz* 40 (1970/1), 391.

Schlesinger, A., *Kitve 'Akiva' Schlesinger*, Jerusalem: Kiryat Sepher, 1962.

Schürer, E., *The History of the Jewish People in the Age of Jesus Christ*, ed. G. Vermes, F. Millar, Vols. I–II, Edinburgh: T. and T. Clark, 1973, 1979.

Seeligmann, I. L., "*Zur Terminologie für das Gerichtsverfahren im Wortschatz des biblischen Hebräisch*," *Suppl. to VT* 16 (1967), 251–278.

Sefer Ben Sira', Ha-Maqor, Qonqordanṣiyah, We-Nituaḥ 'Oṣar Ha-Millim, Jerusalem: The Academy for the Hebrew Language and the Shrine of the Book, 1973.

Sefer Ha-Razim, ed. M. Margaliot, Jerusalem: American Academy for Jewish Research, 1966/7.

Segal, M. H. (M.Ṣ.), "Additional Notes on 'Fragments of a Zadokite Work,'" *JQR* N.S. 3 (1912/3), 301–311.

____________, *Diqduq Leshon Ha-Mishnah*, Tel Aviv: Dvir, 1935/6.

____________, "*Le-Va'ayot shel Megillot Ha-Me'arot*," *Eretz Israel* 1 (1951), 39–44.

____________, "Notes on 'Fragments of a Zadokite Work,'" *JQR* N.S. 2 (1911/2), 133–141.

____________, *Sefer Ben Sira' Ha-Shalem*, Jerusalem: Mosad Bialik, 1971/2.

____________, "*Sefer Berit Dameseq*," *Ha-Shiloaḥ* 26 (1912), 390–406, 483–506.

Septuaginta, ed. A. Rahlfs, 2 vols., Stuttgart: Württembergische Bibelanstalt, 1935.

Shapira, Joshua Isaac ben Jehiel, *No'am Yerushalmi*, 2 vols., Jerusalem: Z. Shapira, 1967/8.

Sharvit, B., "*Ṭum'ah We-Ṭohorah le-fi Kat Midbar Yehudah*," *Bet Miqra'* 26 (1980/1), 18–27.

She'iltot, ed. S. K. Mirsky, 5 vols., Jerusalem: Yeshiva University, 1959–77.

She'iltot, with commentary of N. Z. J. Berlin, 3 vols., Jerusalem: Mosad Harav Kook, 1961.

Shemot Rabbah, in *Midrash Rabbah*, ed. Vilna.

Shem Tov ben Abraham ibn Gaon, *Migdal 'Oz*, in Maimonides, M., *Mishneh Torah*, ed. Vilna.

Shir Ha-Shirim Rabbah, in *Midrash Rabbah*, ed. Vilna.

Siegel, J. P., "The Employment of Palaeo-Hebrew Characters for Divine Names at Qumran in the light of Tannaitic Sources," *HUCA* 42 (1971), 159–172.

———, "Final *mem* in Medial Position and Medial *mem* in Final Position in *11 Q Ps a*," *RQ* 7 (1969–71), 125–130.

Sifra', MS Vatican 31, Jerusalem: Makor, 1972.

Sifra' De-Ve Rav (*Torat Kohanim*), with commentaries, Jerusalem: Sifra, 1958/9.

Sifra' De-Ve Rav (*Torat Kohanim*), ed. I. H. Weiss, Vienna: J. Schlossberg, 1861/2.

Sifra or Torat Kohanim, According to Codex Assemani LXVI, with a Hebrew Introduction by L. Finkelstein, New York: Jewish Theological Seminary, 1956.

Sifre De-Ve Rav (Numbers), ed. H. S. Horovitz, Jerusalem: Wahrmann, 1966.

Sifre on Deuteronomy, ed. L. Finkelstein, New York: Jewish Theological Seminary, 1969.

Sifre Zuta', in *Sifre De-Ve Rav* (Numbers), ed. H. S. Horovitz, Jerusalem: Wahrmann, 1966.

Simḥah ben Samuel of Vitry, *Maḥazor Vitry*, ed. S. Hurwitz, Jerusalem: "Alef" Publishing, 1963.

Skehan, P., "Two Books on Qumran Studies," *CBQ* 21 (1959), 71–78.

Smith, M., "God's Begetting the Messiah in 1 Q Sa," *NTS* 5 (1958/9), 218–224.

Smith, W. R., *The Religion of the Semites*, New York: Schocken, 1972.

Solomon ben Isaac, Commentary, in *Babylonian Talmud*, ed. Vilna.

———, *Rashi 'al Ha-Torah*, ed. A. Berliner, Jerusalem and New York: P. Feldheim, 1969.

Spiro, A., "A Law on the Sharing of Information," *PAAJR* 28 (1959), 95–101.

Stern, M., *Greek and Latin Authors on the Jews and Judaism*, vol. I, Jerusalem: Israel Academy of Sciences and Humanities, 1976.

———, "The Herodian Dynasty and the Province of Judea at the end of the Period of the Second Temple," *The Herodian Period*, ed. M. Avi-Yonah, New Brunswick: Rutgers University Press, 1975, 124–178, 355–360.

Strack, H., *Introduction to the Talmud and Midrash*, New York: Harper and Row, 1965.

Strugnell, J., "The Angelic Liturgy at Qumran—4Q *Serek Širôt 'Ôlat Haššabāt*," *Suppl. to VT* 7 (1960), 318–345.

———, "*Notes en Marge du Volume V des 'Discoveries in the Judaean Desert of Jordan*,'" *RQ* 7 (1970), 163–276.

Sutcliffe, E. F., "The First Fifteen Members of the Qumran Community," *JSS* 4 (1959), 134–138.

———, "The General Council of the Qumran Community," *Biblica* 40 (1959), 971–983.

———, "The Rule of the Congregation (1 Q S a) II, 11–12: Text and Meaning," *RQ* 2 (1959–60), 541–547.

Talmon, S., "The Calendar Reckoning of the Sect from the Judaean Desert," *Aspects of the Dead Sea Scrolls* (Scripta Hierosolymitana IV), ed. C. Rabin, Y. Yadin, Jerusalem: Magnes Press, 1958, 162–199.

———, "The 'Desert Motif' in the Bible and in Qumran Literature," *Biblical Motifs*, ed. A. Altmann, Cambridge, MA: Harvard University Press, 1966, 31–63.

———, "The Emergence of Institutionalized Prayer in Israel in the Light of the Qumrân Literature," *Qumrân, Sa piété, sa théologie et son milieu*, ed. M. Delcor, Louvain: University Press, 1978, 265–284.

———, "*Maḥazor Ha-Berakhot shel Kat Midbar Yehudah*," *Tarbiz* 28 (1958/9), 1–20.

———, "The 'Manual of Benedictions' of the Sect of the Judaean Desert," *RQ* 2 (1959–60), 475–500.

———, "*Mizmorim Ḥisoniyyim Ba-Lashon Ha-'Ivrit Mi-Qumran*," *Tarbiz* 35 (1965/6), 214–234.

———, "*Pisqah Be'emṣa' Pasuq* and 11QPs^a," *Textus* 5 (1966), 11–21.

———, "The Sectarian *yḥd*—a Biblical Noun," *VT* 3 (1953), 133–140.

Targum Onkelos, ed. A. Berliner, Berlin, 1884.

Targum Neofiti. See *The Palestinian Targum to the Pentateuch*.

Targum Pseudo-Jonathan, ed. H. Ginsburger, Berlin: S. Calvary, 1903.

Targum Yerushalmi La-Torah, ed. M. Ginsburger, Berlin: S. Calvary, 1899.
Taylor, C., *An Appendix to Sayings of the Jewish Fathers*, Cambridge: University Press, 1900.
__________, *Sayings of the Jewish Fathers*, Cambridge: University Press, 1877.
Tchernowitz, C., *Toledot Ha-Halakhah*, 4 vols., New York: 1945–53.
Tedesche, S., *The First Book of Maccabees*, New York: Harper & Brothers, 1950.
Teicher, J., "Restoration of the 'Damascus Fragments' xiv, 12–16," *JJS* 3 (1952), 87f.
The Testament of Abraham, trans. M. Stone, Missoula, MT: Society of Biblical Literature, 1972.
Tiklal Shivat Ṣion, ed. J. Kafah, 3 vols., Jerusalem: Eshkol, 1951/2.
The Torah, Philadelphia: Jewish Publication Society, 1962.
Torczyner, N. H., *Te'udot Lakhish*, Jerusalem: Jewish Palestine Exploration Society, 1940.
Tosefot Yom Ṭov. See Heller, Yom Ṭov Lipmann.
Tosefta', ed. S. Lieberman, New York: Jewish Theological Seminary, 1955–.
Tosefta', ed. M. Zuckermandel, Jerusalem: Wahrmann, 1962/3.
Tropper, D., *The Internal Administration of the Second Temple at Jerusalem*, Yeshiva University Doctoral Dissertation, New York, 1970.
Tur Sinai, N. H., *Ha-Lashon We-Ha-Sefer*, 3 vols., Jerusalem: Mosad Bialik, 1959.
__________, *Peshuto shel Miqra'*, 4 vols., Jerusalem: Kiryat Sepher, 1967.
Urbach, E. E., *Ba'ale Ha-Tosafot*, Jerusalem: Mosad Bialik, 1980.
__________, "*Bate-Din shel 'Esrim U-Sheloshah We-Dine Mitot Bet Din*," *Proceedings of the Fifth World Congress of Jewish Studies* II (1972), 37–48.
__________, "*Halakhah U-Nevu'ah*," *Tarbiz* 18 (1946/7), 1–27.
__________, "*Hashlamot Le-Hashlim*," *Tarbiz* 40 (1970/1), 392.
__________, "*Ha-Sod She-Bi-Khetovet 'Ein Gedi We-Noshah*," *Tarbiz* 40 (1970/1), 27–30.
Vaux, R. de, *Ancient Israel*, 2 vols., New York: McGraw Hill, 1965.
__________, *Archaeology and the Dead Sea Scrolls*, London: Oxford University Press, 1973.
Vliet, H. van, *No Single Testimony, A Study of the Adoption of the Law of Deut. 19:15 par. into the New Testament, Studia Theologica Rheno-Traiectina* IV, Utrecht: 1958.
Vulgate, in *Biblia Hebraica*, Vol. I, Lipsiae: Sumtibus Ernesti Bredtii, 1838.
Wa-Yiqra' Rabbah. See *Midrash Wa-Yiqra' Rabbah*.
Weinert, F. D., "4Q 159: Legislation for an Essene Community outside of Qumran," *JSJ* 5 (1974), 179–207.
Weinfeld, M., "*Defusim 'Irguniyyim We-Taqqanot 'Oneshim Bi-Megillat Serekh Ha-Yaḥad*," *Shnaton* 2 (1977), 60–81.
__________, *Deuteronomy and the Deuteronomic School*, Oxford: Clarendon Press, 1972.
__________, "'*Iqbot shel Qedushat Yoṣer Bi-Megillot Qumran U-Ve-Sefer Ben Sira'*," *Tarbiz* 45 (1975/6), 15–26.
__________, "Judge and Officer in Ancient Israel and in the Ancient Near East," *Israel Oriental Studies* 7 (1977), 65–88.
__________, "*Teguvot La-Ma'amarim*," *Shnaton* 1 (1975), 253–259.
Weise, M., *Kultzeiten und kultischer Bundesschluss in der "Ordensregel" vom Toten Meer*, Leiden: E. J. Brill, 1961.
Wernberg-Møller, P., *The Manual of Discipline*, Leiden: E. J. Brill, 1957.
__________, "A Reconsideration of the Two Spirits in the Rule of the Community (1 Q Serek III, 13–IV, 26)," *RQ* 3 (1961–62), 411–441.
Wieder, N., *The Judean Scrolls and Karaism*, London: East and West Library, 1962.
Williams, R. J., *Hebrew Syntax: An Outline*, Toronto and Buffalo: University of Toronto Press, 1976.
Winter, P., "Ṣadokite Fragments IX, 1," *RQ* 6 (1967–69), 131–136.
Woude, A. S. van der, "*Ein neuer Segensspruch aus Qumran (11 Q Ber)*," *Bibel und Qumran* (Festschrift H. Bardke), ed. S. Wagner, Berlin: Evangelische Haupt-Bibelgesellschaft, 1968, 253–258.

Yadin, Y., *Bar Kokhba*, London: Weidenfeld and Nicolson, 1971.
____________, "A Crucial Passage in the Dead Sea Scrolls," *JBL* 78 (1959), 238–241.
____________, "*Le-Hashlim*," *Tarbiz* 40 (1970/1), 390.
____________, *Megillat Ha-Miqdash*, 3 vols., Jerusalem: Israel Exploration Society, 1977.
____________, "The Newly Published *Pesharim* of Isaiah," *IEJ* 9 (1959), 39–42.
____________, "A Note on 4Q 159 (Ordinances)," *IEJ* 18 (1968), 250–252.
____________, "Pesher Nahum (4Qp Nahum) Reconsidered," *IEJ* 21 (1971), 1–12.
____________, *The Scroll of the War of the Sons of Light against the Sons of Darkness*, trans. B. and C. Rabin, Oxford: University Press, 1962.
____________, *Tefillin from Qumran*, Jerusalem: Israel Exploration Society and the Shrine of the Book, 1969.
____________, "Three Notes on the Dead Sea Scrolls," *IEJ* 6 (1956), 158–162.
Yalon, Ḥ, "*Megillat Sirkhe Ha-Yaḥad*," *KS* 28 (1951/2), 65–74.
____________, "*Megillat Yeshaʿyahu 'A*," *KS* 27 (1950/1), 163–172.
____________, *Megillot Midbar Yehudah*, Jerusalem: Shrine of the Book Fund and Kiryath Sepher, 1967.
Yalquṭ Shimʿoni, 2 vols., Jerusalem: Lewin-Epstein, 1941/2.
Yalquṭ Shimʿoni ʿal Ha-Torah, 5 vols., Salonika, 1520/1–1526/7.
Yalquṭ Shimʿoni ʿal Ha-Torah, ed. I. Shiloni, vols. 1–4, Jerusalem: Mosad Harav Kook, 1973–80.
Yaron, R., "The Goring Ox in Near Eastern Laws," *ILR* 1 (1966), 396–496; reprinted in H. H. Cohn, *Jewish Law in Ancient and Modern Israel*, New York: Ktav, 1971.
____________, *Introduction to the Law of the Aramaic Papyri*, Oxford: Clarendon Press, 1961.
Zeitlin, S., *The Zadokite Fragments*, *JQR* Monograph Series 1, Philadelphia: 1952.

INDEX OF CITATIONS

I. Hebrew Scriptures

II. Qumran Literature

Zadokite Fragments

Serekh Ha-'Edah
(Rule of the Community)

III. Apocrypha and Pseudepigrapha

IV. Philo and Josephus

V. New Testament

VI. Rabbinic Literature

A. *Mishnah*

C. *Palestinian Talmud*

D. *Babylonian Talmud*

E. *Targumim*

F. *Midrashim*

INDEX OF HEBREW AND ARAMAIC TERMS

GENERAL INDEX

A

Aaron ben Elijah of Nicomedia, 86 n. 65, 105 n. 44.
Abaye, 152 n. 99.
Abba Saul, 79, 134, 147 n. 27.
Abraham, 33, 46 n. 95.
Abu'l-Fatḥ ben Abī'l Ḥassan 'as-Sāmiri, 135.
Academies, tannaitic, 169.
Accusation, 89, 91–2, 95–6, 100 n. 10, 101 n. 23, 102 n. 24, 104 n. 44, 108 n. 72, 112.
Achan, 126 n. 10.
Adam (and Eve), 33.
Adjuration, 10, 43 n. 30, 50 n. 148, 111–16, 123, 125 nn. 4, 5.
Admonition, 7–9, 12, 93.
Adultery, 112–13, 123, 126 n. 15.
Ages, calculation of, 35.
Agriculture, 176 n. 18.
Akkadian, 145 n. 2.
Alexander Jannaeus, 71 n. 80.
Alexander the Great, 27.
Alexandria, Jewish community of, 28, 45 n. 74.
'Am Ha-'Areṣ, 57.
Amoraim, amoraic period, 24, 35–6, 38, 42 n. 18, 50 n. 149, 59, 61, 69 n. 41, 76, 79, 80, 84 nn. 41, 42, 87 n. 70, 92, 94, 97, 101 n. 16, 102 n. 33, 103 n. 36, 106 n. 57, 109 n. 97, 116, 121–2, 127 n. 15, 129 n. 45, 131 n. 86–7, 134–5, 138, 140–1, 146 n. 23, 149 nn. 53, 69, 152 nn. 105, 113, 169, 176 n. 26, 189 n. 176, 197, 205 nn. 34, 47, 206 n. 55.
Analogy, See: "Hermeneutics, sectarian," "Exegesis, midrash."
Anan ben David, 25, 36, 60, 69 n. 46.
Ananias and Sapphira, 174 n. 16.
Angels, 33, 152 n. 102, 188 n. 168.
Anger, bringing a charge in, 89, 91 93–4.
Animal bones, 127 n. 17, 201, 210 n. 111.
Apocrypha, 11, 18.
Arabic, 176 n. 30, 179 n. 70.
Aramaic, 1, 70 n. 80, 85 n. 47, 103 n. 36, 109 n. 91, 146 n. 10, 149 n. 69, 188 n. 168, 210 n. 110.
Archive, 95, 98.
Aristobulus III, 59.
Assembly, sectarian legislative and judicial. See: "*Moshav Ha-Rabbim.*"
Asseverative statements, 140.
Atonement. See: "Sin and atonement." See also: "Repentance."

B

C

informal, 206 n. 57.
Disability, 33, 34.
Divine Name, 216.
cursing by the, 141–2, 144.
forty-two letter, 153 n. 112.
misuse of, 157, 171. See also: "Tetragrammaton."
profanation of, 136–7, 139, 151 nn. 86, 87.
surrogate, 134–6, 138, 140–1, 143, 147 nn. 24, 31.
swearing by the, 136–40, 144, 214.
Divine Names. See: "Tetragrammaton."
Doctrine, sectarian, 6, 19, 172–3, 217.
Dositheans, 135.
Doxology, 118.
Drinks. See: "*Mashqeh.*"
Dual-Torah Concept, 16, 17.

E

Eating, 191, 194–7.
Ein Feshka, 209 n. 104.
Ein Gedi, 85 n. 48.
Elder(s), 24, 36–7, 48 nn. 126–8, 94, 100 nn. 10, 12.
Elephantine papyri, 24.
Encampment and march, 198, 207 n. 75.
End of Days, 6–7, 12–13, 30, 35, 64, 67 n. 21, 119, 191, 197–200, 202, 215.
Enoch, Book of, 11.
Equal rights, 31–2.
Eschatological war, 35, 56, 100 n. 12.
Eschatology, sectarian, 6–7, 12, 30, 35, 56, 64, 67 n. 21, 119, 153 n. 124, 191, 197–200, 211, 215–16.
Essenes, 1, 8, 13, 24, 37, 62, 64, 68 n. 27, 85 n. 48, 137–40, 144, 149 n. 63, 150 n. 75, 152 n. 107, 156, 163, 168, 178 n. 57, 192–3, 195, 202, 203 nn. 22, 24, 204 n. 31, 205 n. 49, 210 n. 111, 214.
Eucharist, 192.
Evidence, 95.
Examination, 76, 161, 163, 165, 169, 175 n. 17, 181 nn. 79, 82.
Examiner, 29–30, 34–5, 37–8, 63, 73, 78, 81, 95–6, 98, 177 n. 45, 178 n. 49, 215.
Excommunication, 167–9.
Execution, 74, 76–80, 84 n. 40, 87 n. 69, 91, 104 n. 44.
Exegesis, Karaite, 105 n. 44.
Exegesis, *midrash*, 15, 17, 34, 74, 93, 103 n. 33, 112, 120, 123, 125 n. 10, 126 n. 14, 128 n. 38, 184 n. 145, 212–13.
perush, 15.
pesher, 8, 43 n. 44, 60, 99 n. 2, 101 n. 19, 185 n. 152.
sectarian, 2, 7, 9–10, 12, 14–18, 28–30, 34, 39–40, 56–8, 61, 64, 71 n. 89, 74–5, 79, 81, 86 n. 58, 90–1, 93–5, 98, 111–12, 121, 123, 124 n. 1, 167, 170–1, 179 n. 71, 181 n. 90, 182 n. 107, 184 nn. 124, 137, 187 n. 165, 199, 211–13.
tannaitic, 88 n. 88, 91, 114, 119, 123.
Exodus, Book of, 13.
Exorcist, 113.
Expiation, 115, 118–19.
ram of. See "Sacrifices."

I

K

L

P

S

V

W

Y

Z